HARVARD HISTORICAL STUDIES ◆ 187

Published under the auspices
of the Department of History
from the income of the
Paul Revere Frothingham Bequest
Robert Louis Stroock Fund
Henry Warren Torrey Fund

BANKRUPTS AND USURERS OF IMPERIAL RUSSIA

Debt, Property, and the Law
in the Age of Dostoevsky and Tolstoy

SERGEI ANTONOV

Harvard University Press

CAMBRIDGE, MASSACHUSETTS, & LONDON, ENGLAND • 2016

Library of Congress Cataloging-in-Publication Data

Names: Antonov, Sergei, 1977– author.
Title: Bankrupts and usurers of imperial Russia : debt, property, and the law
   in the age of Dostoevsky and Tolstoy / Sergei Antonov.
Description: Cambridge, Massachusetts : Harvard University Press, 2016. |
   Includes bibliographical references and index.
Identifiers: LCCN 2016017879 | ISBN 9780674971486
Subjects: LCSH: Debtor and creditor—Russia—History—19th century. |
   Credit—Law and legislation—Russia—History—19th century. |
   Debt—Russia—History—19th century. | Credit—Russia—History—19th century. |
   Usury—Russia—History—19th century. | Russia—Social conditions—1801-1917.
Classification: LCC KLA1946 .A96 2016 | DDC 346.4707/709034—dc23
LC record available at https://lccn.loc.gov/2016017879

For Katya, Anya, Marina, and Nadya

Contents

BANKRUPTS AND USURERS OF IMPERIAL RUSSIA

Introduction

READERS OF TOLSTOY may recall the scene from *Anna Karenina* (1875–1877) in which Count Aleksei Vronsky, Anna's lover, sat down to organize his financial affairs as was his custom "five or so times a year." Finding out that his available cash could barely cover a tenth of his debts, he divided all of his obligations into three categories. The first consisted of debts of honor, such as a gambling debt that Vronsky had guaranteed for a fellow officer. These absolutely had to be paid upon demand. The second category, requiring only partial payment, came from Vronsky's hobby of horse racing and included debts to the oat-seller, the saddle-maker, and "the Englishman"—presumably a horse trainer or a groom. The third and largest category of debts consisted of bills from shopkeepers, hotelkeepers, and a tailor. These Vronsky considered "not even worth a thought."[1]

The rule that a card swindler was to be paid, but retail merchants were not, was as "unreasonable" and "not very decent" for Tolstoy the narrator as it was "unquestionable" for Vronsky. Although card and betting debts were not legally enforceable, a gentleman's entire financial well-being depended on paying them promptly to reassure merchants and moneylenders about his creditworthiness. Failure to do so would become immediately known, and according to Peter Vistengof, the author of popular sketches of Moscow life in the mid-nineteenth century, insolvent gamblers in the city's fashionable clubs resorted to "most extreme measures" and agreed to exorbitant interest rates for a quick infusion of cash from loan sharks.[2] According to an 1861 police investigation of professional gamblers in St. Petersburg, the opinion that card debt was an "affair of honor" had "taken root in the entire society."[3]

I

In real-life situations, as opposed to fiction, cultural norms and practices relating to debt—and distinguishing it from sales, gifts, or arbitrary
exactions—were anything but unquestionable. Gamblers could choose not to
pay and be blacklisted by their clubs.[4] Yet other debtors, even ones far more
powerful than the fictional Vronsky, made a point of paying their vendors,
landlords, and domestic servants.[5] Credit relations created an intricate pattern of morality, power, and self-interest that was far more complex than the
familiar literary and cultural stereotype of Russian nobles being profligate,
moneylenders vicious, and merchants backward. Assumptions and decisions
about trust- and creditworthy, honorable, respectable, or reasonable behavior,
about ways to identify failure and fraud, what to do when a debtor did not
pay back, and which creditors were to be repaid first were all highly contingent and vigorously contested both in courts of law and by the exercise of
informal influence and patronage. These assumptions were often vague and
articulated only in the breach, but enough of them were shared by legally and
socially fragmented groups of property owners to link them into a vast, but
diffuse, network of personal credit.[6]

This book re-creates the lost world of ordinary lenders and borrowers, and
of not-so-ordinary bankrupts, usurers, and forgers, during the transition
from the conservative reign of Nicholas I (1825–1855) to the period of reforms
that followed his death and Russia's defeat in the Crimean War. The new tsar
Alexander II (1855–1881) abolished serfdom in 1861 and reorganized the
courts and legal procedures in 1864. The new courts featured public adversarial trials, criminal juries, and a newly organized bar. Yet another set of
reforms revitalized Russia's economic and financial structure and its culture
of private property, in what contemporaries praised as the emancipation of
capital. These included a growing railroad network, the use of joint-stock
companies, improvements in the system of taxation, and the rise of private
joint-stock banks, which replaced the state-owned banks established in the
eighteenth century.[7]

Historians often point out that the reforms did not solve all of Russia's
problems and indeed created many new ones. Many fundamental but questionable features of Russian life were left untouched. For instance, Russia
remained an autocracy until 1905 and officially retained its eighteenth-
century social hierarchy of legally circumscribed estates; although censor-
ship was relaxed in the 1860s, for the rest of the century lawyers' courtroom
speech remained the only forum for relatively unfettered expression within
the empire. Moreover, the Great Reforms did not generate immediate

economic abundance, and an industrial takeoff only began in the 1880s. Nineteenth-century Russia participated in the world market primarily as a source of cereals and other raw materials and as a market for industrial products; while its economy equaled or exceeded that of France, per capita incomes remained low.

Interpretations of imperial Russia's economic and social development usually suggest that one of its underlying—and ultimately fatal—problems was Russians' alleged inability to create a robust culture of private property ownership, including credit, and to fully introduce the rule of law.[8] Both capitalism and the law are regarded as either underdeveloped or as importations from Western Europe that failed because they supposedly lacked proper grounding in Russia's society and historical traditions. The significance of private property and credit for these debates may seem self-evident, even when we discard, as Ekaterina Pravilova has done, a simplistic understanding of private property that equates it with modernity, progress, and political freedom and recognize that "other forms of non-exclusive and non-absolute ownership represented the modern alternative to the Western concept."[9]

Yet both personal credit and the culture of private property in imperial Russia are still very poorly understood: existing histories of Russia's Great Reforms, capitalism, and property structures barely even mention credit and do not at all explain its parameters or how its economic aspects were related to social, political, cultural, and legal developments.[10] The only exception is a fascinating specialized literature about the growth of modern banking, which, however, largely overlooks the perspective of the banks' borrowers and clients and completely neglects the variety of informal interpersonal credit arrangements used by the overwhelming majority of Russians without regular access to banks.[11]

My central contention is that informal personal credit pervaded all aspects of life in imperial Russia and underpinned its entire regime of private property ownership and its entire social order; and that it relied upon reasonably effective legal arrangements that were established largely for the purpose of protecting private property interests. The law of debt as conceived and as put into practice thus connected the abstract world of money and exchange with the concrete world of families, neighborhoods, and merchandise.

Part One of this study focuses on the shared culture of credit of Russia's propertied groups. It examines the activities of private moneylenders and places personal debt in the context of social and kinship relations and of cultural attitudes and practices concerning wealth, personal autonomy, and failure. Part Two focuses on engagement between private individuals and the tsarist legal and administrative apparatus, including the police and the courts, legal practitioners, and debtors' prisons. Both parts are closely related and should be regarded as part of a single narrative because the culture of debt to a large extent operated through legal norms and practices, whereas the law cannot be understood apart from the interests and strategies of individuals who used the courts and served on them.

This study is not a work of economic history, although it contains some numbers that are essential for my arguments but are not available from any other published sources; instead, I use perspectives from social, cultural, and legal history as necessary to address a subject as multifaceted as credit. Similarly to several other recent works of Russian history, this study focuses on the lives of ordinary individuals to balance the more familiar top-down narrative of institutions and policies.[12] My sources are largely, although not exclusively, legal cases that have not been previously examined, much less published. Most of them were processed in Moscow, imperial Russia's financial and commercial hub, or in St. Petersburg, its center of government and foreign trade. However, actual transactions and life stories depicted in these cases just as often occurred in other provinces, and so this book can be accurately characterized as addressing the culture of credit in European Russia but leaving out the smaller credit centers on Russia's western and southern periphery, such as Odessa, Berdichev, and Warsaw.

The level of detail in these cases varies, but taken together, they bring to life real nineteenth-century men and women—both rich and poor but almost none of them completely destitute—who left no record of their lives apart from the legal matters in which they were involved. A retired military officer, Andrei Blaginin, issues a debt note to reward a poor townswoman who was taking care of him in his old age and who is now suing the man's heirs. A young nobleman named Petr Veselkin, his wife, and two former merchants set up a complex scheme of mortgaging nonexistent landed estates. An illiterate middle-aged female fish-merchant, Mavra Bubentsova, alleges that as a woman she is weak and inexperienced in business and so should be excused from paying her debts. Some of these stories could inspire a novel, while many are routine, but all of them show that personal debt affected every aspect of Russian life in ways that are at once strange and familiar to the modern reader.

The Early Industrial Culture of Credit

Everyone understands the need to repair homes, to pay doctors, and to educate children and that to this day these tasks can rarely be accomplished without borrowing money. Because debt-free life is virtually inconceivable, borrowing and lending shapes people's perceptions of their material possessions, such as land, homes, personal and intellectual property, and, of course, money.[13] But compared to our world of credit cards and multinational banks, private incomes in imperial Russia and other early industrial societies were even more erratic, cash in circulation insufficient, and credit institutions inadequate. Baron Andrei Delvig, a successful public works engineer and government contractor, reminisced that in 1847 "it was possible to receive a decent education, have a rather considerable turnover in one's financial affairs, and yet to live, as I did, to be 34 years old without having any understanding of banking."[14]

As a result, individuals from all social groups and levels of income, both merchants and consumers, were deeply embedded in a network of debt relations with their relatives, colleagues, and neighbors but also increasingly with individuals they never met in person. This credit network relied not merely on objective information about borrowers' economic conditions and prospects but also on their reputation in the community, which in turn depended on a shared set of cultural attitudes about personal autonomy and responsibility, honor, failure, punishment, and property.

The key features of the Russian culture of credit—informal and personal connections, the moral economy of debt, and its influence on diverse noneconomic aspects of life—were also present in other early industrial societies and are particularly well documented for the Anglo-American world.[15] This literature dispenses with the purely economic view of credit and emphasizes its influence on many aspects of life, from political ideology and literature to family dynamics and gender identities. It also shows how the perceptions and practices of credit changed as part of the West's capitalist transformation, most notably toward treating certain categories of debtors as legitimate risk-takers deserving leniency while reserving a harsh moralistic attitude toward others. In short, the transition to "modern" credit is shown to be incomplete and ambivalent. In light of this literature, the development of Russia's law and practice of personal credit appears to have generally followed that of its Continental counterparts, revealing little or no so-called "backwardness."

Adam Smith and his followers and critics, most notably Marx, treated credit as an impersonal "abstract factor of production," while its cultural and social aspects became less relevant.[16] In the Russian setting, consider an 1852 work on the theory of credit by Professor Nikolai Bunge, who went on to serve as the finance minister in 1881–1886 and oversaw several important economic and social reforms. Bunge acknowledged older definitions of credit, such as that by the Scottish economist John Law (1671–1729), which highlighted its non-economic aspects, including the role of a debtor's honesty and promptness and the protections supplied by the legal system. However, Bunge claimed that these were irrelevant to the bulk of his analysis and dedicated his treatise solely to the "material" underpinnings of creditworthiness. These included the debtor's skills and whether the borrowed money would be put to productive use, but the most important factor was the possession of property that would ensure repayment.[17] Bunge's analysis is particularly remarkable for his haste to dismiss the cultural, ethical, and legal aspects of debt.

An exceptionally influential version of this view can be found in the unfinished third volume of Marx's *Das Kapital* (published in 1894), which posed the dichotomy of usurious and capitalist credit. To be fair, the notion that merchants and entrepreneurs did or should operate in a separate legal and financial universe had existed in Europe for centuries. As Laurence Fontaine argued for an earlier period, the two economic cultures, "feudal" and "capitalist . . . existed together, came close to and clashed with each other but also influenced and merged in each other, emerging transformed from these encounters." According to Marx, pre-capitalist usurious loans were used to support consumption, either by profligate nobility or by subsistence peasantry, and they were predatory in character; that is, the interest rate was so high that such loans could never be repaid and so such loans were used mainly by persons of higher social status to establish and maintain their power. Marx therefore argued that usury had led to enslavement in the ancient world; in a similar vein, the imperial-era historian Vasilii Kliuchevskii argued that usury and debt led to the emergence of Russian serfdom in the seventeenth century.[18]

Marx's framework underpinned all Soviet-era and many post-Soviet analyses of credit, which have been compartmentalized within the subfield of economic history and focused upon the emergence of modern capitalist banking. Personal and informal commercial credit in these works is treated briefly if at all and equated with misery, failure, and stagnation. For example, the Soviet historian Saul Borovoi, in his groundbreaking study of government-owned and capitalistic banks in "feudal" pre-reform Russia, recognized that private lending was also widespread and that it was the background against which government credit policies should be measured, but he was still obligated to follow the Marxist framework and so assumed "usury" to be an archaic predatory activity without examining it even superficially.[19] Standard Western works by Alfred Rieber, Thomas Owen, William Blackwell, Arcadius Kahan, and Jerome Blum rely on works by Borovoi and other Soviet historians.[20]

The same framework is also used in the handful of Soviet and post-Soviet studies of early modern credit, especially those focusing on merchants of the Petrine era and on the large medieval Orthodox monasteries that conducted extensive and diverse credit operations and that have been viewed as precursors to modern banks. These works suggest that the network of private credit in Russia was extensive, active, and diverse for centuries before the Great Reforms of the 1860s and even before Peter the Great. However, they do not connect private debt with larger social, political, and cultural developments.[21]

More recent historiography focuses on changes in cultural and legal attitudes toward debt that accompanied the European commercial and industrial expansion of ca. 1750–1850. Craig Muldrew has shown that in England this expansion was preceded in the sixteenth century by an explosion in consumption, borrowing, and debt-related legal disputes. In the course of the eighteenth century, financial failure and bankruptcy—at least for the wealthy—began to be viewed by politicians, theologians, and lawyers as no longer a moral failing deserving punishment but rather a risk inherent in, and useful for, commercial operations. Bruce Mann has done the same for colonial America and the Early Republic. Debt came to be seen as an opportunity rather than a burden, and the law changed accordingly: by the late nineteenth century most major Western legal systems introduced bankruptcy discharge and limited or abolished debt imprisonment and anti-usury laws.[22]

The transition to capitalist credit in the West was ambivalent and incomplete, as moral and political considerations continued to hold considerable sway over economic calculations. Even in Great Britain, which experienced a revolution in credit and finance much earlier than Russia, debt relations that were informal and deeply moralizing—and more punitive and restricting toward the lower classes—persisted into the twentieth century. In the United States, the modernization of laws relating to bankruptcy, debt imprisonment, and interest rate restrictions proceeded in fits and starts throughout the nineteenth century, so that a permanent bankruptcy statute appeared only in 1898. According to Lendol Calder, even in the twentieth century the development of modern consumer credit in the United States was enabled by persisting older values of "prudence, saving, and industry" that paradoxically opposed excessive borrowing. Similarly, in France—on which Russia's laws of bankruptcy and many others were largely modeled—the traditional anti-debtor moralistic attitudes remained very strong for most of the nineteenth century. In the German region of the Palatinate, "the nineteenth century was a high point for the free disposition of property in a market," yet the terms of market transactions were determined by personal relationships that "wove around a multitude of cultural assumptions about trust, independence, competence, manhood, and family expectations about the uses of property."[23]

In the Russian case, there are only a handful of studies briefly touching upon social and legal aspects of credit: Yurii Lotman and Jerome Blum argued that pre-reform nobles were crippled by debt, whereas Kahan, Rieber, Owen, and Blackwell in their histories of Russian capitalism and capitalists suggest that merchants' activities were handicapped by a lack of credit and a lack of trust more generally.[24] More specialized works disagree: for instance, Iosif Gindin argued that the development of large-scale banking in Russia did not lag very much behind that in other Continental nations. Gindin and other historians who examined the noble debt burden to the state before the serf emancipation, especially focusing on the often-quoted figure of two-thirds of all privately owned serfs being mortgaged to government banks by 1859, found this burden to be not nearly as staggering compared to the overall assets available to serfowners. Boris Litvak in particular argued that the more efficient noble estates were also more heavily in debt and that borrowing therefore indicated economic vitality and prosperity rather than insolvency or unprofitability. But the impact of debt upon the Russian nobility is still very poorly understood, in contrast to the rich discussion of English aristocratic debt.[25] Similarly, Andrei Vvedensky's superb study of the Stroganovs' commercial empire in North Russia noted that their initial fortune arose in the fifteenth century from credit and mortgage operations but unfortunately spent less than a page discussing these operations.[26] Viktor Zakharov's work on Western European merchants in Petrine Russia conveys a sense of simultaneous collision and accommodation between Muscovite and Western cultures of debt but unfortunately does not make this argument explicit.[27]

In the absence of academic works documenting the changes in social, cultural, and legal aspects of credit, one must turn to fictional descriptions by some of Russia's leading novelists and playwrights. Perhaps the most recognizable is the classic play *It's a Family Affair—We'll Settle It Ourselves* (1849) about the culture of traditional Muscovite merchants written by Alexander Ostrovsky, a son of a lawyer and himself a former court clerk. Originally titled *The Bankrupt,* the play—in my own departure from conventional interpretations—captures a growing acceptance of bankruptcy, and legal regulation in general, as a regular aspect of commerce in Russia; the way bankruptcy highlighted age-old tensions between morality and power; and the way it irreparably damaged the traditional practices of credit based on personal character and reputation.[28] The late stage of this transition is depicted in perhaps the most detailed fictional portrayal of capitalism and credit in imperial Russia, Dmitrii Mamin-Sibiriak's 1895 naturalist novel, *Bread,* about the rise of a modern joint-stock bank in a small town in the Urals. The owners of the bank quickly take over grain production and liquor distillation in that rich region and disrupt the old system of credit that was based on long-standing social and kinship relations. Paradoxically, the growth of organized capitalist credit in the novel also leads to more lively traditional "usurious" operations instead of replacing them.[29]

Perhaps the main reason why these fragmentary though fascinating insights concerning the development of credit in Russia were not developed further has been the widespread use of idealized Eurocentric and especially Anglocentric models of credit and capitalism. The above-mentioned literature on the culture of credit in Western Europe and North America shows that in practice these models turn out to be as fractured and contested as they were in Russia, and that their rules were, as Paul Johnson has argued, "neither natural, nor neutral, nor ... in any conventional sense socially or economically optimal."[30] Nineteenth-century Europeans and Americans were anxious and divided about many key aspects of modern capitalism, such as limited liability, bankruptcy discharge, paper money, white-collar crime, the courts and the legal profession, and the morality of the entrepreneurial class. As Sarah Maza has proposed in her study of the "myth" of the French bourgeoisie, "It is high time ... to stop projecting the Anglo-American model, with its inevitable linking of capitalism, liberal democracy, and middle-class individualism, onto continental societies. And it may be time to start wondering whether that Anglo-American model does not constitute the exception rather than the norm in the development of Western culture."[31]

More fundamentally, earlier works on Russian, as well as Western, capitalism assume that the ideal itself, however defined, is an unqualified good and that the proper response by all clear-thinking Russians at the time would have been to emulate it as closely as possible. This premise is something that newly invigorated literature on the development of capitalism in the West is now continuing to undermine, using a rich variety of sources and reconceptualizing some discomforting connections between capitalism and genocide, slavery, imperialism, and criminality. Daniel Lord Smail in his study of the legal and economic culture in early modern Marseilles has reasserted the connection between coercion—legal and extralegal—and economics as "a lubricant that eases the transfer of wealth from one to the other," suggesting that this insight continues to hold true in our own day. Similarly, the well-known theory of Douglass C. North that "free" institutions must result in economic growth and cheaper credit has been questioned on empirical grounds. Even private property itself, as Ekaterina Pravilova has noted, is now increasingly seen as a disciplinary project "symbolically associated with state coercion and prescriptive rules."[32]

As in any other European country, private credit in nineteenth-century Russia departed from some of the prevailing practices of its day, and was in step in others. As a living daily practice of capitalism, the culture of credit was fractured among various personal and institutional interests and it merged practices of coercion—virtually never of the extrajudicial variety, as opposed to the early modern period—with those of accommodation and consensus. In sum, why Russia was not Britain is an important question but one that for the present purposes is subsidiary to understanding what Russia actually was.

Society, Property, and Capitalism in Russia

The persistence of informal personal credit in Russia, among other "old-regime" structures and practices, can be easily misinterpreted to blend into the grand narrative of Russia's fundamental inferiority, or "backwardness," which regards all the major aspects of its civilization as having failed in some way. Even historians labeled as "optimists" contend, for instance, that imperial Russia remained fragmented along early modern estate divisions, that peasants failed to become capitalist farmers, that nobles—and then educated professionals—failed to become an effective ruling class, that merchants and other urban groups failed to develop a Western-style bourgeoisie, that capitalism failed to develop, that the government was dysfunctional, and that the rule of law and private property was rudimentary or completely absent. It is not unheard of in academic literature to claim, for instance, that "Russian nobles often possessed land, but never enjoyed private property." While only a few works contain these claims in such a concentrated form, they are almost invariably accepted at their face value.[33]

This narrative of failure is being revised by works taking advantage of post-Soviet access to archival materials that were not available to earlier generations of historians. Recent scholarship incorporates the long-absent microhistorical perspective into existing narratives of institutions and policies and thereby destroys some of the most cherished myths about Russian peasants, nobles, and merchants.

One key scholarly debate concerns the fact that Russian society was officially compartmentalized into legal categories, or estates, which persisted until 1917 and continued to impact people's lives long after the Revolution. The estate system—consisting primarily of peasants, nobles, the clergy, and several urban and commercial categories—is usually understood as a major limiting factor in Russia's social development, hindering social mobility and the formation of shared identities. At the same time, newer identities based on property and education resulted in what Catriona Kelly calls a "convergence of taste" of Russia's landowning, commercial, and service classes, in a similar way to the process that occurred in a slightly earlier period in Georgian England. Alison Smith has shown the estate system to be imbued with a multiplicity of meanings—"as obligation, as opportunity, as belonging, and as hierarchy"—which were contested and negotiated by the agencies of the tsarist government, by local communities, and by private individuals.[34]

Russia's culture of private property and credit was similarly complicated, and debt relations did not fit neatly into the estate structure. Although individuals often preferred to deal with persons of similar status, debt connections also cut across social and economic boundaries and formed between persons who were not even personally acquainted. An act of borrowing, even when it was the only interaction between persons of vastly different position, had to rely on a set of shared assumptions and experiences. These could be that debts must be repaid, that relatives usually helped each other, or that the lender would be willing and capable of using the courts to induce repayment.[35]

Another fundamental stereotype about Russia presents its vast peasant population as an exotic, undifferentiated mass of subsistence farmers who were poor, ignorant of market relations, and lacking any appreciation for "Western" law. By contrast, David Moon, Jane Burbank, Tracy Dennison, and Alessandro Stanziani have found that peasants were differentiated by wealth and occupation, actively participated in the market, and readily used the law to resolve property and other disputes. These factors, added to the seasonal and unpredictable patterns of the agricultural cycle, made credit indispensable for peasants who worked the land, for the nobles who ruled over—and lived off—a large proportion of them, and for the government that collected taxes from both, directly and indirectly.[36]

Serfowning nobles themselves are often regarded as wasteful and ineffi-cient and, therefore, hopelessly indebted but still jealous of their economic privileges.[37] However, these older accounts focused on the wealthiest layer of fewer than 3,000 proprietors who could afford princely lifestyles and vast debts and ignored the tens of thousands of educated but mostly conservative and religious landowners who could afford to live comfortably but needed to manage their properties effectively to do so. Works by Seymour Becker, Michelle Lamarche Marrese, Katherine Pickering Antonova, and Valerie Kivelson show a variety of legal and social strategies used by such middling families. These included the legal rules allowing married women to own and control property, extensive horizontal and vertical social and kinship ties, and even the often-criticized custom of partible inheritance. In a similar vein, Ekaterina Pravilova has examined the emergence of the notions and prac-tices of public, as opposed to private, property in imperial Russia. These works analyze patterns of property ownership—complex and never abso-lute or exclusive—that closely resemble their nineteenth-century Western counterparts.

Studies of the nobility also reinterpret the longstanding view of provincial life as a stagnant backwater: in addition to Antonova, works by Susan Smith-Peter, Mary Cavender, and Catherine Evtuhov show varied and rich provin-cial lives in which no Chekhovian desire for the city is evidenced; in fact, the city was viewed as undesirable.[38] In contrast to Lee Farrow's and William Wagner's interpretations of "clan" structures as backward, middling gentry networks allowed for a self-sufficient and apparently self-satisfied rural cul-ture that was conservative but not reactionary.[39] Provincial self-sufficiency was not, however, possible without credit ties, which, as Antonova notes, were deeply interwoven with all other social interactions on a noble estate and simultaneously linked serfowners to the state, to their relatives and other peers, and to their peasants and other dependents. Money and debt are therefore shown as part and parcel of the nobles' daily life rather than a disaster or an unrealized aspiration.

Finally, urban and commercial groups in Russia consisted primarily of merchants, who had to pay a special annual tax to retain their privileges, and of townspeople *(meshchane)* and craftsmen *(tsekhovye)* whose prosperity varied but who like merchants possessed their own corporate organization. All but the wealthiest merchants were subjected to conscription, taxation, and corporal punishment, just like peasants. Historical memory has not been kind to these people: condemned during the Soviet era for being capitalist and critiqued in the West for not being capitalist enough, traditional Russian merchants became an object of ridicule and exoticization, dismissed as unable to lead Russia's capitalist development due to their alleged backwardness, dishonesty, and a caste-like mentality that supposedly separated them from the rest of society.[40]

As with provincial life, other, mostly recent, studies of these groups show a vibrant civilization distinct from, yet closely connected to the world of nobles and peasants and already fully fledged in the eighteenth century. William Blackwell, in his 1968 study of Russian industrial development in 1800–1861, argued that it was driven in part by the entrepreneurial abilities of the merchants, among other groups. David Ransel's close reading of a diary by a late-eighteenth-century merchant dispelled the legend of their ignorance and vulgarity and depicted the merchantry "not as a stolid, hermetically sealed social backwater, but instead a more dynamic and colorful social space where characters like Tolchënov could flourish, fail, and start anew." Alexander Kupriianov has shown that pre-reform commercial elites were actively engaged in urban governance and able to assert their interests vis-à-vis the bureaucracy.

In his recent study of Moscow as an "imperial social project," Alexander Martin explored the state's effort to build Moscow's urban population into a modern bourgeoisie competitive with those of Western powers. For a variety of reasons—the devastation of 1812 by the French among them—Muscovites did not become Parisians or Londoners, but Martin does show how heterogeneous middling sorts nevertheless increasingly lived together, enjoyed leisure time together, and experienced unavoidable intersections of business and work.[41] While not concerned with credit directly, these works show that merchants and other urban property owners cannot be reduced to dusty stereotypes that alternately emphasized their dishonesty and their excessive reliance on trust-based networks as opposed to formal sources of credit.

Law in Imperial Russia

In addition to shared cultural norms and credit intermediaries, Russia's large but amorphous credit network depended on formal legal mechanisms, which

borrowers and lenders used to resolve and even prevent disputes when individual honor, ties of kinship, and patronage networks failed. Even when loans
were not disputed, the law still determined the key parameters of the culture
of credit, including debt documents and the categories of individuals who
were included or excluded from the credit network. Craig Muldrew has documented a similar key role for the legal system in early modern England
after the volume of credit transactions sharply increased in the mid-sixteenth
century and the traditional reliance on communal networks of trust no longer
proved sufficient.[42]

But while Western works about the history of debt merely depict the legal
system as a site of contestation and reciprocity inherent in debt relations,
without questioning the foundations of the law itself, in the case of Russia,
the very place of law in Russian society and culture is a major historiographical controversy. Much like capitalism, law is often seen as an importation
alien to traditional Russian culture.

Many specialists and laypersons believe in a Russian legal exceptionalism:
that attitudes toward law and its role in politics and society fundamentally—
and unfavorably—distinguish Russia from the rest of Western culture. A
number of influential studies of imperial-era legislation and legal scholarship
have argued that law in Russia was not simply defective or underdeveloped
but was a marginal and superfluous activity or even, taken to an extreme, a
"cultural fiction"—that is, a set of rhetorical texts never meant to be applied
in everyday practice.[43] This failure is explained variously by the lack of an
organic legal tradition (John LeDonne, Laura Engelstein), peasants' inherent
lawlessness (Jörg Baberowski), a lack of political and social institutions
that could foster the growth of the rule of law and challenge the autocracy
(LeDonne and Elise Kimerling Wirtschafter), and even an Orthodox
Christian mentality that was allegedly intrinsically incapable of operating in
the same way as that of law-abiding Westerners (Uriel Proccacia).[44]

This ultra-critical narrative has been modified by works that focus on the
ways law functioned in actual practice, as opposed to reform-focused jurisprudence and journalism, and show conclusively that Russia does in fact
possess a rich legal tradition. Works by Vladimir Kobrin, Nancy Shields
Kollmann, George Weickhardt, Richard Hellie, and other historians on
pre-Petrine civil and criminal law establish the existence in Muscovy of a
vibrant, sophisticated, and widely used legal system with well-developed
procedural rules.[45] Victor Zakharov, Alexander Kamenskii, and Olga
Kosheleva reveal an equally vibrant legal culture in the eighteenth century,

especially demonstrating that legal formalities were integral to Russian merchants' practices, whereas George Munro has shown that St. Petersburg merchants in the eighteenth century created a functioning system of commercial credit that relied on the legal form of the *veksel* (commercial bill of exchange).[46] Michelle Lamarche Marrese's outstanding study of property ownership and control by Russian noblewomen in early imperial Russia (before 1861) reveals a close connection between the legal system and individual property rights and interests that could be identified, asserted, and defended in court. Richard Wortman's groundbreaking work shows that a body of highly trained and motivated jurists appeared in Russia during the first half of the nineteenth century and created the intellectual and ideological conditions for the reforms that followed. Jane Burbank's excellent study of local peasant courts in the early twentieth century documents peasants' law-abiding practices and willingness to use the law to resolve disputes, as well as the fact that debt litigation made up a significant proportion of the local courts' caseload.[47]

The present study builds upon this literature in two ways. First, I adopt an evolutionary rather than a revolutionary perspective on Russia's legal development in the mid-nineteenth century. At first glance, this may seem counterintuitive: after all, the judicial reform of 1864 was perhaps the most spectacular single event in the history of Russian law, bringing it in line with the highest technical standards of its era. The legal universe created by the reform is commonly viewed as the sole event in the history of Russian law that merits sympathy and detailed study.[48] But, as far as Russia's culture of debt was concerned, 1864 was only one important waypoint in a chain of developments that included incremental but important innovations under Catherine II and Nicholas I, and even earlier, as far back as the Law Code of 1649.

The 1864 reform itself concerned only court procedures and did not directly affect substantive rules relating to property and debt, which changed only incrementally and mostly remained in force until 1918. Indeed, some of the most important reforms affecting credit were only enacted in the late 1870s, long after the Great Reforms had ceased to be a novelty. Many of these changes were indeed striking, but so were the continuities—not only in the substantive laws that were not immediately affected by the reform but also in the fact that property owners in the mid-nineteenth century had to engage both the new courts and the old ones; moreover, personal possessions, documents, and interests did not change overnight in 1862 when the principles of the proposed reform were drafted, in 1864 when the new statutes were issued, or in 1866 when the new courts were opened.

In this long evolutionary chain, the court system that was originally established by Catherine II in 1775 and that existed until the reform of 1864 has been particularly poorly understood even by specialists and treated solely as a polemical backdrop to highlight the reformers' achievements. Pre-reform courts have been criticized for being vulnerable to administrative interference and corruption, for an archaic estate-based court hierarchy, and for an inquisitorial procedure that relied on a rigid system of "formal proofs," as well as for the low qualifications of its personnel.[49]

This tone was set by jurists who in the late nineteenth century defended the reformed court system against conservative attacks. Many scholars of imperial Russia are familiar with the passage penned by the Slavophile Ivan Aksakov, an elite student of jurisprudence in the 1840s who had extensive experience with pre-reform criminal justice and who forty years later described how his hair rose on his head and "a chill" rippled his skin at the very memory of the "old justice."[50] In line with this thinking, Richard Pipes claimed that there was essentially no such thing as law in Russia before the 1860s, and Jörg Baberowski claimed that pre-1864 courts were indeed adopted from Western models but nonetheless failed because they did not cater to the peasants' interests any more than their post-reform counterparts.[51]

Accepting that the hair-raising scenarios described by Aksakov and other critics did take place—and indeed, adding a number of new ones—pre-reform court cases discussed in this book nonetheless add up to a legal system that despite its flaws did not reveal any extreme or exceptional dysfunctionality apart from the predictable exercise of patronage or economic power by private individuals and government officials—a common occurrence even in the most highly praised Western legal systems. Although the wealthier, higher-ranked, or more experienced individuals were more likely to win their legal battles, such results were never pre-ordained. Even the pre-reform legal system was not a law of the jungle, and the tsar's justice continued to attract millions of property owners, who preferred to go to court rather than employ some other alternative venues to resolve their disputes or protect their interests. In short, this study argues that Russians became accustomed to defending their property interests in court long before the 1860s, and undermines the view that the reforms were imposed on a population whose legal culture had no use for these innovations.

My second conceptual contribution to the study of Russian law is to clarify the standard of evaluation used in discussing Russia's legal culture and legal practice, and especially the standards of comparison—explicit or implicit—between Russia and other major Western legal systems. The details of such comparisons vary, but they are ultimately traceable to the ideal known in English as the rule of law, with different versions found in different legal systems in different historical periods. The English variety in use during the Victorian era encompassed three major principles: (1) "individuals' legal equality, irrespective of their status and economic conditions"; (2) the existence of a parliament as "the supreme legislator"; and (3) the protection of individual rights, most importantly the rights of liberty and property. In the United States, these principles were modified by the existence of a written constitution and by the judicial review of federal and state legislation, although such review was rudimentary and incoherent before the twentieth century.

Another influential nineteenth-century model of the rule of law was the German concept of *Rechtsstaat*, or the law-based state, which in its more liberal rendering called for a fully representative parliament, protection of individual rights, and independent courts, but from 1848 to 1919 focused on the formal aspects of law "as a system of impersonal, abstract, general, and non-retroactive rules" that were created and could be changed at will by the legislator and had to be respected by the other branches of government. These values are also emphasized in Max Weber's "formal-rational" ideal type of legality.[52]

It is not surprising that tsarist Russia with its autocratic government and absence of many political freedoms failed to fully live up to these standards of the rule of law, and especially to the Anglo-American version.[53] However, the standards themselves are vulnerable to criticism both on empirical and on conceptual grounds.

Empirically, it is important to remember the many failures of the rule of law in other major legal systems, including Britain, Germany, and the United States, despite the fact that their citizens elected many of their officials and that their political rights were better protected than in Russia. The list of these failures is long indeed, including a pervasive court-sanctioned racist regime in the United States; national, class, and gender oppression in Victorian Britain; and the history of political oppression in Germany. As Nancy Kollmann has noted with respect to an earlier period of Russian history, "On the ground, European "rationalizing" states look less rational and Muscovy's proclaimed "autocracy" looks less autocratic."[54] By contrast, historical and empirically grounded conceptions of the law are more suitable for comparisons of specific practices in Russia and elsewhere, such as punishment for intentional bankruptcy or prosecution of usury, or women's property rights, with the aim of identifying general patterns, which Russia may or may not share with other major legal systems. In short, relying on an idealized image of English or American law and finding that Russia failed to measure up is no more helpful than would be, for example, claiming that Orthodox Russians were not truly Christian because they failed to live up to some "Western" Christian model.

Conceptually, although there has not been a study systematically and vigorously applying Weber's ideas about law to the Russian case, sociologists of law have complicated such a project by arguing that Weber himself, despite all of his partiality for "formal-legal" rationality, was ambivalent about its possible benefits and realized that it could never be achievable in practice. Weber's theory of law arguably viewed Western legal systems as riddled with "irreconcilable tensions between process and substance—between formal and substantive rationality" rather than as the triumphant progression of the former.[55]

But despite these problems with the standard definition of the rule of law and the rational versus despotic dichotomy, I am far from suggesting that law has been merely an instrument of social and political oppression, in pre-reform Russia or anywhere else. Many historians and legal scholars have examined the law as a process of contestation and negotiation, which is typically subject to individual and group discretion, and which does not necessarily serve as a noble tool of dispute resolution but could be just as easily deployed as a weapon of social strife. For example, Paul W. Kahn has argued against legal scholars' focus on the abstract image of the rule of law—which he compares to theology—and their consequent emphasis on the project of legal reform. Instead Kahn prefers to see the law as a "set of sites of social conflict, and a set of resources—institutional and rhetorical—for those involved in these conflicts."[56] E. P. Thompson in his study of one of the most notorious examples of corrupt class-based legislation in eighteenth-century England nonetheless came out in defense of the rule of law, which, he argued, could support existing power structures only by being perceived as occasionally operating to benefit subordinate individuals and groups: "If the law is evidently partial and unjust, then it will mask nothing, legitimize nothing, contribute nothing to any class's hegemony. The essential precondition for the effectiveness of law, in its function as ideology, is that it shall display an independence from gross manipulation and shall seem to be just. It cannot seem to be so without upholding its own logic and criteria of equity; indeed, on occasion, by actually *being* just."[57] In

Russia, too, the legal system was susceptible to extrajudicial pressures and was itself a battlefield for competing interests. However, it retained enough integrity to occasionally punish a corrupt official and to rescue a wrongfully accused serf, and even before the reform of 1864 fulfilled—however imperfectly—its ideological, as well as practical functions.

Government and the Law

A guidebook to Moscow published in 1827 proudly introduced the "enormous . . . beautiful building of the newest Architecture," which housed the municipal and provincial governmental offices *(prisutstvennye mesta)* It was located on a prominent spot just outside the Kremlin and Red Square, to the right of Resurrection Gate, on the site of today's Lenin Museum. The building, depicted on the Figure 6.2 below, was originally a seventeenth-century Mint complex, converted to offices under Catherine II and given its final neoclassical appearance after renovations completed in 1820.[58] Perhaps symbolic of the general state of the Russian bureaucratic world, the elegant exterior was the complete opposite of its busy and cramped inside, which was divided into hundreds of small chambers, staircases, and corridors, with the debtors' prison occupying part of its left wing (see Figures 7.3 and 7.4). The guidebook listed all the offices located in the building—in addition to the courts of law, it housed such key provincial and municipal institutions as the city council, the main police office, the Noble Board of Trustees, the provincial Treasury, and the provincial administrative office—and then noted with a touch of irony: "each of our readers, I think, has some knowledge of the function of each of these governmental offices."[59] There were several other important official buildings, including the Board of Trustees of the Imperial Orphanage on Solianka Street (built in 1825), the Senate building inside the Kremlin (1788), and the 17 police precincts spread throughout the city. The two most important city officials, the governor general and the police chief, each had a spacious residence in the city center, where he conducted business and received visitors and petitioners.

The guidebook's readership, no doubt mostly persons of some property, could hardly avoid visiting these buildings, either in person or through a representative, on a multitude of errands and matters that bound the early industrial state and its subjects, whether it was to register a debt transaction, to request a police debt collection proceeding, to purchase the stamped paper used for all official business, or to pursue a court case. Much like this architectural landscape, the legal and administrative framework of the Russian Empire—summarized in Tables 0.1 and 0.2—was largely erected by Catherine II's Provincial Statute of 1775, but ultimately it rested on the personal power of the tsar and on the ethos of state service, both of which originated in the Muscovite period.

Peter the Great's reforms introduced the Governing Senate as the highest administrative body in the empire, but by the mid-nineteenth century it served primarily as the highest court of appeals. Another major Petrine innovation was the replacement the Muscovite system of ranks with the Table of Ranks—reproduced in Appendix B—which divided all civil servants and military officers into fourteen classes and legally separated them from lower-level servitors of the tsar such as noncommissioned officers and chancery clerks. The table provided an automatic avenue of advancement to personal and potentially hereditary nobility; it also made it easier to determine an official's position in the service hierarchy.[60]

Table 0.1. Russian Legal System before the Judicial Reform of 1864

Level	Institution	Date Est.	Primary Function
Central	Emperor		Issue laws and decrees, accept pettions
	State Council	1801	Legislation; statutory interpretation
	Governing Senate	1711	Appellate court
	Third Section	1826	Special investigations of civil and criminal matters
Province	Provincial Chambers of Civil and Criminal Justice	1775	Non-estate first-tier appellate courts; special cases
	Equity Courts	1775	Minors; parents vs. children
	Commercial Courts	1808–1833	Bankruptcy; commercial disputes
Local	County, Magistrate, Aulic Courts	1775	Estate-based trial courts

Table 0.2 Court Caseload in 1858[a]

Court	Criminal		Civil
First-tier courts	137,950		143,194
Provincial Chambers	62,407		108,866
Equity		1,639	
Commercial (incl. bankruptcy)	n / a		4,219 (394)
Senate	3,643		17,449
Senate Joint Session	66		404
State Council		26	
Ministry of Justice	2,328		2,589
Total	251,568		232,864

a. Data include all cases processed by the courts, even if they were not decided during the year. Administrative and technical *(rasporiaditelnye)* proceedings are not included. *Data source: Zhurnal ministerstva iustitsii* 4 (1860), 24-33.

Catherine's legislation above all established a uniform system of provincial administration, dividing the entire empire into provinces *(gubernii),* each with originally the equivalent population and generally corresponding with the regions *(oblasti)* of contemporary Russia. At the top of the local hierarchy was the civil governor, with some exceptionally important regions like St. Petersburg and Moscow also assigned the higher-ranking military governor general. Governors' power steadily grew in the early nineteenth century, so that an 1837 law referred to governors as "masters of the province." These powers included the authority to expel undesirable persons, such as swindlers and "usurers," to oversee the police, which collected debts and conducted criminal investigations, and to exercise a limited set of judicial functions. Represented in fictional works as local tyrants, provincial governors are shown by archival-based research to have been limited in several ways, not only by their minders from the secret police but primarily by the necessity to find accommodation with local elites.[61]

Formal restrictions were also significant, especially with respect to judicial institutions. Provincial Chambers of Criminal and Civil Justice—second-tier courts—carried out the bulk of justice administration before the 1864 reform; they were all-estate courts, staffed by trained lawyers. Their chairmen were confirmed personally by the emperor from candidates proposed by the

Senate, although in the nineteenth century candidates in most provinces were elected by the nobility. Assistant chairmen were selected by the minister of justice, and lay assessors were selected by nobles and by the provincial urban community (two from each).[62]

Although the police and the administration subordinate to the minister of the interior were better funded, more numerous, and more powerful than the judiciary, it is still a gross exaggeration that the pre-1864 system commingled judicial and executive functions and that therefore Russia had no real justice system before 1864. In addition to the chambers, provinces had several ancillary courts: Commercial, Equity (Conscience), Verbal, and the Orphans'. Commercial courts were particularly important because they were responsible for commercial litigation and for overseeing merchants' bankruptcy proceedings. They were officially equal to the chamber, despite their smaller caseload and relatively narrow jurisdiction. Provincial institutions also included various elected bodies that enabled local elites to participate in government in at least a limited way.

Finally, the chambers oversaw and reviewed the proceedings of the first-tier trial courts, whose jurisdiction was divided according to Russia's system of legal estates: the County Court *(Uezdnyi sud)* tried cases involving nobles and peasants, the Magistrate Court *(Magistrat)* had jurisdiction over merchants and townspeople, and, in the two capitals, the Aulic Court *(Nadvornyi sud)*—over government officials who did not own property there and over the *raznochintsy* (i.e., individuals who did not belong to any estate). In addition to these courts, each county also had its own administrative system. This court hierarchy existed until the new courts opened after the reform of 1864, and another set of reforms greatly expanded the local elected component, but otherwise this administrative framework remained in force until 1917.

Alexander I (1801–1825) added two important central institutions: he established the Council of State (1810) as the highest legislative body, but its other function was to serve as essentially a form of constitutional court, handling a small number of appeals that rested on the interpretation of a particular statute or decree. Second, the ministerial system established in 1802 included the Ministry of Justice, which was charged with the oversight of all courts of law in the empire, except for the ecclesiastical and military courts.[63]

Under Nicholas I (1825–1855), the two major administrative innovations pertinent to this study were, first, the establishment of the Third Section of His Imperial Majesty's Own Chancellery as the empire's "highest" police responsible personally to the tsar. Most of its officials belonged to the militarized Corps of Gendarmes, so that in this study, and in most existing literature, the Third Section and the Corps of Gendarmes are used interchangeably. The Third Section is remembered today for its role in suppressing political dissent, but at least before the Great Reforms, it in effect constituted a parallel system of justice with extensive authority to investigate particularly important criminal cases and property, inheritance, and family disputes that were brought to their attention. However, the Third Section was not authorized to actually try cases, and in private-law disputes it was limited to serving as a mediator.[64]

The second great innovation was the massive codification effort carried out under the direction of the statesman Mikhail Speranskii. This included the Complete Collection of the Laws that had been issued after 1649, published in three series beginning in 1830; and the Digest of the Laws, which compiled the laws that were actually in force and went into effect in 1835, with subsequent editions issued in 1842 and 1857. The Digest is often described as not a true "code" in the sense that it did not claim to establish general legal principles in the manner of the French Napoleonic Code, but this view is misleading because the Napoleonic Code was itself drawn from existing legal tradition and was a compromise between old-regime legal rules, revolutionary innovations, and Napoleon's own views.[65]

The Digest, despite its imperfections and frequent casuistry, was a functioning code of law with separate volumes on substantive criminal and civil law and codes of procedure in addition to massive administrative regulations. In making their decisions, judges only had to refer to the Digest, not to the legislative acts from which it was extracted. Viewed in a general nineteenth-century context, when codification was often painfully drawn out and incomplete, it was as remarkable an achievement as its 1649 predecessor, reflecting an interest on the part of Russia's elites in promoting legality.

Finally, the judicial reform of 1864 was a landmark event in the history of Russian law, although it only affected court structure and procedures, not substantive laws. The courts' authority and prestige were greatly strengthened, and civil and criminal procedure were streamlined by the introduction of public oral trials with criminal juries and the professional bar. The system of formal proofs that limited judges' ability to evaluate evidence was discarded, as were the first-tier, estate-based courts. The reform also established a system of local justices of the peace for smaller claims and disputes. Their equivalent for the peasants were the local township *(volost)* courts established by the emancipation reform of 1861 and administered by the peasants themselves. Because these courts were limited to the peasants and because their decisions could not be appealed to the regular court system, these courts have been misleadingly criticized for fragmenting the legal system. They were in fact concerned with small matters that were not meant to clog up the regular courts in any legal system. Moreover, Jane Burbank has conclusively demonstrated that their foundations in peasant "custom" did not result in any kind of legal anarchy.[66]

Private Credit and Legal Regulation

In addition to the legal structure, the culture of credit was shaped or at least heavily affected by two sets of government policies. One was closely related to official efforts to compartmentalize Russian society into separate legal estates. This long-term project encompassed legislation that sought to create two separate networks of private debt—one for commercial loans and one for noncommercial ones—by regulating the legal forms required for each category. This thinking reflected the common European sentiment that merchants as risk takers were entitled to a separate legal regime, upholding different values than nobles or peasants, even though the two legal and economic cultures could sometimes merge and influence each other.[67]

Pre-Petrine law did not formally distinguish between commercial and non-commercial debt. Legally enforceable credit transactions required witnesses and had to be registered at a court or an administrative office. As a practical matter, borrowers were required to provide some property as collateral or to have other individuals guarantee the loan.[68] Western European merchants who began visiting Muscovy more frequently toward the end of the seventeenth century introduced another form, known in English as the bill of exchange (*Wechsel* in German and *veksel* in Russian, pl. *vekseli* or *vekselia*).[69]

Bills of exchange were invented by European Renaissance bankers to facilitate long-distance commerce: a merchant, instead of transporting cash, deposited cash with a banker, who issued a document asking another banker in a different city to pay that amount to the bearer.[70] Bills of exchange were convenient because they required fewer formalities; for example, they did not require witnesses or registration.[71] They also benefitted from a stricter enforcement mechanism, including the quick imprisonment of a delinquent debtor or a quick sale of his property, and were more difficult to challenge in court because any legally relevant information had to be inscribed on the document itself, and no extraneous evidence was admissible.[72]

Vekseli soon became popular in Russia, although mostly specifically as debt documents rather than as instruments for long-distance money transfer.[73] The first *Veksel* Statute was adopted in 1729, during the brief reign of Peter II, with its text inspired by German models and published simultaneously in German and Russian.[74] In practice, by that time both native Russian and European merchants doing business in Russia had already switched to using *vekseli* for commercial credit transactions.[75] By the late eighteenth century, Russian merchants had de facto created a system of short-term commercial credit based on the use of *vekseli*, as shown by George Munro.[76] Subsequently *veksel* law was modified by the Bankruptcy Statute of 1800 and replaced by another complete statute—this time with strong French influences—in 1832, and then again in 1903.[77] This legislative attention to what is usually assumed to be a minor area of the law is remarkable, given that the fundamental civil and criminal statutes in imperial Russia were updated extremely slowly if at all.

From the beginning of their use in Russia, *vekseli* were viewed as a special privilege of merchants, although under Russia's original *Veksel* Statute of 1729, this privilege extended to all persons who had financial dealings with merchants, and so a person of any estate could issue a *veksel* to a merchant or accept it from one. However, the government soon became alarmed by the easy availability of *vekseli* and sought to limit their circulation, ostensibly to protect nobles and peasants from excessive debt, although the measure could not effectively affect predatory moneylenders.[78] The restrictions on the use of *vekseli* were part of a larger and unsuccessful policy to separate nobles' and merchants' financial dealings. For instance, the government tried to prevent nobles from standing surety for merchants; however, this cannot conceal the fact that the two major propertied groups actively cooperated to take advantage of each other's unique privileges, often by acting as each other's front men.[79]

Peasants were prohibited from issuing *vekseli* in 1761.[80] This prohibition was extended to nobles by Paul I's Bankruptcy Statute of 1800. As finalized in 1832, the privilege to issue *vekseli* was available only to persons specifically listed in the statute; as of the 1857 edition, which was in force during the Great Reforms, these were (a) merchants enrolled in a guild; (b) nobles enrolled in a merchant guild; (c) foreign merchants; (d) *meshchane* (townspeople) and *tsekhovye* (craftsmen) in the two capital cities; and (e) peasants engaged in commerce with a special license.[81]

Yet another restriction was that married women and unmarried daughters who were not legally emancipated from their parents were not allowed to issue *vekseli* without their husbands' or fathers' permission—even if they belonged to the five categories just named—unless they engaged in commerce in their own name. This restriction against women came to Russia directly from the Napoleonic Code and did not fit within Russia's regime of separate marital property. As imperial-era legal scholar Gabriel Shershenevich noted, the restriction also raised the practical challenge of determining whether a given debt related to commerce and whether a woman was emancipated. After all, a woman could own vast property in her own name but live with her parents and, conversely, it would be impossible to determine whether a young woman was "emancipated" if her parents did not own any property that could have been transferred to her. However, *vekseli* issued by individuals not legally entitled to issue them did not become void but merely lost the special advantages conferred by *veksel* law and became equated with ordinary debt documents.[82]

The Bankruptcy Statute of 1800 also envisioned a separate credit system for the noncommercial classes, especially nobles and peasants, based on the "loan letter" *(zaiomnoe pismo)*.[83] It required witnesses and registration, but these requirements were relaxed for the "private" *(domovoe)* loan letter, as opposed to the "registered" *(krepostnoe)* one, which provided the lender with enhanced legal protections.[84] A loan letter did not legally require collateral or surety, although lenders were of course free to demand them. While the statute provided sample forms for different types of loans, a loan letter could be written in any form, as long as the word "borrow" *(zanimat)* was present. A separate model was provided for loans secured by land *(zakladnaia krepost* or—in the abbreviated form more familiar to readers of Russian literature— *zakladnaia)*, requiring a description of the property being mortgaged. In practice, actual loan letters closely followed the models provided in the statute, showing that legal rules and legal forms in imperial Russia were far from fictitious or superfluous but, rather, were closely integrated into Russia's culture of debt and its regime of private property.

But although the legal forms had real practical effect on the culture of debt, this effect naturally differed from what was intended by the legislation. The technical legal distinctions between *vekseli* and ordinary loan letters remained blurry. Eighteenth-century decrees voided *vekseli* issued to pay gambling debts and also treated *vekseli* issued by nobles who were in state service as ordinary debts that were to be paid out of their salaries rather than by seizure of their assets.[85]

In practice, borrowers also often tried to ignore the rule prohibiting them to claim that a bill of exchange was "moneyless"—that is, that no money changed hands during the transaction.[86] This objection was frequently raised by borrowers with respect to loan letters not subject to the *veksel* protections. Russia's first scholar of *veksel* law, Dmitry Meier, noted that even some official documents in the mid-nineteenth century listed all debt documents as *vekseli*. But this confusion is not present in any of the cases examined in this study. On the balance, perhaps the extra registration requirements for loan letters did occasionally prevent a dissolute nobleman from signing away his fortune with a stroke of his pen. However, professional and predatory lenders were well versed in the legal requirements and could not be thwarted by the use of a different type of debt document. When necessary, they had notaries and witnesses ready to assist with the transaction. As for noncommercial borrowers who had sufficient reason to go beyond their usual network of relatives and friends to secure a loan, making the required legal forms more complex was not going to deter them.

The restrictions on using *vekseli* largely disappeared with the law of December 3, 1862, which extended the privilege of issuing them to all persons except for clergy, noncommissioned military personnel, and—significantly— peasants without landed property in their own name, unless they took out commercial licenses.[87] After 1862 loan letters gradually went out of use, especially since the pre-reform courts, where they used to be registered, closed by the end of the decade in the core provinces of the Russian empire.[88]

In practice, the *veksel* reform benefited primarily the nobles who were about to lose their serfs, and the law of 1862 should be viewed as a byproduct of the emancipation, attempting to enable the nobility to improve their financial condition through borrowing. The law also improved access to credit for the wealthiest and most enterprising peasants. The restrictions were further liberalized in 1875, when even soldiers were allowed to issue *vekseli* as part of Miliutin's project of creating a citizen army; all peasants were allowed to issue *vekseli* in 1906. However, the restrictions against women and clergy remained in force until the end of the imperial period.[89]

These changes in *veksel* law served to liberalize Russia's private credit and thus the property regime in general and should therefore be counted as a significant, though little-known "Great Reform" in its own right. Most individuals from the upper and middle classes could eventually borrow without much formality or regard for their personal reputation or for the condition of their properties, if any. In practice, however, it appears that the reform ironically made Russia's credit system even more dependent on personal connections and trust: once almost anyone could write a *veksel*, although *vekseli* written by respectable merchants continued to circulate like cash, ordinary individuals still had to work as hard as before to find a lender willing to trust them with an unsecured loan.

The second major set of policies designed to shape imperial Russia's credit relations established a succession of government-owned banks offering much cheaper loans than the private market. The first such bank appeared in 1754 as a way to assist and in effect bribe the serfowning nobility. It was of limited effectiveness because most of its sums were issued to a small group of courtiers close to Peter Shuvalov, Elizabeth's favorite. The volume of the bank's business remained small into the early nineteenth century.[90]

Under Catherine II, financial support for the gentry was placed on a firmer basis when several institutions were established that provided cash loans secured by serf "souls" at the low legally sanctioned five or six percent annual rate. The most important ones were the Moscow and St. Petersburg Orphanages; by the mid-nineteenth century, they accounted for about ninety percent of all government loans to the nobility. Each of them ran a "Safekeeping Treasury" *(Sokhrannaya kazna)* through its Board of Trustees *(Opekunskii Sovet)*.[91] Board loans issued from 1775 onward were originally limited to 5,000 rubles (admittedly, a hefty sum for all but the wealthiest nobles) and payable within five years, which ensured the Boards' solvency and prevented the highest aristocracy from leaching their funds. In the first half of the nineteenth century, the loan terms were gradually liberalized: the repayment term was extended to twelve years in 1819, to twenty-four years in 1824, and finally to twenty-six and thirty-seven years in 1830.[92] Unpopulated lands and houses could also be mortgaged for smaller sums.

State-run credit institutions reached their apogee during the reign of Nicholas I (1825–1855), when they started to accept unlimited deposits, which paid a generous four percent interest rate that could be compounded. Maximum loan amounts were greatly increased from the original 10 rubles per serf "soul" to 150–200 rubles, depending on the value of the estate.

Table 0.3 lists the total amounts of serf-secured mortgages issued by the Moscow Board of Trustees in the 1850s, before such loans were discontinued in 1859. In terms of overall loan portfolios, in 1855 the Moscow Board held loans worth 192.2 million rubles, accounting for nearly half of the government's credit operations. St. Petersburg Board loans were worth 133.4 million, and the Loan Bank in St. Petersburg that serviced the highest court aristocracy held another 30.1 million. All the provincial Offices of Public Welfare held loans worth 42.4 million. By 1859, when a banking crisis induced the

Table 0.3 Moscow Board of Trustees Loans to Serfowners, in Silver Rubles

Year	1852	1854	1856	1858
Amount	14,566,216.64	9,716,892	8,597,904	16,719,290

Data sources: TsIAM 424.1.2081 (1852), 2083 (1854), 2085 (1856), and 2087 (1858).

government to stop making these loans, the accumulated gentry debt amounted to 425.5 million rubles, secured by sixty-six percent of all privately owned serfs. (The total amount for 1855 was 398.2 million.)[93] The average loan amounts issued annually are difficult to estimate, but the average annual increase of gentry debt to the state in 1823–1859 was 9.3 million rubles.[94] This average increase was smaller than the new loan numbers for the 1850s for the Moscow Board alone, suggesting that gentry borrowing did not taper off once most of the eligible serfs had been mortgaged but rather that it continued until the 1859 closure of government banks, with serfowners paying off some of their loans and then remortgaging their estates.

The financial success of the government banks was enhanced by their privileged legal status. Their loans had priority over all other debts and obligations. Even when a loan was not in delinquency, the Board retained considerable control over the mortgaged property. Borrowers were required to mortgage entire estates with resale value as opposed to a few serfs at a time. Police and the courts could not enforce any acts with respect to mortgaged property without the Board's approval, including moving peasants to another estate. If a delinquent estate was sold, and there were fewer serfs or less land than originally declared, the Board collected the difference from the borrower, and if he was insolvent, from the officials and government institutions that had permitted the situation to occur. It was virtually impossible to take the Board to court or dispute its proceedings.[95]

Success was also ensured by efficient administration. Nineteenth-century government banks were very strict about requiring regular payments, even if they could allow a "remortgage"—that is, issue a new loan secured by that portion of an estate that was "cleared" through repayment. Moreover, instead of selling delinquent properties, state banks preferred to inventory the estates, appoint a trustee, and collect the income until the debt was paid.[96] For example, in Simbirsk province, in 1856, out of 800 mortgaged estates, 33 were inventoried, 14 actually seized from their owners, and only 1 sold; in 1860, out of 897 mortgaged estates, 119 were inventoried, 109 taken over, and 2 sold.[97]

In Riazan province in 1857, out of 2,554 mortgaged estates, 194 were inventoried, taken over, or sold.[98] These statistics do not indicate how many of the mortgaged estates were actually delinquent.

No doubt landowners with appropriate connections could influence the Board to fudge the rules, but for typical landowners, all evidence points otherwise. Moreover, it appears that the small numbers of auction sales were due not to any difficulty of collection but to the difficulty of finding buyers for bankrupt properties. As discussed below, at least the Moscow Board of Trustees turned a healthy profit on its mortgage loans. A public sale was a last-resort measure, which explains its rare occurrence.

Court cases illustrate the circumstances that resulted in a sale by the Board. The estate of Collegiate Secretary Petr Zubov—approximately 3,000 serfs in Arzamas and Makariev Counties of Nizhnii Novgorod province—had been in extreme financial disarray for several generations, yet the Board was content for many years with appointing a trustee but keeping Zubov as the legal owner.[99] Andrei Chikhachev, a middling landowner from Vladimir province, wrote an article for the *Agricultural Gazette* lamenting the indebtedness of provincial serfowners, noting that estates were being taken under trusteeship, but did not mention any actual sales at auction. Aleksei Galakhov in his memoirs recalled the panic experienced by indebted provincial landowners when reading their weekly mail, although he also noted that most of them managed to negotiate with the government or find private loans to keep their estates.[100]

Thus, by the middle of the nineteenth century, the government banks—the four largest ones being the Loan Bank, the Commercial Bank, and the St. Petersburg and Moscow Boards—accumulated nearly 1 billion rubles in deposits—an astronomical amount at the time, enough to fill the empire's budget for several years.[101] As Soviet historian Iosif Gindin has suggested, these funds could have been used more productively to finance the development of Russia's economy. Instead, the larger portion of the amount was used to cover budget deficits, and a relatively small proportion was invested in additional loans to serfowning nobles. But Gindin did not want to exaggerate the claim of Russia's lagging behind: whereas large joint stock depository banks appeared in the United States and Britain in the 1830s, in France, Austria, Germany, and Italy such banks began to appear only in the late 1840s and early 1850s—that is, approximately ten years before they appeared in Russia.[102] Ivan Pushechnikov, a conservative landowner and memoirist from Oryol province, thought the Board of Trustees had been "a most beneficent mediator between depositors and borrowers," in addition to carrying out its philanthropic work.[103] This is in contrast to the late-imperial and Soviet Marxist view that the government's policies in effect enserfed capital and that the banks were essentially "feudal" institutions.[104] It is true that the mortgage banks mostly assisted the nobility, but it is not at all clear why we should consider as deviant or backward the fact that elites enjoyed financial and other economic benefits.

For the majority of Russia's property-owning classes, who owned relatively few serfs or none at all, the state banks could not be of much help.[105] However, the benefits that they provided extended much further than other historians have acknowledged: indeed, the very distinction between government and private lending was not completely clear-cut. The funds loaned to serfowners were often then transferred into the network of private credit by being reissued to other individuals at higher interest rates. Even more interestingly, some serfowners deposited their loans back in the same government banks at four percent interest and then used their deposit receipts—which circulated like cash—to issue private loans and collect additional interest.[106] Moreover, the Commercial Bank, despite its reluctance to make risky loans to entrepreneurs, did support economic development by purchasing commercial debt documents and thereby supporting the system of commercial credit.

In 1859, the state banking system was shut down. Technically, this happened because after the Crimean War there was too much cash in circulation without enough potential borrowers; servicing the swelling volume of deposits became expensive, inducing the state to reduce the interest rate. This led to a run on the banks and to their financial collapse, as recounted by Stephen Hoch.[107] Memoirists remembered the event with bitterness. Pushechnikov thought it was "not only a reckless affair, but a blasphemous one, and even the most ardent enemy of Russia would not dare to commit such barbarity." In his view, the government held such valuable collateral that it could easily borrow money in Europe to deal with the crisis.[108] It was also hinted that the bank fiasco was a subtle way to wrestle serfowners into acquiescing to the impending emancipation.[109] As Seymour Becker has noted, government-issued mortgage banks for the nobility were successfully revived toward the end of the nineteenth century, even though they made far riskier investments.[110]

Government banks were established to make private credit cheaper for privileged property owners, especially serfowners but also merchants. The banks were also unique sites where public and private credit and finances intersected—although this aspect of their activity is still poorly understood. Despite all of their unprecedented authority to collect their debt and discipline their debtors, largely in circumvention of the court system, the banks and government policy in general left a surprising amount of decision-making to private individuals. For instance, there were no restrictions on what the borrower could do with the money borrowed from a government bank. Compared to the state-run credit system, private lending was even less restrictive; most importantly, there were no requirements, such as licensing or registration, on who could act as a lender, making the world of "usurers" a financial free-for-all.

Part I

THE CULTURE OF DEBT

Figure 1.1. V. G. Astrakhov, *At the Market. Playing Checkers* (1857)
Source: State Historical Museum (Moscow)

CHAPTER 1

Usurers' Tales

She was a tiny shriveled old thing, around sixty, with sharp and mean little eyes, with a small sharp nose and uncovered head. Her flaxen-blond hair—barely touched by gray—was thickly smeared with oil. Her thin and long neck, rather like a chicken leg, was wrapped in some kind of flannel rag, and on her shoulders, despite the heat, was flapping a tattered and yellowed fur jacket. The old thing was constantly coughing and wheezing.[1]

This of course describes Aliona Ivanovna, the fictional pawnbroker from *Crime and Punishment*. The university students and young army officers who were her clients said that she was "able to hand out five thousand all at once, while never snubbing a ruble's pawn."[2] The most striking element of the cultural stereotype captured by Dostoevsky is not simply Aliona Ivanovna's pathetic appearance or viciousness but also her social marginalization, which is exaggerated to the point of caricature. Her only known social interaction is to bite her half-sister Lizaveta, her clients appear as parasitical as herself, and her wealth would remain lost to society even after her death by being bequeathed to a remote monastery.[3] Consider also Grushenka, the femme fatale of Dostoevsky's last great novel, *The Brothers Karamazov:*

It was also known that the young woman, especially during the past year, embarked upon what is known as "gesheft," and that in this respect she turned out to have extraordinary abilities, so that in the end many christened her a true Jewess. Not that she lent money on interest, but it was known, for example, that for some time, in partnership with Fedor Pavlovich Karamazov, she had really been engaged in buying up bills of exchange for a trifle, ten kopecks to the ruble, and later made a ruble to ten kopecks on some of them.[4]

To Dostoevsky's early readers, this passage would illustrate the moral defectiveness of both Grushenka and the soon-to-be-killed Fedor Karamazov because individuals who bought up bad debt and then used their knowledge of legal procedures to collect it were known as *diskontery* (for "discounting" a debt document, which means buying it from the original lender for less than its face value) and considered to be "the most greedy and predatory" type of usurer.[5]

Real-life Russian moneylenders and pawnbrokers, in contrast to their prominent fictional counterparts, were hardly ever discussed in the press or remembered in memoirs, even when they were murdered. Even imperial-era works on rural usury, such as those by Roman Tsimmerman (Gvozdev) and Georgii Sazonov, provide detailed information about credit networks and lending practices but very little information about lenders as human beings as opposed to abstract economic actors. These authors show wealthy peasant lenders (known as *kulaks*) as fundamentally in opposition to their communities even while arguing that any peasant would gladly turn into a *kulak* if given a chance. Incidentally, this point also applies to histories of credit in Western Europe and North America, which are written entirely from the debtors' perspective.[6]

Similarly, Marx's framework, which guided the few brief explorations of "usury" by Soviet historians, equated private informal lending with the archaic "usurious" variety, which he interpreted as predatory and nonproductive and therefore not worthy of a detailed analysis except as the backdrop for the development of modern capitalist banking. The data presented in the few Soviet-era studies of "usury" in early modern and Petrine Russia do not at all fit this theory, showing that although credit could indeed be expensive and even exploitative, the web of credit ties linked all social strata, and private lending could not be characterized as unambiguously or predominantly predatory or archaic or as financing mainly wasteful consumption.[7]

Nineteenth-century lenders likewise were a diverse group, ranging from the wealthiest aristocrats to illiterate peasant pawnbrokers, and from a multitude of one-time investors to a few individuals who can be character-ized as professional usurers. It is as difficult to single out the latter group of high-risk lenders as it is to identify the rates they charged. Moreover, even "professional" lenders still depended not upon Aliona Ivanovna–style hostile estrangement from the world but upon being successfully embedded in existing networks of kinship, state service, and locality. Like the motley group of entrepreneurs who prepared the way for Russia's capitalist transformation or the jurists who prepared the legal reform, these individuals—who had to fit in in the absence of large banks—prepared the way for the Russian finan-cial revolution that began in the 1860s.

Equally importantly, lenders relied on their knowledge of legal rules and procedures. Their legal knowledge and skill level varied but nearly always made the laws limiting maximum interest rates practically unenforceable except in rare circumstances.[8] The task of upholding private property and supporting the elites who owned it required the security of private-law trans-actions, including loans and mortgages, even though actual interest rates exceeded the legal limit. This contradiction potentially subverted the tsar's law and his officials' authority and caused no small concern to the latter. Governors, police officers, and jurists needed to determine whether they could effectively regulate private credit and, if so, where to start. For instance, how were they to gather the necessary information, and how were they to justify their intervention in legal, political, and moral terms? Provincial gov-ernors with their extensive police powers, and the officers of the Third Section of His Imperial Majesty's Own Chancellery—Russia's political police in 1826–1879, with broad authority to monitor and regulate public morality—did find the time in their busy schedules to examine private lending by con-ducting surveillance operations that were remarkably sophisticated for the mid-nineteenth century and by gathering and responding to individual com-plaints and secret reports about individual lenders. In the process, officials had to make important judgments about such things as individual authority, responsibility, and failure and, above all, about the tension between morality and the law.[9]

Whereas the authorities suppressed political dissent quite rigorously and had no qualms about using *agents provocateurs* and secret informants to sniff out other kinds of organized crime, I have not located any instances of sim-ilar kinds of entrapment being used to catch usurers. Virtually all private lenders were left unmolested, with the exception of a few individuals per-ceived as not playing by the rules, such as by offending powerful interests or attracting an unusually high volume of complaints. If possible, these were prosecuted in court, but more commonly the government combined out-of-court negotiations and extra-legal—or, rather, quasi-legal—sanctions, including police surveillance and administrative exile. Ultimately, none of these measures could satisfactorily address deep-seated anxieties about the morality of the market and the government's role in regulating it, but then what could?[10]

Morality, Policy, and the Law

Dostoevsky's deep aversion to moneylenders was fueled by his well-known personal experiences with debt, but ultimately it was grounded in a long-standing cultural and religious tradition extending far beyond Russia. Aristotle condemned usury as unjust and unnatural because "interest was money born of money," and money was an arbitrary medium of exchange that was not supposed to breed. The Biblical and Christian denunciations of usury could be interpreted as allowing it under certain circumstances but still considering it incompatible with life in a peaceful community.[11] The most common Russian word for usurer—*rostovshchik*—was a term of abuse that could easily lead to a lawsuit for insult and slander.[12] A brief anonymous tale from the late seventeenth century depicted a usurer who died and fell directly into hell when he was buried; his lot was improved after his widow donated all of his wealth to the church and to the poor, but only after long negotiations and with the participation of a folk minstrel *(skomorokh)*. The devil in this tale—vicious and mistrustful—appears to be little different from the usurer himself, and the negotiations closely resemble the procedure of collecting a debt.[13] In nineteenth-century fiction, for example in Nikolai Nekrasov's 1841 short story, usury involves a "hardening" of one's soul and is associated with vengeance and sexual predation: the lender enticed his victim, a skilled but modest artisan, with an interest-free loan just so he could eventually engineer his ruin and attempt to possess his wife.[14] In our own day, it is commonly accepted by economists and laypersons alike that low interest rates reflect a nation's "intelligence and moral strength."[15]

Occasionally, oppressed debtors took matters into their own hands. The barely veiled threat of popular violence is expressed in one of Ostrovskii's plays published in 1872, in which a character from Moscow's lower middle class opines that "these usurers should be robbed, my friend, because thou shalt not drink another's blood."[16] After public criminal trials were introduced in Russia in 1866, several notorious cases involved the murder of a usurer by his or her client: only weeks before the first installment of Dostoevsky's *Crime and Punishment* was published in 1866, a Moscow University student, Danilov, killed a usurer and her servant.[17] In 1879, another prominent usurer, Vlasov, was murdered in St. Petersburg by his client and friend, Karl Landsberg, an officer in the Imperial Guard, who became worried that the lender intended to ruin his upcoming marriage by revealing his precarious financial condition. After slitting the usurer's throat with a razor blade and then killing his maidservant as well, Landsberg found out that Vlasov had just written a letter forgiving all his debt as a wedding present.[18]

More coordinated attacks were also possible, especially when a lender happened to be in a vulnerable position. In 1864, a sixty-four-year-old merchant and moneylender, Andrei Lukin, was imprudent enough to visit the inner chambers of the Moscow debtors' prison. He was attacked by a group of inmates, who beat him, called him a scoundrel *(podlets)* and a usurer, and told him in the presence of a police officer who was helpless or unwilling to intervene that he was being beaten for "charging a very large and merciless interest rate, namely fifteen percent per month."[19] Rural usurers risked a visit from robbers and highwaymen. In 1838, a gang of approximately twelve men led by an escaped convict broke into the house of Mr. Glinka, a rural landowner in Smolensk province. Glinka, who lived in a dilapidated house with only three girls and one boy as his servants, was known for his wealth and miserliness. The robbers had no difficulty breaking the rotten window frames and subduing the servants, after which they took away a chest containing pawned property and cash.[20]

The majority of the population who were law-abiding took their grievances to the authorities. Popular complaints about usurers preserved in legal and official documents show no awareness of ancient philosophical arguments, such as the Aristotelian critique of usury as unnatural and unjust. Nor were the Biblical and Christian denunciations of usury of much help: early modern Russia had a centuries-long tradition of interest-bearing lending that was pioneered by its greatest property owner, the Orthodox Church.[21] Finally, it was futile to claim that moneylenders were useless parasites similar to Aliona Ivanovna because, much as we might admire the art of Dostoevsky, Ostrovskii, and Nekrasov, real-life usurers were exceedingly well integrated into society, generally much more so than their clients. Consider the well-known memoirs by Elizaveta Yankova (1768–1861) recorded by her grandson Dmitry Blagovo. One of Yankova's relatives, a girl from the old Muscovite

Mamonov family, married an old and wealthy moneylender, Stepan Shilovskii. His craving for money allegedly resulted in chest spasms whenever someone would come to ask him to pay household expenses, and apparently he eventually died from despondency after losing a large investment.

The narrator noted that even if these stories were not true, they still showed that Shilovskii was thought to be capable of severe depression on account of money, something apparently considered bad form among old gentry families.[22] Reading this passage, it is easy to miss the fact that Shilovskii, described as a stereotypical miser found in fiction throughout the world, was nonetheless deeply and comfortably entangled in the network of kinship, property, and influence that Yankova's memoirs describe so vividly. Indeed, Shilovskii's son Peter rose to become a member of Russia's Council of State.[23] His daughter Anna married a member of the prominent Voeikov family but apparently continued his father's occupation as a moneylender and a woman of business.

Rather than condemning usury as such, the typical victim's narrative submitted to the courts or to the police alleged excessive avarice and shrewdness that preyed on personal misfortune and subverted the tsar's law through its loopholes and imperfections. For example, a civil servant in Petersburg, Grigorii Popov, complained to the police in 1859 that

> On January 20 of this year, in extreme need of 300 rubles, I followed the advice of dressmaker Schlesinger and turned to Collegiate Secretary Mikhail Ivanovich Yefimov who after long negotiations agreed to loan me that amount minus 30 rubles as interest and on the condition (1) that I would take from him an old piano that he valued at 600 rubles; (2) would issue him a document for 2,000 rubles due in two months and guaranteed by two persons and moreover, would give him a receipt for the entire amount. For a long time I would not agree to such conditions and decided to accept them only because of my inexperience and extreme need of money and having believed Yefimov that he would treat me honorably, take the debt document only to protect himself, and never actually charge me that kind of interest, and that if I could not pay him the debt, i.e., 900 *[sic]* rubles after one month, he would wait for another month.[24]

In fact, Yefimov sued for the entire amount only one month later, but there was virtually nothing a borrower like Popov could do to defend himself when a usurer had followed the letter of the law.

A more persuasive set of arguments against usury invoked societal interest and came both from the victims and from police officials. For example, this is how one Moscow merchant of middling wealth complained in 1863 about a pawnbroker who had embezzled his collateral:

> [This case reveals] the dark side of the faithlessness not only on the part of the Draevskys [the pawnbroker and his wife], but of all such enterprising usurers who entice poor folk with an attractive bait of lending out money secured by collateral—for moderate interest and on attractive conditions, as published:—but then, based on some fictitious receipts, using poor people's extreme need, lending a dime for something worth a ruble,—allow themselves, not binding themselves by any conditions—to embezzle at will the property they are entrusted with—without any mercy or pangs of conscience, solely for their enrichment; depriving nakedness of its last cover ... With such means, and with non-suppression of this evil by the Government, such enterprising types, given such principles of their enrichment, are capable through their avarice of fleecing the entire poor class of entire Moscow!—Into which category, under the stated enticement, I likewise fell unforeseeably, with my pawned items, into the hands of the Draevskys. Who embezzled my things, while the term of the loan had not yet expired, and while I was paying the interest![25]

Although this merchant owned several fur coats and so could hardly qualify as poor, arguments that the government had a policy interest in preventing the ruin of an entire population class or group were readily heard by the authorities. As already discussed, mortgage banks for serfowners were ostensibly established to protect them from high interest rates charged by private lenders. But the government also targeted usury directly through police surveillance, as well as formal anti-usury legislation. Surveillance was carried out by the Third Section and its military arm, the Corps of Gendarmes. Aside from their well-known function as political police, they were also tasked with keeping an eye on various nonpolitical undesirables, such as gamblers, swindlers, and usurers. It is to the gendarmes that we must be grateful for revealing information about the real-life counterparts of Dostoevsky's Alena Ivanovna that is simply not available from any other sources. Incidentally, the most detailed lists of usurers and the most colorful anecdotes about their activities come from 1859–1867— the precise time of Russia's revolution in banking and finance—as if the government strove not simply to educate itself about existing private lending practices but to become convinced that the existing practice of "usury" was deeply flawed and in need of reform.

At the same time, even at the highest levels the government realized that it was both impossible and undesirable to eliminate interest rates that exceeded the legally mandated maximum. For example, an 1861 memo prepared by one of the tsar's closest aides and a general in the Corps of Gendarmes, Ivan Annenkov, recognized that usurers in Russia enjoyed "complete immunity" but urged that "we must not [condemn as usurers] all persons who loan money for interest, even if under private agreements such interest would exceed the limit defined by the law. Everybody knows that no one has so far placed his capital in private hands in return for the legal 6% . . . [government's policies] must not touch upon those private obligations and conditions that are founded upon mutual benefit." Annenkov proposed a systematic procedure of identifying as many individual lenders as possible and then focusing on those known to engage in particularly abusive practices.[26]

One method of compiling information was for the agents to openly visit notarial offices and examine their records, to search through court records, or to summon and interview individual lenders at the Third Section. Another method was to collect personal complaints against individual lenders, as well as anonymous denunciations and reports by paid informers. In 1859, the gendarmes produced two lists of Petersburg lenders. The first list, extracted from notarial records, focused on lenders to young aristocrats. It contained 39 names, all but 3 of them males, and almost equally split between noble and commercial estates. The range of the numbers of borrowers per each usurer—only 8 had more than 10, and 12 had only 1 or 2—and the differentiation in the amount of the lenders' portfolios—from about 200 rubles to over 300,000—show that this list was compiled without much system or pattern. The gendarmes targeted several truly wealthy lenders but also those who were rather modest by St. Petersburg standards, since the median size of the portfolio was just over 10,000 rubles. The investigation then produced a short list of 16 lenders, with 2 new names added, but 10 of these held debt worth less than 50,000 rubles. An even shorter list identified those lenders who were considered especially infamous: Collegiate Secretary Yefimov, tailor Greib, notary Kalugin, and nobles Fokin and Bogomolets. To give the gendarmes justice, they were interested not simply in the volume of a lender's operations but in lending practices they viewed as prejudicial.[27]

Colonel Fedor Rakeev, the Corps of Gendarmes's expert on financial crime, argued that the list contained two individuals who "did not at all engage in reprehensible lending." One was a wine merchant, Ivan Odintsov, and the other was Lieutenant Margarit, "known under the nickname of Margaritka [Margaret], who has for a long time been a supplier to the Guard Corps, and virtually all of his lifelong profits dispersed into hopeless loans."[28] Journalist Mikhail Pyliaev in his well-known collection of anecdotes about Petersburg eccentrics claimed that Margarit was from the Greek colony in the Ukrainian town of Nezhin and that he had served as a spy as well as a peddler. Apparently Margarit was the first Petersburg merchant to sell khalva and Turkish delight, and he ended his life tragically, being knifed down by his ward. He lent primarily to military officers and, according to Pyliaev, owned documents worth hundreds of thousands of rubles.[29] This is much more than Rakeev's estimate of 20,000 rubles; we may only speculate about the reasons Rakeev was so eager to protect Margarit by personally vouching for him, but it is important to remember that although gendarmes were not permitted to incur debts, they sometimes did; moreover, the position number thirty-five was suspiciously omitted from the list. It therefore appears that lists such as this were far from routine inventories but instead encapsulated intricate strategizing and negotiation among the individuals involved.

The second list from 1859 included 68 individuals (four women), who allegedly "participated in various fraudulent activities and in enticing young men to issue debt documents for large amounts."[30] As in the first list, these lenders' legal identities were split equally between nobles/civil servants (32) and the urban and commercial estates, including merchants (10), craftsmen, townspeople, and foreigners (20), as well as 5 peasants. It is important to explain, however, why only 17 of the lenders had also featured in the first list. One possibility is that the investigation was haphazard. Another explanation is that the second list may have specifically targeted lenders of particular backgrounds, including relatively high-ranking lenders—for instance, a major general, a colonel, and a state councilor—and craftspeople, such as three tailors, three carriage makers, a glove maker, a barber, and a turner's son.

Finally, a third list preserved in the Third Section archive included 81 lenders and was compiled in 1867.[31] Uniquely, it included each lender's religion, age, and home address, as well as notes about their conduct and character. Unlike the earlier lists, it featured 23 women (38 percent), either because women were more active in moneylending after the financial liberalization of the 1860s or because the 1859 investigation chose not to prosecute women. Of the 64 lenders whose religion was listed, there were 39 Orthodox (plus at least 8 more, judging by their names), 10 Lutherans, 8 Jews, 4 Catholics, 2 Reformed, and 1 Old Believer. Thus, at least in the 1860s, we cannot claim that any particular ethnic or religious minority was disproportionately represented among the lenders, given that the Orthodox comprised at least 58 percent of the group. As to the lenders' age, 82 percent of them were between 28 and 51 years, with the average age being 39. Only 3 lenders were over 60, making the stereotypical image of an old miserly usurer a rarity. It is also remarkable that only one lender on this list also appeared in the lists from 1859, suggesting that the careers of those moneylenders who happened to attract the Third Section's attention did not exceed seven years.

In addition to statistical data, the Third Section's lists of usurers contained information about moral character. This consisted of several elements. One was the lenders' "reliability" *(blagonadezhnost')*, which in the context of nineteenth-century Russia generally meant political loyalty but here must have also referred to the lenders' willingness to cooperate with police. Out of the eighty-one lenders from the 1867 list, seven were marked as "reliable," including goldsmith Karl Georg Falk—incidentally the only lender also found on the 1859 list—who was accused of fraud in 1853 and placed under permanent police surveillance, but from that point on had acted in an "excellent and reliable manner in all respects." Ten of the eighty-one lenders were identified as having been involved in illegal activity. This included complaints from the borrowers, accepting stolen property as collateral, engaging in "dirty speculations" and being swindlers *(aferist)*, embezzling the collateral, and even—in the case of townsman Vasilii Stabrovskii—being a notorious pickpocket. Townsman Alexander Anglin was known to immediately pawn the collateral entrusted to him to other lenders. Four lenders either intended to go out of business or were said to be too poor to act as lenders.

Finally, the lenders' personal lives was also important. Being a family member of another usurer was a minus, whereas having family or owning property appears to have been a plus: for instance, noblewoman Yuvalia Baranovskaia had a son and a daughter, and two lenders owned a house. In a different list of pawnbrokers from 1866, merchant Boris Zakharov lived with a mistress, Mr. Miller had a family, and merchant Kon (Kohn) was married.[32] Retired civil servants Shtein and Kuzmin had nice furnishings but bad business reputations. This interest in the lenders' character—paralleled by similar inquiries for the debtors they imprisoned—therefore served to ground the morality of market transactions in such characteristics as personal "reliability," crime-free life, and personal conduct.

Taken together, these lists of course only show us what the Third Section chose to see, but they indicate remarkable variety among Petersburg moneylenders and pawnbrokers in terms of their social position and volume of operations, as well as suggesting huge turnover among practitioners during the financial revolution of the 1860s and possibly a large influx of women.[33] Above all, these lists must be conceptualized not so much as mechanical accumulations of data but as products of active, behind-the-scenes negotiation and influence-peddling, likely accompanied by bribes to police agents who nevertheless may not have held all the trump cards. The stakes were high: one could be shortlisted as a particularly harmful usurer, avoid the list altogether, or even be characterized favorably in the report to higher-ups. Gendarme surveillance can thus be regarded as a variation of the more familiar procedure of a lender or rating agency checking a borrower's credit, except that here lenders rather than the borrowers were scrutinized.

The gendarmes themselves acknowledged that their surveillance techniques were far from perfect and blamed their instructions, which limited investigations "solely to malicious [zlovrednye] usurers and especially those of them who entice young men into debt instead of extending the investigation to all usurers without any distinction."[34] In 1859, the previously mentioned Colonel Rakeev complained that such instructions hamstrung his efforts, since it was impossible to determine a priori which of the lenders were malicious usurers. Moreover, the procedure of summoning moneylenders to the Third Section for questioning did not produce any results since none of them were willing to admit any wrongdoing. Nor was it possible to question the debtors unless they first submitted a complaint, which very few were willing to do out of fear of "losing credit among the usurers."[35] For example, during an 1859 investigation, only two debtors were willing to complain, and the gendarmes could do nothing because they did not have evidence to initiate a formal criminal investigation.

Colonel Rakeev argued that a much better way to collect information would be through personal contacts with usurers or with their relatives and acquaintances.[36] At least once, in 1866, the Third Section acted on this advice by sending an officer to 28 pawnshops in Petersburg, offering the same watch—worth 35 rubles—as collateral and recording the terms of the loans at each shop.[37] The agent compiling the report noted that there were so many pawnbrokers in Petersburg that it was impossible to list them all, but there were more than 20 who regularly advertised themselves in newspapers, whereas all the others worked without any publicity. Out of 28 lenders, 6 (21 percent) were women, and their social background was, as before, extremely diverse, as listed in Appendix C. Only 14 of them were also on the above-mentioned list from 1867, which was so large and well detailed that this lack of continuity suggests high turnover more than it does the likelihood of buying one's way out of the list.

This list is fascinating not simply for its attention to the lenders' personal circumstances and character but also for the fact that it is the only document that provides anything like objective data for the monthly interest rates actually charged by Russian lenders.[38] It varied from 5 to 12 percent, with 10 being the norm (i.e., the most commonly charged amount as well as the average and the median). The average loan for the 35-ruble watch offered as collateral by the agent was 11.6 rubles, with 10 rubles being the median and the most commonly offered amount. Sixteen of the lenders offered a "grace period," presumably referring to a period during which the interest was not compounded, ranging from one month to "without limit." Superficially, these conditions appear to be rather harsh, but not when compared to other high-risk or payday operations in other countries in the nineteenth and twentieth centuries, which charged astronomical rates.[39] More importantly, this exercise by the Third Section indicates that even this unregulated pawnbroking in the age of Russia's financial liberalization and transformation operated as a market, within a range of commonly accepted terms and conditions, and was therefore a far cry from the predatory free-for-all that is presumed in existing literature.

Whereas the gendarmes were specifically looking for professional high-risk lenders, a more systematic examination suggests that such lenders were completely outnumbered by one-time investors seeking a better return on their money than the low interest rate paid by government-owned banks or those helping relatives or friends. Looking at the debt registers at the Moscow Civil Chamber, we may suppose that individuals issuing multiple loans in a given year were more likely to be "usurers" than those recorded only once. For example, there were only 5 such lenders out of a sample of 138 in 1852, 7 out of 122 in 1854, and 2 out of 55 in 1864.[40] For the purposes of comparison, a loan letter register from the backwoods town of Temnikov (Tambov province) in the first three months of 1820 shows that out of 35 creditors, four made more than one loan, including one person who made six loans.[41] In-town mortgage loans were more attractive for professional moneylenders: for instance, in 1855, 11 out of 100 lenders loaned more than once (and 11 out of 132 in 1860, though only 3 out of 97 for rural mortgages in 1862).[42] As a comparison, transactions between close relatives were more common: 12 in 1852, 14 in 1854, and 8 in 1864 for loan letters. In the early 1700s, debt registers from Moscow and several other towns also contained very few repeat lenders.[43]

All population classes were thought to be vulnerable to predatory lenders and need police protection. The police paid particular attention to usurers catering to young aristocratic borrowers, whose relatives' complaints were likely to trigger investigations. Lenders to the rich had to tread carefully, unless of course they were aristocrats themselves. But the problem was not thought to be limited to the upper classes. The agents during the 1866 investigation noted that "as regards the victims of such usury, they are primarily the middle class [srednii klass], i.e., petty officials and poor individuals who barely get by through work and are induced to make such loans mainly because pawning property in the government-run pawn shop is fraught with difficulties and takes a long time."[44] Lenders to the laboring classes usually evaded notice but were sometimes targeted, no doubt due to their religion (if they were Jews), vulnerability, and lack of literacy and social connections.

Formal anti-usury legislation was also available against lenders who failed to take adequate legal precautions. For centuries, European laws regulating usury vacillated between prohibiting all interest, setting a legally permissible rate, and banning only practices viewed as predatory, especially compounding the interest. As Western attitudes to credit became more permissive by the late eighteenth century, usury laws were gradually relaxed but usually not abolished altogether. In England, the five percent interest ceiling established in 1713 was abolished completely in 1854, by which time some rather sophisticated legal schemes had been designed to evade the restrictions.[45] Pre-1789 French laws prohibited interest-bearing loans but in the eighteenth century included many exemptions, while Napoleon's statute of 1807 set the maximum rate at five to six percent.[46] In the United States, most states kept interest ceilings into the twentieth century and occasionally even lowered them, although usury laws contained many exceptions and were generally ignored in practice. The general tendency in the United States was to keep minimum rates but to expand the exceptions and to reduce penalties to voiding the loan or imposing a moderate fine.[47]

In Dostoevsky's Russia, the legal annual interest rate was six percent, with some exceptions for commercial debt that could also carry collection fees of an additional eight percent.[48] Several laws issued in the first half of the century relaxed these restrictions considerably. In 1834, lenders were allowed to charge a penalty on delinquent mortgage loans. An 1849 law abolished a longstanding rule found in many legal systems limiting the overall amount of accruing interest to the amount of the principal. Finally, an 1854 law permitted compounding the interest.[49] The prescribed punishment for usury was sometimes severe earlier in the eighteenth century and could include confiscation of the lender's property, but after 1786 it was limited to a fine in the amount of excessive interest, which was tripled by the Penal Code of 1845, with short prison sentences added for repeat offenders. Importantly, borrowers were still responsible for paying both the principal and the legally permissible interest.[50] While a criminal conviction itself entailed social and legal disadvantages, the legal punishment for usury did not involve the loss of one's legal rights, imprisonment, or penal exile, thus showing unambiguously that the law regarded usury as one of the least dangerous crimes. Compared to other major Western legal systems, there was therefore nothing fundamentally defective or even substantially different about the Russian approach to regulating private lending.

A moral and religious aversion to usury did exist, and the highest government officials believed that private lending involved important policy considerations; that said, long before the reforms of the 1860s and 1870s, the law was clearly moving toward gradually relaxing the restrictions. While the Russian legal system had many peculiarities that are discussed throughout this book, the legal regulation of usury does not stand out from the common Western experience and cannot be interpreted as hampering the development of capitalism in Russia in the way that the development of corporate law has been claimed to do.[51]

Gendarmes and Usurers

One individual whose travails illustrate these competing concerns and whose story is unusually well detailed came to the government's attention in March 1859, when the all-powerful chief of the gendarmes and director of the Third Section, Prince Vasily Dolgorukov, received a petition from the elderly General Nikolai Buturlin (1801–1867), a decorated veteran of campaigns against Poland and Turkey and a member of the tsar's Military Council.

General Buturlin complained that two years previously, his son, who then served in the elite Chevalier Guard regiment in Petersburg, had fallen victim to a gang of swindlers who were in the business of taking advantage of young men from wealthy families by encouraging their habits of luxury and loaning them small sums of money, in exchange for which they took debt documents for exorbitant amounts. The younger Buturlin was receiving only 6,000 rubles per year from his father, a modest allowance considering the expenses expected for someone of his station, and so could hardly survive without borrowing.[52]

The alleged gang of usurers included two merchants, Gavrila Mironov (formerly a peasant) and Alexander Lipgardt, shoemaker Ivan Goze, and retired civil servant Vasily Chestnokov. Together they took from Buturlin debt obligations amounting to a staggering 280,000 silver rubles. Considering that Chestnokov's rank—collegiate assessor, corresponding to army major—was far superior to that of the other members, he was the primary target of General Buturlin's petition and of the investigation that ensued. The main issue was not so much that Chestnokov did not actually issue all that money to the young man but rather that he took advantage of the younger Buturlin's inexperience and induced him to write three letters in which he admitted to several criminal offenses. Allegedly this was done to provide Chestnokov with additional leverage to induce repayment, since he no doubt realized that with people as prominent as the Buturlins, the usual legal channels were less effective than threats to their honor and reputation. In the first letter, the young man asked Chestnokov for a loan and claimed to act as his father's legal agent, tasked with purchasing a property for which he supposedly needed to get cash quickly. Chestnokov later claimed that he thought that he was in effect lending the money to General Buturlin rather than to his dissolute son. In the second letter, the youth admitted that he had lied about representing his father and in fact used the loan to pay his prior debts; in the third letter, he also admitted that he had earlier deceived Chestnokov about his age by claiming to be over twenty-one. This was important because in Russia, individuals under that age were strictly prohibited from entering into any property transactions such as lending or borrowing money.

General Buturlin had to act quickly because Chestnokov, having failed to get an acceptable settlement from him or from his son, and given that the loan was void due to Buturlin's minority, initiated criminal proceedings, in which the youth—having admitted to writing the letters—was sure to be convicted. The general acknowledged his son's "heavy guilt" with a "crushed and torn heart," while at the same time he portrayed himself as a gruff old servitor of the tsar primarily concerned with the public welfare, which would inevitably suffer if Chestnokov, the real wrongdoer in the case, managed to evade punishment and continue to "harm public morals, to ruin noble families and to inflict personal misfortune upon raw youths." General Buturlin also attempted to play on the frequently sour relations between the regular police and the Third Section that was tasked with overseeing its actions: he ended his petition by requesting that the case be taken over by the Third Section because Chestnokov had previously served in the Petersburg police and would likely "enjoy the special patronage of regular police authorities."[53]

Although this story was very much like many other complaints against moneylenders, General Buturlin's wealth and connections were exceptional. Within a few days the complaint was reported to the tsar himself, who was told that in addition to Buturlin, there were other aristocratic youths in Petersburg who were being similarly ruined by usurers. Alexander II ordered the Third Section to form a special secret commission composed of officials from the city police, the governor's office, and officers of the Corps of Gendarmes, including Captain Chulkov, who was said to be familiar with many of the individuals involved in the case.[54] A month later, in April 1859, the gendarmes also appointed Colonel Fedor Rakeev, a high-profile officer also "familiar with many of the local usurers."[55] The military sent its own representative, Major General Dubensky, who was supposed to protect the younger Buturlin's interests as a member of the military establishment.

Forming a commission with the involvement of the gendarmes was the standard way of addressing complaints against usurers, which were common in Petersburg as well as in Moscow, especially when borrowers took the risk of losing credit with other lenders and complained as a group. The record of the commission's activities provides a unique glimpse into Russia's legal culture on the eve of the court reform of 1864 and into the numerous and previously unstudied nonpolitical cases investigated by the Third Section. Existing studies have paid no heed to the fact that the Third Section's Second Expedition served primarily as a forum for civil law disputes and that particularly important criminal cases were handled by the First Expedition (cases against nobles) and the Fourth Expedition (cases against peasants). Taken together, the Third Section during its entire existence doubled as a parallel system of justice curiously approximating the English equity jurisdiction, with its task of handling cases for which the regular court system could provide no remedy.[56]

The commission's first step was to search legal, police, and Third Section archives for information about the alleged usurers' prior offenses. It turned out that Chestnokov had been accused earlier of malfeasance when acting as the executor of a will of another civil servant and even of forging a payment receipt. While these allegations were never substantiated and were indeed routine in debt, property, and inheritance disputes, they no doubt engendered additional prejudice against Chestnokov, given that the commission was undoubtedly already aware that his influence and connections could not hope to match those of Buturlin. There was much more compromising material against the merchant Mironov, technically a fruit vendor, who was known for selling fruit on credit at a large interest rate to wealthy students at boarding schools in Petersburg, where the menus were monotonous even at the most elite institutions and in any case insufficient for healthy boys.

Moreover, the Third Section had "information" that Chestnokov, Mironov, and the jeweler Lipgardt "engage in buying and reselling debt obligations, often act in concert, and use reprehensible means in the course of their financial transactions." This allegation was particularly important from a legal standpoint because it raised the possibility of prosecuting Chestnokov and other moneylenders as a "gang" *(shaika),* which—unlike usury alone—was punishable by lifelong exile to Siberia.[57] These provisions punished even secondary members of a *shaika* and applied even if the gang failed to complete any of its crimes, although a conviction in a court of law was required, which, as we will see, proved to be a problem for the Third Section's case. However, Chestnokov was no doubt aware that Siberian exile could not be ruled out for him.

In addition to searching the archives, the gendarmes also "unofficially" assembled information about the "way of life" of Chestnokov and the others, most likely by questioning neighbors and servants. In 1859 Chestnokov was fifty-three years old and had served his tsar for almost thirty-one years, most of it as a police officer specializing in complex criminal investigations. After serving as a police chief in a rural district, he advanced to the rank of junior police chief in Kiev and eventually moved to Petersburg, where he investigated crime and served in the city's central police office, tasked, among other things, with supervising debt collection. His final assignment in the eight years before his retirement was as the office supervisor for Petersburg's head police chief, a central position in the city's law enforcement. In contrast to the stereotypical figure of a conniving and corrupt petty official of the Nicholaevan era, dismissed with prejudice from one posting after another to end up eventually as a private pettifogger or worse, Chestnokov's positions were prestigious and potentially lucrative.[58]

By 1859, Chestnokov owned a mansion near the Kharlamov Bridge in a prestigious area of Petersburg, worth approximately 150,000 rubles. His overall fortune was said to be 500,000 rubles. This was much less than General Buturlin's estate, which Chestnokov thought to reach 10 million rubles, but it was still sufficient to maintain a modest provincial noble family in comfort for at least a century. Chestnokov's level of wealth should be compared to that of other prosperous moneylenders, such as Moscow's Second Lieutenant Aleksandr Tersky who died in 1856, leaving his heirs with 16,000 rubles in cash and 60,000 in debt papers.[59] A smaller lender, Nikolai Popov, was an honorary citizen from the small town of Kashira who inherited around 15,000 rubles from his father and invested it in loans, which allowed him to live more like a well-dressed Parisian *rentier* than a Muscovite merchant, spending his days courting pretty seamstresses and taking strolls in central Moscow.[60]

Compared to other lenders who ended up on the Third Section's list during the investigation, Chestnokov's portfolio was large in its overall amount (43,000 rubles) but included only six transactions, unlike the portfolios held by real "usurers" such as Tersky or Chestnokov's alleged partner Mironov, which were composed of dozens of transactions. Moreover, while the Third Section list of 38 alleged usurers included 20 portfolios over 10,000 rubles, none of them came even close to the extravagant sum that Chestnokov allegedly loaned to Buturlin. This suggests that Chestnokov was either an investor rather than a professional moneylender or that he loaned his money through Mironov or another front man, which was not at all unusual.

The Third Section's 1866 investigation of Petersburg pawnbrokers showed that out of 28 lenders—all of them of moderate wealth—5 were known to operate with other people's money.[61] Because it was considered to be unethical for Russia's traditional merchants to sell other merchants' bills of exchange to the Commercial Bank, they used brokers who dealt with the bank directly.[62] Highly ranked aristocrats who wished to engage in business frequently operated through merchants: Prince Boris Yusupov did so in the nineteenth century, and Catherine II's top financial and judicial official, Prince Aleksandr Viazemskii, preserved his reputation for exceptional honesty by conducting business through the wealthy usurer and tax farmer Vasilii Zlobin.[63] Even in the late nineteenth century, when Russia already had a modern banking system, individual investors were still known to use go-betweens to place their money.[64]

Aside from his wealth, Chestnokov was known to be widowed and living with a lady friend and housekeeper *(khoziaika)*, "a young and very interesting person." He also had a married daughter and a son who was a for-pay military cadet. Chestnokov had ambitions for his son, but because he did not qualify for one of the government-paid spots usually reserved for sons of officers, he most likely was not fully accepted as part of the service establishment. Finally, Chestnokov also cared for three small, orphaned nephews and had a brother with whom he was close enough to entrust him with submitting legal documents on his behalf. Everyone agreed that Chestnokov lived modestly and was not involved in any "questionable affairs," although he was rumored to be worried about his loan to Buturlin because he feared that "this matter has been reported to the Sovereign in a bad light." He was also said to be a "rather efficient *[del'nyi]* and quite clever man, of strict character." Another report that was prepared by General Dubensky, the military's representative, also described Chestnokov as an "old dealer [*delets*—which has a negative connotation, unlike the positive *del'nyi*], with practical experience and nimbleness acquired at different times in different positions." The only—most likely false—rumor sullying Chestnokov's personal life was that he at one point had his son imprisoned for some minor prank, and that the young man died while at a penal company *(arestanskie roty)*.

In short, after spending over twenty years in St. Petersburg, Chestnokov was positioned in a dense web of personal, family, and business relationships, much like Moscow's Stepan Shilovskii, mentioned above, and completely unlike the stereotypical image of a miser or a usurer found in contemporary fiction. One of this image's central motifs—also found in Western European literature, such as in Dickens's *Nicholas Nickleby*—was the mistreatment of the miser's own family members. For instance, Ostrovskii's Krutitskii starved himself and his wife for twenty years, and Nekrasov's Korchinskii caused his wife to run away with their son. Whereas the real-life Chestnokov obviously took great care of his family; it is remarkable in fact to see the popular rumor imposing the familiar cultural stereotype around his actual person.[65]

After the commission gathered this preliminary information, it interviewed all the parties involved. Surprising both to General Dubensky, who advocated more forceful action, and to the modern reader, who would have expected it, the gendarmes did not conduct any sudden raids or seizures, explaining that they did not want to be punished in the event that Chestnokov ended up winning the case and giving Chestnokov and the others sufficient time to remove any inculpating evidence. Only after preliminary interviews of Chestnokov and Buturlin proved inconclusive did the commission ask the chief of the Corps of Gendarmes for special permission to search the targets' houses.

The men were never detained aside from a prohibition against leaving the city, and at least Chestnokov was able to study the materials of the investigation freely at his home and make extracts from these materials to prepare his own responses. This treatment was radically different from that of political suspects, who were reasonably well-housed and fed but often not even informed of the nature of the charges against them or given much opportunity to defend themselves. At one point the gendarmes wanted to inspect Chestnokov's notes, but he abruptly refused, stuffed them in his pockets, and even allegedly shouted abuse. Again the gendarmes did not insist any further. The restraint of the gendarmes is surprising because while Chestnokov was wealthy and experienced in legal matters, he was by no means aristocratic or particularly well connected, and there was no obvious reason to tolerate any behavior on his part that they thought to be inappropriate. Needless to say, this restraint is also surprising in light of the stereotypical image of the Russian gendarmes that persists in fiction and academic literature alike and does not encompass much respect for personal privacy.

Before the investigation proceeded any further, merchants Mironov and Lipgardt announced that Buturlin never owed them any money at all, although Buturlin himself said that he issued them debt notes for 120,000 rubles. Their behavior shows how moneylenders' strategies when engaging with tsarist bureaucrats varied along with their social standing and connections in the official world: even though Mironov and Lipgardt lost any possibility of collecting this debt, they were hoping to avoid further trouble with the powerful Buturlin family. Shoemaker Goze, however, held out, determined to collect his much smaller—and, more likely, genuine—debt of 8,700 rubles and maintaining that he had friendly relations with Buturlin, despite the difference in their official rank. Chestnokov, likewise, was fully intent on collecting his debt of 121,500 rubles plus interest; we may suppose that if Buturlin had not actually owed him a large sum of money, Chestnokov would have probably given up his claim at that point.

As discussed throughout this book, it was a common practice for provincial governors or Corps of Gendarmes officers to attempt to broker a settlement: such attempts are usually carefully recorded in case files. Nor was it unusual for lenders to reject such proposals. In the Chestnokov case, the gendarmes seem never to have attempted to broker a deal but proceeded directly to assemble their case.

The procedures employed do not resemble the high-handed arbitrary imposition commonly associated with the Third Section and pre-reform justice in general. Officers carefully recorded and compared testimony from both sides, incorporating the results of searches—when these were finally ordered—and face-to-face meetings (known as *ochnye stavki*) between the parties, as well as comments from General Dubensky, who provided something of an outsider's perspective on the investigation. Chestnokov also submitted several carefully crafted petitions to the chief of the Corps of Gendarmes Dolgorukov and to the tsar personally. His petitions to Dolgorukov eloquently and emotionally appealed to the prince's "hereditary" love of truth and loyal service to the throne, even invoking the historic Prince Yakov Dolgorukov, who fearlessly argued with Peter the Great himself; Chestnokov's petitions to the tsar appealed to his image as the enlightened reformer and liberator of the serfs.

As to Chestnokov's specific arguments, he categorized them as legal and "moral." First, he raised the stakes by formally accusing Buturlin of fraud. This offense—unlike usury—was punished by penal settlement in Siberia and would be easy to prove according to Russia's rules of evidence since Buturlin himself admitted it in writing. As a military officer, Buturlin would be demoted to the ranks and deprived of his noble status. Russian law set the age of majority for criminal cases at seventeen, and so he would be fully responsible for any criminal offense, even though he was still underage for the purposes of civil law.[66]

The "moral" issues of the case seemed to be more important to the Third Section because no one disputed that the law was on Chestnokov's side. He argued that, having lived in Petersburg for twenty years, he only had financial dealings with seven individuals who were all questioned by the gendarmes and did not report anything negative about him. If he really was an unprincipled usurer, it would be impossible for Petersburg courts, police, and notaries to retain no records of his dealings with his borrowers, unless (we might add) he followed the practice of the time and used a front man for his transactions. Instead, Chestnokov claimed that his main occupation was "scholarship." Merchant Mironov, he claimed, was actually Buturlin's accomplice, and it was the two of them who formed the real "gang" that fleeced him. Chestnokov's account portrays Buturlin as a young aristocratic swindler, curiously resembling Moscow's infamous Jacks of Hearts Club of the 1870s, a loose network of swindlers and forgers, many of them from upper-class families, who often chose wealthy merchants and moneylenders as their victims.[67]

Chestnokov's narrative also included a fascinating personal attack against General Buturlin, whom he accused of encouraging his son to borrow money irresponsibly while underage, knowing that his loans would be uncollectable, and of inducing his creditors to keep silent, "knowing the moral principles and powerful connections of the Buturlins." Eventually the younger Buturlin lost all credit with moneylenders and turned to open fraud. General Buturlin's behavior, according to Chestnokov, was in line with his "family trade—to loan money to private persons at interest." In other words, he accused General Buturlin of actually being a much bigger usurer than himself. Chestnokov also claimed that usury was the Buturlins' hereditary occupation:

> Such huge profits, I think, even his mother, Yekaterina Pavlovna Buturlina, never received; and this woman, as everyone knows, acquired too large of a reputation in this occupation, to which her son was also called. Beginning with a tiny estate she acquired—through the noble enterprise of collecting interest [blagorodnyi protsent] and selling the items that were pawned to her—over 4,000 serfs and 18 million assignat rubles that her son inherited. If His Excellency, utilizing his hereditary talent, acquired the same fame through his own exploits, then he has even less reason to insult through slander a man who cannot in a conscionable and legal manner be convicted or accused of any action contrary to the honor of a nobleman.[68]

In this account, the general's mother appears as a real-life—and far more successful—counterpart to the fictional Arina Petrovna who was so eloquently imagined by Mikhail Saltykov-Shchedrin in his famous novel, *The Golovlyov Family* (1875–1880). Arina Petrovna created a fortune through the clever manipulation of landed property only to lose everything through her inability to manage her family relations.[69] We can also recall another gentry capitalist fortune, this time in real life, created by the powerful and eccentric Agathoclea Aleksandrovna Poltoratskaia (1737–1822) and developed by her son Fedor Markovich Poltoratskii (1764–1858).[70]

The subject of aristocratic usury in tsarist and imperial Russia is still poorly understood, for obvious reasons: the aristocrats themselves were not eager to publicize such activities. However, moneylending seems to have strengthened and sometimes created aristocratic patronage networks centered on the great princely families. For example, the fabulously wealthy Morozov boyar family in the second half of the seventeenth century was involved in extensive credit operations with their peers and subordinates alike.[71]

While initially merchants rather than aristocrats, the Stroganov family spearheaded Russia's early modern expansion into the Urals and Siberia and built a fortune vastly exceeding that of princes and boyars. While their trading and salt-mining operations are well documented, less well known is the fact that the original wealth that allowed them to undertake this expansion arose in the late fifteenth century from moneylending.[72]

The legendary Yakov Bruce (1669–1735), one of Peter the Great's closest collaborators, was a wealthy and active usurer.[73] Yet another famous example is Prokofii Akinfievich Demidov (1710–1788), from the clan of industrialists and merchants, who became a prominent agent and sponsor of the Russian Enlightenment. After selling most of his factories and mines, he financed his fabulous charitable and scientific projects with income from lending to Russia's top aristocrats and Catherine the Great herself.[74]

In the nineteenth century, Prince Boris Nikolaevich Yusupov (1794–1849) was remembered for liberating his serfs. However, he was also a practical man who acquired vast new properties and, according to the whistleblower Prince Peter Dolgorukov, vastly increased his fortune by secretly engaging in usury: "Thanks to his noble profession as a usurer, Prince Boris had an office in Petersburg, and in Moscow he employed as his agent the famous industrialist Gavrila Volkov, who told me once: 'The late Prince Boris Nikolaevich was a commercial man; he and I never missed; we shot fat black grouse and small snipe alike.'"[75]

Unlike even wealthy non-aristocratic lenders, individuals with famous surnames could feel themselves quite safe from police harassment. For example, Prince Fedor Andreevich Golitsyn, despite his modest rank of collegiate assessor, in 1863 felt free to be cheeky with gendarmes and with the tsar's own aide-de-camp, General Boris Perovsky, without any repercussions whatsoever.[76]

Compared to the likes of the Yusupovs, Stroganovs, and Golitsyns, the branch of the Buturlins discussed here were nouveau-riches in terms of their wealth, if not their pedigree, illustrating the onion-like character of Russia's networks of power and property ownership.[77] High service rank and entrepreneurship often went hand-in-hand, and General Buturlin's youthful bravery on the battlefield quickly turned into a lucrative expertise in army logistics, especially food supply. Considering the reputation of Nicholaevan-era supply officers for embezzling on a massive scale, this aspect of Buturlin's service must have conveniently complemented his moneylending activities.

Interestingly, General Dubensky freely admitted Chestnokov's allegation, while attempting to present it in a favorable light: "His Excellency, as far as I know, by issuing loans out of his capital, truly benefits many persons with insufficient means, in return for the legally permissible interest or even without any interest at all, but in any event not according to the rules of malicious "debtofacturers" [Dubensky's neologism rendered in the original Russian as *dolgopromyshlenniki*].[78] We do know that at least some of Buturlin's operations extended to Moscow, since a random look into that city's debt registers indicates that in 1854 he issued 5,400 rubles, unsecured by any collateral to retired Lieutenant Sergei Korob'in, and in 1860 loaned 25,000 rubles to retired civil servant Prince Aleksei Golitsyn, secured by a masonry house in the prestigious Tverskaia precinct of Moscow.[79]

In his defense, the younger Buturlin portrayed himself as an innocent victim, claiming that he only received approximately 15,000 rubles from Chestnokov and Mironov and wrote the letters that inculpated him at the dictation of his creditors, who wanted additional security in the form of a threat of criminal prosecution. However, Buturlin did admit that he signed the letters and that he did lie about his age. This admission was potentially damning to the young officer, although it did not necessarily help Chestnokov, who by law was not entitled to rely on someone's claim to be of age without requiring additional proof.

The only factor that worked in the young Buturlin's favor, aside from his father's influence, was his youth and lack of experience in financial matters. General Buturlin asserted that his son would have been too illiterate to compose the letters in question. Colonel Rakeev, the Corps of Gendarmes's expert on financial crime, agreed: "Chestnokov's loan to Buturlin was formalized through receipts and letters of such content that could only be composed by Chestnokov who was skilled in business affairs, and not by Buturlin who barely possessed the ability of simply expressing his thoughts on paper."[80]

General Dubensky agreed, reporting that Buturlin was "unable to compose such letters even to save himself from a death sentence or from a horrible death by starvation." Rakeev also wrote that "one only had to be present during one of the face-to-face meetings of Chestnokov and Mironov with Buturlin . . . to become completely convinced morally in the fraudulent scheme of these persons, with which Mr. Chestnokov in particular had entangled the thoughtless young man." All this sounds plausible enough, although one might still wonder how an officer of the Imperial Guard, no matter how stupid and poorly educated, would have agreed to sign a letter openly admitting dishonorable, as well as criminal, behavior, if he were entirely blameless.

After collecting the evidence, the commission faced the difficult task of drawing its conclusions. Its reasoning curiously resembled that of Chestnokov, again highlighting the tension between the morality of business transactions and the requirements of the law that was incapable of ensuring it. Part of the problem was that according to the rules of evidence that existed before the court reform of 1864, a conviction required documentary proof, personal confession, or testimony from at least two witnesses. But because the Third Section was not a court of law, it was not officially bound by these rules and was free to employ circumstantial evidence and rely on "moral conviction."

Both the documents and Buturlin's personal admission unambiguously spoke in Chestnokov's favor. However, while there were no "direct factual proofs" of Buturlin's position, there was "enough basis," in the opinion of the gendarmes, "to form a moral conviction that Buturlin's loan did not take place in the way described by Chestnokov." Conversely, even before they gathered all the facts, the gendarmes became sure that Chestnokov's guilt "cannot be denied, although it is impossible to prove with positive facts." Colonel Rakeev likewise argued in his memo that "it is impossible not to form a moral conviction" that General Buturlin's complaint was well founded. In order to justify their "moral conviction," the gendarmes then conducted a logical analysis of the kind that would be perfectly acceptable for any criminal investigation after the 1864 reform, or indeed in our modern day, but that the system of formal proofs was specifically designed to prevent.[81]

The first basis for the "moral conviction" of the gendarmes was that they thought it implausible that Chestnokov would lend 120,000 rubles without first gathering information about Buturlin's finances, checking whether he really did have the authorization from his father, and which property he was intending to purchase. This was customary even for relatively small loans of only a few hundred rubles. However, Chestnokov replied to this argument that he knew that General Buturlin had a fortune of 10,000,000 rubles, and so it was perfectly reasonable to entrust 120,000 rubles to his son, who swore on his honor as an officer in the Chevalier Guard, and who was not asking for a loan for the purposes of carousing but in order to fulfill his father's commission.[82] Debt transactions by other individuals the gendarmes suspected of being predatory usurers were all exponentially smaller in amount (usually just a few thousand rubles), suggesting that Chestnokov did in fact think that he was lending to the older Buturlin. This entire exchange is yet another indication of the deeply conflicted mindset of Russian elites on the issue of credit: while ostensibly upholding an officer's honor, the gendarmes at the same time assumed that this honor was worth nothing and had to be carefully checked.

Second, a key argument that damned Chestnokov in the eyes of the gendarmes was that when they searched his house, they found account books in which he recorded the tiniest details of his household expenses but not an account book that detailed his financial dealings. Chestnokov claimed that he never had one. The gendarmes did not believe this, and they were no doubt correct to conclude that Chestnokov had hidden or destroyed it.

Nonetheless, other legal cases from the mid-nineteenth century show that Russia's merchants and entrepreneurs never revealed their real account books to police investigators or bankruptcy boards, if possible, but doctored the accounts or claimed to have lost them or never to have kept them in the first place. They did this even under threat of the criminal prosecution mandatory for insolvent merchants who did not keep account books according to prescribed forms. While Chestnokov was neither a merchant nor a bankrupt, and possibly not a professional lender either, he must have shared that same concern with preserving his partners' and clients' business secrets.

Third, the gendarmes reasonably thought it suspicious that Chestnokov could not provide the dates and numbers of the bank deposit receipts that he supposedly issued to Buturlin. It was not plausible that someone would keep 120,000 rubles at home without writing down this information somewhere in the event the notes were lost or stolen, because the bank would then be unable to render the money. Suspiciously, Chestnokov did keep detailed information for stock certificates that he also owned, which did not require the same precautions as anonymous bank notes.

The rest of the gendarmes' reasoning on this point was more questionable. They visited the *Sokhrannaia kazna* (the government bank used by Chestnokov) and checked to see which particular 10,000-ruble notes were presented for redemption in 1857, on the premise that Buturlin would redeem the notes as soon as he received them from Chestnokov. However, the gendarmes failed to check whether any 10,000-ruble notes were redeemed in 1858, which would be likely since Chestnokov made his loan at the very end of 1857. The gendarmes also tried to check Chestnokov's story by looking at his calculations of interest due on the notes, whose amount would help to determine the day on which the notes were originally issued and thus could identify the particular notes that Chestnokov allegedly issued to Buturlin. In this case, it was General Dubensky, the military's representative on the commission, who pointed out the idiocy of the gendarmes: such a calculation would require 164 billion mathematical operations.

The gendarmes also doubted that Chestnokov would have issued Buturlin the entire 120,000 rubles that he was trying to collect. They reexamined the information that General Buturlin sent two of his agents to buy out Chestnokov's claim against his son. Both agents testified that Chestnokov at one point offered to settle for 75,000 rubles. The commission made much of this evidence to conclude that Chestnokov did not actually issue the entire 120,000 rubles if he agreed to be repaid a smaller amount. This reasoning is completely spurious: many creditors in the mid-nineteenth century would have been perfectly happy to get almost two-thirds of an original investment that had turned sour. Something like 25 percent was more common and 10 percent not unheard of.[83]

The gendarmes also thought that Chestnokov would not have agreed to lend to Buturlin without expecting a "considerable reward for his risk"—that is, including a huge interest payment as part of the official debt document. In the same vein, Colonel Rakeev estimated that Chestnokov would have required a 300 percent interest payment for the risk. This sounds reasonable in light of what we know about credit practices in Russia at the time. That said, it is notable—though Chestnokov himself did not make the point— that the gendarmes calculated the 300 percent interest to be the market price of the risk of lending to someone as irresponsible as Buturlin yet still held it against him. Another point Chestnokov did not bring up but perhaps should have is that these risk calculations made sense for a loan to the unreliable younger Buturlin but not if Chestnokov actually did think that he was lending money to his capitalist father.

Taken together, the four arguments set out by the investigation of the gendarmes sound spurious enough to make one wonder whether the allegedly archaic system of formal proofs could be more fair in this case than the free evaluation of evidence that was practiced by the gendarmes and that would no doubt be similar to arguments by a defense attorney had Buturlin come before a jury trial in a post-reform court.[84]

At the end of the investigation, the commission still could not decide which of the two protagonists had committed a crime, finding "thoughtlessness" on one side and "unscrupulousness" on the other. All of the logical analysis discussed above did not add anything to the body of legally admissible evidence *(uliki)*, which showed the case in a completely different light than the inherent sense of justice of the gendarmes or, alternately, their duty to please their superiors and especially the tsar. The commission was therefore determined to avoid a full-scale trial because they were certain it would end in Chestnokov's favor. The most amazing, though not elegant, articulation of this legal and political dilemma came from General Dubensky, who argued that "if we had a trial by jury, then it is certain that it would have taken into deep consideration the feelings of the same moral conviction, and would have loudly thrown stones at Chestnokov and Mironov, condemning them as notorious usurers and would protect Buturlin."[85] Dubensky then concluded that

> a trial by jury, *which in our country is replaced by the Third Section,* would find that ... the thread of this entire case combines completely in the hand of Chestnokov, who elected to satisfy his and [his accomplices'] avarice with the most reprehensible type of usury: intentionally enticing a member of a noble Russian family into fraud and dishonor that can be nullified in no other way than through the exemplary punishment of the usurers, by applying to them with Supreme confirmation of that article of the law that commands to remove such persons from the capitals through administrative proceedings."[86] *[emphasis added]*

In retrospect, the analysis and calculations of the gendarmes do not rule out the possibility that Chestnokov really was a professional moneylender who took the usual precautions when dealing with a young aristocrat; however, to a modern observer they raise the strong likelihood that he was an investor who occasionally dabbled in lending but in this case thought he was dealing with the famous capitalist General Buturlin and believed his son's word of honor. But ultimately the "true" occupation of Chestnokov is not as important for the purposes of this study as showing what the parties involved in the case thought was possible or likely when they presented their conflicting testimony or—in the case of the gendarmes—evaluated it and presented it to their superiors.

Lenders on Trial

The most important reason Chestnokov and most other lenders could not be convicted was that none of their activities could be proven to have violated the letter of the law. Even before the judicial reform of 1864, the government was firmly determined to uphold the institution of private property and not to intervene in private debt agreements without sufficient evidence of criminal wrongdoing. In contradiction to the commonly held view that the imperial Russian government tended to subordinate the rule of law to the arbitrary authority of executive officials—the Third Section being portrayed as one of the worst offenders—the previously mentioned 1861 policy-making memo by Corps of Gendarmes General Ivan Annenkov urged exactly the opposite. Noting that usurers were careful to observe all legal formalities, he urged that "to maintain credit among private persons the government cannot fail to demand the strictest fulfillment of lawfully executed private agreements" and that "the procedure in the courts of law must not be infringed under any pretext."[87] As the Third Section officers were well aware, debtors recognized this and so were reluctant to complain to authorities and risk losing credit with all other lenders.

Court records show that usury prosecutions were undertaken successfully only under a very peculiar set of circumstances, such as a careless admission by the lender or witness testimony. The lender whose apartment is so vividly described in Nekrasov's 1841 short story took a great risk by inviting several clients at once who could potentially testify about his activities in court.[88] Contrary to General Dubensky's optimism, jury trials, once they were introduced in 1866, did not improve the chances of conviction. As a result, when the police wanted to make an example of a particular lender, their best option was to utilize the power of administrative exile, which, as will be seen, was not foolproof either.

Perhaps the safest way to avoid legal troubles was not to act as a lender at all but to use a front man (or woman), but this of course raised the problems of reliability and profit-sharing. Those lenders who operated under their own names commonly wrote up the loan as a different type of transaction.

One way was to write up the transaction as accepting the amount of the loan for "safekeeping." Such documents, favored by "professional" money-lenders, were known as *sokhrannye raspiski* (safekeeping receipts). The agreement for safekeeping *(poklazha* or *otdacha pod sokhranenie)* was written up as a hire of movable property, such as cash. Technically speaking, the debtor did not borrow money from the lender but accepted it temporarily for safekeeping.

The safekeeping receipt had several possible uses but in practice served primarily as a legal fiction allowing creditors to dispense with the form of the loan letter and some of its inconveniences.[89] First, the "safekeeping" transaction was only subjected to a "simple" stamp duty rather than to one in proportion with the amount borrowed, as was the case with loan letters. The second practical advantage was that the lender gained more secure rights in his or her investment because unlike with a regular loan, a safekeeping transaction was not subject to Russia's ten-year statute of limitations, and so the lender's rights to sue were limited only to both parties' lifetimes.[90] Finally, this type of transaction received preferential treatment in bankruptcy proceedings. In order to prevent this type of agreement from replacing regular loans in practice entirely, the law contained unusually detailed requirements, such as the requirement of a detailed description of the type of property that was being transferred, including the numbers on banknotes and their denomination, as well as the type and year of issue of the coins. This last requirement was, of course, easily circumvented in practice, for example by listing common types of coins that were easily replaced. However—typically for all Russian anti-usury measures—the law stopped short of the one requirement that would have effectively stopped the use of the safekeeping transaction for disguising loans, which was sealing the money package to ensure that it was not spent and then replaced. This indicates that although the tsars and their ministers and senators sought to protect borrowers through formal legal precautions, they at the same time avoided making private credit too inconvenient and too expensive and refused to eliminate a well-known practical adaptation of the law.

A contract for the safekeeping or a formal pawning of movable property still provided the borrower with some rights, a risk that many pawnbrokers were not willing to accept, and so a common strategy was to write up the debt as a sale of the item being pawned. This of course placed borrowers completely at the pawnbrokers' mercy and created easy opportunities for fraud and embezzlement.[91]

In 1863, a merchant from the town of Sergiev Posad near Moscow, Vasily Smirnov, read a newspaper advertisement by Mikhail Draevsky, a noble-born clerk at the First Department of the Moscow Aulic Court who owned a small landed estate and added to his income by pawnbroking. Smirnov then sent his grown son Pavlin to borrow 65.50 silver rubles, secured by his wool-covered fox fur coat (worth over 125 rubles), a new wool suit worth 35 rubles, his wife's silk overcoat with fur lining and collar (75 rubles), and his son's wool overcoat worth 30 rubles. Between June and October, Smirnov paid Draevsky 10 percent interest each month, but when he wanted to redeem his property in October, with the cold weather approaching, it turned out that the usurer and his wife had sold everything without giving Smirnov any notice. Because a pawnshop transaction was executed as a sale, the only recourse left to Smirnov was to submit a petition to Draevsky's superiors and the police. At first, Draevsky was able to fend off Smirnov's complaints to his superiors, but he eventually had to leave government service. However, Smirnov appears never to have recovered his property.

Lenders who used a formal debt document such as a loan letter, bill of exchange, or mortgage note took advantage of the fact that the law only prohibited excessive interest but not all interest-taking. In other words, it was up to the borrower to prove that he or she was charged a usurious rate. The key problem here was Russia's system of evidence that relied on so-called formal proofs. As noted previously, proving a criminal case required either documentary proof, a confession, or the sworn testimony of two witnesses. Written evidence, of course, would be the most helpful variety in any case involving debt, but high interest rates were very easy to disguise; the lender would simply list the legal six percent interest rate on the debt document and charge higher amounts in practice by issuing the borrower with a smaller amount than what was stated in writing and making him or her sign a paper acknowledging the receipt of the entire amount.[92]

Court cases suggest that it was common for moneylenders to make their borrowers sign debt documents for at least twice the amount actually borrowed, ostensibly to protect their investment in the event of default. For example, in the insolvency case of the young Count Dmitrii Nikolaevich Tolstoi, his father's lawyer argued that the main creditor, merchant Gorodetskii, always took debt documents for twice the amount actually issued.[93] In another case, Gubernial Secretary Dmitrii Sheremetevskii claimed that in 1855 he borrowed 100 rubles from Moscow townsman Nikolai Ivanov but had to write debt documents for 200 rubles and a few months later was sued for the entire amount.[94] In post-reform villages, usurers always demanded debt documents for over 100 rubles to have access to the regular court system and thus to avoid the jurisdiction of local peasant courts, which would be biased against them.[95] The Annenkov memo found that high-risk lenders routinely required documents for twice the amount actually issued, although Annenkov considered this practice to be abusive. Even more abusive was the practice of taking documents for the amount the lender wished to borrow and then issuing a fraction of the amount over a period of time, in effect opening a secured line of credit.[96]

In most cases it is difficult to determine whether the excess of the amount stated on the debt document over the amount actually borrowed constituted hidden—but reasonable—interest, additional security to ensure repayment, or a predatory practice taking advantage of a borrower's particularly vulnerable circumstances—or, indeed, all of the above. Among such vulnerable individuals were young aristocrats like Buturlin and Dmitrii Tolstoy, who expected to someday inherit their parents' vast fortunes. Another situation was the borrower being drunk or otherwise mentally agitated. For example, in 1860 Moscow townsman Mikhail Ulitin had another townsman Aleksei Klimov write out a large number of bills of exchange with different dates and to different persons, but allegedly gave him only a few rubles.[97] A similar predicament befell a wealthy Moscow merchant, Klavdii Yeremeev, who in 1871 fell victim to a group of swindlers and signed numerous debt obligations in a prolonged bout of drunkenness. Because most debt documents were short-term, if a debtor did not make a timely payment as required by the usurer, he or she could be asked to sign a new debt document for a still higher amount.[98]

Whereas debt documents themselves were unlikely to inculpate a money-lender, other written evidence was likely to be insufficiently specific. The case of Gubernial Secretary Dmitrii Sheremetievskii illustrates why usury was so difficult to prove even when there was some written evidence: given that the law did not require the amount borrowed to be transferred immediately upon the signing of the debt document, Sheremetievskii, having signed debt papers for 200 rubles and, as he alleged, having borrowed only 100 rubles, had no way to prove this fact other than by producing his letter to the usurer describing the situation. The court ruled that the letter was not specific enough to show that it applied to that particular loan transaction.[99] This case was judged under the pre-1864 evidence rules that gave judges little discretion in weighing evidence; under a legal system giving judges more discretion, the letter would no doubt have been considered more probative.

With pre-reform evidence rules, it was generally possible to prove usury only when there was a careless admission by the lender or sworn testimony by more than one witness. In Russia's legal practice, such cases were rare occurrences indeed. For example, one Moscow pawnbroker, Count Sheremetiev's serf Epistimiia Durkina, was convicted for usury in 1861 after she loaned 44 rubles to townsman Sergei Ivanov at an annual rate of 60 percent, secured by two gold watches and an icon frame, and, apparently needing money herself, in turn pawned the watches elsewhere. Durkina appears to have been ignorant of the law because she easily testified that she was charging 5 percent per month—ten times the legal amount—and that the accumulated interest of 76 rubles made it impractical for Ivanov to attempt to redeem his collateral, which he then asked her to sell.

The Chamber of Criminal Justice, taking into account Durkina's admission, sentenced her to be fined 64.8 rubles, nearly three times the amount of excessive interest minus the legal interest. The original sentence by the Moscow Aulic Court was to convict Durkina of fraud for embezzling pawned property, to strip her of her legal rights, give her 50 lashes, and place her in the workhouse for eighteen months; this was typical of pre-reform criminal sentences, which were initially overly harsh and reduced after review by the higher-up Criminal Chamber.[100]

Witness testimony also led to criminal conviction on rare occasions. In the 1840s, a Dmitrov townsman Demian Pastukhov had an arrangement with a Kishinev merchant Mikhail Gendrikhov, whereby they collected debts on each other's behalf; by 1851, Pastukhov had collected 3,159 rubles, but he never delivered the money because he claimed it was the interest owed to him for his services. In a conversation with Gendrikhov, Pastukhov claimed that "he never took less than 15% interest per year and that even better people than Gendrikhov pay up." These words were overheard by merchant Provotorov and townsmen Plotnikov and Sovelov. Because three witnesses were more than the two required for conviction under Russian evidence laws, the Moscow Aulic Court sentenced Pastukhov to three days' arrest, and the decision was affirmed by the Criminal Chamber and the governor general of Moscow.[101]

In a similar case, collegiate registrar's wife Elizaveta Shustitskaia (Pereshivkina in her second marriage) was prosecuted for usury in 1843, after she took personal effects worth 1,335 paper rubles from Moscow townswoman Ekaterina Bulasheva and gave her 284 paper rubles at an annual rate of 80 percent. Bulasheva paid interest at the end of each month but eventually could not afford this high rate and had to permit Pereshivkina to sell a fox fur coat for 500 paper rubles to pay off the debt. Her witnesses were Class 9 official Ivan Sokovin, chancery clerk Glazatov, and Second Lieutenant Vladimir Schmidt, who all heard Pereshivkina claim that she was charging 7 percent per month. Because there was an issue of Bulasheva bribing a witness, the lower court ruled that usury had not been proven and instead convicted Bulasheva for attempting to influence witnesses, but the Criminal Chamber ruled on December 21, 1856, that Pereshivkina's usury was proven by three witnesses under oath and punished her with the triple fine required by law. However, her conviction was vacated pursuant to the tsar's amnesty manifesto of March 27, 1855.[102]

Because existing legislation and court procedures made criminal conviction for usury so difficult, the only effective measure was administrative exile, widely used throughout the nineteenth century to remove various categories of undesirable individuals from large cities and other sensitive areas. It was so broadly used by provincial governors in the first half of the century that the tsar's decree of December 2, 1855, restricted its use to the central government. This restriction was not practical, and many governors of individual provinces saw these powers restored in the 1860s and 1870s, including those of Moscow and St. Petersburg in 1879—that is, even before the famous security law of August 14, 1881, which at once permitted administrative exile in all provinces to which the law applied but limited exile to five years and required approval by the Interior Ministry.[103]

With respect to usury, administrative exile was typically applied when unhappy debtors—usually a group but sometimes one powerful individual, as in the case of Buturlin—complained about a particular lender or lenders. The authorities usually attempted to mediate a settlement and sometimes threatened the lender with expulsion. This would in effect shut down his or her business, although some semblance of procedure was provided and the borrowers were still legally obligated to repay their loans. This is what happened to Chestnokov. He could take comfort in the fact that the gendarmes found no evidence of a criminal gang.[104] But on August 31, 1859, less than six months after the beginning of the investigation, Prince Dolgorukov, chief of the Third Section, ordered Chestnokov's exile to the small town of Yarensk in northern Vologda province, although unlike political prisoners he had another five weeks to organize his affairs before he was actually removed from Petersburg. In December of that same year, he was transferred to the larger and more civilized town of Ustiug because of an illness, so that he could have access to a doctor.

Before 1881, administrative exile did not yet have a legal time limit, and Chestnokov consequently continued to petition the authorities for a pardon, and in 1862 was finally allowed to choose his place of residence anywhere outside Moscow and Petersburg provinces. He chose the town of Tver, which lies approximately halfway between Moscow and Petersburg, within a relatively easy train ride from each, for which reason it was an attractive place of penal exile in the nineteenth century, as well as in the twentieth. Merchant Mironov likewise chose Tver for his residence after he was allowed to return from his exile in another northern town of Kem in Arkhangelsk province. Mironov was 13 years younger than Chestnokov and was able to build a new life for himself, although this new life also involved making new enemies. One of these alerted the gendarmes to the fact that the Moscow–Petersburg railroad effectively undermined police control since exiled undesirables could always come to Petersburg for a few days to carry out their financial dealings.

Chestnokov was also allowed to rebuild his life, but by the time he settled in Tver, his seventeen-year-old son Aleksei had been expelled from the First Cadet Corps, and his Petersburg house run by a hired manager was in a bad shape. Then, in February 1863, soon after Chestnokov's terms of exile had been relaxed, his son—who by that time had entered government service in Petersburg—fell gravely ill, so that Chestnokov asked for permission to visit him. Whereas Mironov had no difficulty making brief illicit visits to the city, Chestnokov was either unable or unwilling to do the same. Petersburg Governor General Prince Arkadii Suvorov proposed to allow him to return for six months, and the Committee of Ministers that examined Chestnokov's petition also recommended leniency, but the tsar personally rejected it.

Chestnokov's story shows the extent to which even a wealthy person skilled in legal procedure was no match for a millionaire with court connections, and that administrative exile—while mild by the standards of the twentieth century or compared to Shlissel'burg Fortress, where the most dangerous revolutionaries were imprisoned in the nineteenth century— could have very real and ruinous consequences. Such consequences could be more devastating for those lower-middle-class individuals who acted as lenders and pawnbrokers for Russia's mass of poor laborers, a group that was steadily augmenting the urban population in the decades after serf emancipation.

For example, in 1879, twenty years after the Chestnokov case, the Moscow Governor expelled several groups of Jews who had been legally residing in the city as artisans and retired soldiers or soldiers' wives.[105] These included the retired private Levik Bich and soldiers' wives Khaia Markovich, Khaia Schumacher, Malka Baranishnikova, and Sara Landar. Moscow's police chief persuaded the governor to exile them for the alleged offense of "positively ruining the factory folk. Issuing in exchange for the pawned items a sum that was most minuscule compared to their value, these Jews use all means possible to appropriate the items they accept as pawns, leaving the workers without clothing and shoes and thus provoking their disaffection and complaints."[106] In addition to official anti-Semitism, these women's plight also resulted from the war against the Ottoman Empire that had started in 1877. According to their wives' petitions, the soldiers stationed in Moscow were suddenly sent to the Balkans, leaving them without any other way of making a living but by peddling and pawnbroking.

But while all these individuals were exiled to the remote provinces of northern Russia, such as Viatka, Vologda, and Olonets, the degree to which their economic activities were disrupted varied greatly, depending on their wealth and social status. Baranishnikova's family ranked slightly above the rest: her husband owned a shop in the center of Moscow, and Baranishnikova herself had taken out a commercial license. It is also conceivable that the Baranishnikovs were able to spend some money on bribing the police. As a result, Baranishnikova, who had a newborn baby and five other children, was permitted to go to her original hometown of Mogilev in Belorussia instead of to the north, while her husband continued to trade in Moscow, although his petitions to allow his wife to come back to him were denied. The grounds for the denial were that Baranishnikova had opened a ready-made clothing store in Mogilev, which the officials considered to be a cover for continuing a moneylending operation; it seems that despite her exile, Baranishnikova was able to remain within the middle class.

Other pawnbrokers whose husbands were rank-and-file soldiers likewise petitioned to be sent to their homeland in Poland but were denied, although none of them had newborn babies. Once in Russia's north, they had a more difficult time integrating into small-town life. For example, the 65-year-old retired soldier Mendel Londar owned a smithy in Moscow with hired workers, but in exile, after finally finding a location where his skills were in demand, he had to rent a workshop to make a living. However, by 1882 all these individuals had been freed from police oversight and were permitted to choose their residence anywhere except the two capitals and their outlying regions. As in the case of Chestnokov, it was essential to continue to submit petitions to the authorities in hopes of a change of policy.[107] Also it is important to note that the government was open to relaxing the punishment within a relatively short time.

Provincial governors retained their authority to exile undesirable money-lenders until the end of the imperial period, but the policy toward usury changed several times after the Great Reforms. By that time, the government recognized that the legal interest rate of six percent was impossibly low. The implication was that a law that by definition could not reasonably be obeyed tended to undermine the integrity of the legal system. One anonymous individual who denounced a well-known usurer from the 1860s, Vladimir Karpovich, pointed out that the law against usury was easy to circumvent and argued that "if the law . . . is not timely or not satisfactory in our mercantilist age, the government should change or abolish it instead of promoting disrespect for the law.[108] Finally, the decree of 1879 abolished all restrictions on loan interest rates in line with the larger Western nineteenth-century trend and also in line with several other measures that liberalized Russia's financial and credit market in the 1860s and 1870s.[109]

The law of 1879 specified that special rules were to be introduced at a future date to regulate predatory lending practices that were to be prosecuted as usury; when finally introduced in 1892, the new rule, much like its European counterparts, replaced the mechanical limitation of a permissible interest rate by a more flexible and discretion-based circumstance test designed to prevent the abuse of particularly vulnerable individuals, most importantly peasants.[110]

This was of course not the only potential solution: it was also possible to retain some minimum restrictions but to ensure that exceptions and loopholes would continue making lending profitable, for example, for commercial lending. The maximum interest rate was almost immediately restricted again by the law of June 8, 1893, to 12 percent. Once again, special rules were added to restrict so-called rural usury, which was seen as a distinct affliction of the Russian countryside.[111] However, public trials for usury continued to be rare. One colorful case was reported by the lawyer Grigorii Rozenzweig, in his collection of anecdotes from Russian legal practice; it involved Vladimir Pashkevich, a retired major-general serving as a professor of mathematics at the prestigious Mikhailovskaia Artillery Academy in Petersburg and a well-known expert in ballistics, who was put on trial in the late 1890s for charging 36 percent interest to his numerous debtors, all of them from prosperous social groups. Pashkevich was convicted even though he used a go-between to act as the legal lender to shield him from legal problems, and he later argued that the loans in question were issued before the new anti-usury law went into effect. On appeal, the Senate accepted Pashkevich's argument and overturned his conviction.[112]

Although large joint-stock banks appeared in Russia in the 1860s, individual lenders, whether "usurers" or investors, continued to be crucial for the system of private credit until the end of the imperial period, much as they did in other legal systems.[113] Cultural understandings of usury had by then long departed from the longstanding technical meaning of charging any interest at all or charging interest in excess of a low legal limit. Instead, usury in Russia and in other major Western legal systems came to connote predatory practices that took advantage of a borrower's difficult circumstances and exceeded what was considered to be a reasonable reward for lending to high-risk clients. Usury indeed came to stand for the unjust and even irrational aspects of capitalism in general.[114]

Intellectuals in late imperial Russia saw this point clearly, and their observations and interpretations did not at all correspond to Marx's model, in which capitalist credit appeared alongside its allegedly archaic usurious variety and the latter continued to exist to finance consumption and small-scale producers.[115] For example, an 1875 pamphlet published under the name N. Goremykin argued that Russia's new commercial banks closely cooperated rather than merely coexisted with usurers who had transformed themselves into credit brokers. Banks preferred to minimize their risk by lending to these intermediaries who then distributed the money at a much higher rate to merchants and entrepreneurs.[116]

Similarly, in Dmitrii Mamin-Sibiriak's 1895 novel *Bread*, examining capitalism in the post-reform Trans-Ural region, the new local capitalist bank quickly seized control over most local industry and commerce, but instead of sidelining usury—practiced, for example, by a village priest—banking greatly stimulated it by making it more socially acceptable and in effect merged with it. The economist Roman Tsimmerman in his 1898 study of rural usury argued that even the most ruthless and exploitative usury was not much different from supposedly advanced capitalist entrepreneurship because it stemmed from similar motivations and employed the same legal and social mechanisms that involved the destruction of traditional communal and family ties. In Tsimmerman's description, the peasant usurer *(kulak)* was an agent of unstoppable capitalist transformation and not anything like Marx's vaguely outlined archaism.[117] Rather than being regarded as an outdated model to be discarded, usury thus continued to problematize the nexus between private and public morality and the culture of capitalism and entrepreneurship, as well as the limits of the legal regulation of all of them.

Even the most ruthless high-risk lenders were almost always protected by unassailable legal forms, and predatory lending therefore undermined the integrity and credibility of the law as strongly as the potential solutions of either removing the legal barrier altogether or subverting the legal process through administrative intervention. One of the Russian government's paramount concerns was to uphold the well-being of its propertied elites and consequently the regime of private property, including the system of private credit that could not exist without effective legal mechanisms and procedures. Paradoxically, this concern at once required some restrictions against predatory lending, as well as assurances that delinquent debtors would quickly lose their land, homes, serfs, and other possessions, and potentially be subjected to personal arrest as well. This contradiction explains why Russia's anti-usury laws were mild, why usury prosecutions were rare, and why occasional round-ups of "usurers" were limited in scope.

It is also important to remember that "professional" high-risk lenders, who were sometimes little more than swindlers and confidence men and women, constituted a small proportion of all lenders, and their activities, fascinating and revealing as they are of credit practices in the age of Russia's financial revolution, cannot constitute a comprehensive survey of the system of private credit. The next question for this study is, therefore, who were the lenders and the borrowers if, as a general rule, they were not innocent dupes preyed upon by ruthless predatory usurers?

CHAPTER 2

Nobles and Merchants

THE MODEL ESTATE manager and memoirist Andrei Bolotov was anything but a spendthrift, even in his younger days as a promising army officer during the Seven Years' War. While careful to avoid excessive debt both in Russian-occupied Königsberg and then in Petersburg, he was nonetheless involved in credit relationships that transcended geopolitical, ethnic, and social divisions. For example, he owed his Prussian hosts for a year's worth of lodging; he took up an offer to borrow 150 rubles for relocation expenses from his own serf manservant; he relied on his wealthy and powerful boss, baron N. A. Korf, to loan him money to get settled in St. Petersburg; and in turn, he loaned 30 rubles to his regiment's physician, somewhat reluctantly because he barely knew the man. Upon coming to the capital in 1762, Bolotov had to raise another 100 rubles to buy one of the fancy uniforms introduced by the new tsar, Peter III. Some of the tailoring could be done on credit, but only after a partial cash payment, for which Bolotov was offered a friendly loan by a fellow officer slightly higher in the service hierarchy.[1]

Conspicuously missing from Bolotov's account are organized banking and usury, the two types of relationships until now thought to be the sum total of private credit in imperial Russia. Borrowing from the recently established Noble Loan Bank was never considered, most likely because it was only available to a small group of borrowers with court connections. Nor did Bolotov feel the need to go to one of the usurers said to be exploiting and often ruining profligate nobles. As discussed above, high-risk lenders did exist, but most loans took place outside the framework of "capitalist" versus "usurious" credit. Borrowing money inherently involved power and inequality, but not necessarily wasteful consumption or ruthless exploitation.

Instead, we find that men and women in all positions in society and the service hierarchy operated in a complex network of relationships, whose size and composition have been so far left unexplored in any systematic way. This lack of attention stands in sharp contrast with the relatively well-known history of banking in imperial Russia, which emphasizes the scale and influence of government-run credit operations before large private banks appeared in the late 1860s. However, individual debt portfolios and official debt registers show that private credit greatly exceeded state credit operations. In other words, private lending was not, as was previously assumed, a somewhat embarrassing appendage to organized credit, but was instead at the center of Russia's economic and social structures.

Moreover, the alleged burden of debt was not as oppressive as is often claimed. Property-owning Russians in the nineteenth century were as a group wealthy enough and prudent enough to evade bankruptcy and financial ruin. Even more importantly, we should not assume that large-scale indebtedness necessarily implies failure and that a debt-free life necessarily means prosperity.

Finally, just as in Bolotov's day, nineteenth-century credit ties combined "horizontal" and "vertical" connections, which were also common in other early-industrial societies. As Laurence Fontaine noted for early-modern France, "far from strengthening the compartmentalization of society, the web of credit cuts through it vertically, links together social groups, institutions and regions in dependencies in which each one finds himself both a lender and a borrower."[2] Russians certainly liked to borrow from individuals of the same rank or social status, but they were unable or unwilling to do so exclusively. Therefore, Russia's peculiar social and cultural divisions—and especially its robust system of legal estates that persisted until 1917—cannot be said to have fostered a qualitatively different or particularly fragmented system of credit relations, although credit paradoxically divided persons and communities while at the same time connecting them.

Private Credit Network

Recall that by 1859, two-thirds of all privately owned serfs were mortgaged at state-owned banks for 425.5 million rubles and that the average annual increase of gentry debt to the state in 1829–1859 was 9.3 million. These large and well-known figures have obscured the relative size and importance of private credit even for those few historians who were mindful of private lending.[3] In contrast to the accounts of state-owned banks, records of private transactions were virtually impossible to study systematically before the post-Soviet opening of the archives and even today require some detective work. The one commonly cited estimate of private indebtedness in the mid-nineteenth century put the total private gentry debt in southern Russian Voronezh province in 1859 at 17 percent of the debt to the state.[4] This number came from research by military statisticians who provided surveys of all the provinces and seem to have relied on provincial authorities for their data. In the absence of more reliable data, this estimate has also been used by modern scholars,[5] although Nikolai Pavlenko has argued that lending was the single most important non-agricultural activity for eighteenth-century nobles—more important than government contracts, distillery, commerce, or industry.[6]

A more careful examination indicates that earlier estimates should be greatly revised upward to rival and almost certainly exceed government-issued credit. Private lending no longer appears as the marginalized and somewhat disreputable activity portrayed in most existing literature but must be reconceived to be at the heart of the empire's system of private property and, by extension, its social order.

I have estimated the size of Russia's network of private credit by considering each major type of debt transaction separately, beginning with the three most common varieties: "loan letters," or ordinary promissory notes originally designed to be used by nobles; mortgage notes that could be used by any owner of real estate; and commercial bills of exchange *(vekseli)*.

Loan letters came in two varieties. First, there were "registered" loan letters that enjoyed certain enhanced legal protections. In Moscow, the value of such transactions was 6 to 7 percent of the annual value for government-issued loans. For example, in 1850 the Moscow Chamber registered debt transactions for nearly 930,000 rubles, and in 1852 for 1,118,073 rubles; in 1854, at the height of the Crimean War, the amount was down to 636,238 rubles; in 1864, when more convenient bills of exchange became available to all nobles and cheap government credit was no longer available, the partial amount was 606,900 rubles.[7] It is important to note, however, that unlike government debt, loan letters could be registered in any provincial capital, and, moreover, county *(uezd)* courts, such as the Moscow County Court, kept their own debt ledgers—unfortunately poorly preserved—and so the actual number even for "registered" loans must have been much higher.

The other variety was the "private" loan letter. These letters were not required to be executed and registered at a court and did not require witnesses, although they did have to be notarized within a week of being signed. The ledgers for this category are not as complete as for the registered loans, and at least in Moscow they were preserved only for the first half of the century. In 1850, there were 40 entries in the amount of 218,685 rubles, and the average and median amounts did not differ from those for registered loan letters.[8] There is no indication that a certain type of borrower or lender was likely to favor private letters. This suggests that there was no strong rationale to use one form or the other except convenience or a desire for additional legal protection.

The second widely used type of transaction was a loan secured by mortgages. These loans came in two varieties, each with its own set of registers. One set included mortgages of rural properties, most importantly serf-populated estates but in some cases also vacant lands that could be owned by merchants or wealthy peasants. In 1862, the amount of such loans recorded by the Moscow Chamber was 1,899,045 rubles.[9] Mortgage records are not ideally preserved, but when estimating the amount for the earlier years, it is important to account for the wartime slump of 1854–1856, considering that the Crimean War negatively affected both state-issued mortgage loans and private loan letters. But the impact of the wartime slump should not be exaggerated, considering that government-issued credit was not as readily available to the gentry during the Crimean War, when the state took money from the Board of Trustees to make up for its increased expenditures, and so private lending would have had to make up for the difference. For the pre-1854 period, competing government mortgage loans were more readily available to landowning nobles, potentially reducing the demand for private loans but perhaps not greatly, since the demand for credit was clearly very high. Moreover, private loans secured by land would have been preferable to unsecured loan letters during a time of economic instability.

Mortgage loans could also be secured by various urban properties, including houses, shops, and even empty plots of land. These seem to have been comparable to the value of registered loan letters, based on the evidence of 1850, when such mortgages amounted to 1,158,587.95 rubles.[10] In 1855, the amount was 518,843 rubles; both ledgers appear to be incomplete.[11] Considering that 1855 was much worse for Russia's credit than 1854 because of the Crimean War, it is remarkable that the amounts for urban mortgages issued in 1855 were only slightly less than amounts for loan letters for 1854

(636,238 rubles). This type of loan would have been proportionately larger for Moscow and other large cities with many eligible buildings, such as Petersburg, Warsaw, and Odessa.

The third major type of documented debt was the *veksel*, or commercial bill of exchange. Before 1862, the use of *vekseli* was restricted by law to individuals enrolled in a merchant guild, to peasants with commercial licenses, and several categories of townspeople, whether or not they were engaged in commerce. Already in the early eighteenth century, "the overwhelming majority of merchants conducted their commercial operations on credit."[12] One way to estimate the volume of commercial credit in the nineteenth century is through the operations of the State Commercial Bank, which discounted the bills issued by individual merchants. In 1853 the bank discounted bills for 25.8 million silver rubles; during the Crimean War, this amount decreased (under 20 million), but in 1859, due to the post-war economic upturn and inflation, it reached 47.7 million rubles. The discounting operation was primarily conducted in the bank's Petersburg office, the only office permitted to purchase the bills using the bank's privately deposited funds and not just its relatively small principal capital.[13]

Yet another way to estimate the volume of commercial credit is by looking at the great annual fair at Nizhnii Novgorod, which the imperial-era economist Vladimir Bezobrazov described as a crucial element of the Moscow-based credit system. The fair served as a great credit exchange for merchants and industrialists coming from all over European Russia, furnishing a unique forum for borrowers and lenders to meet face to face, conduct business, and evaluate each other's further prospects.[14] According to ethnographer and novelist Pavel Melnikov (Pecherskii), ready cash was a rarity at the Nizhnii fair, "where almost all commercial deals are executed on credit."[15] He estimated that ready cash available at the fair was sufficient to cover less than 17 percent of the merchandise traded and that less than 7 percent of the 40 to 50 million rubles of actual overall sales were made for cash during the economic downturn of the 1840s.[16] In sum, even allowing that some bills of exchange never made it to Petersburg or Nizhnii Novgorod, the annual credit operations of Russian merchants were far more extensive than those of the much more numerous nobles.

In addition to the three major varieties of debt documents, there were several other forms that were not specifically contemplated by imperial legislation and, moreover, are still more difficult to estimate because the evidence is very fragmentary. One category included the "safekeeping receipt" *(sokhrannaia raspiska)*, which, as discussed already, employed the legal fiction that lenders entrusted their borrowers with a sum of money in exchange for a fee. This form was favored by professional and high-risk lenders. A connected type of operation were the pawnshops and pawnbrokers, who preferred to document their transactions as sales. One estimate for their business is available for the licensed *(glasnye)* pawnshops in Petersburg in the early 1870s: 3 million rubles in loans annually.[17]

Another distinct category of debt was informally documented or not documented at all, including oral transactions and informal receipts that occupied an ambiguous in-between zone. According to Melnikov's calculation for the Nizhnii Novgorod fair, such debt accounted for up to half of all transactions there.[18] It was similarly widespread among the merchants in the important commercial town of Rybinsk.[19] Memoirist Yulia Karpinskaia recalled that the noble-born entrepreneur Pavel Mikhailovich Yablochkov became involved in a massive liquor contracting operation based on oral agreements: "They of course did not observe any formalities, back then people still trusted each other's word."[20] Such obligations were legally enforceable but were difficult and often impossible to prove in court and, moreover, ceded priority to debt documents that observed all formalities.[21]

For example, in the insolvency case of the peasant Mavra Bubentsova who was a fish trader in the late 1860s, most claims against her were not documented.[22] In the 1859 bankruptcy case of a far wealthier merchant, Vasily Prokhorov, almost half of his debt was not documented.[23] The Old Believer Artemii Riazanov, another bankrupt merchant from the same period, testified when explaining the reasons for his insolvency that undocumented debt was commonly used by Moscow's merchants.[24] A middling Moscow merchant, Ivan Yelmanov, claimed to his creditors that he had transferred his shop to a friend to pay an undocumented debt of 2,000 rubles. Whether true or not, it is important that Yelmanov thought it plausible enough to offer as a defense.[25]

The debt registers and most legal cases examined in this book come from Moscow provincial courts, but private credit could also originate in any of the other provinces and regions of the empire, as well as in Poland with its robust economy, and in the Grand Duchy of Finland, with its close links with Petersburg. It is therefore important to discuss Moscow's position within Russia's overall credit system. The transactions recorded by pre-1859 government banks makes Moscow's predominant position very clear: its Board of Trustees held almost half of all loans to serfowning nobles. The

Moscow and St. Petersburg Boards informally divided up European Russia between themselves, with only a small overlap in the geographic distribution of their clientele. St. Petersburg was preferred by the nobility from St. Petersburg, Novgorod, and Pskov provinces, as well as those of Belorussia, Lithuania, and right-bank Ukraine up to and including Kiev. Eastern and northern Ukrainian and south Russian gentry went to Moscow, as did the borrowers from all the central, northern, and Volga provinces.[26] This geographical distribution was dictated by cultural preferences and ease of communications, and so it most likely held true for private borrowing as well.

As to private lending, Moscow's predominant position was already evident in the early 1700s, when the city's recording office registered thousands of debt transactions, whereas smaller commercial centers like Astrakhan and Yaroslavl registered a few hundred at best.[27] Nineteenth-century statisticians directly linked Moscow's position as the empire's primary hub for domestic commerce with its role as the largest source of private credit. Merchants from other provinces preferred Moscow to Petersburg not only because of its geographic location but also due to its position as a center of credit: "Many entrepreneurs and merchants who could receive everything necessary for their factories and commerce directly from St. Petersburg prefer to turn to Moscow, both because it is closer, and because they already have credit with Moscow's capitalists."[28] Bezobrazov claimed in 1882 that "[through credit] all of our internal trade and all of its local representatives are dependent upon the commercial and manufacturing centers of [the central industrial region] and especially upon Moscow itself." Even the Ukrainian network of rural and small-town fairs, aside from the southwest periphery, was known as "Moscow's market" *(moskovskii torg).*[29]

In addition to contemporary opinion, the financial leverage of Moscow's merchants can be conceptualized through a sample ledger of rural mortgages for 1862.[30] It shows that urban and commercial borrowers accounted for nearly half of the total loan amount, even though the merchants' credit operations did not typically involve land, and though the nobles' share was presumably increased for 1862 because by that time all of their credit needs had to be met with private loans.

By contrast, the merchants and moneylenders in Petersburg primarily serviced foreign trade and foreign merchants operating in Russia. These of course dealt with merchants and entrepreneurs in the interior of Russia, but the power of such credit links seems to have been somewhat weaker than that of Moscow. For instance, in 1847 a group of prominent Petersburg merchants had to go so far as to engage an officer of the Third Section to act as their debt collector in a number of small towns deep inside Russia. The merchants complained that they had exhausted all other, less drastic methods of debt collection.[31]

In addition to credit networks based on Petersburg and Moscow, other smaller but still important credit centers also existed. For example, in the early eighteenth century, these were Yaroslavl, located closer to the White Sea with its European trade, and Astrakhan, whose moneylenders serviced Russia's trade with Iran.[32] In the mid-nineteenth century these were replaced as credit centers by Odessa, Warsaw, and Berdichev.[33] Their volume of business is difficult to establish precisely, as the military statisticians discovered in the 1850s. The officers sent to Odessa found an ingenious way to do so through the volume of private cash transfers sent through the imperial post. In all of Russia in 1848, postal customers received 210.8 million rubles; of these, Moscow and St. Petersburg taken together amounted for one-third sent and two-fifths received, with Odessa in third place.[34]

This calculation did not include cash equivalents and debt documents that were also sent through the mail, but if it does indicate the two capitals' relative financial power, their combined share of Russia's private credit market can also be estimated as between 33 and 40 percent, which is, however, only half the amount of their combined share of government-issued credit, which reached almost 90 percent in 1855. Another relevant statistic for Odessa is the value of its grain exports, which relied on credit because of the seasonal character of agriculture and lack of liquid cash.[35] This value in 1853 was 25.7 million rubles, and in 1856 (in the midst of the Crimean War) it was 17.8 million.[36]

Finally, in 1857 there were forty-nine bankruptcy proceedings in Odessa over debts that totaled more than 3 million rubles.[37] These numbers suggest that Odessa's private credit system was very strong even though smaller than that of Moscow or Petersburg. In right-bank Ukraine, the major center was the town of Berdichev, where the annual credit turnover was estimated at 20 million rubles in the late 1840s. According to the military statisticians, the town's fees for registering bills of exchange and loan letters were enough to pay for the town's government, court, and hospital.[38] In smaller towns and villages, local sources of credit including both nobles and wealthy peasants (free or enserfed) were also available—in smaller numbers, it would seem from the fragmentary available information—but capable of issuing loans of up to several thousand rubles.[39]

Taken together and estimated conservatively, annual private credit transactions greatly exceeded government loans; the earlier 17 percent estimate is unlikely to be accurate even for Voronezh province, to say nothing of the rest of the empire. Moreover, the very distinction between government and private lending is somewhat artificial because the same funds could simultaneously circulate in government and private credit networks: serfowners who borrowed from the state could reissue their loans to other less privileged individuals at higher interest rates. Even more interestingly, some serfowners deposited their loans back in the same government banks at 4 percent interest and then used their deposit receipts to issue private loans and collect additional interest.[40] Credit in imperial Russia, therefore, operated largely outside the government's direct purview.

Debt as a Burden

Existing discussions of private debt in Russia, tantalizingly brief as they all are, differ on whether it represented an opportunity or a burden. Aleksei Bugrov has argued that most debts in the seventeenth century remained unpaid and that private credit was therefore too expensive and predatory, based on the fact that only a small fraction of the extant debt agreements contain notations of partial repayment (in fact, documents that were repaid or forgiven were returned to the borrower who would presumably immediately destroy them).[41] Earlier histories of Russian capitalism assume that capitalist credit was desirable for Russia and suggest that it was not sufficient.[42] Tracy Dennison, in her study of the institutions of Russian serfdom, draws on the field of development economics that emphasizes the benefits of credit for promoting economic growth.[43] But historians of the Russian landowning nobility are far less optimistic. To this day perhaps the most culturally prominent image of the role of debt in Russian society and culture is centered on an irrationally wasteful nobility, whose "Westernization" in the eighteenth century was expensive and required huge amounts of debt that simply could not be repaid.

However, the data used by Arcadius Kahan to make this argument can be just as easily interpreted to show that the costs of "Westernization" were actually quite modest.[44] Moreover, anecdotal evidence compiled by Karnovich, Romanovich-Slavatinskii, and Lotman only examines the tiny top stratum of Catherinian grandees who indeed accumulated staggering debts and does not take into account the spectacular financial benefits offered by association with the imperial court.[45] Equating nobility with wasteful consumption became commonplace in histories of imperial Russia.[46] The question is, then, whether private individuals, nobles and others, could or did opt to avoid debt or, to be more precise, to avoid excessive indebtedness that could not be supported by their income, available assets, or financial prospects.

Those Russians who reflected on the issue of debt at the time did often speak of it as a burden, or even an illness. One of the most important literary statements on the development of capitalism in Russia, Dmitrii Mamin-Sibiriak's novel *Bread* (1895), features a sympathetic young entrepreneur who felt the "invisible bonds" tightening around him when he borrowed 30,000 rubles from a wealthier associate.[47] During that time, forty years after emancipation, rural usury was described as a second serfdom.[48] Officers aspiring to join the prestigious Corps of Gendarmes were not supposed to have debts.[49] Even earlier, in the eighteenth century, the previously mentioned Andrei Bolotov was reluctant to incur debt, and he spent much of his long life at his country estate, engaged in scholarly and agricultural pursuits.[50] Unknowingly echoing Bolotov, in 1846 a middling serfowner from Vladimir province, Andrei Ivanovich Chikhachev, wrote in the *Agricultural Gazette:* "Few of us are not afflicted with the dangerous and malignant illness of debt . . . [which] has now become so widespread that the present generation will not likely be able to get rid of it."[51] And in another of his numerous articles Chikhachev lamented that, "Only the rare postal delivery fails to bring a summons to appoint a trustee over [someone's] estate." The notion that noble estates could easily be ravaged if not entirely taken away by government-appointed trustees or even private moneylenders would have been extremely unsettling to landowners conceiving themselves, as Katherine Pickering Antonova has shown in her microhistory of the Chikhachev family, at the center of a patriarchal village-based community. Chikhachev's personal response was to limit his consumption and to improve his estate's economic condition in partnership with his wife, which enabled the family to continue its lifestyle of rustic nationalism by paying off their substantial inherited debt.[52]

A similar life strategy was adopted by another middling nobleman and landowner, Nikolai Petrovich Makarov (1810–1890), best remembered today for his Franco-Russian dictionary and for popularizing classical guitar in Russia. Before settling down to a quiet life on his country estate, Makarov left the Imperial Guard to become an entrepreneur and an associate of the liquor tycoon Vasilii Kokorev, and also dabbled in moneylending only to eventually go bankrupt. A graphomaniac like Chikhachev, Makarov claimed as one of his life principles, "without extreme necessity, unavoidability, so to say, never to borrow, go into debt. And when it were unavoidable, then do it only in small amounts, and for a short time, and only borrow from my close acquaintances, who know me completely and trust me unconditionally. And then, even if I had to 'lay down my life', to repay the debt entirely and on time."

Makarov's principles vacillated between those of a prudent manager and a miser: he professed to have never gambled and, moreover, to have "constantly denied myself not only expensive pleasures, but also cheap ones." However, he added: "I did not spare money only for those things, which a decent [or "respectable"] man could not do without." As a young officer in the Imperial Guard, Makarov once had to stay in bed after a riding accident and was left without food other than milk and bread because the government did not pay the officers on time. According to his own story, it would have been the easiest thing to ask for a small loan from his friendly company commander, who lived right across the staircase. However, Makarov's principle was that "to ask for a loan from someone who might be the most wonderful person and a comrade, but with whom you were not on [sufficiently familiar terms], this would be so against my rules or concepts, seemed to me so monstrous, that I did not even once consider it." The commander still forced Makarov to take the money as soon as he learned about his difficulties.[53]

A few families and individuals seem to have attempted to live entirely without debt. One example is shown in the memoirs of feminist educator Elizaveta Vodovozova, née Tsevkovskaia (1844–1923). After her father, a landowner and a small-town judge in Smolensk province, died in the 1848 cholera epidemic, her mother paid off all of their inherited "town debts," many of which were incurred to cope with the illness, and retired to her modest country estate with all the children and servants.[54] From then on, the family strove to minimize expenses by purchasing as little as possible for cash and producing as much as possible on the estate; most household serfs were sold or forced to work the land. As a result, the family gave up many of the customary attributes of the genteel lifestyle, such as sugar, tea, coffee, and white bread. A lack of suitable clothes and of a decent carriage severely limited the family's social engagements with nearby landowners and even trips to the local church.[55]

While Tsevlovskaia's story is perhaps not common for the better-off serfowners, it may have been more familiar to the nearly 84 percent of the nineteenth-century gentry who owned few or no serfs. For example, the children of Lieutenant Colonel Aleksandr Iukichev, who died in 1851, inherited only twenty-seven serfs, bringing 100 rubles of total income. When the mother needed the money in 1854 to prepare one of her sons for military service, she preferred to do so by accumulating arrears on her taxes rather than by borrowing from private persons. In 1861 she did have to borrow a few hundred rubles from fellow gentry, but already by 1863 she had repaid some of the debt.[56]

Similarly, deceased Moscow merchants and townspeople whose minor children were placed under court-ordered trusteeship often left a debt-free inheritance, whether they were poor townspeople or merchants worth several thousand rubles in cash.[57] This is remarkable even taking into account possible undocumented debt and the custom of paying off one's debts when old or ill.[58] First, creditors would not have hesitated to submit undocumented debt for collection even if they were ultimately unsuccessful.[59] Second, if these individuals were indebted during their lifetimes, it is significant that they were able to repay before their deaths. It was far less common, but still possible, even for wealthy merchants to conduct business entirely without using credit, as Vladimir Vasilievich Pegov did in the 1860s, when institutionalized commercial credit had already become far more accessible.[60]

Perhaps more common were individuals who never aspired to complete self-sufficiency but who avoided excessive debt by paying close attention to managing their properties and regulating their level of luxury consumption.[61] Their stories should be seen as counterbalancing those of aristocratic spendthrifts, who in any case were becoming less common as the nineteenth century progressed. In addition to Chikhachev, Makarov, and Bolotov (all three representing the middling gentry), much wealthier and more powerful nobles managed to rebuild their own or their family's fortunes. For example, Prince Pavel Aleksandrovich Urusov—married to the daughter of Count Sergei Uvarov and therefore expected to maintain a grand lifestyle— in the early 1850s painstakingly worked on clearing his wife's property, populated with 6,400 serfs, from private debts of 140,000 rubles. Originally the estate was producing no income, but Urusov remortgaged it to the government bank, paid off private debts, and made improvements so that in a few years he was receiving an annual income of 101,000 rubles. In addition to servicing the bank loan and maintaining his wife and children, Urusov used approximately 20,000 rubles each year for improvements. For instance, Urusov claimed to have purchased a steam engine, built two distilleries, and bought elite livestock.[62]

Even individuals who were much more heavily burdened with debt had the ability and the will to either repay it completely or make substantial progress toward repayment. One type of documentation showing this is the trusteeship records of the Moscow provincial Noble Trusteeship Board (*Moskovskaia Dvorianskaia Opeka*), an elected body that appointed guardians for the estates of underage, profligate, and legally insane noble landowners. For example, the guardians over the children of Actual State Councilor Prince Iurii Ivanovich Trubetskoi (d. 1851) encountered debts of almost 600,000 rubles to the Board of Trustees and of over 80,000 rubles to private lenders; by 1857 this debt had shrunk to under 500,000 and just over 50,000 rubles, respectively, with annual maintenance payments made to the prince's widow and children amounting to tens of thousands of rubles.[63] The estate of more than 10,000 serfs brought 84,000 rubles in 1851 and 100,650 rubles in 1857, and it could have allowed an even faster repayment.

For example, in 1825, the governor of Moscow placed the young Prince Nikolai Fedorovich Golitsyn under trusteeship because of the "weakness" of his behavior, which involved incurring private debts of over 165,000 rubles. His property was enough to repay his debts in just a few years while at the same time paying Nikolai the staggering annual stipend of 40,000 to 60,000 rubles for his living expenses.[64] Another somewhat smaller estate (2,395 serfs) that had belonged to Guard Captain Rakhmanov and was inherited by his legally insane wife, also in 1851, was burdened with over 66,000 rubles in debt to the Moscow Board, and that debt was completely paid off by 1857.[65]

Nobles whose property was not under trusteeship still routinely made payments on their loans, even when they eventually became bankrupt. Even those debtors who were ill and elderly, like Guard Captain's widow Anna Bestozheva, refused to deal with debt in the manner of an ostrich: when she petitioned for insolvency in 1870, 6 out of her 21 loans were partially repaid.[66] Another widowed debtor, a teacher's wife, Pevnitskaia, when faced with the persistent legal action of her creditors who were trying to sell off her property, managed to fend them off at least from 1847 to 1853 by making partial payments, which she, in turn, could afford by retaining control over her estate.[67]

Finally, in contradiction to the stereotypical image—immortalized by Tolstoy in *Anna Karenina*—of an aristocrat disdaining the task of repaying his retail debt to innkeepers and vendors, real-life cases provide examples of meticulous attention to such obligations. For example, the trustees over the estate of the Princess Natalia Saltykova-Golovkina, who died in 1860, specifically gave priority to wages owed to her servants, to unpaid rent for her apartment, and to small debts owed for supplies and provisions.[68] It was considered good form and even a point of honor for a gentleman to repay his consumer debts when leaving town. For example, in 1801, the recently enthroned tsar Alexander I commanded that one of the aristocrats who led the coup against the late tsar Paul, Count Peter von Pahlen, leave Petersburg within three days. One of Pahlen's aides, lawyer and memoirist Vasilii Gettun, recalled that the count was forced to sell his house cheaply but still made sure to set aside 25,000 rubles—a huge amount—to repay his petty debts. However, the clerk entrusted with the task embezzled the money, and the count, already in the carriage and ready for the road, was beset by peddlers and shopkeepers asking for payment. The count opened his personal money-chest and paid them in person.[69]

It is also often assumed that because of the generous terms of government loans, as opposed to high-interest private ones, debtors were not in a hurry to repay them.[70] However, claims that the government banks were financially unsteady or that the Russian state propped up the nobility via credit are inaccurate.[71] On the contrary, during the difficult years of the Crimean War and the financial crisis, it was the nobility that propped up the state with its loan payments and bank deposits that the state used to bolster its finances.[72] Although government-run banks were indeed originally established to support the nobility, and though estate owners in provinces stricken by famine or rebellion received payment holidays, the banks' chief consideration still was to ensure a steady income stream. Accurate payments were required even by the less successful eighteenth-century banks.[73]

During the last ten years of its existence, the Moscow Board of Trustees consistently enjoyed a significant positive balance in its accounts; that is, the nobles paid back more than they borrowed, in contradiction to the commonly held view that the government loans were essentially a subsidy for the nobility. According to the Board's account books, in 1852 it collected 7,397,497 rubles more in principal and interest payments than it issued as loans; in 1854 this figure was 7,489,978; in 1856 it was 8,757,878; and in 1858 it was 5,615,996.[74] The Loan Department *(Ekspeditsiia zaimov)* of the Board routinely transferred up to 10 million rubles at a time to the Deposit Department and to the government directly. Thus, it was actually the gentry that subsidized the government rather than the other way around. A similar pattern existed for commercial credit: the records of the Commercial Bank in St. Petersburg show that out of hundreds of millions of rubles' worth of *vekseli* that it purchased at a discount during its existence, bad debt amounted to a trifling 1,510,229 rubles.[75] This shows that Russia's merchants as a group were likewise able and willing to pay their debts.

And further contrary to the common view, the Russian nobility was neither ruined nor excessively burdened by debt.[76] Its overall debt to the state (the often-cited 425.5 million rubles accumulated by 1859), even augmented to account for private indebtedness, still did not represent an unmanageable amount compared to the nobility's assets. According to the Soviet economic historian Iosif Gindin, the state-owned mortgage banks held 936 million rubles in deposits in 1856,[77] which exceeded the amounts deposited in post-reform Russian or even German banks until the mid-1890s.[78] By 1859, this amount grew to 970 million.[79] Some historians have pointed out that, given the estimates of the value of the noble-owned real estate between 1.375 billion rubles in 1853 and 2.1 billion in 1859, in addition to their cash deposits and other assets, the overall debt to the state of 425.5 million cannot be considered particularly large.[80]

Thus, the average amount of debt taken out on each serf soul (approximately 60 rubles) actually did not come close to the full amount that could have been borrowed (150–200 rubles). This was known to the nobles themselves: for example, Ivan Pushechnikov, a landowner from Oryol, recorded in his annual notes in 1859 that the government's alleged reason for closing its credit operations—fear of a run by its depositors—was completely unfounded because its loans were secured by property worth two or three times more, and so in the event of a run on the banks, it could easily find a low-interest emergency loan from foreign bankers. At the time of the emancipation, he thought that one-third of noble properties would end up being sold for debt.[81] This seems like a large amount until we realize that two-thirds were thought to remain solvent even after losing much of their value. One can of course object that these riches could have been very unequally distributed within the gentry. However, even contemporaries noted a lack of correlation between debt and wealth. Interior Minister Sergei Lanskoi noted in 1856 that landowners in the wealthy Saratov province owed almost as much as those in destitute Vitebsk province.[82]

Lendol Calder has argued that the development of modern consumer credit in the United States in the beginning of the twentieth century paradoxically rested upon on "traditional," "Puritan" values of economic discipline, and "prudence, saving, and industry" because installment plans, on which consumer credit was based, could not exist without a habit of regular timely payments.[83] I do not claim that Russia had modern consumer credit in the nineteenth century—some important elements were missing—but it is noteworthy that the two most important groups of property owners in Russia were taught financial discipline long before the financial revolution of the 1860s. First, serfowner borrowers were taught discipline by being required to make accurate payments to government banks. Civil and military officials were taught financial discipline because if they defaulted on their debts, a portion of their salary was subtracted each month until the debt was repaid.[84] Some private lenders found that lending to civil servants provided an easy stable income, and at the beginning of each month they methodically visited various government offices to collect their debtors' wages.[85]

Although academic literature and Russian cultural memory contain some memorable images of spendthrift nobles ruined by excessive debt, this stereotype must be placed in the context of another widespread model of behavior: avoiding excessive indebtedness through the careful management of resources and/or giving up immoderate consumption. Moreover, the image of consumption-oriented nobility must be placed in the overall context of the considerable assets available to the nobility and of the collective pattern of accurate debt repayment that was characteristic of nobles and merchants alike.

Individual Debt Portfolios: "Horizontal" and "Vertical" Connections

The system of clearly defined but permeable legal estates codified by the eighteenth-century tsars—including nobles, clergy, several types of merchants and townspeople, and peasants—is crucial for understanding Russian life well into the twentieth century. Estate identity determined one's tax and service obligations; it limited some opportunities—cultural, educational, and economic—and created others. But far from being merely a top-down set of rules, the estate system involved complex negotiation and contestation among the various government agencies, local communities, and private individuals.[86] Imperial law sought to create separate credit systems for nobles and for merchants, and it is important to ask whether individual debt portfolios generally followed or violated these estate boundaries. The answer proposed here is at once simple and complex: they did both. Alfred Rieber has argued that each social group in late imperial Russia included a "hard, unyielding core" in addition to the more amorphous and porous periphery. If this is the case, debt relations can be described as partially resting on the "denser interior" of each estate group but at the same time routinely bypassing that core, together with the "soft outer pulp."[87]

The central point here is not whether borrowing and lending destroyed or even undermined traditional structures and categories. Rather, debt existed in addition to and alongside them, bypassing them and superimposing a new identity and creating new alignments—however amorphous—of middle- and upper-class property owners. Debt relations in the mid-nineteenth century can thus be viewed as an example of what the U.S. sociologist Mark Granovetter has termed "weak" social ties. He defined the "strength" or "weakness" of an interpersonal tie as "a . . . combination of the amount of time, the emotional intensity, the intimacy (mutual confiding), and the reciprocal services which characterize the tie." Granovetter showed that, in the twentieth-century United States, diffuse networks of acquaintances, as opposed to tightly knit clusters of close friends, were essential for disseminating information throughout society and thus for promoting plurality, for enabling social mobility especially in educated middle-class and professional groups, and for "effecting social cohesion" by helping communities organize for common goals.[88] In short, Granovetter argued that weak ties are instrumental for individuals to adapt to modern societies. Given that imperial Russia's propertied classes are usually thought of as amorphous and incapable of common action, especially political action, the role of "weak" ties during the imperial period awaits more detailed study. Here I argue that credit transactions between distinct, often tightly knit social clusters enabled the existence of Russia's large, although diffuse, system of private credit.

Credit relations in Russia had been socially diverse for centuries, routinely bypassing the complex Muscovite social and service hierarchy. Seventeenth-century debt networks connected aristocratic boyars, lower-level military servitors, merchants, peasants, and Orthodox monasteries.[89] Petrine-era borrowers and lenders continued to be "motley" in terms of their social origins, including individuals from all social strata.[90] Moscow merchants, in particular, may have loaned money almost entirely to other merchants but themselves drew on a much wider source of capital: in addition to other Russian merchants, they routinely turned to foreign ones, as well as nobles, petty government clerks, clergy, and trading peasants.[91] Nobles' borrowing patterns in imperial Russia have not yet been studied in any depth, but noble lenders, judging by Nikolai Pavlenko's data for 1732, strongly preferred to diversify their investments and issued 40 percent of their loans to non-nobles; indeed, noble-to-noble loans comprised only 27 percent of Pavlenko's overall sample, which also included lenders from other estates.[92]

Nineteenth-century individual debt portfolios show that many individuals did prefer to form "horizontal" links with social peers. Most notably, the wealthier gentry liked to borrow from fellow aristocrats, and merchants and entrepreneurs dealt with other merchants. At the same time, individuals of all social ranks and levels of wealth routinely formed "vertical" and "extrinsic" links with persons of different social and legal status. This is very much in line with Laurence Fontaine's argument that credit links in early modern Europe often involved moving out of one's core social group. However, her observation that social proximity led to better treatment by one's creditor was not something reliably true in the Russian context.[93] For example, memoirist and historian Dmitrii Nikiforov recalled how a dashing cavalry officer named Luka Pokhvisnev inherited a rich estate from his father in the late 1850s, which he promptly squandered, and was then "rescued" by Anna Voeikova, daughter of the well-known usurer Stepan Shilovskii, who undertook to help him with his debts and eventually ended up with the best portion of Pokhvisnev's estates.[94]

Different patterns of borrowing had their own advantages and disadvantages. Borrowing within one's kinship and social network allowed debtors to hope for better loan terms and more lenient treatment in the event of default. However, it could involve a sacrifice in one's personal autonomy that would not be involved in a more arm's-length transaction; that is, a closer tie with the borrower could just as easily translate into economic pressure—for example, when a delinquent borrower would be forced to surrender his remaining assets at a discount. From the lender's perspective, the same considerations applied: one could have greater confidence in getting the debt paid from someone one knew well, but the relationship also could impose an awkward strain in case of default or a lawsuit.

Other distinctions from the Western European practices also existed: for instance, Jonathan Sperber notes that whereas lending to one's subordinates and peers was common in the nineteenth century in the German region of the Palatinate, borrowing from a subordinate was considered a social embarrassment.[95] No such qualms existed in Russia; indeed, many nobles whose serfs grew rich from trade were known to be hopelessly indebted to their own movable property.[96]

Aristocratic Debt

Wealthy serfowners were the only category of the population eligible for large, long-term, and low-interest loans from state banks and thus able to minimize private indebtedness and potentially to turn to their equally wealthy relatives and friends for a quick infusion of cash. On the eve of the emancipation, there were approximately 4,000 proprietors with 500 or more serf "souls."[97] Such serfowners' debt portfolios show that in the nineteenth century, government loans could be so enormous—reaching into the hundreds of thousands of rubles—that they completely overshadowed private indebtedness but that, in absolute terms, private debt was still considerable.[98] Moreover, even very large estates could still be laden with private debts exceeding the Board loans.[99] For middling and small serfowners, a larger proportion of private debt was more typical.[100]

In addition to their wealth providing access to cheap government credit, members of Russian aristocratic families enjoyed the benefits of extensive kinship and patronage networks.[101] One of the benefits of these networks seems to have been access to private credit that could allow nobles to avoid paying excessive rates to professional lenders. Nonetheless, lists of creditors included in several types of legal documents suggest that credit relationships with peers based on kinship and patronage were far from universal. Nobles routinely either preferred, or were driven by circumstances, to borrow from their social inferiors, while the most common pattern was to mix the two types of borrowing.

The estate of Guard Captain Muraviov is one example of a preference for credit ties with one's peers. At the time of his death in 1848, he owned 3,655 serfs in five different provinces (Orel, Riazan', Voronezh, Vladimir, and Kaluga) and held a total of six loans from the Moscow Board of Trustees, amounting to 164,455 rubles. His much more modest private loans were from the privy councilor's wife Davydova (3,500 rubles) and from *rotmistr* (cavalry captain) of the guard Pokrovskii. Muraviov also guaranteed a loan of 5,500 rubles incurred by his relative, State Councilor Aleksandr Muraviov.[102] While a few thousand rubles do not seem a large sum compared to the nearly 165,000 rubles of Board loans, it should be remembered that 3,000 rubles annually would allow a comfortable existence to a gentry family, and when issued all at once in cash was not a trifle even to the likes of Muraviov. Almost half a century earlier, the privy councilor's wife Ekaterina Naryshkina, who was born into an old but undistinguished gentry family, the Opochinins, and married into an illustrious family of the old Muscovite aristocracy, followed the same pattern in her borrowing: in addition to modest Board loans, around 1813–1815 she owed sums of 1,500 to 5,000 rubles to several other old Muscovite gentry families, including some relatives, such as an Opochinina, an Orlov, a Mansurov, and a Naryshkin.[103]

By far the most extensive horizontal private credit network I found is that of Anna Bestozheva *(sic)*, widow of a captain in the Imperial Guard, who became insolvent around 1870, fell ill, and died in 1873 without any property but with debts totaling almost 160,000 rubles, all of them private because the government had discontinued its mortgage loans in 1859. Except for four merchants, the rest of Bestozheva's twenty-one creditors were officers, gentry, and civil servants. Of the entire amount, only 38,000 rubles were Bestozheva's own debts. The rest she had guaranteed for other individuals, presumably her relatives and friends.[104]

Those aristocrats who engaged in commerce also liked to deal with their peers. One prominent example of an aristocratic entrepreneur is Prince Andrei Golitsyn, who participated in one of several ill-fated attempts to establish a silk-growing industry in Transcaucasia. Golitsyn became insolvent after the death of his partner, who had provided the necessary sericultural expertise. The list of his twenty-one creditors is notable for the presence of other aristocratic names, such as Demidov, Iurgenev, Kurakin, Potemkin, Voeikov, Baroness Dunka, Counts Orlov and Bobrinskii, and the wealthy and well-connected capitalist, Titular Councilor Yakovlev. The list included only two merchants and one townsman, who, incidentally, was the one creditor who actively pursued the lawsuit against Golitsyn, whereas most of his aristocratic creditors recognized his insolvency as a misfortune and refused to sue.[105]

Other aristocratic debt portfolios combined debts to peers with those to clear social inferiors. For example, Actual State Councilor Prince Iurii Ivanovich Trubetskoi upon his death in 1851 left private debts amounting to 81,115 rubles (which were dwarfed by his Board debt of almost 600,000 rubles) and an estate of 10,645 serfs, bringing in over 70,000 rubles annually. Trubetskoi's debts included loan letters from his equals, such as his sister Agrafena Mansurova, and Nadezhda Karnilieva, widow of a collegiate assessor (equivalent to an army major). But Trubetskoi also borrowed 10,000 rubles from a very junior civil servant and slightly less from a townswoman and from a high school student *(gimnazist)*, all three of whom were probably professional moneylenders because their loans were executed as the "safe-keeping receipts" typically utilized by high-risk lenders. However, despite Trubetskoi's occasional sudden need for money, his largest single private loan by far of over 18,000 rubles was from his sister.[106]

Aristocratic debt portfolios could be more diverse, such as that of Privy Councilor Prince Vasilii Alekseevich Khovanskii, who died in 1850 and who held estates in Ruza and Dmitrov Counties in Moscow province. Khovanskii and his daughter, who was married to an equally ranked Privy Councilor Bulgakov, owed money to five nobles, five merchants, one townswoman, and two serfs. One of the serfs must have been a trader, as his debt was only 384 rubles, but the other serf creditor, Egor Duduev, despite being owned by a noblewoman named Shepeleva, must have been either a moneylender or a prosperous merchant since he loaned 6,233 rubles. Interestingly, all but one of Khovanskii's noble creditors were very highly ranked: Khovanskii's own wife, a colonel's wife, a state councilor's wife, and a collegiate assessor (Class 8). Their loans were much larger than the 6,000 paper ruble loan from the "noble-born maiden" Shemanskaia, likely a professional moneylender.[107]

Those nobles who were involved in commerce and manufacturing only as an aspect of their management of extensive serf-populated estates also tended to have diversified lists of creditors. One of the more dramatic bankrupts, Actual State Councilor Krotkov, attempted—ultimately unsuccessfully—everything from agriculture to technological innovation to manufacturing and government contracts. His debts of almost 300,000 rubles were held by 39 creditors, of whom 21 were military officers and civil servants, 17 merchants, 1 townsman and 1 foreigner. Of the first category, 12 held a senior rank (Class 8 and higher), suggesting that despite the chaotic character of Krotkov's entrepreneurship, he still found the most ready and willing source of credit among his social and service peers. At the same time, his involvement in manufacturing and government contracts brought him into close contact with merchants.[108]

Other enterprising wealthy serfowners also borrowed from creditors who were far beneath them in station. For example, Collegiate Secretary Petr Zubov, in addition to inheriting 3,000 serfs and several factories from his brother, also took over his brother's debts to eleven persons, including three civil servants, one unspecified member of the gentry, one foreign merchant, three Russian merchants, and three townsmen. To these Zubov added his own additional debts to an army lieutenant and to a civil servant's wife. The only highly ranked creditor was a collegiate councilor's wife (Class 6). Whether any of Zubov's noble creditors were wealthy landowners like himself is not indicated in the record, but half of his debts were owed to persons of the commercial and urban estates; what is clear is that Zubov, despite his considerable wealth and his allegedly desperate attempts to improve the estate's condition, was either unwilling or unable to form most of his credit connections with peers.[109]

We know even less about the activities of cavalry Lieutenant Nikolai Engelgardt, from the famous family of aristocratic farmers in southern Kherson province, who accumulated private debts reaching 300,000 rubles.

The list of his 39 creditors included 7 military officers, 6 civil servants, 1 unranked member of the gentry, 9 merchants, 2 townsmen, 7 peasants, 5 foreigners, and 2 skilled mining craftsmen. Only a few of these people can be considered Engelgardt's peers: a landowner Count Raniker, a Count Tolstoy, two Swedes, and another Engelgardt. Clearly, Engelgardt took advantage of the available opportunities to form debt connections with his peers, but either these were either not sufficient for his needs or he did not want to get excessively entangled with his friends and relatives.[110]

The limitations on the kinds of loans that were available from one's peers are clearer in the case of the young Count Dmitrii Nikolaevich Tolstoy, a remote relative of the great writer, who lived with his father and went deep into debt to buy himself fine horses and other luxuries. Because Tolstoy had neither his own property nor an established legal personality separate from his father (despite being of age), he had not been able to form the kind of connections with fellow aristocrats that would include the possibility of extending credit. Thus, all four of the officers and civil servants among Tolstoy's creditors were of low rank. At least some of Tolstoy's creditors were being investigated for their alleged usurious practices, and so some of these may have been high-risk lenders. Other creditors were most likely vendors who supplied Tolstoy with luxuries, including three merchants, one townsman, two serfs, one craftsman *(tsekhovoi),* one soldier, and one free peasant.[111]

It is important to remember that the lists of creditors found in court cases are not necessarily complete because they include only individuals who either initiated a lawsuit or learned about it from newspapers and joined in. Thus the complete debt portfolio of a living, active, and solvent propertied person must have been somewhat different, including amounts owed not only to acquaintances, professional lenders, and business partners but also for the servants' wages and retailers' bills.

Most of these claims never showed up in court records, but one exception was the case of the aristocratic privy councilor's wife Princess Natalia Saltykova-Golovkina, who died in 1850, leaving a fabulous property with 10,300 serfs. Saltykova's recorded debt included some debts for only a few rubles. Among the 49 creditors were three junior civil servants, 13 merchants, 18 serfs and free peasants, 12 townspeople and craftsmen, 1 soldier's wife, and 1 foreigner; only one, the Aulic Councilor Tuchkov, from whom Saltykova rented her city apartment, could be considered her social peer. The merchants and peasants were mainly personal servants and retail vendors, including a cook and purveyors of bread, coal, hay, firewood, clothing, medicine, miscellaneous goods, and horse harnesses. There were 16 tradesmen's bills, as well as 17 claims for servants' wages and 14 money loans. Finally, there was the merchant Iulii Zhianini, to whom Saltykova had pawned various pieces of movable property for 3,300 rubles. Several of these loans were marked as partially paid, and there were no suspicions about Saltykova's solvency; nor did she owe to the Board of Trustees, or even have large private loans. Thus, unlike many other debt portfolios discussed in this chapter, Saltykova's probably represents a "normal" case that came to the courts accidentally because of her untimely death rather than because creditors despaired of any other way to collect their money.[112] The case also shows that credit relationships involving significant cash loans should be augmented by numerous financial links with servants and retailers.

The Urban Classes

Although common for the wealthier nobles, mixed borrowing practices were simply unavoidable for the "middling" urban groups. Although the cultural and—in the case of Moscow—even spatial division between the noble and servitor group and Russia's traditional commercial classes was perceptible throughout the nineteenth century, and "horizontal" and intragroup credit ties were still very important, members of the "middling" groups could not rely on having friends, relatives, or patrons with ready cash and could scarcely avoid borrowing across social and estate lines.[113]

Consider, for example, the memoirs of Alexander Petrovich Miliukov (1817–1897), a minor literary figure born into a traditional family of Moscow textile industrialists. His father, however, was a mere clerk who had to struggle to give his son an education. In order to enroll him in Moscow's then-only high school, he had to raise 700 rubles for the fee to sign Alexander out of their local community of townspeople *(meshchane)*. Of that sum, 100 rubles came as a friendly loan *(tovarishcheskii zaiom)* from the local priest who oversaw Alexander's elementary education, and 500 more were borrowed from the father's employer, a factory owner, and were going to be subtracted from his wages, although eventually the boss wrote off half of the loan. The last 100 rubles were the hardest to obtain: first, Alexander's mother managed to borrow 40 rubles from a wealthy merchant with whom she was acquainted. He owned a prosperous business that dyed cheap furs to make them look expensive, but he positively refused to loan the entire 100 rubles. Finally, the mother gathered everything that was valuable in the household—table silver, an old fox coat, her wedding shawl, some small jewelry, and even the heirloom icon frames—to take to a pawnbroker in a different part of Moscow in exchange for 100 rubles. This property was redeemed only a year and a half later, minus the shawl and the jewelry used to pay the interest. It is clear that the Miliukovs' credit network consisted entirely of members of the urban and commercial classes, including the local priest, but curiously not including members of their own family. It is also notable that this network was ultimately not sufficient, and the family had to resort to a purely market transaction with a pawnbroker, one selected from outside the family's network of neighbors and acquaintances.[114]

Merchants who generally dealt with their peers could also form more diverse credit connections. For example, the honorary citizen Nikolai Kuznetsov was a wealthy merchant who began his business already burdened with a 300,000-ruble debt inherited from his father. In 1865 he was put on criminal trial for fraudulent bankruptcy; he owed debts to seventeen creditors, all of whom were either merchants or townspeople. Kuznetsov had long-term relationships with most of his creditors, since they held up to nine of his bills of exchange for different amounts. However, five of his creditors were specifically listed as being from outside Moscow.[115]

Merchants also occasionally borrowed from nobles and civil servants. For example, Moscow merchant Zhivov had six creditors at the time of his death in the early 1850s, with individual loans varying from 2,800 to 555,000 paper rubles. Of these creditors, four were also merchants, and only the smallest debt of 1,000 silver rubles came from a titular councilor, Shapovalov. However, Zhivov's house was mortgaged to Messrs. Orlov for 17,428.53 rubles.[116] A much more modest merchant, Iakov Chistiakov, owed 2,710 rubles to seven creditors, of which five were merchants, one a merchant of Armenian or "Tatar" (Turkic-Muslim) origin, and one was the titular councilor Nikolaev, to whom Chistiakov owed 350 rubles, less than the average amount.[117]

A much more diversified debt portfolio was incurred by a modest female merchant Mavra Bubentsova, who sold fish and was not even enrolled in a merchant guild. Her debts were worth over 40,000 rubles (while her merchandise stock was worth 962 rubles); however, almost all of these creditors (claiming debts worth 38,000 rubles) could not present any written proof, making collection virtually impossible. Out of Bubentsova's nine creditors, three were peasants, three merchants, and three civil servants (one belonging to the lowest Class 14 and two – to Class 12). These estate-crossing links are remarkable given Bubentsova's low social status. Also notable is the fact that

Table 2.1 Debts of Liubov' Pevnitskaia, 1852–1854

	Men	Women	Servitor	Clergy	Urban and Peasant
No. of loans	12	10	8	6	8
Total amt.	19,306	4,358	7,276	8,739	7,649
Average amt.	1,609	435	909	1,456	956

Data source: TsIAM 92.6.741 / 1, l. 6.

Bubentsova's higher-status creditors all had documented debts that could be pursued in court, while the much larger debts from peasants and merchants, as well as the lowest-ranked civil servant, were not documented.[118]

Urban property owners who were not enrolled as merchants were likewise unwilling or unable to borrow exclusively or even largely from their peers, although they did like to form some horizontal credit connections as part of their social and financial network. Consider the debts of the collegiate councilor's wife Liubov' Pevnitskaia, who owed approximately 24,000 rubles and was accused by her creditors of being a compulsive borrower because she incurred more debts even as it became clear that she was unable to repay most of them. Despite her ownership of 228 serfs in Ruza County, and her husband's officially high rank (collegiate councilor corresponds to army colonel), she was also connected to Moscow's clerical circles because her father had been a priest of noble birth, as well as to the world of *raznochintsy* (individuals of "various ranks," educated and employed in "white-collar" occupations but neither nobles nor merchants), since her husband was actually employed as a high school teacher. Her debt portfolio reflected this diverse background of clerical, noble, and middling urban elements. Out of 22 creditors, 8 were military officers and civil servants and 6 were clergy (two priests, a bell-ringer, two deacon's wives, and a priest's wife), with the latter being Pevnitskaia's largest creditors both in terms of the total and average loan amounts (see Table 2.1). At the same time, her creditors also included four merchants, two townspeople, and two serfs. Thus, Pevnitskaia's debt portfolio suggests that her social milieu continued to be her single most important source of credit, but it was not by any means the sole source. Table 2.1 shows that while the loans from men were four to five times as large as the loans from women, loans to Pevnitskaia from members of other estates did not differ drastically, suggesting that Pevnitskaia's social cluster should be viewed as a single "middling" urban class that brought together individuals of varying legal status.[119]

Successful entrepreneurs who were nonetheless unable to form sufficiently extensive connections in elite circles had to diversify their credit relationships, as shown by the example of the military engineer Colonel Nikolia, who dabbled in a variety of businesses and governmental contracts in the 1840s and 1850s. By the time Nikolia became insolvent, he owed money to 48 individuals, of whom 28 were nobles, officers, and civil servants, 12 were merchants, 4 peasants, 3 foreigners and 1 clergyman. Similar to Pevnitskaia, Nikolia liked to borrow from other military engineers—there were five of them among his creditors—but could not rely on them for credit to any significant extent. Interestingly, the quickest and most informed creditors who were placed in the first category during the insolvency proceedings and thus were most likely to get repaid included thirteen persons, of whom only one was a merchant.[120]

Other non-merchant debt portfolios likewise show a combination of strong links between the gentry and Moscow's commercial classes, some links within one's milieu, as well as connections with one's social superiors. For example, the debts of the retired cavalry captain Mikhail Levenets may have resulted from some commercial activity because he owed 35,773 rubles to a Dutchman named Luk and 26,875 rubles to Collegiate Registrar (the lowest Class 14) Zamkov. But at the same time, some of his debt may have been consumer related, such as the 360 rubles to townsman Alatyrtsev and 200 rubles to craftsman Kumisov, while yet another group could be called his "social" debt, such as the 2,500 rubles owed to staff-captain of the guard Dashkov and 8,158 owed to Privy Councilor Prince Iurii Alekseevich Dolgorukov. While Levenets's service in the cavalry, an expensive branch of military service, implied substantial wealth, it also no doubt led to useful credit connections not available to more modest urban property owners. Levenets even acted as a surety to the higher-ranked Collegiate Councilor Monkevich. At the same time, his credit connections remained diverse, with only one of his twelve creditors being a fellow military officer, five civil servants, three merchants, two townspeople, and one foreigner.[121]

An even clearer example of the intertwined relationship between entrepreneurship, credit, and social status or connection is the case of collegiate councilor Platon Vasilievich Golubkov (1786–1855). Born to a low-ranking civil service family in Kostroma, Golubkov eventually grew exceedingly wealthy through trade, government contracts, and, most importantly, ownership of gold mines in eastern Siberia.[122] The list of Golubkov's creditors shows no less clearly than does his patronage of the arts how economic success and the prestigious character of gold mining improved his social status and led him to aspire to join the likes of the Demidovs and Stroganovs. At the time of his death, Golubkov owed money to fourteen nobles, including a Golitsyna, a Trubetskoi, and a Shakhovskoi, and to only two merchants and one peasant. It is interesting that Golubkov's largest single debt of 35,000 rubles was held by the peasant freedwoman Aleksandrova, who later enrolled in a merchant guild and was one of the two creditors who initiated the lawsuit.[123]

Whereas Pevnitskaia, Nikolia, and Golubkov were able to incur substantial debts and to resist collection proceedings perhaps in large part because of their social connections, individuals of similar station in life but without either the landed wealth or a social network had more difficulty resisting insolvency. For example, a British subject named Nikolai Dzhakson (Jackson) owned a house in Moscow jointly with his mother and brother but made his living by giving lessons and translating literature from English into Russian. He also was pursuing two legal cases: one for 20,000 rubles in the Moscow District Court against the heirs of Major General Poliakov and the other in St. Petersburg against another British subject, Gen [sic], for 1,000 rubles. By the time Dzhakson became insolvent in 1872, his debts reached 54,000 silver rubles owed to 16 persons, of whom 6 were civil servants, 4 merchants, 1 townsman, 1 foreigner, 1 midwife, 1 "maiden" (presumably of gentry origins), and 1 nobleman. Not only did he not borrow from other Englishmen or other Westerners residing in Moscow, aside for one Prussian merchant, but he was involved in a lawsuit with his own countryman.[124] This apparent lack of social ties no doubt contributed to his financial ruin, although in the end most of his creditors took pity on him and his family.

A gentlewoman of very modest means, staff captain's wife Avdotia Zerkal'nikova, owed money to seven persons, of whom one was a cavalry officer of the same rank (Class 10) as her husband, and two were a gubernial secretary and his daughter (Class 12), one merchant, one townsman, one foreigner, and one postman's wife. Notably, Zerkal'nikova either could not or did not want to borrow from persons of superior status, but her credit connections show a strong degree of integration in Moscow's credit community, which in her case linked such considerably different persons as a cavalry officer and a postman's wife.[125]

Even very short debt lists could be diversified; one example is that of the insolvent retired Collegiate Secretary Petr Glushkov, who owed 2,000

Table 2.2 "Vertical" and "Horizontal" Debt Connections: Relative Disparity in Rank between Lenders and Borrowers

	0^a	1–2	3–4	5–6	7+	Serv.^{b}/ Non-TR^c	Serv./ Other^e	Serv./ Urb.^{d}	Urb./ Urb.	Other/ Other
Reg. loan letters, 1852	18	37	29	12	4	15	4	16	1	2
Urban mortg., 1855	3	7	14	4	2	0	5	30	35	0
Rural mortg., 1862	8	10	13	6	8	0	7	22	15	8

a. Disparity in rank according to the Table of Ranks; b. Persons classified under the Table of Ranks; c. Nobles not in state service and servitors not classified under the Table of Ranks; d. Honorary citizens, merchants, townspeople, craftspeople; e. Foreigners, clergy, peasants. *Data sources:* TsIAM 50.14.2363 (1852); 1597 (1855); and 1629 (1862).

rubles to Collegiate Assessor Mikulyshin, another 2,000 to the second-guild merchant Sulaev, and 1,156 rubles to townsman Andreev.[126] Considering that there was a significant social gap between Glushkov's Class 10 rank and Mikulyshin's rank, it is interesting that Glushkov chose to borrow from a superior.

In sum, credit links formed by members of urban and commercial propertied groups were considerably more varied than those of the wealthy landowners. Borrowing within one's own group remained attractive, but the middling groups' lesser wealth and their inability to utilize formal credit institutions led them to form mixed debt portfolios with members of other social groupings. This conclusion is also confirmed by an analysis of several types of debt ledgers kept at the Moscow Chamber of Civil Justice, categorized according to the service rank and legal estate of the participant. Table 2.2, showing the relative disparity in rank between lenders and borrowers, reveals clusters of transactions between peers, as well as ones crossing estate boundaries. Moreover, it was far more common for nobles and civil servants to do business with merchants and townspeople than with individuals within their own estate but on the opposite end of the Table of Ranks. Borrowers and lenders definitely liked to deal with their peers but were unable or unwilling to do so exclusively or consistently.

Lenders

Another question that emerges from this account is whether lenders also tended to favor their social peers. Lists of debtors are obviously much less common than those of creditors, since lenders were interested in keeping this information private. In St. Petersburg, the Third Section occasionally sent its officers and secret agents to investigate alleged usurers, but such inquiries were limited to lenders who catered to wealthy and aristocratic borrowers. More helpful are lists created when a lender died, became insolvent, or was subject to full-scale prosecution. Such lists suggest that even those lenders who worked with a particular type of borrower also formed connections outside their social and cultural circles.

One example of a lender favoring his own kind was Lieutenant Vasilii Nilus, who died in 1852, whereupon the trustees appointed over his estates attempted to sort out his assets and debts. While Nilus owned 147 serfs in the agriculturally rich Orel province, most of his income must have come from his ownership of four residential buildings in Moscow, as well as from his moneylending activities. He strongly preferred to loan money to other officers and civil servants: two of his debtors were staff-captains, one was a titular councilor, one was an Aulic councilor (equal to lieutenant colonel), and one was an unspecified nobleman. Nilus did, however, diversify his investments in other ways, by making several medium-sized loans (of around 2,000; 2,000; 3,000; 6,800; and 8,200 rubles) rather than a few large ones by lending money to one person from St. Petersburg and by securing the loan to one Mr. Krenenberg with a mortgage on a house in the town of Orel. The loan to Titular Councilor Pavlov (for 8,208.50 rubles) must have turned sour because Nilus was engaged in a lawsuit at the time of his death that was being appealed all the way to the Senate. In turn, Nilus himself actively borrowed money: he mortgaged his estate for 14,140 rubles and one of his houses for 1,464 rubles to the Moscow Board of Trustees, possibly in order to loan that money out at a higher rate, and he also mortgaged at least one of his houses for 7,000 rubles to "Mrs. Shamsheva." Finally, Nilus also took out a cash loan of 865 rubles from townswoman Pisareva, and he owed an unspecified sum of money to his brother.[127]

Table 2.3 Loans Owed to Aleksandr Terskii, 1856

	Men	*Women*	*Servitor*	*Merchant*	*Urban*
No. of Loans	22	5	20	4	3
Total Amt.	50826.15	8343	50686	7275	2208
Average Amt.	2420	1669	2668	1819	736

Data source: TsIAM 50.5.13.

Table 2.3 lists loans issued by Second Lieutenant Alexander Terskii, who died in Moscow in 1856. He was a prosperous lender, frequently listed in the city's debt registers, both as a party to a transaction and as a witness. He catered primarily to nobles and officials, but it is remarkable that over a quarter of his portfolio consisted of merchants and townspeople.

Another example of a lender's portfolio comes from an honorary citizen from the town of Kashira, Nikolai Popov, who inherited 10,000 rubles from his father and lived by lending this money out, allegedly at the legally mandated interest rate and secured by real property. The list of his debtors showed a clear preference for other merchants who were also from Kashira and, if possible, his relatives: out of eight debtors, six were also merchants—of those, four were from Kashira (and of them, three were related to Popov). At the same time, Popov did show some attempt to diversify his investments: one of his debtors was an army captain, and one was a major general. Also diversified were the kinds of debt obligations that Popov accepted: only two were actually mortgages for a factory in Moscow and a house in Kashira, and one was a contractual obligation of unspecified sort, one was a less commonly used safekeeping receipt, and the others were loan letters, which were taken from all categories of borrowers, including officers, a townsman, and an honorary citizen from Kashira.[128]

In addition to various practical reasons, several likely general considerations explain why Russia's credit network routinely involved dealings across the boundaries of estate and service rank. One is that nobles possessed assets vastly exceeding their own indebtedness and were also willing to engage in commerce themselves, whether as passive investors or active entrepreneurs. Second, while there was a cultural gap between noble/servitor and commercial groups, it varied in time and space and was bridgeable through marriage and social interaction. Even wealthy aristocrats who preferred to borrow from their peers or from the government still shopped on credit, owed wages to servants, and in need turned to professional moneylenders. Members of the urban and commercial classes in the course of their credit dealings routinely crossed the barriers between merchants, officialdom, and the gentry.

Individual debt portfolios and debt registers kept by local courts show that the most common arrangement was to combine horizontal ties with peers and ties across social lines. This prevalence of mixed debt portfolios suggests that personal and informal debt connections, in addition to reinforcing traditional Russian hierarchies of legal estate and state service, also simultaneously undermined them by uniting a "middling" propertied stratum that included the lesser gentry and civil servants, merchants, and better-off peasants and townspeople. Although property owners in nineteenth-century Russia were a diffuse and amorphous lot, they shared a place of habitation, engaged in the same economic activities, and intermarried. Moreover, as anthropologist David Graeber has also noted, debt relations necessarily involve assumptions of equality that coexist with power and hierarchy.[129] In order to engage in debt transactions at all, people have to share a set of attitudes and practices relating to honor, trust, failure, mutual dependence, and reputation in the community as well as determining who could be included in the credit network.

CHAPTER 3

The Boundaries of Risk

WHILE THE NETWORK of private debt in imperial Russia was extensive and diverse, it was by no means all-inclusive. Lenders and borrowers operated within a complex web of cultural and legal norms and assumptions linking property ownership with understandings about personal autonomy, personal responsibility, trustworthiness, and risk taking. Some of these norms were legislated as strict, bright-line rules and are therefore a good place to begin to examine the cultural underpinnings of credit.

Perhaps the clearest and most unambiguous legal rule pertaining to credit in imperial Russian law was the absolute prohibition on minors under twenty-one from engaging in any property transactions without the written approval of their legal guardian. The way this law applied in practice is notable not only because the image of a young, rich spendthrift was so recurrent in nineteenth-century culture but also because this ostensibly strict legal rule was enmeshed within other, more fluid legal and social regimes attempting—as they did in all other major legal systems—to regulate and discipline financial life and risk taking.[1] Such regulation was to be accomplished primarily by excluding individuals deemed to be incompetent or untrustworthy, not only minors but also—since children did not always become financially responsible when they came of age—spendthrifts who accumulated massive debts that threatened to ruin their entire kinship group.

Another crucially important set of legal rules that sought to police the credit network was the institution of bankruptcy. For centuries, bankruptcy in the West was viewed as something of a symbolic and legal death, publicly expelling the culprit from the civic realm of property relations, a process hardly more pleasant than being convicted of a crime or declared insane. To an important extent, this attitude persisted in the nineteenth century. The bankrupt's suicide was a familiar cultural model.[2] Consider, for example, the noble-born entrepreneur, Nikolai Makarov, who in 1860 lost his business because of the financial crisis and a falling out with his much more famous companion, the liquor tycoon Vasilii Kokorev. Makarov later wrote in his memoirs, "Ruin I could have weathered with fortitude and patience, but insolvency—never. This is why the very thought of bankruptcy chilled my blood and breathed on me with a deathly chill." Before deciding to give himself a second chance by writing and publishing, Makarov seriously considered suicide, and one of the self-published novels that he produced to try to fix his finances features a bankrupt nobleman. He wrote, "The thought of the impending bankruptcy paralyzed all of his abilities, killed in him all activity. He could not engage in anything because everywhere he saw the horrible words—bankruptcy, bankrupt."[3]

At the same time, by the nineteenth century bankruptcy increasingly came to be seen in most Western legal systems as the outcome of accepting the risk of failure, which under certain circumstances could be viewed as acceptable and result in the discharge of one's remaining debts. The Russian Bankruptcy Code of 1800 asserted that "a bankrupt must not be considered dishonorable because honor or dishonor do not consist in the title of bankrupt, but solely in the action that led a person into bankruptcy."[4] The legal proceedings therefore involved a highly discretionary evaluation of the debtor's character and conduct. In practice, therefore, the laws protecting the integrity of the credit system resulted in a rather tangled relationship between legal rules and personal interests and discretion. Even the clearest legal rules were contested, reinterpreted, and modified in practice, much like every other element of personal credit.

Innocents and Wastrels

The image of an aristocratic spendthrift (in Russian rendered as *mot, rastochitel', tranzhir, rastratchik,* or *prozhigatel'*) ravaging his patrimony through a combination of inexperience and lack of restraint was prominent in nineteenth-century literature and journalism and has influenced subsequent historians. We have already noted the problems with the traditional account of Russia's allegedly wasteful nobility: contrary to popular belief, its indebtedness was not excessive compared to its available assets and, more-over, many landowners with large debts were enterprising and prosperous. But the spendthrift image was not entirely invented by moralists and foreign observers: younger nobles and merchants routinely fell into debt from drinking, gambling, and other forms of carousing. Spendthrift behavior no doubt revealed the less rational aspects of human nature and can only in part be explained by the youngsters' frustration due to their inability to take full advantage of their families' wealth. Lack of financial education and socializa-tion was another likely factor.

However, many stories of alleged wastrels had less to do with an irrational pursuit of pleasure and luxury than with the necessity of maintaining and advancing one's social and official status. For many young nobles, life in Petersburg and service in the Imperial Guard was a financial gamble—but not necessarily a wasteful or irrational one.[5] Nor was it quite as hopeless as it might appear from the letters and petitions of indebted aristocrats hoping for a bailout from a gracious monarch. A social, cultural, and above all legal framework was also in place to restrain inexperienced or wasteful members of the propertied classes. This framework is particularly fascinating because the strict legal rule about borrowing by minors was interwoven with a less formal ad hoc regulation of adult "spendthrifts" and because formal legal rules in Nicholaevan Russia invariably complemented, and underlined the importance of, private discretion and private initiative.

Profligate nobles from nineteenth-century fiction are too many to list here, from the indebted nobles in Faddei Bulgarin's bestselling novel *Ivan Vyzhigin* (1829) to the young Count Rostov from Tolstoy's *War and Peace,* who lost 43,000 rubles in one night to an unscrupulous cavalry officer.[6] These characters had real-life counterparts. Consider the young Count Dmitrii Nikolaevich Tolstoy, who was declared insolvent in 1863, with debts approaching 30,000 rubles, some of them secured by various expensive mov-able properties such as furs. This amount was enough to maintain a very wealthy noble family for a year, while falling short of the six-digit debts of some of Russia's grandest aristocrats. A large proportion of this money Tolstoy seems to have spent on fine horses, some of which turned out to be worthless. These debts had no discernible connection to any expenses of the military or other state service, since the young count served at the Moscow Noble Assembly apparently solely to avoid imprisonment for his debts. In the end, he was lucky in having his father pay his debts and get the case closed.

Far less governable was the young Lev Verigin, son of a naval officer, who showed "bad inclinations" from a young age and ran away from home, from foster care, and from several boarding schools. After his seventh escape, in 1865 he was put on a naval vessel *Izumrud,* bound for Japan. He continued to incur debts throughout the trip and was eventually expelled from the ship in Nagasaki for forging a banknote. In 1868, several months before Lev came of age, his father successfully petitioned to continue to be his guardian to avoid wasting away his property.[7]

The expectation that the scion of a wealthy family could be tempted to lead a merry life resulting in massive debt was also shared by the creditors of Moscow's commercial class. For example, in the bankruptcy case of Moscow honorary citizen A. Kalashnikov from the 1870s, one of his creditors wanted to put him on criminal trial for intentional bankruptcy because "being a son of wealthy parents, he early became acquainted with a quite dissolute and merry *[razgul'naia i veselaia]* life and . . . began to borrow money from various persons in order to later announce himself insolvent."[8]

After Alexander Terskii, a prominent Moscow moneylender, died in 1856, his son inherited 16,000 rubles in a bank and almost 60,000 in debt documents. After receiving the cash and collecting from his father's more reliable debtors, "Terskii started to live lavishly *[barski]*, recklessly, acquired friends and mentors; he had extensive credit from lenders, tailors and other craftsmen and innkeepers; the inheritance was quickly squandered; he was also borrowing recklessly and signed debt obligations." Terskii was declared insolvent in 1860 but continued to borrow until being placed in debtors' prison.[9]

The only son of another wealthy moneylender from that period, Ivan Briukhatov, likewise began a life of carousing after his father's death that included participating in a mock religious funeral, leading to a criminal trial for blasphemy in 1878. His co-defendants were members of a group of swindlers known as the Jacks of Hearts Club, and it is important to note that both the swindlers and their victims in that case included rather colorful young merchants who lost all sense of financial reality due to alcoholic stupor. One of the most important victims was a twenty-one-year-old merchant, Klavdii Yeremeev, who had a young wife and a fortune of 150,000 rubles. His bout of drinking and carousing in 1871 also involved issuing debt documents worth around 60,000 rubles, which he could barely remember. Another young merchant, Vasily Pegov, son of a prominent Moscow industrialist, drank and partied so much that his father eventually expelled him out of his house, after which Vasily began to forge bills of exchange in his father's name.[10]

Moderately wealthy Muscovites who could not rely on wealthy relatives also signed debt documents while drunk and gambling. For example, in 1863 a young Moscow University student named Ivan Chulkov refused to pay his debt on the grounds that he had been underage at the time and testified that he became drunk and lost a card game, after which "the friendly game suddenly became serious," and his partner, nobleman Khlopovitskii, forced him to sign a bill of exchange. He claimed to have been so intoxicated that he only remembered writing something to Khlopovitskii's dictation but did not remember what it was. Chulkov's story of intoxication, craftiness, and betrayal was completely rejected by his creditor, who claimed that they had never played cards but that he had loaned money to Chulkov so that he could pay his other debts.[11] Another example is the case of townsman Aleksei Klimov, who in 1865 borrowed money from another townsman, Mikhail Ulitin. While drunk, Klimov wrote seven backdated bills of exchange for different dates and to different persons, but according to his claim, he received no cash from Ulitin except for some money for a cab.[12]

It should be noted that not all reckless spendthrifts were men: women, and widows in particular, were also known to go into heavy debt. For example, a wealthy noblewoman, Elizaveta Dolgovo-Saburova, moved to Moscow in 1839 and signed numerous debt documents, both in her own name and as the guarantor for other persons, while suffering from the "white fever" (*belaia goriachka,* referring to alcoholic delirium) that "made her completely insensible."[13]

Not all spendthrift behavior resulted from stupidity or alcoholism, and in some cases it actually indicated an attempt to establish and maintain oneself close to the imperial court, to important grandees, or especially in a prestigious regiment. The memoirist Andrei Bolotov, coming to St. Petersburg in 1762 to serve as General Nikolai Korf's aide-de-camp, was clearly reluctant to spend large amounts on horses and gilded uniforms, which could not be accomplished without borrowing, but found that he had no choice if he wanted to retain his advantageous position.[14] Twenty-three years later, the young Prince I. M. Dolgorukov, another well-known memoirist, noted that "judging by the common opinion, I established myself in [St. Petersburg] society on a good footing, but look at what this cost me. I am not talking about boredom, strivings, petitions and various whims that I had to withstand here and there. Most of all I was beginning to be oppressed by debt, this ever-wakeful worm that afflicts city dwellers! . . . Foppery made my head dizzy."[15] At the end of 1785 Dolgorukov discovered that he owed as much as

2,000 rubles to clothiers, hairdressers, and cabmen. He did not have his own horses or a house, nor did he indulge in any significant gambling and carousing, and so these expenses seem to have stemmed mostly from his position as an officer in the Imperial Guard close to Grand Duke Paul.

These demands had not changed much by around 1860, when a member of another ancient Russian aristocratic family, the young Prince Nikolai Pavlovich Obolenskii, was unable to obtain a position in the Imperial Guard after finishing his education due to his poor performance in school and had to content himself with entering the less prestigious Elisavetgrad Hussar Regiment. From the very beginning of his service, Obolenskii bombarded his uncle and guardian with letters, which, while disavowing a desire to "stick it to him" in financial matters *(uschityvat')*, begged him for more money: it turned out that even a regular cavalry regiment required the officers to provide themselves with expensive horses, uniforms, and equipment. Officers who had not acquired a horse quickly enough were transferred to the infantry, the shame of which the young prince could not even contemplate. As the year went on, Obolenskii's letters became more desperate: although he initially vowed to have not "the slightest intention of taking on new debts," the gilded Hussar uniform turned out to cost more than 1,700 rubles, and he had to acquire a horse before the inspection by the divisional commander; in his Christmas letter to his uncle, the young prince confessed to having "out of necessity made some debts." Thus, although Obolenskii regarded his Hussar regiment as beneath his family pedigree, it still proved to be beyond his means, and he had retired from service by 1862. His motivation of maintaining his family's longstanding prestige is clear from his letters, but it is interesting that his uncle did not seem to think that these debts were inevitable or even useful.[16] State service, especially in the capital cities, did demand significant expense, yet the line between luxury and perceived necessity was apparently not always easy to determine.

However, potential benefits of debt-financed service in St. Petersburg were also considerable: family status and future income resulted from valuable assignments, promotions, gifts from the tsar, military loot, and government contracts. Aristocratic financial success stories have not attracted as much scholarly attention as spectacular aristocratic bankruptcies. Consider, for example, Catherine II's key administrator, Prince Alexander Viazemskii, who came from an old but utterly impoverished family and accumulated a fortune of 2 million rubles. In the nineteenth century, Moscow's flamboyant governor general, Count Arsenii Zakrevskii, came from a modest provincial family but after attracting Alexander I's attention was arranged to marry one of the wealthiest heiresses in Russia.[17] Taking a risk to advance one's position and connections appears in this light to be entirely compatible with the eighteenth- and nineteenth-century ideal of a rational economic decision-maker.

Aside from being rescued by relatives or—for the select few—directly by the monarch, spendthrifts and unsuccessful risk takers were protected by a complex web of legal rules prohibiting certain categories of individuals from incurring all or some types of debt. These rules were part of the fundamental legal principle that property transactions could only be effected by persons deemed legally competent. The French Napoleonic Code of 1803 was a particularly influential example of a civil law system setting the bounds of legal competence, granting extensive authority to the patriarchal adult male head of the household, to be exercised over women, children, and other dependents, including poor laborers.[18] Similarly, the laws in force in nineteenth-century Russia placed partial restrictions on the legal competence of, for example, foreigners, Jews, monks, and government officials.[19] In addition to these partial prohibitions, the law prohibited from entering into any legal contract all persons who were not legally competent, such as those subject to an appointed trusteeship.[20] The largest and most clearly defined category of legal incompetents was minors. Whereas in the Muscovite period boys who reached fifteen entered the tsar's service and were considered legally competent, Peter the Great's legislation raised the age of majority to eighteen for transactions with movable property and twenty for dealing with real estate.[21] Peter's 1714 law of primogeniture provided that documents issued by persons under twenty were not to be honored. This rule was reiterated in 1752, 1821, 1826, and 1830 and was included in the Digest of the Laws of 1832. These decrees also specified that a minor over seventeen could still incur debt with their guardian's permission.[22] In 1785, Catherine II's law allowed persons who reached seventeen to manage their real estate but not sell or mortgage it without their guardian's permission until they reached full majority, which was set at twenty-one.[23]

Despite its commendable intent, this rule was bound to cause problems—and not simply because people lied about their age. A rather serious technical problem was that by setting the full age of majority at twenty-one while granting a limited capacity to manage property to persons over seventeen, someone who was technically a minor could appear to be independent of their families in most aspects: a young man could be in civil or military service, and a young woman could marry and move under the jurisdiction of her husband. An additional practical challenge was determining a person's precise age. In the nineteenth century, this was not always easy, since metrical records could be lost or unavailable, especially for certain categories of the population, such as for Russia's numerous and economically active Old Believers whose sacraments were not officially recognized.[24] Other less conclusive ways to prove age included tax rolls *(revizskie skazki),* confession records, and circumstantial evidence such as witness testimony. Not surprisingly, abuses and errors were rampant.

To address potential abuses, some European legal systems chose to retain some debt responsibility for minors to prevent unjust enrichment, especially when a minor posed as an adult, as was the rule in Austria. Another option that Russian law could have adopted was to discard the concept of limited legal capability at seventeen or to provide for a court-ordered emancipation that was already available in Russia's Baltic provinces.[25] By contrast, Russian law—in line with the pre-reform tendency not to give judges too much interpretive leeway—adopted the strict rule that the only factor that mattered was the person's actual age at the time of the transaction; neither anyone's subjective belief nor any deception employed could make the transaction valid. In practice, the Senate in the 1860s modified the rule by requiring any minor who issued a debt obligation by certifying his or her age by illegal means to compensate the creditor and by permitting the court to require the adult person to repay a debt incurred before the age of majority if he or she admitted that debt after coming of age.[26] These decisions introduced some measure of safety for defrauded creditors at the expense of additional procedures, uncertainty, and judicial discretion, and only served to account for the most extreme cases without modifying the basic rule.

In turn, individual creditors and debtors were aware of the rule and took precautions. For example, the registries of loan letters at the Moscow Chamber of Civil Justice included the borrowers' age in some entries, as well as the guardian's permission and signature for those actually underage. But despite these precautions, youths apparently often lied in an attempt to take advantage of their creditors. In such cases, the creditors' best recourse was to complain to the police and initiate a criminal investigation, hoping that this threat would induce repayment.

This mechanism is illustrated by the otherwise unexceptional debt collection case against the previously mentioned student of the Imperial Moscow University, Ivan Chulkov. He was born in 1843 to a serf-owning army major and a serf woman, Agafia Rodionova. At first his parents signed him up as a townsman *(meshchanin),* as required by law for the children of such unions, but later his mother paid the merchant's tax for her son "just so he could have that rank."[27] As the young man later stated to the police, on July 14, 1863, he was playing cards with his friend, nobleman V. I. Khlopetskii, who "took advantage of his inexperience" and took from him a bill of exchange for the weighty sum of 4,500 silver rubles. When the police came to Chulkov's home to collect the money, he claimed that he issued this document as a minor because of his inexperience but never received any money. On the document, however, Chulkov wrote that he was twenty-two years of age. He was freed on the surety of his landlord and told to bring his birth certificate to the police.

As the investigation continued, Khlopetskii testified that he had not played cards but had loaned the money to Chulkov so that he could pay his debts. He claimed that he had not known that Chulkov was underage but that the broker *(makler)* who was recording the transaction began to doubt Chulkov's age and asked him to write it on the debt document. However, none of these circumstances turned out to be legally relevant. While legally Chulkov could not be required to repay his debt, the police started a criminal investigation of his intentional misrepresentation of his age, and this threat effectively induced him to come to a settlement with Khlopetskii. Eventually, the two of them petitioned the court to discontinue the case, emphasizing that Chulkov "could easily have made a mistake about his age." The investigator chose to drop the charges, although he was not legally obligated to do so.

What could have happened if Chulkov had not settled his case is illustrated by the fraud proceedings against noblewoman Agrafena Krivtsova, who in 1849 signed a loan letter for 5,000 rubles and falsely claimed to be twenty-five, which her husband Nikolai falsely witnessed.[28] Krivtsova claimed that she only found out her age when the loan letter was first presented for collection because "as a maiden living in her parents' house she had no necessity to know her exact age and upon marrying she was deprived of any means to obtain correct information about it." Her husband unsuccessfully attempted to avoid trouble with the law by claiming that his signature only meant that he certified his wife's identity and not her age.[29] Krivtsova's original sentence from the Moscow Aulic Court was to leave her "under strong suspicion"—the pre-reform equivalent of a suspended sentence—but free her from the debt collection because of her minority.[30] The province-level

Criminal Chamber held her to be potentially liable to a sentence of one year in the workhouse but freed her from punishment pursuant to the tsar's amnesty of August 26, 1856. If not for this manifesto, Krivtsova would have lived the rest of her life with the blemish of a criminal conviction, which could have affected her in various ways, even if she had not had to spend any time in prison or the workhouse. Still, although the Senate freed Krivtsova from having to repay the loan, it noted that the creditors still had the right to recoup their losses through additional criminal proceedings. However, the case file contains no indication that such proceedings occurred.

These two cases show how a debtor could attempt to use the inflexibility of the law to his or her advantage, whether or not Chulkov or Krivtsova did know their true age at the time of their transactions. Considering that Chulkov was a university student, it is likely that he was better informed about his age than the average Russian of the period. At the same time, these cases show—independently of the question of what the most effective legal rule would have been—that the pre-reform legal system was not nearly as inefficient and inflexible as portrayed by its critics and in practice found a way to enforce through potential criminal sanctions the bright-line prohibition of borrowing by minors.

The rule was effective even when the circumstances of the case made the action against a debtor swift and difficult to resist in court, such as the 1845 proceedings against the Senate registrar's wife Mel'nikova.[31] She was sued by a captain's daughter Olenina for 840 rubles but claimed that she never received the money and had issued the note without knowing she was doing so because of her inability to read shorthand. The police applied Russia's system of formal evidence to rule that because Mel'nikova admitted the signature on the note was hers, she had to pay, and the Aulic Court affirmed this ruling and sent her to debtors' prison even as she was further appealing the decision. However, someone must have advised Mel'nikova of the law about minors, and as soon as the court was informed that she was only sixteen when she signed the debt note in 1842, she was freed from arrest.

The courts enforced the law even at the expense of parental authority, which the imperial regime usually strove to protect. While normally parents were automatically their children's guardians, the issue was more complicated when parents and children were on the opposite sides of a transaction, and the former could not be expected to exercise impartial judgment. This was the issue in litigation between a wealthy Moscow merchant Dmitrii Savinov and his daughter, who was married to an army lieutenant,

Aleksandrov. It was common for parents and parents-in-law to use loans—real or fictitious—to secure their power and authority over the younger generation, and this was the case for Savinov. At one point, perhaps due to some personal conflict, he decided to exercise his authority and collect from his daughter an enormous debt of 350,000 rubles that was secured by a mortgage on part of his daughter's lands.[32] The daughter claimed that she had signed the mortgage note at the insistence of her father and that she was then only eighteen, as confirmed by the birth and baptism certificate from the Moscow Spiritual Consistory that she provided to the court. Given that her father must have been aware of his daughter's age, she argued that he therefore could not legally make her sign the mortgage without appointing a separate guardian to review and approve the transaction. Furthermore, the daughter or her husband unearthed another questionable transaction, an 1841 gift to her brother Dmitrii of four brick shop buildings that were originally purchased in her name in 1838. When the gift was registered at the Moscow Civil Chamber, Savinov named himself as his daughter's guardian, without being affirmed in this capacity by any official institution. Over Savinov's objections, the Equity Court found that he was not recorded anywhere as being his daughter's official guardian and, therefore, ruled against him.[33]

Parents could also attempt to benefit from this rule by having their children sign a debt document in their place, perhaps to avoid having to pay back the debt, although in the case of an old merchant, Artemii Riazanov, there was some doubt as to who was ultimately the victim of deception. At his trial for fraudulent bankruptcy, one of the charges against Riazanov was that in 1860 he had his eighteen-year-old son Vasilii claim that he was twenty-two and sign a 900-ruble bill of exchange to merchant Tikhomirov, and when Tikhomirov tried to collect the money, Vasilii said that he was a minor and had only signed the bill of exchange on his father's command. However, the senior Riazanov claimed that he had carried out that trick at the request of Tikhomirov himself, who would only agree to loan him the money if the loan was in Vasilii's name, with the father's signature to guarantee it. If this is true, it is possible that Tikhomirov intended to cause Riazanov to violate the law in order to hold the threat of a criminal prosecution over him and Vasilii, thus motivating the senior Riazanov to repay the loan.[34] Another similar case that took place in 1859 and involved a young aristocratic officer of the Imperial Guard in Petersburg suggests that this strategy was not uncommon within Russia's culture of debt and that creditors could use the rule against borrowing by minors and the threat of criminal sanctions for their own purposes.[35]

In sum, the prohibition against borrowing by minors was technically simple and straightforward, stemming from a rational intention to protect young property owners and their families by placing the entire burden on creditors to ensure that borrowers were competent to contract the debt. Pre-reform justice has been alternately criticized for being too formalistic and for focusing exclusively on substantive justice. It is therefore intriguing to see that borrowers and lenders alike found ingenious ways to adapt the law to their interests and strategies. The fact that the rule did not operate exactly as intended should not be seen as particularly surprising or as suggesting that Russian law was in some way defective or fictitious. The fact that criminal sanctions were used to deter abuses does not suggest a weakness but has been a strategy widely used by other legal systems as well. Finally, the cases applying the rule reveal the surprising extent to which basic legal knowledge was available to the general population in nineteenth-century Russia.

In a situation where the wasteful individual was over twenty-one, families had several other options. In addition to simply paying the debt or separating the debtor from the household, it was possible to petition the government to establish a trusteeship *(opeka)* over the spendthrift's property. This measure existed in all major legal systems, both in Roman law and the legal systems derived from it, including the Napoleonic Code, and in common-law jurisdictions.[36]

Early examples in Russia date from the 1760s and show an extraordinary procedure requiring a special decree from the empress to establish a trusteeship and then remove it if the spendthrift corrected his behavior.[37] The legal definition of spendthrift behavior emphasized behavior not "proper to [one's] station in life," "immoderate expenses," and gambling and selling off one's property "for the purpose of drunkenness or satisfaction of other passions."[38] The procedure used the framework of Catherine II's Provincial Statute of 1775, which granted provincial governors the authority, subject to review by the Senate, to prevent and curtail excessive luxury and dissolute behavior.[39]

Originally this provision did not include the power to establish trusteeship over wastrels' property, but the law of 1817 did extend the rule to include wastrels.[40] Governors could establish trusteeship over a spendthrift even without a petition from family members, and after the court reform of 1864, this power was also given to District Courts upon a motion by a district prosecutor.[41] The law applied not only to nobles but also to merchants and townspeople, for whom the rules were finalized only in 1859.[42] However, the law did not apply to spendthrift peasants, who could still be disciplined by their local communities.[43] Interestingly, the two cases of spendthrifts that led to the 1817 decree involved not aristocrats but the wife of Gubernial Secretary Levashov (the lowly Class 12 on the Table of Ranks) and retired noncommissioned officer Bykov.

The effect of placing a wastrel's property under *opeka* was to deprive him of the ability to enter into any legal transaction or agreement and thus prevent him from mismanaging his remaining assets. The rules were found in several different statutes and were often unclear. However, the overall effect of a trusteeship was that, as long as creditors had not grown too impatient and the wastrel had not had the chance to ruin all of his remaining property, the trustees could make partial payments or negotiate with creditors to prevent insolvency and summary sale of the property. Creditors, in turn, would be more likely to be patient seeing that the debtor's financial affairs were being put in order.

Thus, the *opeka* had the practical effect of limited bankruptcy protection, although these protections did not in any way limit creditors' rights to sue and to seize debtor's property, unlike certain other closely related provisions. For example, special debt commissions were established mostly in the eighteenth and early nineteenth centuries by imperial decrees as a favor to individual aristocratic debtors; mediation commissions, set up by an 1827 law, were available only to solvent debtors and trusteeships imposed over the estates of serfowners who defaulted on their debts to state credit institutions, such as the Moscow Board of Trustees.[44]

For some families, having a wastrel's property taken over by a trustee was therefore beneficial, despite the negative effect upon that family's reputation caused by newspaper announcements. For example, in 1825, Actual Chamberlain Prince Fedor Nikolaevich Golitsyn petitioned Moscow's governor general to place his son Nikolai under trusteeship, arguing that "due to the weakness of his behavior [he] incurs considerable debts and, thus wasting away his capital, may with time lose all of his property." He also petitioned to appoint Privy Councilor Prince Sergei Mikhailovich Golitsyn and Privy Councilor Senator Lev Alekseevich Iakovlev as guardians for as long as they considered it necessary; the father also wanted to publish newspaper announcements that would prevent Nikolai from incurring new debts. The governor forwarded this petition to the provincial administration, which declined to impose trusteeship because Nikolai did not own property in

Moscow province. However, the governor overrode this decision, arguing that the father already had control over Nikolai's property, and ordered the trusteeship established specifically over his person *(lichnost')*.

Interestingly, merely limiting Nikolai's ability to dispose of his property was insufficient since he was not prevented from signing debt obligations, and he had to be equated with a child or a mentally incompetent person.[45] Occasionally, trusteeship could be denied, most commonly when spouses wanted to take over their wives' or their husbands' property because of their alleged mismanagement. One example was Prince Pavel Alexandrovich Urusov, who unsuccessfully attempted to take over his wife's property in 1855, alleging "ruin" and "mismanagement."[46]

However, if a property's condition was beyond repair or the relatives could not agree on a strategy, insolvency could still result after a trusteeship had been imposed. For example, in 1858 the Moscow military governor Count Zakrevskii, known for his dislike of the commercial classes, ordered a trusteeship established on the grounds of "wastefulness" over the person and property of Moscow merchant Vasilii Prokhorov, a member of a prominent Russian capitalist family who owned a shop of "Russian goods" (Russian-styled textiles for which the Prokhorov dynasty was famous). Zakrevskii's order averred that Prokhorov led a "life improper for his position in society and not corresponding to his station in life *[sostoianie]*" and that "there is no hope for his correction." Prokhorov's uncle and father-in-law—who headed the family business—became the trustees. Whether because, as Prokhorov himself claimed, the trustees mismanaged the shop or because the business at that point was already beyond repair, Prokhorov was still held to be insolvent in 1859.[47]

Negotiating Failure: The Culture of Bankruptcy

Alexander Nikolayevich Ostrovsky's first play, *The Bankrupt* (1849) was the first high-quality literary depiction of traditional Russian merchants, and it instantly propelled the author to enduring prominence.[48] The play features an old merchant, Samson Bolshov, who declares bankruptcy in order to pass his successful business on to his sly and scheming son-in-law without paying off his debts, and intending to remain in actual control. The play depicts a new commercial world based on self-interest and formal legal rules appearing alongside the old culture of commerce based on trust and kinship, to which the legal formalities were only subsidiary. Ostrovsky's critics, focusing on traditional merchants' alleged lack of morals, miss the fact that in Bolshov's world, the institution of bankruptcy—by all accounts a crucial element of capitalist transformations—is accepted and widely practiced.

Just like their English, French, or—after 1898—American counterparts, Russian merchants judged that the danger of fraud was counterbalanced by the benefit of arranging for an orderly distribution of the assets of the debtor, who in turn was incentivized to cooperate by the opportunity to get his debts discharged and make a fresh start. An anonymous pamphlet published in Petersburg in 1848 claimed that in 49 bankruptcy cases out of 50, creditors were willing to grant full discharge, whereas, in its author's view, only 1 case out of 50 would in fact involve some misfortune warranting debt forgiveness.[49] Ostrovsky's plot, then, is driven not so much by Bolshov's faithlessness as by the prosaic fact that his son-in-law, now the legal owner of his property, is offering to repay only 10 percent of the debt on Bolshov's behalf, whereas the creditors are demanding the more commonly expected 25 percent.[50]

Real-life stories of bankrupt merchants and nobles contain some of the most illuminating detail about Russia's culture of debt precisely because of this element of negotiation and contestation. Bankruptcy discharge was institutionalized in Russia in 1800, around the same time as in most other major legal systems. However, as was the case with most nineteenth-century Russian legal and administrative practices, its application depended to a surprising degree upon the discretion of private individuals—in this case the individual creditors who staffed bankruptcy boards.

Borrowers who lost their creditors' trust had to surrender their remaining assets and then provide testimony explaining their failure and typically acquiring a performative and even dramatic aspect that was generally lacking in regular Russian court procedures before the 1864 reform.[51] Creditors who staffed bankruptcy boards then decided—subject to approval by a court—whether to grant a discharge. Circumstances deemed beyond the borrower's control, or, conversely, fraudulent actions such as concealing property or account books, of course tended to sway the creditors. But, just as significantly, creditors were motivated by the possibility of negotiating a partial repayment of the debt, which could lead them to disregard obvious fraud. The possibility of debt forgiveness in effect served as just another factor in out-of-court negotiations between the debtor and his or her creditors, who were motivated to get their investment back if possible, if necessary by threatening the debtor with debtors' prison or a criminal prosecution and by holding out the possibility of a discharge as a reward for cooperation.

Legal practice in mid-nineteenth century Russia balanced the two approaches to debt that had existed—and collided—in the West since at least the eighteenth century. The older view assumed that insolvency was caused by a debtor's immorality and recklessness, while the newer attitude, revealed at first in practice but increasingly also in legislation, shifted some of the risk of failure to creditors when the insolvency stemmed from circumstances beyond the debtor's control. In Western Europe and North America, the treatment of debtors in the eighteenth and early nineteenth centuries gradually shifted away from regarding debt and bankruptcy as a moral failing that was to be dealt with through harsh legislation. Although much of day-to-day debt relations continued to rely on personal acquaintance and traditional notions of honor and character, the emerging consensus was that debt was necessary and even beneficial for commerce and that insolvency was primarily an economic, rather than a moral, failure, meaning that individuals taking business risks were no longer to be punished for it.[52]

Thus the early modern English bankruptcy laws that were penal in character were replaced with the statutes of 1825 and 1849, which offered greater protections to insolvent merchants, and the statute of 1869, which extended bankruptcy protections to non-traders.[53] The French law of 1807 was harsh toward debtors, focusing on enabling creditors to identify, seize, and distribute a debtors' assets, with the result that voluntary agreements between creditors and debtors became the norm in practice and that subsequent legislation strove to correct the imbalance and provide some protections for debtors.

The effect of the new European bankruptcy laws was that cooperating debtors could enjoy a complete discharge of their debts and could start with a blank slate, free of oppressive legal sanctions and virtually free of social disapproval. At the same time, though, debtors continued to view their condition as limiting their personal autonomy as citizens.[54] As to those individuals whose debts were too small to be eligible for bankruptcy protection—the poor and the laboring classes—they were increasingly viewed not as objects of charity but as delinquents who needed to be restrained and punished.[55]

In imperial Russia, a broadly similar movement was also taking place. The landmark Law Code of 1649 did not provide for bankruptcy discharge or specify how a debtor's assets were to be distributed, but it did require a payment moratorium of up to three years when insolvency resulted from fires, floods, or brigand attacks; after that, all the negative consequences, such as indentured service, still ensued.[56] Although the first bankruptcy statute in Russia was enacted in 1740, it never actually went into effect, and during the second half of the eighteenth century bankruptcy practice relied on several fragmentary decrees.[57] The important Senate decree of 1767 followed Dutch commercial law and ruled that the majority of the creditors who held most of the debt were to make the decisions. In 1784 this was refined to also give the authority on a bankruptcy board to a minority of the creditors who held the majority of the claims.[58] A complete bankruptcy statute was enacted in 1800, and so in this respect imperial Russia was in-step with the overall Western trend. A slightly different version of the statute was adopted in 1832 and remained in force until 1917, with only minor changes.

Russian law defined bankruptcy as the inability to repay one's debts in full. Other signs of bankruptcy included personal admission or flight. Technically, this definition would make virtually any merchant or property owner into a bankrupt and, consequently, made the entire bankruptcy regime completely dependent upon creditors' confidence. A debt-ridden individual could stay in business for years and, conversely, someone declared bankrupt could actually be completely solvent by today's standards. Noble landowners who were not technically insolvent could petition the government to establish a "mediating commission" composed of their creditors for the purpose of the orderly distribution of the debtor's assets.[59]

Although there was some debate in Russia about whether to extend bankruptcy procedures to nobles, there was no widespread resistance and apparently nothing like Sir William Blackstone's position, which was widely shared in England, that only merchants could possibly become insolvent through no fault of their own, whereas everyone else could only do so through dishonesty.[60] As in other major legal systems, Russian law contained separate provisions for commercial and noncommercial bankruptcy, but with its relatively clearly defined system of social estates, the attempt to distinguish between commercial and noncommercial bankruptcy presented particular difficulties for noncommercial debts incurred by merchants, as well as commercial debts incurred by members of other estates. In 1846 this issue was clarified, and commercial bankruptcy rules were extended to persons from all estates, as long as they took out commercial licenses. Finally, another legal issue, likewise not unique to Russia, was what kind of activity should count as trade. According to Gabriel Shershenevich, imperial Russia's leading expert on commercial law, the judicial consensus was that it was not necessary to engage in a series of transactions: it was enough to show the intention to engage in trade, for example, by purchasing merchandise on credit with intent to resell it.[61]

The law of 1800 also established the framework—already present in the eighteenth-century drafts—of three types of bankruptcy: accidental, reckless, and intentional. Nineteenth-century French bankruptcy law also followed this categorization, distinguishing *faillite, banqueroute simple*, and *banqueroute frauduleuse*. The default rule requiring no special showing was to hold an insolvent debtor to be "reckless," whereas in order to have his or her debts forgiven, an insolvent debtor had to prove that there were external circumstances that affected his or her ability to pay. Among the conditions for this full discharge were a natural disaster or an enemy invasion, or "other accidental decline or bankruptcy, an extraordinary fall in the prices of merchandise, if it will be proven that other merchants suffered the same fall at the same time . . . and other similar circumstances, which he could not prevent."

Conversely, if creditors found that the debtor concealed property that could be used to cover the debt or engaged in any other fraud, they held bankruptcy to be "malintentioned" *(zlonamerennoe bankrotstvo)*, which automatically resulted in criminal prosecution. Unlike usury, fraudulent bankruptcy was punishable with exile to Siberia. The creditors' findings were reviewed by the Commercial Court and often resulted in litigation, especially when challenged by creditors who were not satisfied with the majority's decision.[62]

One example of how the decision was reached in practice is provided by the case of the military engineer Colonel Vladimir Nikolia (Nicolas) who became insolvent in 1870, with debts totaling nearly 185,000 rubles. By that time, he had retired from commerce and worked for the Warsaw-St. Petersburg Railroad, but in the 1850s, he had been heavily involved in municipal engineering projects and government contracts. His misfortunes started in 1859, when his uninsured grain barge on the Volga burned down. Later he built an embankment in the town of Rybinsk, which was destroyed by ice before he officially turned over his work; then he lost money in an "unlucky enterprise of an oil-making factory," as well as through managing a steamship company in 1851–1863 and designing a water-supply operation in the city of Kazan'.[63] Nikolia's creditors concluded that this kaleidoscope of projects was evidence of "recklessness," which was punishable by up to five years in a debtors' prison. Superficially the decision suggests that Russians at that time had not yet adopted the more debtor-friendly attitude to commercial failure that just then prevailed in Great Britain; but considering that Nikolia's creditors eventually settled the case, agreeing to set him free to pursue yet another project in exchange for continuing to make payments on his debt, a more likely interpretation is that the creditors were simply trying to pressure Nikolia to agree to favorable settlement terms.[64]

While it is less clear whether it was Nikolia's mismanagement or misfortune that most contributed to his insolvency, other cases make much clearer the string of "social" and natural disasters that could build up over years and bring to nothing even wealthy people's attempts to rebuild their finances. These cases make for some of the most dramatic reading in pre-reform court documents. For example, Prince Andrei Borisovich Golitsyn inherited a debt-ridden estate from his father in 1822, suffered crop failures for two years, massive peasant disobedience, and on the top of that the ruin of his investment in the Sericultural Company in Transcaucasia when one of his partners who had the necessary expertise died and the company was taken over for its debt to the imperial treasury.[65] Many of his creditors, especially those of his own social circle, chose to discontinue their claims, considering his bankruptcy to be unintentional, but others continued the suit.

A similarly detailed and dramatic testimony was offered by Collegiate Secretary Petr Fedorovich Zubov, who had estates in Arzamas and Makarievsk counties in the Volga region, with nearly 3,000 serfs. Zubov chose to take over this debt-ridden estate from his brother and for several years attempted to improve conditions for his peasants by paying them to develop additional lands, transferring newly bought serfs from central Russia to work on empty lands, and developing a timbering operation (which came to nothing because his creditors shut it down). All these efforts eventually failed, according to Zubov, because of the "unfortunate confluence of circumstances" that included several crop failures, fires destroying both Zubov's and his peasants' structures, and the serfs suing Zubov to gain their freedom and refusing to pay their rent, which, in turn, made it impossible for him to repay the mortgage to the Moscow Board of Trustees. The Board then had a trustee appointed over the estate to collect its income, which put an end to Zubov's attempts to regain his financial autonomy. For his daring in taking on this debt-ridden estate, Zubov was held to be a "careless" bankrupt, although actually arresting him proved to be impossible, since after being expelled from his estate Zubov went into hiding, apparently at his friends' estates.[66]

That the outcome of cases like Zubov's or Golitsyn's depended completely upon the creditors' goodwill and discretion is showed by another almost identical case that did lead to a full discharge. The misfortunes of Actual State Councilor (equivalent to army major general) Sergei Ivanovich Krotkov began in 1847, as soon as he received—as was commonly practiced by the Russian landowning gentry—his portion of his future inheritance while his father was still alive. This transfer was accompanied by various debilitating conditions and was followed by three years of bad harvests in 1847, 1848, and 1849, when Krotkov had to borrow to pay his living expenses and the interest on the Board of Trustees loan, as well as to feed his hungry peasants and their livestock and rebuild their houses. At that point, Krotkov had not yet given up but decided to convert his distillery plant to a textile factory to take advantage of low prices for raw wool. Although this required yet another loan, Krotkov was able to repay much of his debt and made a profit for four years, until the Crimean War ended in 1856 and the demand for woolens went down because the government was no longer buying new uniforms. Then Krotkov tried himself out as inventor, traveling to London to attempt to sell a patent for an "electro-magnetic guard." However, he was swindled and had to come back to Russia after spending another 20,000 rubles for the trip. On returning to his estate in 1860, he organized a mechanical sawing workshop to manufacture "cheap men's clothes" out of the woolens made at his factory. For a while he was paying off his debts, but then a clerk sent to Nizhnii Novgorod stole 10,000 rubles' worth of merchandise. At that point, Krotkov was finally ruined; once serfdom was abolished, he needed cash to continue to operate his factory, which he could not raise because of his debts. He therefore had to lease out the factory, thus losing the income, and had to begin a pyramid scheme of borrowing money solely to repay his old debts.

Krotkov became insolvent, in his own words, "despite the fact that throughout his life he never allowed himself to live above his station, and even less to spend his money lightly, while to the contrary using all of his strength and ability to preserve his fortune." The final blow was delivered in 1874 by a colonel's wife, Aleksandra Shenshina, who brought to the recently established District Court his letter begging her to wait because his other creditors had forced a sale of his properties for less than half of their value, and so he was left with no means to make any more payments. The court clerk underlined these lines with a pencil and wrote "debtor's admission." Unusually for Russian bankruptcy proceedings, none of his thirty-nine creditors had any objections to Krotkov's testimony and in 1876 held him to be an "accidental" bankrupt.[67] It is difficult to argue that Krotkov was any less "reckless" than, say, Zubov; for instance, both stories included references to natural disasters that according to the Bankruptcy Statute entitled the debtor to full discharge.

One possible reason for the leniency to Krotkov was the more liberal attitude to insolvents in the 1870s, leading, for example, to the partial abolition of debt imprisonment in 1879; judging by the earlier examples, Krotkov might not have been so lucky in the 1850s and early 1860s. But it seems that another important reason was that many of Krotkov's creditors were his relatives—with his wife alone accounting for almost one-third of the total amount of the debt—and thus able to influence the proceedings of his bankruptcy board.

Overall, however, it seems that full discharge was not an outcome that could be taken for granted, although this conclusion could be affected by the nature of my sources.[68] In contrast to the Krotkov case, in the case of Nikolia discussed above, creditors were clearly pressing the debtor to reveal any hidden assets or make some other arrangement for repayment, while in the Zubov case, it is unclear what motives, other than malice and frustration, induced his creditors to declare him "careless," since there was no chance that Zubov retained any significant property or could acquire any in the future.

What is clear is that the discharge could be agreed on as part of a deal between the creditor and the debtor: this is precisely what happened with Moscow merchant Borisovskii, who, legally speaking, was anything but an "accidental" bankrupt, since he was caught hiding merchandise and various household furnishings with his relatives. However, the creditors voted to ignore this inconvenient evidence that would have committed Borisovskii to a criminal trial and thus would have prevented him from repaying any of his debts in the future.[69]

Conversely, creditors could pressure debtors despite good evidence; for example, Artemii Riazanov (the elderly Old Believer merchant) received no sympathy despite very good witness testimony that said he was "an honest old man" who had become insolvent because of his inexperience in running a textile factory and because of bad prices for raw materials. Cases that I have reviewed contain very few instances of full bankruptcy discharge. The explanation for this is probably that, given that the creditors' agreement was required for a discharge, those that were sympathetic to the debtor would have already reached a settlement during the early stages of a bankruptcy proceeding.

In addition to the balance between debtors' financial and business decisions and those circumstances that were beyond their control, such as natural
disasters and widespread price fluctuations, another important factor influ-
encing the way debtors were treated in bankruptcy proceedings was information about their personal character, such as honesty, family commitment, and
sobriety. To some extent, this notion was inherent in the very rules of Russian
criminal procedure, which were applied in cases of "intentional" bankruptcy.
Before the 1864 reform, these included a procedure (known as *poval'nyi
obysk*) similar to early medieval juries in the West: the court investigator
questioned twelve and sometimes more members of the defendant's community of the same legal status (i.e., merchant, peasant, etc.) about the defendant's behavior and character. In nineteenth-century practice, the answer
was virtually always positive, except that in a very few instances, the person
so questioned "did not know" anything about the defendant. While this
particular procedural element had lost its practical meaning by the mid-
nineteenth century, the question of debtors' character continued to be crucial
in bankruptcy proceedings, considering the central role of the creditors' discretion and thus of their good opinion about the debtor.[70]

Another type of evidence that shows the balance between outside circumstances and personal character in determining how debtors were treated was
a list of less wealthy debtors who were imprisoned in Moscow in 1826 and
were considered for redemption on the occasion of Nicholas I's coronation
festivities, which prompted many charitable donations. These prisoners were
all members of Moscow's "middling" class, including junior civil servants,
lesser merchants, townspeople, and peasants engaged in commerce. The list of
71 prisoners included detailed annotations of their character and of the reasons for their debt. These fall into two groups. The first set of 45 persons had
debts related to business. To give just a few examples, the foreign merchant
Petr Temerer could not repay 630 rubles related to his collapsed cartwrighting
business. Merchant Zimin could not repay a 1,000-ruble *veksel* (commercial
promissory note) because his money disappeared in bad debt extended to
others. The merchant Kozma Ulianov owed over 4,000 rubles in rent to the
city for keeping fisheries on its property and could not repay because of a
flood, which also may have ruined townsman Ignatii Lubkov, who owned a
mill. Another merchant, Petr Malyshev, rented space for an inn from General
Poltoratskii but was ruined when the nearby theater closed down, leaving
Malyshev in debt for 2,500 rubles. These were all considerable debts for
mid-nineteenth century Russia, vastly exceeding the amounts earned by

manual laborers, for example, but still far short of the large commercial bank-ruptcies with their toll extending into hundreds of thousands of rubles.

The second set of debtors consisted of victims of a wide variety of everyday life circumstances and included individuals of all social estates. For instance, a collegiate registrar's wife, Maria Aleeva, became heavily indebted because of the slow progress of a legal case in which she was involved. Army Staff Captain Afanasii Bakhterev could not repay 4,000 rubles because his 100 serfs were refusing to pay their quitrent. No fewer than five individuals ended up in prison because they had to borrow to pay for their daughters' weddings: soldier's wife Maria Fomina owed 400 rubles; craftsman Ilia Rodionov owed 1,500 rubles; and three other townspeople owed 291, 200, and 600 rubles, respectively. Illness was another common cause, ruining foreigner Fedor Ride and townsman Gerasim Gavrilov (300 and 200 rubles, respectively). Irina Kozlova owed 700 rubles for rent and the expenses of signing up as a Moscow townswoman. Katerina Prakhova, a townswoman, owed 2,800 rubles because her late husband had borrowed from the wife of a civil servant who was later convicted for embezzlement. Townsman Sergei Smirnov still owed 800 rubles for timber used to rebuild his house after the French inva-sion in 1812. Townsman Konstantin Danilov owed 3,000 rubles that he had borrowed to ransom himself from serfdom. Craftsman Sergei Maksimov had borrowed 280 rubles to pay his taxes.[71] This list could be continued, but what is already clear is that aside from such misfortunes as illness, peasant unrest, or legal expenses, the single most common cause of crippling indebt-edness for these relatively humble individuals was a too-expensive attempt to better one's social condition, whether by giving one's daughter a respectable wedding, rebuilding a house, or escaping serfdom. This suggests an important social role for debt that is difficult to document *en masse* from any other single source.

Although the debtor's character and actions as well as his or her behind-the-scenes negotiations with creditors seem to have been the two most important factors affecting how they were treated, there is some evidence that mid-nineteenth-century Russian legal practice was at least beginning to recognize that simply engaging in commerce made debt inevitable and insol-vency highly possible—even in the absence of famines and enemy invasions.

First, Russian merchants and government officials alike tended to conflate large debts and large business turnover. For example, in the criminal bank-ruptcy trial of the elderly merchant Fedor Solodovnikov and his sons, his creditors and the court that reviewed their decision recognized that the

Solodovnikovs' annual business turnover of 800,000 to 900,000 rubles "obviously could not occur without using credit."[72] This statement was made in a much later period than that covered in this study; however, the Solodovnikovs' business and related indebtedness that eventually resulted in a bankruptcy did go back to the 1850s and 1860s.

Earlier, in 1863, the Moscow governor general dispatched his special aide, Titular Councilor Count Konovnitsyn, to oversee renovations in the debtors' prison. In his report arguing for improved conditions for wealthier debtors, Konovnitsyn noted that "almost always the greater the amount of debt, the larger the debtor's affairs must have been, [he must have] had more money, and therefore was used to a better life." The governor did not agree, but Konovnitsyn's opinion could not have been completely eccentric if it was offered up to the governor in an official report.[73]

Second, as mentioned earlier, the Bankruptcy Statute did list market fluctuations as a basis for debt discharge, and actual bankrupts did bring up the vicissitudes of commerce to explain their insolvency. For example, the 75-year-old Old Believer merchant Artemii Riazanov unsuccessfully ran a small textile factory and for his debts was imprisoned for over four years and eventually put on trial for criminal bankruptcy. Explaining his failure, Riazanov mentioned high prices for raw cotton and low prices for finished goods that forced him to sell at a loss, in addition to the common stories of theft and the purchase of defective materials. Riazanov was unique among Russian debtors whose cases I reviewed as he described his emotional depression as a contributing factor in his financial misfortune and as explaining his unsatisfactory testimony to the bankruptcy board. Here I have tried to preserve his grammar:

> I traded in cotton goods and because fortune did not accompany my commerce, my business went badly, and therefore I gradually lost myself and fell in spirit, paying little mind to my thoughts and cares, and came to a kind of sickly condition which included not only a lack of focus but also forgetfulness. And for that reason when proceedings were instituted regarding my inability to pay the debts pursuant to documents issued to creditors for the amounts indicated in them, then I, given my circumstances, agreed to everything as long as I was not constrained and could come back to myself—expecting some more favorable circumstances, which happen frequently in commerce, when a rich man becomes poor and a poor man becomes rich, and so I testified about my

insolvency indeterminately and haltingly, expressing myself for the most part with phrases 'I don't know' and 'I don't remember'... and all of this was attributed by my creditors, who became my judges, to my intention to conceal capital and merchandise to their detriment, whereas my testimony clearly spoke to my mental condition.[74]

Less expressively, the brewer and innkeeper Prokhor Bodrov, who became insolvent in 1867, explained his failure as a general decline of the beer trade, the loss of a large sum in bad debt, trade losses resulting from competition by tax farmers, who until 1863 administered Russia's alcohol monopoly, and the loss of up to 12,000 rubles that resulted from his attempt to renovate his inn. This went along with a less convincing story of thieves stealing a chest with his account books and debt documents worth up to 20,000 rubles.[75] While in those cases that I was able to review creditors usually suspected foul play and were not very inclined to listen to debtors' stories of declining prices and markets,[76] at least the courts that had to review and affirm the initial rulings of bankruptcy boards staffed by creditors approved the notion that market failure could be a mitigating factor. For example, the Moscow Commercial Court, aggressively pursuing an elderly Moscow merchant named Ivan Borisovskii, contrasted his story of an unsuccessful investment in the purchase of several houses in Moscow with an "accidental decline" *(nechaiannyi upadok)* in trade that could get him more lenient treatment.[77] Taken together, it seems that the notion of unfavorable business circumstances leading to indebtedness and bankruptcy was used by debtors and their creditors and judges alike but did not acquire the force of a general outcome-determinative rule, since the lenient treatment did not reliably extend to instances of unsuccessful individual investment and risk taking that was interpreted to be reckless.

After the 1864 reform, fraudulent bankrupts were tried by juries, who always retained the option of acquitting even those defendants who were obviously guilty, and so the post-reform jury trial should be viewed as one additional—and final—element in Russia's bankruptcy procedure. Individuals who were formally guilty because they, for example, had destroyed their account books, could still be discharged of their debt in effect by being acquitted by the jury. For example, in 1876 a 49-year-old Moscow merchant, Ivan Yelmanov, was indicted for selling his bread shop to a friend, merchant Lepekhin, and for pawning to him all of the movable property in his apartment. Yelmanov claimed that his insolvency resulted from bad debts by bakers but could not provide their names; he also destroyed his account books. His brother, who worked as his clerk, testified that his trade on credit was in very small amounts and that there were no bakers among his debtors. Lepekhin denied being handed over the shop to avoid debt. The jury acquitted Yelmanov.[78]

Another form of quasi-legal proceeding was the debt lottery, a privilege occasionally granted to high-profile, aristocratic debtors. This was one of the ways in which the central government and the tsar himself could occasionally become closely involved in specific debt cases, especially when a high-profile debtor became bankrupt or died. This intervention occurred through parallel extra-legal procedures rather than through subversion of the court system. Debt lotteries were an interesting alternative to using the court system and were primarily intended for the heirs of Russia's wealthiest debtors. One example occurred in 1821, when Count Nikolai Golovin, the great-grandson of Russia's first admiral of the Petrine era, died, leaving 3 million rubles' worth of property and 7 million rubles' worth of debts. The late count's heirs sensibly refused to take on the inheritance, and the government was obligated to authorize a lottery sale administered by a special commission with the minister of the interior as its head. The commission issued 170,000 tickets, each worth 50 rubles. The four winning tickets included portions of Golovin's extensive landed estates, but there were also 6,009 money prizes ranging from 50 to 200,000 rubles. The drawing was conducted by twelve children from the Gatchina Imperial Orphanage, and information about the lottery and the drawing was published daily in the leading St. Petersburg daily newspaper. The winners included individuals from many different provinces, of various estates (gentry, civil servants, soldiers, merchants, townspeople, and even a serf of Count Sheremetev, who won 25,000 rubles).

The lottery had huge resonance across Russia because individuals from many provinces and from different social ranks bought tickets and were eagerly hoping to win. Memoirist Vasilii Gettun bought a ticket for 50 rubles and sent it to a young lady as a sign of affection. Novelist and ethnographer Melnikov-Pecherskii, in his *Grandmother's Tales,* wrote, "In her last years grandmother prayed every day to the point of fainting .... At that time there was a lottery for the Golovin estate; grandmother bought three tickets and she wanted very badly to win Vorotynets [the estate constituting the main prize]. She prayed for it so hard that every day she would be put to bed unconscious. The lottery was drawn, grandmother lost, but she did not want to believe it and every day prayed for the rich Vorotynets with its gardens, wharfs, picture galleries, and all the riches of the fabulous estate." Another reaction, exemplified by characters in Nikolai Leskov's unfinished novel *A Family in Decline* (1874), was shock at the fact that human beings (Golovin's serfs) were being sold at a lottery.[79]

A similar case occurred when Chamberlain Aleksandr Sergeevich Vlasov, another eighteenth-century grandee, died in 1825, and his heirs refused to take on the estate because of its staggering debts, in his case incurred by acquiring a fabulous art collection of paintings, engravings, bronzes, marbles, porcelain, books, antique weapons, and so on. In this case, 2,154 items were to be drawn at the lottery, likewise established by Alexander I's special decree explicitly as an alternative to court procedures, which were thought to be ill equipped to deal with a case of such magnitude.[80] However, the tickets sold so poorly that the lottery had to be canceled and replaced by the more typical auction sale.[81] This kind of alternative procedure seems to have become a notable feature in the culture of debt, even if it was used only sporadically. For example, in 1860 there was a widely publicized lottery of an estate in Warsaw province, which consisted of five sections, each divided into three classes. Prizes were staggering: in only one of the several sections the main prize was 425,700 rubles.[82] Official permission was necessary to stage a lottery, which was sometimes denied (perhaps because it was seen merely as a way for the debtor to get out of paying).[83] Public lotteries were only used sporadically, but should be seen as an alternative form of bankruptcy discharge and as something of a social safety valve for high-status individuals burdened with hopeless debts.

In sum, Russian bankruptcy laws provided for the full discharge of debts for individuals who fell victim to natural disasters, enemy invasions, and sudden market fluctuations that ruined their business. However, actual cases show that the three-fold classification of bankruptcies as unfortunate, reckless, and malintentioned—clear enough on paper but not corresponding to the real practices of Russian merchants and other entrepreneurs and dependent on the discretion of the creditors staffing bankruptcy boards—ultimately served as a framework for practical negotiations between creditors and debtors, much as they did in France, for example.[84] Creditors appear to have been more motivated to recover at least some of their investment than to argue about precise legal definitions. Debtors, in turn, were motivated to convince creditors that they did not intentionally deprive them of their money and were not hiding anything of value, or that they still had enough earning potential to recover the loss if allowed to stay in business. Both sets of "bright-line" rules discussed in this chapter were therefore inextricably linked with individual discretion and strategizing and, ultimately, with a set of far less clearly articulated values and assumptions about credit.

CHAPTER 4

Fraud, Property, and Respectability

A NOTHER DEFINING set of ideas about credit connected property ownership and wealth with the much more tangled and often unspoken notions of trust and respectability. A wealthy person was usually deemed to be respectable and thus creditworthy, but the roles of risk, contingency, and trust in any credit transaction are also obvious. A rich borrower could easily prove to be the lender's worst nightmare, by leaving town or engaging in protracted legal battles or simply dying. As Craig Muldrew has pointed out with respect to early modern England, in the absence of modern credit-reporting agencies and large banks, individuals strove to minimize the risk inherent in lending by relying on the legal system.[1] But even with criminal penalties provided for fraud, the legal system was not of much help to a lender whose debtor became penniless. So what did borrowers and lenders do as a practical matter to determine creditworthiness? Markers of trust were complex, including not simply documentary proof of property ownership, rich clothing, and good manners but even more importantly the presence of partners, friends, and relatives who helped to demonstrate the potential borrowers' membership in a network of property owners known to be creditworthy and reputable.

The culture of credit was therefore inseparable from the more encompassing "invisible code of honor" that governed respectable conduct in the nineteenth century and whose boundaries were most clearly articulated in the breach.[2] Existing studies of nineteenth-century honor unfortunately leave out its connection with credit, but Russian debt cases reveal the same focus on appearances, deception, and the concealment of shame that William

Reddy has described as the "essential feature" of the nineteenth-century culture of honor.[3] Potential borrowers needed to project prosperity and inspire confidence even when they were desperate for a quick infusion of cash, and when the time came for repayment, potentially insolvent debtors attempted to convince their creditors that their finances were sound and that postponing the debt would do no harm. As Jonathan Sperber has observed for nineteenth-century Germany, even when both borrowers and lenders were honest, a "gap remained between the knowledge of credit-worthiness, stemming from the face-to-face dealings of individuals, and the broader scope of . . . commerce."[4]

The complex connection between trust, respectability, and concealment and deception—as well as the importance of nineteenth-century information technologies—were particularly apparent in cases where concealment and deception were interpreted as criminal fraud. Nineteenth-century swindlers and forgers were as newsworthy as those of our own day. A prosperous country squire in temporary need of cash or a young nobleman claiming to be an attorney for a prominent aristocrat could easily turn out to be impostors skillfully manipulating the norms of respectability and legal formalities to obtain loans that they had no ability or intention to ever repay. Friends and relatives of the swindler could themselves be accomplices, victims, or innocent dupes. One of the most recognizable fictional swindlers is Nikolai Gogol's Pavel Chichikov from *Dead Souls* (1842), a disgraced former civil servant who went about purchasing dead serfs still listed in the government tax rolls in order to mortgage them to the state bank. Chichikov was attempting to defraud the government, but his real-life counterparts were often far more daring and imaginative in avoiding the pitfalls that quickly unmasked Chichikov's scheme.

In contrast to Gogol's story, real-life private persons were usually far easier targets than the government, and the fact that Chichikov observed all the legal formalities highlights the point that the continuum between lawful and criminal strategies and stratagems was as vague in the nineteenth century as it is for today's "white-collar" criminals.[5] Moreover, stories of real-life swindlers show that fraud did not simply subvert or make use of the norms of respectability but was inseparable from them, given that the ever-more-common middle-class embezzler was typically motivated by the desire to maintain his respectability and social standing and that most fraud cases appeared in almost every way to be indistinguishable from legitimate transactions, just as they seemed to the victims.

Creditworthiness and Wealth

In the nineteenth century, individual trustworthiness and creditworthiness were primarily underpinned by property ownership. The rules of the Moscow and Petersburg Boards of Trustees, which before 1859 issued loans secured by serf "souls," required only a certificate sent directly from provincial authorities that the borrower actually owned the stated number of serfs. The certificate also needed to affirm that the property was "reliable for a loan" *(blagonadezhnoe k zalogu),* but as a practical matter this proof of "reliability" was not explained or problematized: provincial authorities seem to have issued reliability certificates more or less automatically. No special inquiry was expected to be made into estate owners' character, reputation, or existing indebtedness.[6] The same principle applied to private transactions, both in fiction and in real-life cases. A rather foppish character from Ostrovsky's play *Mad Money* (1870) exclaims that "fifty thousand is good money; in Moscow it can get you credit for a hundred thousand and there you have a hundred and fifty thousand."[7] Elsewhere he claims to be completely content to be penniless and in debt, although some of his creditors could get angry and imprison him in the Debtors' Pit for a couple of months: "And then they will let me out, and I will be free again, and have credit again because I am a good fellow, and I have eleven aunts and grandmothers and I am the heir to all of them."[8] A rich merchant from another of Ostrovsky's plays, *Jokers* (1864), responds to a request for a loan from a virtuous but poor young woman: "What am I going to do with your word? Can't make a fur coat out of it."[9] The memoirist and worldly legal official Vasilii Gettun remembered after acquiring a large silver snuffbox that "it does not hurt to own things because when in need of money they can be pawned either in a pawnshop or to a private person."[10]

Similar sentiments are found in many debt-related legal disputes. For example, the defrauded creditors of a young civil servant, Nikolai Dmitriev, who borrowed money with forged credentials, noted in their complaints in the late 1840s that they had known him for many years, loaned him money previously, and he had always paid back on time.[11] In another case, nobleman Khlopetskii, who allegedly loaned money to university student Ivan Chulkov, noted in 1864 two precise grounds for extending credit: one was Chulkov's claim that he was going to receive an inheritance from a relative and the other was that Khlopetskii had gathered up information about Chulkov and received good references to the effect that he repaid his debts to other persons in a satisfactory manner.[12] The young Count Dmitrii Tolstoy likewise was able to borrow from usurers because he was the sole heir to his wealthy and elderly father and was also expecting to get married and thereby obtain financial independence.[13] Townsman Aleksei Klimov, disputing his debt to another townsman, Mikhail Ulitin, in 1866, claimed during an *ochnaia stavka* (a face-to-face meeting between the defendant and the victim or a prosecution witness) that he could not possibly have entrusted him with a large amount of money because Ulitin did not even know where Klimov lived. Ulitin responded that that was true enough but that they had instead gone together to the Moscow Magistrate to obtain information about the inheritance Klimov was about to receive.[14] In 1855, Collegiate Registrar Dmitrii Sheremetievskii borrowed 100 rubles from townsman Nikolai Ivanov (or 200 rubles, according to Ivanov) with the expectation that he was going to get money in a few months, after selling some land.[15] A failed entrepreneur and aristocrat, Actual State Councilor Prince Vladimir Sergeevich Golitsyn, was considered to be more creditworthy because he was the heir to a wealthy aunt, and he claimed that his insolvency in part resulted from the fact that she later changed her will and disinherited him.[16]

Another case shows how wealth could be interpreted as automatically rendering someone incapable of dishonorable behavior. Consider Nikolai Popov, a moderately wealthy Moscow moneylender whom we have already encountered. On a spring day in 1859, this 26-year-old native of the nearby town of Kashira went on a stroll with his friend, a 27-year-old merchant Chelnokov, who lived on the rental income from his house, accompanied by two women: Chelnokov's 21-year-old wife and a 20-year-old seamstress, Kravitsyna. Walking down the sidewalk on the Ordynka street, Popov saw a paper envelope lying on the pavement, probed it with his cane, and picked it up, whereupon several men tackled him and his companions and accused them of being criminals. It turned out that a merchant's widow who owned the house next door had received an anonymous threatening letter demanding 300 silver rubles, and her friend State Councilor Folz then proposed to ambush the blackmailer. They placed a paper envelope under a rock on the sidewalk just as was demanded and placed a groundskeeper *(dvornik)* and two of Folz's serfs in an ambush. According to these servants, Popov turned over the rock and picked up the envelope, which he would not have otherwise seen hidden under the rock. Popov and his companions claimed that the envelope was not hidden at all and that they picked it up out of simple curiosity. Popov's girlfriend, Kravitsyna, claimed that Popov was not actually caught but brought the envelope to the house and asked to see the landlord.

The most interesting fact about this case is that the Moscow Criminal Chamber ruled that Popov was "involved in this case accidentally" and immediately set him free. Whether this was because the facts tended to exonerate him or because Popov paid off the officials is unclear, but the police did make a careful record of Popov's lending activities and financial circumstances, with the obvious potential for extortion. But even if Popov *was* set free because he paid a bribe, it is significant that court clerks formally wrote up the case in such a way as to suggest that Popov's respectability—his ownership of a considerable sum of money, his nice clothes noted by the witnesses, and a leisurely lifestyle that allowed him to spend his days taking strolls with friends and a young seamstress—showed that he could have no possible reason to blackmail or play a prank on the widow and that such crimes were generally limited to members of the lower classes.[17]

The Boundaries of Trust

The connection between property and creditworthiness was not always as direct as it may appear from these stories. It is true that in Western Europe and North America, as well as in Russia, cultural attitudes were shifting toward viewing debt and bankruptcy in economic rather than in moral terms, and all major legal systems sooner or later introduced bankruptcy discharge and relaxed or abolished usury laws and debt imprisonment.[18] However, the transition to modern impersonal credit was far from complete: even in England, informal debt relations persisted into the twentieth century, as did the moral economy of debt. While sanctions against merchants and other "respectable" bankrupts were gradually relaxed in the age of free trade, working-class debtors began to be treated more severely after the Victorian prison reforms and were regarded as dangerous delinquents rather than as victims of misfortune.[19] At the same time, Victorian journalist and essayist Walter Bagehot, in his influential exploration of the nineteenth-century banking system, still claimed that "the 'credit' of a person—that is the reliance which may be placed on his pecuniary fidelity—is a different thing from his property." Nineteenth-century gentlemen bankers from the City continued to rely on trust, common educational background, and kinship ties every bit as much as the merchants from the proverbial Muscovite "Kingdom of Darkness."[20]

In the case of Russia, it is still not entirely clear how and when, and to what extent, attitudes to credit underwent the same transformation. In the early 1700s, commercial credit generally had to be secured by collateral or by a large number of sureties.[21] It may turn out that the connection between credit and trust was reaffirmed and reiterated in the seventeenth century, similarly to the way gentlemanly honor was placed as the linchpin of the early modern English scientific community, as shown by Steven Shapin.[22] As we discussed earlier, Russia's traditional merchantry has been alternately depicted as particularly prone to lying and cheating and as placing high value on honor and trust. Economist Ivan Babst wrote in the mid-nineteenth century that commerce in grain and other commodities in the important northern town of Rybinsk reached 30 million rubles per year, "whereas the form of credit bears the same imprint of [relying on] trust. Merchants entrust each other with significant sums pursuant to notes on a simple sheet of paper without observing any formalities, and the provisional Rybinsk office of the Commercial Bank, where [such notes] are presented annually in the amount of 100,000 rubles, cannot accept them." A parish school teacher in the small town of Medyn' in central Russia emphasized in 1848 that, when dealing with each other, the local merchants are "faithful and honest without any written documents," while they are hostile and deceitful with nobles and other out- siders. Senator Pavel Sumarokov, who visited the famous Nizhnii Novgorod fair in 1845, noted that "honesty among the merchant estate is held to be sacred, due to necessity: any penalty, delay, or change in what was promised brings shame upon one's name, discontinues trust and disrupts commercial affairs. It is desirable that we, nobles, also be governed by the same manda- tory obligation."[23]

A similarly ambiguous relationship between property and trust was observable in Moscow in the early 1850s: according to Dmitrii Nikiforov, "most people" (that is, his social circle of property-owning gentry and mer- chants) knew each other's means "and so only a few tried to bedazzle the others *[puskat' drugim pyl' v glaza]*."[24] This statement implies that if these people did not possess accurate information about their neighbors' and acquaintances' finances, they would have found it advantageous and effective to fool each other by pretending to be wealthier than they were in reality.

Ostrovsky's play *Mad Money* (1870) shows how rumors were perceived to have operated in the 1860s. The entire plot revolves around various property- owning or at least genteel individuals judging and (mostly) misjudging others' financial condition; thus, a group of young dandies tricked the

Cheboksarov family, mother and daughter, into believing that a gruff provincial entrepreneur, Vasil'kov, actually owned a gold mine; the latter, in turn, convinced everyone through his lack of outward luxury that he was an upstart of little means, whereas in truth he was a successful railroad contractor. Yet another character, Kuchumov, convinced everyone that he was a wealthy man, largely through his manners and sociability.[25] Similarly superficial elements could also cause someone to be denied credit. As noted previously, most commerce at the Nizhnii Novgorod fair was conducted on credit. However, several categories of merchandise were sold only for cash, and several categories of non-Russian merchants—those from Bukhara, Armenia, and Iran—were said to have no credit in Russia and had to conduct their business entirely in cash.[26] In a similar vein, Ostrovskii's character from *Mad Money* claimed that "young and pretty women cannot borrow money because it is not polite to remind them when they forget about the debt, and it is even less polite to sue them. You either graciously refuse them or you just give them the money."[27]

The previously mentioned noble entrepreneur and a graphomaniac Nikolai Makarov bragged in his memoirs that his habit of repaying his debts promptly gave him a reputation for trustworthiness: his fellow officers used to say that "to loan to Makarov is just like putting the money in a bank." His butcher was excited by his promptness: "Dear Sir! Even if you did not pay me for the entire year, I would not be concerned at all. The money is much safer with you than in my own chest. If someone steals from me, it's gone. But with you it will always be intact; even if it gets stolen, you will surely repay me. I will never forget how you could easily not pay me a kopeck, because it was my own fault, yet you paid me without any argument or doubt." According to Makarov, a perceptive Parisian shopkeeper guessed his creditworthiness by just looking at him and entrusted him with a pair of binoculars without asking for his address or even his name: "You will bring the money, you certainly will, I am sure. I know who I am dealing with; I haven't been sitting here for twenty years for nothing." Makarov contrasted this episode with a wine merchant in Petersburg who would not sell him two bottles of cheap wine on credit but would sell only one bottle secured by a golden ring worth 15 rubles.[28]

Indicators of respectability and trustworthiness ranged from attractive physical appearance, speech, and manners to personal possessions and living spaces, as well as one's social circle. As a starting point, good looks were helpful, especially given the nineteenth-century belief in physiognomy, that is, that a person's appearance reflected his or her character.[29] Roman Mikhailovich Medoks (1795–1859), a famous Napoleonic-era confidence man, took advantage of his "English" looks when he was touring the Caucasus in 1812, pretending to be a Guards officer and the tsar's personal representative, raising a mountaineer militia.[30] Sonya the Golden Hand, a late-nineteenth-century swindler so legendary that it is now impossible to reconstruct her reliable biography, used her feminine charms to engage in a wide array of frauds and thefts, many of which involved credit.[31] Sergei Mikhailovich Fokin, an equally remarkable but completely unknown—aside from his public trial for trigamy in 1867—nobleman swindler was no Apollo by today's standards, described as "very corpulent . . . with a round full face, thin black hair parted in the middle, thick black eyebrows, small bulging dark eyes, small black round beard."[32] However, his corpulence did not detract from his masculine appeal to his multiple wives and companions and presumably worked in his favor as a sign of prosperity.[33]

Most signs of respectability were independent of nature and served to indicate one's level of wealth, as well as more subtle factors such as the degree to which the individual was rooted in his local community and the degree to which his wealth was sufficiently secure to provide the basis for future repayment.[34] Even wealthy and powerful people were sensitive to this principle. For example, in the early years of the nineteenth century, Petersburg's Governor General, Count Peter Tolstoy, was to attend a grand ball and realized that his wife's jewelry had been pawned at a state-run pawnshop. Because of his position, he was able to borrow the diamonds for the day of the ball, but at the last moment changed his mind, telling his wife, "you almost led me into imposture [sharlatanstvo]." It was less of a dishonor to have his wife not wear her best jewelry than to wear pawned items and send the wrong message about one's financial condition.[35]

In the eighteenth century, Prokofii Akinfievich Demidov, remembered as Russia's first modern banker, used contemporary signs of respectability to induce debt repayment: one aristocratic woman, for instance, in order to borrow money, had to sign a note in which she admitted her sexual licentiousness. On another occasion, Demidov had to loan money to Catherine the Great herself, but to make sure she repaid, he made her lover, Orlov, sign the debt and pledge that he would take three smacks on the head if it was not repaid.[36] Hugh Hudson has interpreted Demidov's eccentric ways as a form of protest against corrupt aristocratic habits and an effort to promote the rights of the middle class, but from the perspective of the culture of debt,

Demidov simply forced his debtors to provide the only form of collateral that could effectively secure the loan.[37]

To be sure, some perfectly genuine aristocrats were actually swindlers. The young Prince Marcellus Lubomirsky, from perhaps the most illustrious and fabulously wealthy Polish family, fled from St. Petersburg by ship in 1849 after selling his wife's and his father's properties, including the entire town of Dubno, to several individuals simultaneously and pocketing nearly 1 million rubles.[38] All that the police could do in the aftermath was to ascertain a list of the prince's deceived creditors and business partners.

Vsevolod Andreevich Dolgorukov, one of the key members of the loose network of swindlers dubbed by journalists as the Jacks of Hearts Club in the 1860s, came from the senior branch of his princely family, though his father's marriage was eventually held to be invalid, and Vsevolod was officially not permitted to use his title.[39] One of Sergei Fokin's accomplices held the rank of *kamer-iunker* of the imperial court, which the gendarmes thought to have facilitated his frauds. And still another infamous swindler from the 1870s and 1880s, Lieutenant Savin, claimed to have come from a wealthy family and retained his properties long after beginning his criminal career.[40]

However, most nineteenth-century swindlers needed to be skillful at acquiring the outward trappings of a much wealthier person and then translating the signs of respectability and wealth into cash loans. Sergei Fokin's story is a typical example of how a successful swindler combined skillful acting, appropriate external trappings of wealth, and a social network that inspired confidence in his targets. After Fokin fled to Moscow from his Petersburg victims in 1859, the gendarmes reported that "Fokin's usual method of deception is the role of a wealthy landowner that he artfully performs. An excellent apartment, acquaintance with some persons of the highest circles and a life that is luxurious in appearance complete the rest." One of the victims, the 75-year-old civil servant Aleksandr Petrovich Munster, upon Fokin's "incessant invitation, found him in a luxurious apartment; that same luxury was manifest in the servants, in rich outfits of his wife, in stylish carriages and in all the external furnishings."[41] In the late 1850s, Fokin took out numerous loans—that he had neither the means nor intention to repay—by claiming to have inherited as many as 2,000 serfs and 400,000 rubles in cash. In reality, as the police and the creditors eventually found out, Fokin's entire family—consisting of his mother, two sisters, and two brothers, in addition to Sergei himself—owned only between 400 and 600 serfs in Simbirsk, Vladimir, and Tver provinces.[42] Fokin's official rank was the unimpressive retired first-rank chancery clerk. His mother was widow of a second lieutenant *(podporuchik)*, and one of his brothers, Nikolai, was retired lieutenant *(poruchik)*. In his younger days, Fokin had taken advantage of the Crimean War to evade the official 1852 ban from residing in Petersburg, and in 1856 he enrolled as an officer cadet in a grenadier regiment that was stationed in the capital, where Fokin managed to stay upon his prompt retirement. Given his large family, Fokin's alternative to becoming a confidence man would have been service in the lower echelons of bureaucracy or otherwise the modest life of a provincial landowner, completely dependent on the agricultural cycle and on his peasants' work habits. For nobles and government servitors who did not have even those resources, engaging in illegal schemes was a way to hold on to the respectability that separated even poor nobles from the common folk, especially given that petty fraud and embezzlement often went unreported and were punished informally, if at all.[43]

The same strategy of combining a genuine genteel upbringing with fictional aristocratic wealth and manners was bread-and-butter for the group of swindlers known as the Jacks of Hearts who operated in post-emancipation Moscow. The several real-life impoverished noblemen from among this loose partnership of criminals were saved from life on the street by their enterprising but uncouth accomplices and given housing and furnishings to stage intense performances as visiting provincial aristocrats or—in one case—as an up-and-coming industrialist from south Russia (something of an economic Promised Land in the mid-nineteenth century). Swindling performances in hotel rooms and luxury apartments was a delicate matter: extrapolating from David Sunderland's illuminating study of the signs of respectability and trust in Victorian Britain, each knick-knack, each notebook, and each picture in the office or hotel room of a make-believe "industrialist"—as much as of a real one—would carry a symbolic meaning for visiting creditors and business partners. In the case of the Jacks of Hearts, this included fake business correspondence strewn around the desk, fake account books in expensive gold-lettered bindings, and photographs of the products of non-existent agricultural estates.[44]

Moreover, it seems that such performances would have required the acting skills of a seasoned professional. To go back to the Napoleonic-era Roman Medoks, although he was the son of a British entrepreneur who moved to Moscow and founded its first public theater (eventually to become the Bolshoi), he had to impersonate a Guards officer for months and participate in social activities of the local elite, exchange gifts, and keep his story free of contradictions. Sonya the Golden Hand seems to have posed as a wealthy noblewoman without any knowledge of foreign languages beyond a few phrases that she, however, could pronounce with a perfect accent.

Even what Catriona Kelly has described as a common culture of gentility left much room for variation between aristocrats and lesser nobles.[45] For example, when Sergei Fokin went on a swindling spree in several European countries in the early 1860s, the high-born Russian ambassador at The Hague described him as having the "methods and manners of a man who is affluent but nonetheless simple and uneducated" and in particular that he spoke "like a commoner" *(prostoliudin)*.[46]

Another recent escapee from imprisonment in Russia, anarchist Mikhail Bakunin, received a visit from Fokin in London in 1862. The swindler was offering Bakunin and his friend Alexander Herzen introductions to wealthy friends who were allegedly willing to donate at least 50,000 francs, which, Bakunin emphasized in a private letter promptly intercepted by tsarist agents, "the <u>cause</u> now desperately needs" (underlined in the original). Nonetheless, the aristocratic Bakunin "strongly disliked" Fokin upon introduction and sized him up right away as "a strange gentleman . . . from top to bottom a landowner of Tatar extraction from [the province of] Simbirsk." Despite his contempt for the less privileged and less educated provincial gentry, Bakunin was still desperate enough to lend Fokin his ear at least initially.[47]

In addition to swindling, Fokin had some expertise in procuring money, since an unrelated investigation by the Third Section in 1859 listed him as one of Petersburg's most notorious usurers, operating in partnership with another man, Anton Bogomolets. Incidentally, that same investigation also listed Fokin as being heavily in debt to another suspected usurer, Gubernial Secretary Andrei Dmitriev.[48]

The emphasis on acting and pretense was even more important to those swindlers who lacked a genuinely respectable background, and cases of fraud by individuals who did not properly belong to the culture of gentility highlight the ease with which some of the signs of respectability could be manipulated and imitated. In one case with an exceptionally detailed record, the swindler was a citizen of Hamburg, Nikolai Bedeker (born around 1839), who operated in Moscow and inspired trust in his victims through his knowledge of French, his pleasant manners, his beautiful handwriting, and his neat dress and clear, clean-shaven face, which made him stand out among Moscow's clerks, artisans, and tradesmen.[49] Of his background we only know that he had no property or older relatives, that his Lutheran family must have seen more affluent times, that he had two slightly younger sisters also living in Moscow who belonged to the estate of townspeople *(meshchane)*, and that his many friends and acquaintances were mostly from the lower orders, including one girlfriend who was a peasant and another who was a townswoman from the southern town of Bolkhov, although one of his friends owned an inn. Bedeker had no permanent dwelling of his own but spent his nights with friends or in various rented rooms, and whenever arrested, he stated his occupation as "commerce on commission" or "buying and selling various items."

Already in 1856, Bedeker was prosecuted for forging a receipt in order to receive a mail package and fleeing from arrest. He was sentenced to three months in the workhouse. Subsequently, he seems to have committed his crimes in sprees according to one particular scheme over the course of just a few days. This strategy, while eventually alarming the police more than usual, prevented his initial victims from communicating information about his activities quickly enough to alert other potential victims. One of his favorite schemes in 1861 was to take advantage of the credit-based system of retail commerce. Bedeker would come to a foreign-owned clothing shop, introduce himself in French, and then take a selection of the product, such as fine shirts or linen, allegedly in order to bring it to a wealthy buyer. The owner would send along a servant girl or come herself, but Bedeker would manage to lose her on the way either by running away or by entering a building and leaving by another door while the woman waited outside. The plan backfired when a serf girl employed by Riga citizen Khristina De Lor managed to chase him down Moscow's fashionable Kuzhnetskii Most and onto Lubianka Square, where he was tackled by passers-by and arrested. On different occasions, Bedeker helped himself to such diverse items as pianos, "foreign-made liquid paint," and carpets from Moscow's Gostinyi Dvor. When addressing the soldiers and policemen who arrested him, Bedeker affected the condescending manner of a gentleman. For example, after escaping from arrest and being recaptured, Bedeker claimed that he only decided to run away when a police officer he met on that day screamed at him for being drunk and waved his fist. This affront to his dignity, apparently, was plausible as an excuse for running from the police.

Bedeker's other favorite scheme, used in 1863 in St. Petersburg, likewise took advantage of his "respectable" manners and appearance. He would dress up as a clerk and visit the houses of various important officials and merchants, show them beautifully written notices, and claim that there was a foreign ship in port that carried a package for them. The important person would give Bedeker the shipping money and send with him a clerk or a servant, whom he always managed to lose on the way to the port. This scheme, which only rendered him around 20 rubles at any one time, must have been so unprofitable as to suggest that Bedeker did it out of a sense of adventure or kleptomania. With his handwriting and his manners, Bedeker could easily have been employed as a clerk and would likely have earned at least as much as he made with his schemes.

While his behavior must have been very uncommon for German immigrants in Russia, the outlines of Bedeker's story seem to be not atypical for the younger representatives of Russia's growing and upwardly mobile urban classes who had been exposed to genteel lifestyles but had had no opportunities to earn enough money to adopt them permanently. Bedeker's female—and ethnically Russian—counterpart, townswoman Maria Lebedeva, was trying to provide for her four small children.[50] Lebedeva was the 32-year-old daughter of a Moscow merchant and a widow of a townsman from the nearby town of Podolsk. While she apparently had no material possessions other than the clothes she wore, she made a living by perpetrating fraud and also by teaching music and sewing men's shirts. It was her status as a music teacher—presumably demonstrated by some actual knowledge of music—that enabled her in 1861 to rent four pianos from different pianomakers and music shops and pawn them to different usurers. When pawning the pianos, Lebedeva claimed them as her own ("because otherwise they would not be accepted as collateral") and issued a note of sale customary for pawnshop transactions. When she was caught, Lebedeva claimed that she had acted "out of poverty" and only at the insistence of townsmen Smirnov and Rozanov, to whom she owed money. Lebedeva also replicated Bedeker's stratagem, taking cotton fabric worth 61.16 rubles from the Hamburg-born Anna Winterling, for which Lebedeva's fictitious fiancé was supposed to pay. She even dabbled in the pawn broking business herself by taking a fox coat from state peasant Smirnov worth 160 rubles but giving him only half the amount and then disappearing, as well as taking a 150-ruble fur coat from townswoman Shustova and later claiming that it had been taken from her on the street by two muggers. Lebedeva thus appears to be a virtual double of Bedeker—except that she was completely Russian, female, and at least to some extent motivated by real responsibilities to her children rather than any sense of derring-do. Interestingly, the pre-reform Moscow Criminal

Chamber reversed her original conviction and closed the case, holding that she used neither fraud nor violence and that therefore no crime had been committed!

Other cases highlighting the complex connection between creditworthiness, reputation, and tangible signs of property ownership involved situations when established credit was claimed to have been damaged in a commercial setting by such factors as quarreling with authorities, being slandered, or becoming the victim of trademark infringement. Trouble with police and other officials could be very damaging, as shown by the persistent petitions of an extremely wealthy Moscow Old Believer merchant and textile manufacturer Ivan Butikov, who in 1859 engaged in a bitter feud with the policemen trying to arrest his son for debt. Not finding the son, the police briefly detained Butikov himself and then placed armed guards around his house, which caused the old merchant to frantically petition the chief of gendarmes and Moscow governor general to argue that such actions were illegal and damaging for his business reputation and his credit.[51]

Rumors spread by one's ill-wishers could be just as damaging as actions by Russia's often heavy-handed police apparatus: Moscow townsman Vasilii Kurochkin, a freed serf and later an innkeeper at Moscow's Smolensk Market and estate manager to his former master, Major General Grigorii Kolokoltsev, was accused of embezzlement by the late general's children. In his suit for slander, Kurochkin complained that "through being slandered *[posramlenie]* by Mrs. Kolokoltsev in this fashion, I and my family fell into complete penury and as a man of commerce engaged in various kinds of trade, I thereby lost all trust in my credit *[poterial chrez to vsiakoe doverie v kredit]*."[52] As part of their legal campaign, the general's heirs petitioned the Board of Trustees and the Commercial Bank not to issue any loans to Kurochkin *or* his relatives. The heirs claimed that their investigation of the embezzlement did not have an "official character," and so Kurochkin could not have lost his credit because the allegations were not published in print. Kurochkin's criminal "insult and slander" *(obida i kleveta)* case missed the filing deadline at the Moscow County Court, and Kurochkin was left with far less effective recourse in the civil court.

Finally, even an indirect slight such as trademark infringement could be interpreted as harming one's credit by associating the merchant with inferior-quality goods, as was argued by the Prussian subject Stepan Iakovlev Schiffers, who traded in woolen clothes in partnership with another merchant, Shaposhnikov, selling them to China through the famous Kiakhta trading post in Siberia. Schiffers alleged that Shaposhnikov continued to use their common trademark on his rolls of cloth long after their partnership had ended and thereby "harmed his credit."[53]

The Price of Middle-Class Respectability

Fokin and other swindlers from the lesser nobility seem to more properly belong with Russia's still poorly studied middling classes, which also included junior civil servants, merchants, and better-off townspeople and peasants. Some of their stories reveal a more complex connection between respectability and fraud; much as in Victorian Britain, middle-class fraud in Russia reveals a combination of social pressures brought to bear in maintaining a respectable lifestyle and the ease of confusing potential victims. When arrested, middle-class swindlers and embezzlers narrated long stories of their misfortunes and of their struggle to maintain their finances and to regain respectability.

One example is the merchant Pavel Galitskii, who began his career of fraud both because his merchant status allowed him to issue easily forged bills of exchange and because, according to his testimony, he was striving to support his family and regain his financial soundness. In a proceeding that began in 1880 in the reformed post-1864 court with a jury trial, he pled guilty to forging 236 bills of exchange worth at least 234,000 rubles.[54] In his testimony to the police, he recounted a decades-long saga of struggling to maintain his status as a merchant, to hold off creditors, and to counter the effects of various bad financial decisions made by others. From 1855, he had served as a clerk to another merchant for a salary of 300 and then 700 rubles per year. Soon he married and, while continuing his job, started a separate business in ready-made women's clothes, together with his wife. He was successful at first, accumulated a modest capital of 3,000 rubles, and made useful connections in the business world. However, one of his partners became bankrupt, and the other one—his former employer—embezzled thousands of rubles from their shared business. As Galitskii's debts started to come due, he decided that his only solution was to forge several bills of exchange in the name of two well-known merchants "whose bills were circulated as easily as cash."

He soon turned this into a habit and was initially able to continue his trade until the forged bills became due, their "issuers" became suspicious, his own credit dried up after he left his dishonest partner, and the entire pyramid scheme collapsed. Galitskii decided that there was no escape left and went to the court building to report himself. By turning himself in and spinning his elaborate yarn of hard luck and his tireless efforts to do right despite all obstacles, Galitskii portrayed his motives and many of his actions as fully appropriate for a man of his station in life—thereby leaving bad luck as the only possible explanation for the uncomfortable fact that crimes had indeed been committed. He was convicted but only had to resettle in eastern Siberia for a reduced period of time because the jury recommended leniency.

Another case shows why the victims of white-collar embezzlers might ultimately prefer a nonpublic, informal resolution of their case. The slight twist that saved the swindler in question was that Aleksandr Ivanovich Saltykov was a prominent Moscow barrister *(prisiazhnyi poverennyi).*[55] Aside from his legal practice, he earned his living beginning in the early 1870s by investing his clients' money in loans and mortgages. Earning 7,000 to 8,000 rubles per year, Saltykov was nonetheless burdened with debts incurred in setting up his legal career and by his early marriage, and as early as 1875 he began to embezzle his clients' money and give them bills of exchange written out in the names of fictitious persons. In the 1880s, Saltykov branched out into fake mortgages, which he always closed himself; he also paid out interest on the fraudulent debt, so that his clients, trusting him as their attorney, never bothered to gather any information about the property allegedly mortgaged to them or about their borrowers. Only in 1891 did one of his numerous high-ranking victims, Actual State Councilor Ternovskii, became suspicious.

Saltykov found it necessary to stage his own suicide, assume a fake identity, and move to the city of Kishinev in the southern region of Bessarabia. He stayed there for seven months and then came back to Moscow and surrendered to the police, fully confessing all of his many frauds and mentioning his sense of guilt and his duties to his family as reasons both for committing his crimes and for deciding to surrender. He explained that his schemes resulted from his desire to set things right by incurring more and more fraudulent debt to keep himself afloat long enough to make money from his profession. Thus, by claiming that his crimes stemmed from efforts or intentions to engage in correct or respectable behaviors, Saltykov effectively made what were unquestionably criminal acts seem excusable or even necessary. And this strategy worked: Saltykov was acquitted at the end of his closed-door jury trial. In other words, as with Galitskii, the jury believed that Saltykov's alleged efforts to do right according to the standards of respectability trumped his breaking of the law and that unlike Galitskii, he had enough potential to eventually make good the damage.

Fraud, Kinship, and Social Networks

Nineteenth-century German criminologists and police officials thought, according to Richard J. Evans, that criminals were "virtually a race apart . . . a world of 'crooks' that formed a virtual mirror-image of respectable society" and "aped" the "straight" world. Compared to the early modern underworld that relied on open violence and tended to aggregate in an easily identifiable "criminal quarter," the mid-nineteenth-century criminal, according to Evans, was more "individualistic" and "tended to work on his own," relying on stealth and deceit. To sum up, he said, "the underworld had gone underground."[56] Although armed brigands and outlaws were still active in many areas in mid-nineteenth-century Russia, it appears that swindling, embezzling, smuggling, and counterfeiting became more profitable than open robbery, and so Evans's general point seems to apply to Russia as well. However, this emphasis on the individualistic criminal—indeed observable in some swindlers—obscures the fact that more typically "respectable" criminals depended not merely on their wit, good looks, or acting skills but operated by means of a network of friends, relatives, and business partners of various degrees of culpability who could shelter the criminal, help him manage information, reassure the potential victim about the swindler's alleged wealth and reputation, and, in sum, create the appearance of genuine links within Russia's network of private credit.

Recall the case of Nikolai Bedeker, the déclassé swindler from Hamburg without any possessions or a permanent residence; a superficial look suggests a lone operator relying solely on his wit and charm. However, he would not be have been able to elude the police for as long as he did without relatives and friends. For example, on December 21, 1864, he was being escorted from the prison hospital in Moscow to a police station by two middle-aged soldiers, with whom he at once adopted a tone that marked him as different from a common criminal or from former peasants like themselves. First, he suggested that they take a cab rather than trek across the city to the remote Khamovniki precinct, no doubt offering to pay for the ride. He then talked the guards into stopping by the apartment of his German-speaking sisters, where his "fiancée," a peasant girl Evdokiia Galkina, was also present, and where everyone, of course including the soldiers, proceeded to have tea and vodka. After resuming the trip, Bedeker managed to run away by telling his presumably tipsy guards that he needed to make a stop to pick up some money. Two days later, Bedeker was recaptured at a friend's house in a village just outside the city. As already mentioned, one of his friends kept an inn; on a different occasion, he was captured at the lodgings of another young "fiancée" of peasant origin.

In addition to having accomplices, a successful swindler deployed a complex network of friends and relatives, whose involvement usually remained tenuous enough to evade prosecution. Indeed, one of the key issues for prosecutors in criminal trials was to prove the existence of a criminal conspiracy when the evidence pointed at best to a loose partnership or simply random acquaintance.

One basic strategy was to use one's wife, a sister, or a girlfriend. The wife of one young nobleman swindler discussed throughout this study, Petr Veselkin, was his active helper, although she was not put on trial. The degree of the wives' possible involvement varied greatly; some were swindlers in their own right, such as Sonya the Golden Hand, who consecutively married several men who were her underlings or at best junior partners.

The next level of involvement was for a wife to actively assist her husband—for example, by enticing potential victims. Sergei Fokin effected many of his frauds with the help of his second wife, the widow of a second lieutenant, Elena Plemiannikova, "a young woman of attractive appearance and easy virtue," who enticed young men to visit her husband's home. Another report described her as "always distinguished by her particular ability to lure the inexperienced into her nets, and by these means to assist Fokin's frauds." Plemiannikova seems to have approached the category of being a swindler in her own right or at least was in an equal partnership with Fokin. She had a child with him but agreed to let him claim that she was only his mistress, not legally married to him, so that he could marry a hapless widow named Uresheva and get her property. After Fokin's arrest, Plemiannikova petitioned the authorities on his behalf. She even seduced Kudriavtsev, the secretary of the Moscow Criminal Chamber. In exchange for her promise to marry him, he arranged for Fokin's release from arrest upon his mother's guarantee, allowing him to eventually escape Russia with a forged passport. The secretary even became financially involved with Fokin, providing him with a loan of 6,000 rubles to use as a down payment for a presumably bogus stearin factory in Moscow (worth 35,000 rubles), which Fokin immediately resold to a third party for 26,000 rubles in cash. In the end, Plemiannikova fulfilled her promise and married Kudriavtsev.

At that same time, Fokin seduced a young girl named Aleksandra Opitz, the ward of a wealthy Mrs. Orlova-Davydova, and talked her into robbing her guardian's house. Opitz was caught and arrested, but Fokin persuaded Kudriavtsev to help her escape. Fokin then fled with her abroad, and Opitz, now pregnant and described by the famous anarchist Bakunin as "rather interesting," posed as Fokin's wife and thereby enhanced his respectability. We have no idea what happened to Opitz after Fokin was finally arrested in Wiesbaden in 1865 and extradited to Russia, but the gendarmes filed away her printed article from *The Daily Telegraph* from June 4, 1864, about "Tsar Alexander II's atrocities against the Poles and the Circassians."[57]

More remote relatives could also provide crucial assistance to swindlers and, by extension, to regular borrowers, by convincing lenders of their respectability. Fokin's two sisters, Varvara and Liubov', were described as "rather sharp and resourceful women" who "complement[ed] the seductive circumstances of his evening parties." Fokin invited his elderly victim, Collegiate Assessor Aleksandr Munster, to spend time with his family, and Fokin's mother Ekaterina and his brother Nikolai acted the part of individuals with a large fortune, assuring Munster both verbally and in writing of Fokin's creditworthiness. Nikolai helped Sergei Fokin to identify potential victims, for example, by making the acquaintance of a young widow of a colonel, named Uresheva, and by borrowing from her 3,000 rubles. Uresheva also became friendly with Fokin's mother, his sisters Varvara and Liubov', with his brothers Nikolai and Aleksandr, all of whom concealed the fact that Fokin was already married to Plemiannikova and had a young daughter. After marrying Fokin, Uresheva surrendered to him the control over her house and her money, upon which she was promptly abandoned with her three young children, one of them Fokin's.

Fokin himself was eventually extradited by the Prussians, escaped once again, was caught in Bessarabia, and eventually ended up in Siberian exile, but none of his relatives were even questioned by the police, much less prosecuted. Fokin and his family were careful not to violate the law openly: Moscow gendarmes in May 1859, soon after his arrival to Moscow, collected information, as was their habit, from servants and neighbors and reported that the family created a "most unfavorable" impression, especially Sergei himself and his older sister Varvara, "who are inclined to actions that are demeaning to gentle-born persons." The police described him as a "terrible adventurer and swindler" *(uzhasnyi aferist i obmanshchik)* but never used the term "illegal." In addition to his loans in Petersburg, Fokin borrowed 4,000 rubles in Moscow from an unmarried daughter of a civil servant, secured by his wife's house, which already had a private mortgage for 10,000 rubles. "Fokin is not paying any of his debts," warned the gendarmes. Yet there was no obvious wrongdoing for which he or his relatives could be immediately arrested.

In addition to openly assisting the swindler, relatives and friends could help in small ways by helping the swindler create the impression of having legitimate social relationships. For example, Fokin's third wife, Uresheva, who was also his victim, was not involved in his frauds but still used her name and her property to get fraudulent loans without at first arousing suspicion, since ordinary persons who were not swindlers routinely used their spouse's property to get loans or officially had their houses and shops registered under their names.

Fokin and other successful swindlers understood that it was also important to have a larger circle of unrelated acquaintances and friends, once again in contradiction to the "lone actor" theory of nineteenth-century criminals. Consider once again the Napoleonic-era Roman Medoks: upon arriving to the Caucasus, allegedly to raise a militia to fight the invasion, he immediately created a network of friends, just as any legitimate visiting noble would have done. The network involved exchanging expensive presents, gambling, and entering into sale transactions involving luxury items.

Another case illustrates the importance of a well-centered social network: it involved the previously mentioned petty civil servant Petr Veselkin (twenty-two years old in 1841), a hereditary noble with thirty-two serfs in backcountry Zaraisk county.[58] Veselkin entered government service as a "junior sorter" at the Riazan' provincial post office in 1835 and four years later moved to Moscow to serve as a clerk at the Moscow Office of Crown Lands, both of which posts yielded a meager income to complement an equally meager income from his lands. Not surprisingly, in 1841 Veselkin left service, with good recommendations from his superiors. His other, more profitable, occupation was carried out beginning in 1839 with two partners, a former Moscow merchant, Aleksandr Lefort, who typically posed as the representative of a fictitious Prince Dmitrii Kropotkin of Vladimir province, and another former merchant, Ivan Miliutin, who claimed to represent the equally nonexistent Lieutenant Goncharov from Riazan' province. Veselkin's wife Klavdia and his brother were also in the group.

With forged powers of attorney and other paperwork, Lefort and Miliutin registered mortgages for their "clients'" fictitious estates and then remortgaged them to actual wealthy landowners in the Moscow area who were looking for investment opportunities. Lefort also took a trip to St. Petersburg to look for victims there but was not successful. Only a few weeks after the last such transaction, one of the victims, Collegiate Assessor Glazunov, decided to double-check and found out that the documents were forged. In the presence of witnesses, he confronted Lefort, who lost his composure and allegedly said, "I already know that the certificate and the power of attorney are false."[59] Veselkin and his friends were able to delay and confuse the investigation for several years, until in 1847 Lefort unexpectedly and voluntarily showed up at a police station in Moscow and confessed the entire scheme, claiming that he composed all the fake mortgage papers, as well as forged pawnshop tickets, together with Veselkin, who "enticed him with promises of a great profit."[60]

Many things are striking about this Gogolesque case: Veselkin's youth, Lefort's apparently voluntary surrender and confession, and especially one significant disadvantage of Veselkin's otherwise ingenious scheme—that it was very labor- and time-consuming, requiring complex negotiations, close interaction with the victims, and the forgery of many documents that could be easily checked with the appropriate authorities. For present purposes, the other point to note is that the scheme worked as well as it did despite the effort and great risk involved because of the sheer size of the criminal group. Each member could vouch for and lend an appearance of respectability to the others, which allowed them to earn the trust of their victims.

The same strategy on a larger scale was deployed by the group of swindlers known as the Jacks of Hearts, who operated more than twenty years after Veselkin. The police identified almost one hundred individuals directly connected to the case. Several overlapping loose circles of friends and acquaintances incurred fraudulent loans by posing as wealthy individuals, forged debt documents, engaged in retail credit fraud, and opened bogus businesses. These individuals' interests were so divergent that the prosecution's case rested almost entirely on the testimony of several defectors. The Jacks of Hearts were ready to swindle each other as easily as they would an outsider. But there is more to this case: in addition to this loose partnership, the extensive case record depicts an entire semi-criminal "upperworld" (to borrow George Robb's coinage) that, despite the best efforts of nineteenth-century criminologists, cannot be easily separated from legitimate and semi-legitimate commerce. This was a world not only of swindlers but of usurers and money-lenders, brokers and intermediaries of all kinds, closely linked to local government officials, all of whom were busy buying and selling all types of objects, land, and commercial paper, engaging in loan operations, dealing in smuggled and counterfeit objects, and so on.

It is tempting to connect this criminal demi-monde with the growth of Russia's urban life in the post-reform era, when cities grew and became rapidly filled with peasants trying to find work and gentry who could no longer live off their land. However, it is clear that while the reforms of the 1860s and 1870s boosted these practices, they were building upon the foundation that was already there in the 1840s and 1850s in Russia's largest cities, such as Petersburg, Moscow, Odessa, Warsaw, and Vilna. The Third Section records, for example, refer to a loose community of swindlers in pre-reform Petersburg, where Fokin himself seems to have been trained, and which even the tsar's secret police were helpless to suppress. As far back as 1850, Fokin was "involved in the case of the group of persons living by various types of frauds that was then uncovered in St. Petersburg and who named themselves as "*trubolioty*" (literally, "chimneysweeps," a nineteenth-century slang word also recorded by Dal as referring to being bankrupt or to being a high-society wastrel).

I have not been able to find any information about this particular "gang," but the then-young Fokin avoided further unpleasantness by paying off his victims. In the late 1850s to early 1860s, Fokin's circle closely resembled that of Veselkin in the 1840s and of the Jacks of Hearts in the late 1860s and 1870s. One key similarity was the participation of individuals from all social groups, including nobles and government officials, merchants, and relatively respectable moneylenders, as well as the more shady brokers, commissioners, pawnbrokers, and pettifoggers.

Individual roles within these circles were carefully divided up and practiced. One of Fokin's friends was Aulic Councilor Romanovsky, who owned a house in Petersburg and was employed by the Naval Ministry. He claimed Fokin was his nephew, was a "great aficionado of cards" and was said by the police to "[loan] money secured by various documents, [buy] up loan obligations and in general to be counted among usurers." He was said to have purchased his house very cheaply in some "improper" way. Another important friend was the non-serving nobleman Anton Bogomolets, who acted out the role of manager of Fokin's (nonexistent) estates, allegedly including a large sheep farm producing many thousands of pounds of wool.

This was exactly the same tactic that was later used by the Jacks of Hearts, who liked to employ some real but completely destitute young noble and to pose as his obedient servants and estate managers. Bogomolets acted as a sort of consigliore to Fokin, conducting some legal work for him and sometimes acting as the official front man for Fokin's fraudulent loans or at least serving as a witness to his transactions. Another important actor was the notary named Kalugin, "Fokin's constant assistant in his deceptions and fraud." One of the key Jacks of Hearts was the notary Aleksei Podkovshchikov; in addition, the Collegiate Councilor Sergei Slavyshenskii may have acted as their lawyer before his murder in 1871.

Another key role, in Fokin's case performed by Gubernial Secretary Yakov Yunitsky, was to act as an unrelated party who would reassure ("introduce, persuade, encourage, and sooth") the victim about Fokin's reputation and creditworthiness by telling them about rich estates that he allegedly had seen with his own eyes. One of the tsar's gentlemen of the chamber (*kamer-iunker*), Rudzevich, lent Fokin's operations an additional veneer of respectability.

To the police, and to us in retrospect, it is clear that Fokin and his accomplices were criminals, but the key point here is that it was not clear at the time. This perhaps suggests the reason the government did not stage a large-scale prosecution of Fokin's acquaintances: not only was there the problem of evidence, but exposing the entire group of Fokin's accomplices would have been impossible without it becoming public knowledge, at least in Moscow's commercial circles, which would have severely damaged the entire system of private credit, based as it was on precisely these go-betweens, semi-legal "usurers," and the fact that many officials, aristocrats, and otherwise respectable individuals seem to have been routinely engaged in rather unsavory commercial and financial schemes. For example, the famous Mother Superior Mitrofaniia was convicted of credit fraud and forgery in 1874. Her story points to the lack of a clear boundary between fraud and manipulation of legal rules and interpersonal ties, and although she was unusually highly placed because of her court connections and although she was prosecuted and convicted, which was also unusual, her worldview and her engagement in business schemes were not unusual at all.[61]

However, employing a large circle of friends and accomplices was not merely enabling but also sometimes dangerous for the swindlers themselves: accomplices or even simple acquaintances were more likely than relatives to go to the police or unintentionally divulge incriminating information that would cause a potential victim to get suspicious. For example, in 1865 the retired Staff Captain Georgii Balakan, who made a living by lending money, was saved only by a lucky accident from a fraudulent scheme concocted by the wife of Aulic Councilor Maria Skrebkova.[62] Skrebkova asked Balakan for a loan, but he only agreed on the condition that merchant Ivan Korolev, the affluent former mayor of Moscow, would act as the legal borrower. Balakan visited Korolev in person to make sure he really did agree to this condition, only to find out that he had nothing to do with Skrebkova's loan and that it was his dissolute brother Dmitrii who was posing as the former mayor. Balakan notified the police, staged an ambush, and after a short scuffle caught Dmitrii Korolev and Skrebkova just as they signed the fraudulent debt instrument.

Balakan's case shows that there were certain simple precautions to deter fraud and, in a wider sense, to ensure the reliability of one's investment in the loan. For instance, in real estate mortgages, it was advisable to write to the provincial authorities that registered mortgages and issued the required reliability certificates to ensure that the property in question actually existed and had not been mortgaged to someone else. Failure to do so—out of neglect or some sense of honorable dealing with one's fellow landowner—could have unpleasant consequences. For example, in 1865, Moscow merchantess Kurenkova purchased a *dacha* (a suburban home) in Sokol'niki Park on the outskirts of Moscow from merchant Vasilii Mazurin, paying him 4,500 rubles in advance of the closing. However, Mazurin continued to delay the closing for many months, and Kurenkova eventually found out that the house had been mortgaged to someone else when she and her husband were evicted.[63]

Similarly, the victims of the Veselkin–Lefort–Miliutin trio discussed above did not think to question the authenticity of the gang's powers of attorney and the mortgage certificates that they presented. Even Glazunov, who owned an estate just outside Moscow and eventually unmasked the scheme, only became suspicious a few weeks after handing over his money. At that point, it took him no more than a few weeks to unmask the scheme by obtaining all the necessary information from the Riazan' and Vladimir provincial registers of the powers of attorney, mortgage certificates, and provincial tax rolls. Although he did have the good sense (eventually) to pursue this course, Glazunov was not able to recover his investment. Even less lucky was Gubernial Secretary Aleksei Zaborovskii, who loaned 10,000 silver rubles to Princess Cherkasskaia but was falsely accused by her representative

Konovalov of taking the debt document and never issuing the money.[64] While it is possible to speculate that Glazunov may have been a naïve rustic landlord, Zaborovskii had served at the state-owned Commercial Bank and must have had a fairly detailed knowledge of the risks of his trade, yet he was perhaps the hardest-hit white collar crime victim of all that I reviewed, since he spent several years under the threat of being exiled to Siberia, in addition to losing his money.

In all of these cases, the immediate cause of the scheme's success was that lenders and creditors would not deal with each other directly. This was because Russia's network of private credit had become so large by the mid-nineteenth century that financial links between individuals who were neither acquainted personally nor willing to become acquainted became commonplace. This was a risk that Russia's elites were often willing to take. Thus the previously mentioned Glebov brothers avoided trouble with the law only through their own good judgment in destroying a key piece of evidence, whereas the precautions by Princess Cherkasskaia and the wealthy and powerful clients of barrister Saltykov were perfectly reasonable— after all, what could be more reliable than employing a highly prominent attorney to screen one's borrowers? Nonetheless, they failed due to the fragile character of nineteenth-century attitudes about trust, respectability, and failure.

The culture of credit and notions of creditworthiness were inseparable from objective assessments of individual wealth. However, they equally depended on less tangible markers of respectability and trust, which ensured that wealth was not the borrower's fleeting condition and would continue to be available in the future to repay the debt. Aside from the cases discussed in this chapter, these signifiers of trust and respectability were not explicitly discussed in most cases that I reviewed; they were made explicit mainly in the breach. Cases of fraud show that in addition to the obvious advantages of good looks, good manners, fashionable clothes, and well-furnished houses and offices, an individual's social circle was every bit as important to convey creditworthiness. Swindlers' wives, siblings, and close friends could enable credit fraud largely because these people were seen as vouching for the swindler's good reputation and rootedness in a given locality.

But the converse was also true: the fact that nineteenth-century legitimate commerce was carried out by brokers, lenders, "commissioners," clerks, notaries, and civil servants of questionable morals obscured the line between what was criminal and what was not and created the enabling atmosphere also observed, for example, in the case of Victorian Britain, the prime economic power in the mid-nineteenth century.[65] Finally, it follows that the social and kinship circles described in this chapter were crucial in defining and understanding the very nature of private property in imperial Russia.

CHAPTER 5

Kinship and Family

O F THE VARIOUS TYPES of personal connections that underpinned Russia's system of private credit, family ties were among the most important. Parents and children, husbands and wives, brothers and sisters borrowed from each other, sued each other in court, and served on their relatives' bankruptcy boards. This phenomenon was certainly not unique to Russia; for example, writing about English "middling" classes in the late seventeenth and eighteenth centuries, Margaret Hunt explained a similar reliance on kin by the necessity to allocate scarce resources, especially liquid cash, as well as by a lack of bureaucratic structures that lodged significant authority in individual households, which induced creditors and debtors to rely on the moral pressure of kin ties to procure loans and to ensure their repayment, thus compensating for the inadequacies of business ethics, commercial law, a finance system, and reliable communications.[1]

Similarly, in imperial Russia the lack of formal credit infrastructure combined with an active property market and frequent financial crises led relatives and spouses to help each other to cope with debt and, if necessary, to resist and evade creditors, taking full advantage of legal rules and sometimes adapting and subverting them to suit their ends. Moreover, this personal and informal credit system not only acted as a system of social insurance but also created considerable potential for friction. Patterns of property ownership in early industrial societies, including Russia, emphasized dividing up both assets and debts among relatives. Devolution of property to the younger generations was a lengthy and complex process, sometimes skipping a generation and beginning long before children reached majority.[2]

Whereas existing literature on Russia emphasizes the importance of kin-ship networks centered on the top stratum of the nobility, it is crucial to examine the overlapping circles of communities that included the lesser gentry, as well as urban and commercial classes.[3] Even for moderately wealthy individuals and families, the legal framework was essential for structuring marital and testatory property arrangements, as well as resolving the disputes that often resulted.

In Western Europe, the legal restrictions on female inheritance and mar-ital control of property had an immediate influence on the development of private credit, while being adapted creatively by individuals (male or female) to suit their strategies and property interests.[4] In imperial Russia, the law likewise privileged a patriarchal family, granting the head of a household extensive control over his wife and children. The distinction was that the law allowed married women in Russia to maintain and control their own sepa-rate property. As Michelle Marrese has shown in her groundbreaking book, Russian laws permitting married women to own and control property sepa-rately from their husbands were indeed followed in practice, and noble-women in Russia controlled both urban property and provincial landed estates. Marrese also concluded that Russia's legal system, "for all of its short-comings," allowed women to protect and to advance their and their families' property interests and that noblewomen using the courts "experienced no greater disadvantages than their male counterparts."[5] Similarly, Galina Ulianova has shown that female merchants and entrepreneurs controlled up to 25 percent of businesses.[6]

This chapter adds to this developing field of study by identifying a discrete sphere of activity—borrowing and debt management—that was significantly affected by the law of separate property. I also contribute by focusing on family and kinship structures in which women participated and whose inter-ests they advanced—as did other members—through exercising their partic-ular legal rights. In other words, separate property ownership by a married woman could advance not only her own property interests but also her hus-band's, and families deployed these legal rights as part of their common strategy.

Marital and other family ties helped to secure and promote property rights and interests, both against outsiders and against foolhardy behavior within the family. At the same time, relatives quarreled about debt and used debt to pursue their grievances. Relatives could help each other cope with debt, or they could end up burdening each other with it. The same conclusion, of course, applies to the relevant legal rules themselves: some were enacted to protect kinship groups and others to prevent abuses against third parties, but taken together they served as important strategic tools, whether to maintain the status quo or to change existing property distributions within kinship networks and between generations.

Coping with Debt

Perhaps the most important way in which family and kinship relations affected the culture of credit was for relatives to help each other cope with indebtedness. If family members were unable or unwilling to simply pay the money owed, they had the option to devise strategies, such as hiding an insolvent's property from creditors or ensuring that the debtor owed some money to his or her relatives, who would then be admitted to participate in bankruptcy proceedings. Another way to protect the family's property was to take some preemptive steps through inheritance or trusteeship arrangements that would prevent property from falling into the hands of relatives who were vulnerable to creditors.

The most direct way to help one's relatives was to pay their debts. For example, we have already encountered the young Count Dmitrii Tolstoy, who in the early 1860s incurred substantial debts due to his love of good horses and other luxuries. His father managed to buy up most of Dmitrii's debts and get the insolvency case closed, as well as to foil the sole recalcitrant creditor by complaining about him to the gendarmes, who started an investigation into his predatory lending practices. The father also assisted his son by taking over the burden of the legal proceedings.

Almost one hundred years previously, memoirist Prince Ivan Dolgorukov was similarly bailed out by his own father for his debt incurred by having to maintain a proper lifestyle as an officer of the Imperial Guard in St. Petersburg.[7] According to Dolgorukov's memoirs, this was done with good cheer, presumably in the hopes that the young prince would imbibe the moral lesson and in the future avoid endangering his family's finances.

Less wealthy families likewise supported their relatives by helping them pay their debts and avoid making new ones. For example, another eighteenth-century memoirist, Andrei Bolotov, after moving to St. Petersburg to take up a lucrative position with the police chief baron Korf, received a timely shipment of money from his country relatives just before he had to pay for his elaborate new uniform.[8] Aside from the question of payment, it was not unusual to petition the courts on behalf of one's relatives, especially when they were imprisoned for debt.[9] For instance, the young merchant Nikolai Kuznetsov, on criminal trial for fraudulent bankruptcy in 1865, benefited from his mother's petitions defending his case, which were prepared with the help of top-notch lawyer Aristov.[10]

More sophisticated and long-term strategies for keeping creditors at bay could involve keeping property away from the children's control for as long as possible. Sometimes this resulted in rather curious arrangements. Elizaveta Yan'kova, in her famous reminiscences *(Grandmother's Tales)* written down by her grandson Dmitry Blagovo, recounted that Prince Dmitry Golitsyn, the popular and powerful Moscow Governor General in 1820–1844, depended on his mother financially for most of his adult life, receiving from her an allowance of 50,000 rubles and controlling a village with one hundred serfs. Only seven years before his own death did he inherit from his mother and finally enjoy her fabulous fortune of landed estates with 16,000 serfs.[11] Although his mother, the old Princess Natalia Petrovna Golitsyna, did have a powerful personality, she was also probably trying to preserve the Golitsyns' properties from her son's creditors and his likely mismanagement.

The best option for creditors who did loan to young heirs was usually to be patient. For example, insolvency proceedings against the previously mentioned Dmitrii Tolstoy ran into difficulties when it turned out that he had no property that was legally his own and that his creditors could seize. Although of age, he lived with his father, who owned everything in their apartment, as well as all the carriages and expensive horses.[12] As previously discussed, the expectation of an inheritance was often considered by moneylenders a sufficient guarantee of repayment to extend credit to young persons without any money of their own, which is what also happened in the Tolstoy case. While Russian law provided parents with the option of issuing children their share of their inheritance while they were still alive, and while many parents did choose to do so, the key issue was that neither the children nor their creditors could legally force parents to transfer property during their lifetime, and thus the creditors' only option would be to wait until the parents died and the child came into possession of the inheritance.[13]

Conversely, wealthy individuals could attempt to evade their own creditors by devolving at least some of their property to their children or grandchildren. If executed properly, such divisions could be quite effective, as in the case of the noble entrepreneur and memoirist Nikolai Makarov, who lost his factory, his money, and his landed estate during the financial crisis of

1859–1860 but was able to retire to his children's property near the city of Tula. Makarov's memoir also provided another example, that of his aunt, Alexandra Shipova, who led a very pleasant and hospitable life on her estate but eventually had to sell all of her 600 serfs, her jewelry, and the "unnecessary" silverware to repay her debts. However, her young son still had 400 serfs that he inherited from his father that were enough to pay for his elite education in St. Petersburg.[14] Memoirist Yulia Karpinskaia, writing about another gentry entrepreneur, Pavel Yablochkov, noted that his older daughters, who were given their share of the inheritance early, did not suffer very much from his later business failures, unlike the younger children, who in the end received almost nothing.[15]

But such arrangements could create legal problems as well, most notably when the parent wished to retain some control over the property or when the children were not willing to wait to assume control. Debt in such cases became a weapon for both sides. This was the situation of Yekaterina Naryshkina, the widow of a senator and privy councilor, who in the first half of the nineteenth century held lands populated by over 1,600 serfs. Although she thus belonged to the few thousand of Russia's wealthiest nobles, 1,100 of these serfs were legally owned by her children, having been transferred in 1804 by her mother and sister. According to the arrangement, Naryshkina could manage her children's serfs and enjoy the income for the duration of her life, but she could neither sell nor mortgage them. In 1845, six years before her death, she was subjected to a full-scale criminal investigation initiated by a denunciation from her son Nikolai, a wastrel who had been banned from his mother's house since 1826.[16] A retired army officer heavily in debt and at one point exiled by the government to the northern town of Vologda for his dissolute behavior, Nikolai claimed that his mother had let into her house an enterprising young man named Divarii, who had previously been expelled from the Corps of Gendarmes for seducing a lady and who now allegedly induced the elderly woman to take out mortgages on her vast holdings, including the children's serfs, to satisfy his love of luxury. The governor general of Moscow dispatched a high-ranking aide to investigate, and it turned out that Naryshkina had indeed mortgaged some of the "children's" estates in 1841 to the Board of Trustees for 31,860 silver rubles.

On April 14, 1847, the 78-year-old lady was interrogated in the presence of a procuracy official *(striapchii)* and a deputy from the nobility, State Councilor Stroev. Naryshkina displayed a very detailed knowledge of all of her properties and their legal status, even though neither her relatives nor a legal adviser were present. She denied any illegality, but at the same time claimed that her sole motivation was to deny her son's creditors the ability to seize these lands and that she used the money to make improvements. But she could not convincingly explain why she never revealed the serfs' true ownership on her tax rolls. The authorities placed all of Naryshkina's property and her person under trusteeship, a sanction typically applied to minor children, mentally incompetent persons, spendthrifts, and serfowners who mistreated their serfs more than was socially and legally accepted. However, after Naryshkina exercised her connections in the highest spheres, the trusteeship was left only over the "children's" properties, and the control over Naryshkina's own lands was restored to her, although still without the right to sell or mortgage. The government also seems to have removed her case from the jurisdiction of Moscow's regular courts because her case file stops abruptly shortly after the first interrogation. It seems that Naryshkina actually prevailed in the end because there is no indication that her illegal mortgage was subsequently rescinded.

Given Naryshkina's travails, it is not surprising that property owners were motivated to retain as much control over their property as possible, while at the same time shielding it from their creditors. This was the conundrum of Elizaveta Dolgovo-Saburova, who in 1823 transferred 550 of her serfs to her six minor children and in 1839 moved to Moscow, where she may have engaged in trade and possibly became involved with shady company; she incurred considerable debts, some of them from the known bankrupt Prince Nikolai Engalychev and convicted forger Collegiate Assessor Grigorii Polianskii. Dolgovo-Saburova disputed these debts, but after her death her children stopped pursuing the case, thinking that their property was safe from collection. One can only imagine the shock of the sole surviving son, Ivan, when the creditors tried to take away his estate in the early 1850s and the case was appealed all the way to the Senate, which ruled against him.

The ambiguous wording of the gift acted against Elizaveta and her children. On the one hand, she clearly intended to observe the appearances of giving up her ownership of the property: she listed it as the children's in all official papers and appointed her brother as the trustee over it. At the same time, the Senate ruled that the gift was not finalized and the children never legally came into possession of the property. According to the Senate, the language of the act was that Elizaveta would divide up the property among her children only when they came of age and if they were "respectful." This argumentation sounds bogus because the conditions referred to the future division of the property and not to the gift itself. However, she later sold some of the land and also took out a mortgage from a state bank, and further claimed the property as hers on the tax rolls at least once. Finally, the registration procedure at the Yaroslavl' County Court was never properly completed.

Ivan's arguments were that the children could not officially come into possession at the time of the gift because they were underage, the transfer was clearly meant to be final, and Elizaveta's sale and mortgage activities violated the terms of the gift but could not be grounds for voiding it. She claimed property as hers on the tax rolls due to an error by her bailiff and, finally, the error in the registration procedure meant that some official had made a mistake and not that Elizaveta's children should lose their property.

Having lost the appeal, Ivan petitioned the tsar to stop the sale of his estate. The procedure in that situation was for the Third Section and the minister of justice, Count Viktor Panin, to opine first. The minister's opinion was likewise against Ivan. Whereas we may allow that during the formal judicial proceedings Ivan's creditors could have bribed the Senate officials to rule in their favor, Panin's reasoning indicates a concern for the creditors who allegedly in good faith purchased the claims against Elizaveta from her original, rather shady, lenders. Panin thought that although Elizaveta did give up some of her property rights, the gift was conditional, the children were never formally brought into possession, and she continued to manage the estate without any constraints until her death. More importantly, Panin then argued that Elizaveta's creditors did not know about the gift and assumed when they loaned her the money that she was still the owner. The tsar approved Panin's opinion. In this fashion, the government balanced its concern for preserving property arrangements within noble families with its concern for preventing families from defrauding creditors.

Another complicated and not invariably successful strategy to protect family assets was to register loans to a relative in order to gain membership on his or her bankruptcy board in case of future insolvency. Already in the late eighteenth century, the law recognized only transfers that occurred before the debt to the third party was incurred.[17] Although the other creditors could challenge or even exclude suspicious debt claims, legally it was nearly impossible to prove whether relatives really did or did not physically transfer the money unless the transaction was properly documented. For example, Colonel Count Ivan Zotov, when he died in 1853, was embroiled in a legal dispute with Cavalry Staff Captain Vasilii Mozharov, who maintained that the Zotovs owed him nearly 9,000 silver rubles related to a land sale by the countess. However, the late Zotov's largest creditor, for over 41,000 rubles, was his son Cavalry Captain Petr Zotov. While it is unclear just how far Petr was able to press his advantage, Mozharov's actions were clearly constrained because Petr never tired of pointing out in his court petitions that his debt was much larger than Mozharov's and because Mozharov was ultimately unable to get an insolvency proceeding under way.[18]

However, entangling one's financial affairs with those of relatives could also be a dangerous path leading to one's own insolvency, which is what happened to Collegiate Secretary Petr Zubov, discussed throughout this study, who owned nearly 3,000 serfs in the Upper Volga region. When declared insolvent in 1853, Zubov claimed that he had accepted a debt-ridden inheritance from his brother Aleksandr largely because of the latter's debt of 67,227 silver rubles (300,000 assignat), whereas the other brother, Valerian, wisely refused the inheritance.[19]

For merchants—who rarely owned far-flung landed estates and typically lived near their families and frequently shuffled their merchandise between shops and warehouses—the preferred solution was to hide movable property with relatives. This included not only merchandise but also furniture, silverware, clothing, jewelry, carriages, and horses. This scheme—the subject of Ostrovsky's play *It's a Family Matter*—was not unique to Russia or Russian merchants and so does not testify to the latter's exceptional dishonesty, but it was real and widely used.

One example is the criminal prosecution of two insolvent Moscow merchants, brothers Nil and Aleksei Bakhrushin. In 1864, their brother Ivan, who owned a fashionable clothing shop, became insolvent and, after moving some merchandise to his brothers' shop, in 1864 declared to his creditors that he was too ill to continue in business and transferred the shop to Nil, Aleksei, and his son-in-law. What ensued were prolonged negotiations with creditors, several settlements, and a continuing shift of merchandise between the shops. The shops would alternately be emptied out of anything but the poorest quality goods and then filled up again. The police investigator found phony account books and discovered that the Bakhrushins had also managed to install one of their clerks as a member of their own bankruptcy board.[20]

More remote relatives likewise actively helped debtors hide property. For example, an ex-policeman, Leiba Sumgalter, retired after over 20 years of service but then returned to Moscow to collect a debt from townsman Krasil'nikov, who lost all court proceedings outright but was able to hide his movable property with his mother-in-law, who successfully claimed it as hers.[21] Similarly, the Old Believer merchant Fedor Solodovnikov, who owned a textile factory in the town of Bogorodsk outside Moscow, transferred large amounts of money to his daughters-in-law.[22] Moscow flour and wheat merchant Mushnikov, when sued for debt in 1842 (including 1,000 rubles incurred by his late father), transferred merchandise worth 1,500 silver rubles through his wife to his brother Grigorii Volkov and then absconded. This he did despite apparently being amidst a "great strife" with his relatives, whom he described as "insignificant people without much money" who were taking advantage of his success.[23]

Another merchant, Pavel Lavrentiev, gave fifty-three large cases of tea to his relative, craftsman Lebedev, who in turn gave it to Lavrentiev's sister-in-law Anna Kochnaia, who stored it at *Kaluzhskoe Podvorie,* an inn in Moscow, from which it was removed by some person whose identity the creditors were unable to uncover. As of May 1865, the creditors were at a loss when an unknown person appeared at their office and reported that Lavrentiev was hiding his property at Kochnaia's house. Two of the creditors came to her apartment with the police and found Lavrentiev and more than ten cases of tea, which Kochnaia admitted belonged to him. However, Lavrentiev had another line of defense, not surprisingly involving debt: he claimed that he had pawned this tea to his sister-in-law several months before for 1,000 rubles and thus was not concealing any property. While the conclusion of that case file does not survive, Lavrentiev's defense was likely successful because he produced two witnesses to back up this claim.[24]

More inventive merchants could distribute property among several relatives in such a way that even when an informant could point to the location of the items, it was not easy for the creditors to identify and seize them. For example, we have already encountered the bankruptcy record of Moscow merchant and honorary citizen Ivan Borisovskii, who owned five houses, two teashops, and a vegetable retail business. When he became insolvent in 1845, it turned out that only one of the houses was free of mortgage and could be seized by the creditors. The police search found merchandise worth only 5,000 paper rubles and no movable property. However, Borisovskii's former servant, the peasant Egutatov, denounced him for secretly taking various items out of his house and concealing them with his son-in-law, with townsman Alekseev, and in the shed in the courtyard. The second police search located several carriages, a sleigh, and a horse, as well as icons, mahogany furniture, mirrors, a clock, trunks with clothing and boxes with bronze, porcelain, and glass dishes, two grand pianos, five cases of tea, ten silver-lined horse collars, some old accounting books, and many other items. Borisovskii claimed that all the property belonged either to his wife or to his brother Martemian, although he could not explain why everything was packed in boxes. The pianos had allegedly been gifted by Martemian to Ivan's daughters, and the icons were gifted by Ivan's mother to her grandchildren. The clothes and fur coats were his, and he claimed that he omitted reporting them to the creditors because he alleged that they had only been interested in his furniture during their previous visits. All the property found during this second search was valued at 981.07 rubles.

The creditors were not satisfied with this result, arguing that Borisovskii "occupied a huge two-story house, had seven horses, a carriage, and other things, but according to the inventory and the search he had not a single shirt and not a single suit, except for those on his body, no table linen, and not a single spoon or a saltshaker . . . the best and most valuable things are concealed; for instance, there are seven frames that could hold 37 icons, but the icons themselves are missing, there are glass clock cases but no clocks, there are samovar chimneys but no samovars, carafe stoppers but no carafes, and the tableware is packed in boxes as if for transportation."

Other servants and relatives testified that in Borisovskii's house in the past they had seen numerous valuable items, such as icons in silver frames, bronze clocks, silver spoons, carriages, horses, table linen, and so on, although no one admitted to seeing anything during the official face-to-face meeting *(ochnaia stavka)* with Egutatov at the police station. The creditors not surprisingly complained about the fact that the police failed to find property during their first search and had not found anything truly valuable during the second one. However, despite all these complaints, the Commercial Court took seriously enough the claims by Borisovskii's wife and brother that these items belonged to them or to Borisovskii's daughters and did not allow the sale.[25]

Cases like Bakhrushin's, Lavrentiev's, and Borisovskii's may not have been representative of typical bankruptcy proceedings, which never made it to the criminal court and are thus more difficult to access today. Individuals who did get caught were either too incompetent to hide property well, unlucky enough to get denounced by their servants and acquaintances, or simply unable to come to an early agreement with their creditors. Their remaining property would in any case most likely provide little satisfaction to their creditors: silverware, carriages and fur coats maintained a façade of financial stability but were actually worth relatively little compared to the merchants' debts of tens or even hundreds of thousands of rubles. However, even these relatively unsuccessful attempts to deceive creditors that eventually resulted in criminal prosecution show that distressed debtors in Russia had little chance of resisting their creditors or inducing them to negotiate a settlement without considerable assistance from their family members, other relatives, employees, and domestic servants and that the overwhelming majority of these people remained loyal to their bankrupt patron even when questioned by authorities, showing ties of relation and employment to be usually stronger than the obligation to be forthcoming with creditors and the authorities.

Debt, Inheritance, and Family Conflict

While family ties assisted individuals in dealing with outside creditors, the converse was also true, and debt relations structured a wide range of strategies within family and kinship groups. Debt helped preserve and enhance power and property interest within such groups, but it also helped transfer wealth to the next generation through inheritance and dowry arrangements. It is important to point out that such arrangements were often conflict-ridden, that they sometimes stretched over many years and even decades, and that legal stratagems could easily fail to work as intended.

The simplest strategy would be for borrowers to go to their relatives for loans before seeking help from unrelated individuals. For example, Alexander Terskii, a prosperous Moscow moneylender who died in 1856, held loan letters from his son-in-law and another pair of relatives, most likely his brother and sister-in-law.[26] Registers of mortgages and loan letters show that generally between 8 and 14 percent of all transactions in the mid-nineteenth century took place between close relatives.[27] The true number was probably higher, since creditors lending to their relatives could dispense with the security of a mortgage or the additional legal protections provided by "registered" loan letters and were thus more likely to use simpler "private" loan letters that are less well preserved.

A more complicated use of interfamily debt ties involved inheritance arrangements. For example, individuals who were normally excluded from succession either by law or by custom could use debt to claim their share of an inheritance. The litigation involving the privy councilor's widow Ekaterina Naryshkina has already been mentioned; she died in 1851 and had lived with her daughter Natalia, whereas her wastrel son Nikolai was banned from the house in 1826. Natalia was entitled by law to inherit only one-fourteenth of the real estate and one-tenth of the movable property, and the mother apparently did not want to disinherit her son. But shortly before her death, the mother signed a loan letter to Natalia for 30,000 silver rubles. Natalia was ultimately unsuccessful in enforcing her claim against her mother's estate, the courts openly favoring the dissolute Nikolai, but the attempt to use debt to effect a more equitable property distribution is nonetheless notable.[28]

Another virtually identical arrangement shows that this strategy could be attempted to benefit more remote family members. The aristocratic widow of a colonel, Anna Lopukhina, died in 1842, bequeathing 100 serfs to her second nephew, Actual State Councilor Prince Sergei Dolgorukov, a house in Moscow to her granddaughter, colonel's wife Voyeikova, and absolutely nothing to her niece Tvorogova, who was married to a major general. Tvorogova was the closest person to the almost 90-year-old Lopukhina before her death and executed such sensitive tasks on her aunt's behalf as inspecting her estates and dealing with serf disobedience, and after Lopukhina's death she managed the funeral at her own expense. Although she was officially excluded from the inheritance, Tvorogova produced an unwitnessed "safe deposit receipt" from Lopukhina for 15,000 silver rubles, the form being undoubtedly selected for the legal precedence that it provided in bankruptcy or inheritance proceedings. Dolgorukov fought Tvorogova's suit, as is recounted later in this study, and the case dragged on for years; however, once again, the use of the debt document as a form of inheritance seems to be the most likely explanation of this litigation.[29]

This tactic was also used by individuals from the lower urban classes, as in the case of Lieutenant-Colonel Nikolai Blaginin, who died in 1849. This retired military officer lived alone in a small house in Moscow and was looked after by an illiterate former serf, Anna Antonova. Blaginin gave her a debt note for 600 rubles, a sum she was highly unlikely to have ever possessed. It is less relevant whether Blaginin actually borrowed any money or whether Antonova thought that she should be the proper inheritor of Blaginin's little house in exchange for her labors than that this was the preferred solution rather than simply writing or even forging a will in Antonova's favor.[30]

The reason for a preference for debt documents over a formal will was no doubt not simply the rigors of inheritance litigation but also some social constraint that limited one's choice of official heirs. This phenomenon is possibly what was at issue in the lawsuit by major general's widow Anna von Bussau against a former cavalry lieutenant Prince Nikolai Obolenskii, who apparently borrowed 15,000 rubles from her in 1858, under the supervision of his uncle and guardian, Staff Captain Bové, who served as the County judge in the town of Mozhaisk near Moscow. Von Bussau was seemingly a close family friend; the young prince frequently implored him in his letters to help "poor" Anna Pavlovna, who found herself in "extreme circumstances." However, no blood relation between them is mentioned. What makes this debt look suspicious is the fact that in 1858, Obolenskii was a young military cadet under strict military discipline who could neither need 15,000 rubles nor indeed be permitted to have this money in his possession; thus his story—that Bové made him sign the note, claiming that this was the debt of Obolenskii's father—was probably true. More mysterious, however, are Obolenskii's hints at Anna Pavlovna's "close" relations (the word *blizkie* here suggests intimacy between a man and a woman) with his father, and her taking this hint as a serious insult, about which she complained to the court. Finally, while Obolenskii managed to delay the collection proceedings, he was eventually confronted by his uncle and several military officers and forced to formally acknowledge the debt with them as witnesses. Although we do not have all the facts of this case, it seems likely that this debt was a well-concealed device for Anna Pavlovna to claim a part of Obolenskii senior's inheritance, something that could not have been accomplished openly since Anna Pavlovna was not a relation.[31]

Friction and conflict of interest were no less apparent whenever the older generation intentionally passed on its debts to the younger generation, often thereby jeopardizing or completely ruining its chances of financial autonomy. Prince Andrei Golitsyn was bankrupted in the late 1830s primarily because of his investment in the failed Transcaucasian Sericultural Company and likely also by his mystical fervor bordering on naïveté.[32] But he claimed to have first begun his slide into insolvency when his father transferred to him as his share of his future inheritance an estate of 2,520 serfs and nearly 24,300 acres (9,000 *desiatinas*) of land in the fertile Kursk province, with a saltpeter factory and a liqueur distillery. The reality of being a wealthy landowner turned out to be vastly different from the young nobleman's dreams: he found that the factory was mortgaged, the estate came without any liquid cash, and at the same time he had to pay his father's "private" debts plus the estate's tax arrears, as well as his own creditors (altogether around 73,000 rubles).[33]

A similar fate met another memorable bankrupt, Actual State Councilor Sergei Krotkov. When testifying during his bankruptcy hearings in 1874, he complained that from the very moment he received his portion of his inheritance during his father's lifetime in 1847, he was put in a "false" position whereby the very acquisition of property was the source of his ruin, compelling him to incur further significant debts. The villages Krotkov received were in complete disorder, so that he had to begin by building himself a house and other necessary structures. Even more crippling were the conditions imposed by Krotkov's father in exchange for this early transfer of his share of the inheritance: first, the father kept the income from the distillery located on the estate for three years; second, during these three years, the son was obligated to furnish up to one hundred peasants to work on his father's land for six weeks in the summer during the crucial harvest season; third, the father sold all the grain from the 1846 harvest and kept the money; and fourth, the father remortgaged the estate just before handing it over to the son and, once again, kept the money. Not surprisingly, despite Krotkov's attempts to straighten out his finances over the years, he was starting from a huge disadvantage that certainly helped to bring about his eventual failure.[34]

This kind of debilitating inheritance could also be found in merchant families, as in the case of the young Moscow merchant Nikolai Kuznetsov, who became insolvent in 1865. He had inherited from his father property worth nearly 90,000 silver rubles, including movables for 1,498 rubles, merchandise worth 46,000, cash of almost 1,000, and debt obligations from various persons worth over 41,000. He also inherited clan *(rodovoe)* property consisting of two houses and grain warehouses in Moscow that were worth 85,000 rubles. But once again, out of these amounts Kuznetsov not only had to provide 25,000 rubles for his mother and sister but also pay his father's debts worth over 300,000 rubles. Whether or not Kuznetsov was, as his creditors later alleged, something of a wastrel, he was clearly constrained by this burden, according to his mother's court petition on behalf of her son: given that he did not inherit enough money to repay his father's debt outright, he had to transfer it to his own name, with all the accrued interest, which made it impossible for him to incur new loans necessary for continuing the business, thereby crippling his trade and hastening his insolvency.[35]

Even when there was no apparent abuse on the part of the older generation, unforeseen events such as family deaths could bring financial affairs into disarray, not simply because of debt but also because formalizing an inheritance usually took time, which creditors were not always willing to concede. For example, the English-born Moscow resident Nikolai Dzhakson (Jackson) became insolvent in 1872, with debts of up to 54,000 rubles, and his property was limited to a house that he owned jointly with his mother and brother, whose shares were also burdened with debt. Both relatives died within seven months of each other, which made it impossible for Dzhakson to effect any kind of financial transaction involving the house until his rights of inheritance were affirmed.[36]

In addition to simply passing on their debts to the next generation, property owners could also contrive to use debt to continue to control their children after they came of age and (in the case of women) moved under their husband's supervision. We have already been introduced to the case of the wealthy Moscow merchant Dmitrii Savinov, who married his daughter Maria off to Second Lieutenant Vladimir Aleksandrov in 1839; to provide her with a dowry, he purchased a large estate outside Moscow from the aristocratic Guard Colonel Ivan Musin-Pushkin. At that time, according to the daughter's testimony, Savinov had a talk with his daughter, giving her "many examples of unfortunate marriages, in which husbands, having spent not only their own fortunes, but also those of their wives, left them with the children lacking any daily sustenance, and told [her] that [her] husband was still a young man, little known to [them], and God knows what he will be like in the future." Ostensibly to guard against this uncertainty, Savinov had his daughter sign a 350,000-ruble mortgage note to him for the estate, promising to nullify the debt once Aleksandrov had completed his probation period and gained his approval. Because of her "filial love and unconditional obedience," the daughter did not dare to refuse. Although the entire estate was purchased for only 117,000 paper rubles, the huge mortgage only applied to a small portion of 108 acres (40 *desiatinas*).[37]

While disputes between spouses and other relatives were litigated in regular courts, lawsuits between parents and children in pre-reform Russia had to be litigated in a special province-level Equity Court, which was modeled on its English namesake by Catherine the Great's 1775 legislation. The English equity jurisdiction of the Court of Chancery and the Court of the Exchequer—familiar to the readers of Dickens's *Bleak House*—was established primarily to address wrongs for which the regular court system with its focus on money damages provided no remedy. The Russian incarnation—also influenced by the traditional arbitration courts in Little Russian (left-bank Ukrainian) provinces, was similar in intent but different in form because it processed civil and criminal cases involving minors, insane persons, accusations of sorcery, and disputes between parents and children.[38]

Another important distinction was that English equity procedures were written and secret, actually rather similar to pre-reform procedures in regular

Russian courts; by contrast, Russian courts of equity employed a streamlined oral procedure involving a face-to-face meeting between the parties that at least in theory was more similar to a mediation procedure than a trial. Judging by the records of the Moscow Equity Court, its most common type of civil case involved parents suing children for maintenance payments.

Thus, while similar conflicts between spouses were litigated in ordinary courts, some equally complicated cases like Savinov's had to go to the Equity Court because they were presumed to be less acrimonious and were to be resolved through a mediation-like procedure rather than a full-scale lawsuit. In reality, litigation between parents and children could be anything but amicable, such as the bitter dispute in the late 1840s between townsman Kolpinskii of middling wealth and his son Petr, which centered on a loan letter for 10,000 rubles, which was written out in the son's name but which the father wanted in his possession. The senior Kolpinskii eventually complained to authorities that Petr had expelled him from the house and persuaded the police to seize all of the property on his behalf. Unfortunately for the father, his house had also been signed over to his granddaughter, and in addition mortgaged to the father of his daughter-in-law, serf Tsurikov. Petr was arguing that his father had not been expelled at all but actually went to Moscow to collect a debt from his son-in-law for 550 assignat rubles. It is unclear how the Equity Court would have eventually resolved this bitter conflict, but the father died in August 1848, and the court quickly closed the case.[39]

In addition to Equity Court, another option that avoided the legal system altogether was to petition the Third Section; Russia's secret political police operated in effect as a parallel legal system because its officers had extensive police powers to intervene in civil disputes and to investigate particularly important criminal cases. As discussed throughout this study, the officers of the Third Section and its military arm, the Corps of Gendarmes, used their close connection to the tsar as leverage, as well as their power to impose administrative exile and their ability to take over investigations and thus guard against local and regional influences.

However, these powers were also limited because the Third Section could not try cases by itself and because highly ranked and well-connected individuals felt free to resist its persuasions. This is what happened in the case of State Councilor Alexander Varentsov, who was married to the daughter of Collegiate Assessor Prince Fedor Andreevich Golitsyn. Despite his modest rank, the prince was wealthy and engaged in moneylending. In 1849, Golitsyn gave debt notes for 30,000 rubles to his daughter, Sofia, apparently because he worried about his son-in-law's spending habits and wanted his daughter to use the interest on these notes as her spending money. In the 1850s, the couple had a falling out with Golitsyn, who ended up holding some of Varentsov's debt, asserting that "whoever trusts me, will never be in loss." In 1862, Golitsyn transferred these documents to his agent for collection, and Varentsov and his wife complained to the Third Section. The old prince rejected the officers' advances and adamantly refused to stop his collection procedures. The prince accused his son-in-law of wastefulness and offered to set the amount of the debt aside to be kept for his grandson, Fedor, when he came of age, but refused to make any concessions to Varentsov, asking "can I forgive a man familiar with the rules of Jesuitism, who irritated and incensed my family, a man who threatens and lies instead of asking." There is no indication that the Third Section's influence had any results, but it appears that Golitsyn died in 1869, presumably while the dispute was still going on. There is also information that Golitsyn accused his wife of wastefulness *(motovstvo)* as early as 1842, and that she abandoned him and went abroad. Coupled with the same accusation against Varentsov, this suggests that the family conflict originated in the old prince's mind. But what is historically important from this sad family saga is the way Fedor Golitsyn used debt to exercise control over his family.[40]

Even less amicable were parent–child conflicts that involved fraud and forgery and therefore ended up in criminal court. The famous case of the group of swindlers known as the Jacks of Hearts that was tried in Moscow in 1878 included several colorful family disputes involving credit and money, perhaps the most notable one involving a young merchant, Vasily Pegov, who was expelled from his father's house for inveterate drunkenness and theft and decided to improve his finances by forging his father's debt obligations. This was a bad idea because the older Pegov was well known in the city as one of the few merchants who never borrowed money and who conducted all of his trade in cash.[41]

But the temptation to use one's father's credit was strong, both in the 1870s and long before the Great Reforms. In the early 1850s, a 24-year-old son of a merchant, Klavdii Rudnev, was caught signing debt documents with his father's name.[42] It was the father himself who suggested to the police that Klavdii, "as he had heard," issued "many forged bills of exchange." At first Klavdii fled Moscow, but he soon came back home and was presented to the police by his father, at which point he confessed that he had talked a now-deceased foster son of his father's into forging signatures on the bills of exchange. Klavdii "wasted away" the money thus obtained. At the same time, handwriting experts thought that Klavdii's father may have been the actual forger, and some of the deceived merchants said that they received the fake bills of exchange directly from him. In any event, the old man died during the investigation, after which Klavdii recanted his confession and claimed that his father had forced him to take the blame, which he agreed to do out of his "burning" filial love and sense of guilt for "past transgressions," referring to his alleged mismanagement of the family business during his father's illness. Klavdii even claimed that during the investigation, he learned to imitate his father's signature to make the original confession more convincing. The Criminal Chamber, while upholding Rudnev's sentence of Siberian exile, found that his father's participation was a mitigating factor. While Klavdii's actual culpability in this case is unclear, his father's involvement must have had a significant effect upon Klavdii's motivation, while his testimony adopts the familiar motif of excusing criminal behavior by claiming it was motivated by a desire to live up to respectable ideals—in this case "filial love" and a guilty conscience.

Debt and Marital Property

Both imperial-era lawyers and modern historians have debated exactly why imperial Russia adopted the regime of separate marital property, which allowed women legal control over their dowry, and the acquisition, ownership, and management of property completely independent from their husbands.[43] Pre-reform jurist Dmitrii Meier offered a functional explanation: he pointed out that the rule did not prevent effective joint control over marital property in properly functioning marriages, but it did provide real protection for spouses in poorly functioning relationships. This explanation is certainly sensible but does not explain very much, since there were many perfectly reasonable legal rules in the history of Russian (or any other) legal system that were proposed but never adopted, and vice versa; many very inconvenient rules were stubbornly retained.

Historian Michelle Marrese offered another, historical, explanation in her landmark work on property ownership and control by noblewomen in pre-reform Russia. She found that the rule first became practically effective in the first half of the eighteenth century, and she argued that it offered additional safety for family property when nobles were frequently exiled and dispossessed during the political struggles of that period.[44] She noted that a crucial aspect of the rule—namely, the limitations on the spouses' respective liability for each other's debts—was only finalized in 1846 after prolonged debates. By that time, the government's concern was that spouses would abuse the separate property rule by fictitiously transferring property and making fraudulent loans to each other in order to evade creditors.[45]

To be sure, this concern long predated 1846, but previous legislation was unclear and appeared to distinguish transactions involving nobles and those involving merchants. Decrees issued within the framework of noble property ownership prohibited all real-estate transactions between spouses from 1763 to 1825 out of a concern to protect women from abusive husbands.[46] Laws relating to commerce, bankruptcy, and credit had more complex rationale, equally concerned with protecting creditors from fraud.

For example, the Bankruptcy Code of 1740 that was enacted but never went into effect would have placed wives' property in all forms, including their dowry, at the creditors' disposal, on the rationale that they are "completely obligated to share their husbands' misfortune." However, the law of 1797 ordered that transfers between relatives were valid if executed before the other party incurred the debt obligation. That is, a merchant or an entrepreneur could be protected before going into business by transferring some assets to his or her spouse. This provision was supplemented by the Bankruptcy Code of 1800, which allowed creditors to seize the wife's property only if she conducted business together with her husband.[47]

The law of 1846 for the first time created a practicable arrangement and essentially elaborated tsar Paul's decree of 1797: it required the wife of an insolvent husband (or vice versa) to submit proof of her property ownership and allowed her to keep all property either received as dowry, inherited from or gifted by third parties, or purchased with her own money. Moreover, the wife could keep any property gifted by her husband more than ten years before the insolvency. Even wives who could not submit the necessary proof were still somewhat protected by the rule, in that it secured for them all the women's and children's clothing and half the dishes, furniture, silverware, carriages, horses, and horse harness in the couple's possession.[48] During insolvency proceedings, wives could be admitted to participate as creditors, but only if the money they lent to their husbands was acquired in one of the ways listed above.[49]

The law of 1846 remained unchanged until the end of the imperial period and had great significance for Russia's culture of debt. First, the law obviously did not eliminate opportunities for husbands and wives to support each other's strategizing against creditors by, for example, standing surety for each other, petitioning courts, and participating in insolvency proceedings, as well as invoking the law to resist creditors' attempts to seize property. Second, the separate property regime created the potential for arm's-length debt relations between spouses that could be used for various property arrangements that not only promoted family finances, but were utilized in inter-spousal disputes and litigation—or even caused such disputes. Spouses could use debt to formalize dowry arrangements or to dispute them or even to secure divorce. Dowries could be written up in whole or in part as a loan, while women could use their husbands' debts to themselves as leverage to make them cooperate in divorce proceedings.

One commonly used way to take advantage of spouses' separate legal personalities was to guarantee each other's debts. There are many examples in the cases that are discussed in detail throughout this book: the collegiate councilor's wife Liubov' Pevnitskaia had some of her debts guaranteed both by her husband and by her father, the priest Rozanov, while she likewise guaranteed some of her husband's debt.[50] In 1825, Moscow merchant Marshchev was imprisoned for debt to the Treasury connected to liquor tax farming, whereupon his wife petitioned the governor to release her husband "at her guarantee".[51] Thirty-five years later, when another insolvent merchant, Vasilii Prokhorov, quarreled with his relatives, so that none of them would agree to be his surety to keep him out of debtors' prison, eventually his wife Iuliia Fedorovna guaranteed his debt, although the documents at the end of the case file show that creditors became suspicious and were inquiring whether she actually owned any property of her own that she could use to guarantee her husband's debts.[52]

Even when a wife did not own debt-free property but merely was engaged in a "secured" legal case against someone else, it could prove enough to rescue a bankrupt husband. This happened, for example, with Actual State Councilor Prince Vladimir Sergeevich Golitsyn, who became insolvent after unsuccessfully attempting to run a textile factory near Moscow in partnership with several aristocratic women, including a Bakhmetieva and another Golitsyna, as well as his own wife. Golitsyn himself owned seven serfs plus a salary of less than 550 rubles. In 1849, Golitsyn's wife Praskovia successfully petitioned the Moscow County Court to guarantee some of the claims against her husband, totaling almost 40,000 paper rubles, by her own claim against Colonel Nikolai Borisovich Golitsyn for 60,500 paper rubles, which she had been trying to collect since 1826. Unsurprisingly, the creditors refused to in effect take over Praskovia's ancient lawsuit, but she then petitioned to consider their claims as not concerning her and her property, leaving the creditors with the option of going after her husband's estate with its seven serfs.[53]

Much as with parents, wives' assistance extended to their husbands' legal proceedings, especially if they were in a debtors' prison and could not easily advocate for themselves. For example, in 1844, Moscow townsman Ivan Monakhov became insolvent because of his cartwrighting business—mostly, it seemed, due to dishonesty by the merchant Dmitrii Evdokimov, who was refusing to pay his debt to Monakhov of over 10,000 rubles, while presenting his own claim for half that amount. As part of the prolonged case that stretched into the 1850s, Monakhov's illiterate wife Anna, with the help of townswoman Elizaveta Filipova (who signed her petitions for her), successfully complained to the governor as part of Monakhov's appeal process and offered to stand surety for her husband.[54]

Yet another related strategy was for wives to contrive to be included among their husbands' creditors. For example, in the Krotkov insolvency case that has already been discussed, his creditors included his wife Varvara, with a claim of over 47,000 rubles, twice as much as the next largest claim. Adding this to the large claims by several other relatives, it is not surprising that the creditors eventually voted to grant him full bankruptcy discharge.[55] Another wealthy debtor, Privy Councilor Prince Vasilii Khovanskii, who died in 1850, likewise had his wife listed among the creditors, with the hefty claim of 13,148 rubles.[56] Needless to say, despite the legal restrictions on debt and other transactions between spouses, couples continued to purchase property in each other's name. For example, gentleman capitalist Pavel Yablochkov was cheated by numerous relatives whom he had appointed as his agents while in the liquor tax farming business: they had managed to transfer all of their extensive properties to their wives and thereby made themselves collection-proof.[57]

While all these strategies utilized the fact that the wives of insolvent husbands remained off-limits to creditors and could actually count themselves among them, the law of separate marital property was also useful in another common type of situation: when creditors attempted to seize property that belonged to the debtor's spouse. For example, in the Moscow Equity Court case of merchant Savinov discussed in the preceding section, in which he sued his daughter on the basis of a mortgage note for the estate that he purchased for her as dowry, the father attempted to argue that he actually took this mortgage note in exchange for 200,000 rubles that he gave to his daughter's husband. He backed up this argument with some letters written by his son-in-law. However, the daughter reasonably maintained that she had no idea whether her husband and her father had any debt relations, but "according to existing laws" she was not to be held accountable for them because the letters did not mention her in any way, and her husband was not mentioned in the mortgage note.[58]

The issue of separate marital property came up even more often when creditors simply appeared at a debtor's house and attempted to inventory or take away movables. For example, in the case of Moscow brewer and merchant Marshchev, who was imprisoned for government debt in 1825, the police searched his apartment but were forced to conclude that all the property there belonged to his wife. Thus, even the government, while usually very jealous of its financial interests, had enough respect for the law to interpret it to favor the wife.[59]

In another case, Lieutenant Nikolai Tolstoy managed to mix up his property with that of his wife Natalia so thoroughly that the police could not untangle the question of ownership and in 1851 sent the case to Moscow County Court "as is." The court not surprisingly objected that it was unclear what property, if any, belonged to Tolstoy's wife and found that some of the claims were actually against the wife alone and that "it is even more impermissible to mix up the collections against him with those against his wife simply because this court is only examining the case of Mr. Tolstoy." The court then sent the case back for additional investigation. When the police came to his house to inventory his movable property, Tolstoy claimed that everything in the house belonged to his wife, who submitted the proper "explanation" and refused to let the police into the house.[60]

Similarly, in another case, the collegiate assessor's wife Maria Serebriakova refused four times to let the police inventory property—furniture, horses, and carriages—that she claimed was hers. The court eventually held that half of that property was still subject to seizure, but Serebriakova was referring to a 1842 dowry contract that showed all of this property as hers.[61]

Even in situations when wives were unable to protect their property, the rule of separate property permitted them to contest the police and creditors. In the 1841 case of a modest and not very well educated Moscow merchant Ivan Ignatiev, who was accused of forging a bill of exchange and imprisoned at a police precinct, the authorities inventoried and sealed the merchandise in the shop of his wife Avdotia and obstinately resisted petitions to reverse their decision. According to Ignatiev's complaint to the governor, a corrupt and malevolent police clerk falsely wrote in the interrogation transcript that the shop belonged to him. In fact, Ignatiev only "managed and oversaw" the establishment, which his wife legally owned, financed with her own capital, and provided with merchandise of her own manufacture.

We do not know whether Advotia eventually managed to get her property back, but it is clear, first, that both she and her husband were fully aware of the law of separate marital property despite their modest social status, and in fact probably set up their joint business with this rule in mind, and second, that the policemen's obstinacy may have resulted from the fact that it was Ignatiev who managed the business and contracted debt and thus appeared to be the owner. Because townspeople, unlike merchants and peasants, did not need to enroll in guilds or obtain trading licenses, it would have been very difficult for the court to ascertain who actually owned the business. While this confusion of course harmed the Ignatievs' finances while their business was shut down, the case shows that even in a situation involving serious police misconduct, the law of separate property prevented the Ignatievs from losing their shop outright.[62]

In situations when the property clearly belonged to the husband, the creditors and the courts seem to have followed the requirement of granting the wife's half of the husband's movable property. For example, in the case of merchant Artemii Riazanov, half of his property was given to his wife Matrena Anisimova Riazanova, and the other half was sold at an auction, except for the family's icons, which were also given to the wife.[63]

The rule about separate marital property also applied when it was the wife who had become insolvent. For example, the collegiate councilor's wife Liubov' Pevnitskaia did not allow the police to take property from her house, claiming that all of it had belonged to her husband before their wedding, although it turned out that two years earlier she had acknowledged this property—including furniture, three horses, horse harness, and an icon—as hers. Thus, the Moscow County Court ordered in 1852 that Pevnitskaia's movables be taken away "without accepting any more refusals from her." But three months later, her husband was still not allowing the police to take the valuables to an auction, claiming that all the property was his, that his wife's debts could be paid out of the income from her rural estate, and that in any event he had the right to consider half of these possessions as his "untouchable property," thus applying to himself the law of 1846 that on its face was designed to protect wives and was specifically couched in feminine language.[64]

While it is clear that debtors were attempting to use the law of separate marital property to advance their interests vis-à-vis their creditors, the extent to which the latter were actually taken advantage of is not clear in some cases. For instance, Prince Vladimir Golitsyn was sued and declared insolvent because all the debts of the textile factory that he was running were in his name, although his wife and her two partners were the actual owners. Intriguingly, Golitsyn mentioned in his testimony that although the losses from the fire in the factory constituted his wife's share, they "fell" on him, perhaps because he was responsible for the accident. It is also possible that Golitsyn contracted to run the factory at his own expense.[65] It does, however, appear that the creditors were not able to positively establish who owned the factory and that this confusion was possibly created on purpose to make debt collection more difficult and to shelter the property of the three female investors.

While it was obviously difficult to catch someone of Prince Golitsyn's status in any obvious wrongdoing, the law was indeed strict toward another common abuse of the separate property rule, which consisted of one spouse issuing debt documents in the name of the other, without the appropriate power of attorney. As Margot Finn has shown for Victorian England, wives' ability to pledge their husbands' credit resulted in a great deal of litigation and legal uncertainty.[66] In Russia, this situation could result in a criminal proceeding, as beset the humble Moscow townsman Mikhail Loskutkov, who was placed on trial for issuing bills of exchange in his wife's name in 1853; he signed the documents because of his wife's illiteracy, which created an additional problem when she claimed that she never borrowed any money and never gave that authority to her husband. Loskutkov himself admitted during the interrogation that his wife knew nothing about these debts, although a creditor's servant testified that when he was sent to ask the Loskutkovs for repayment, it was the wife who requested a postponement. The wife, however, claimed that she was merely asking for a postponement until her husband returned home and was able to respond himself. The Chamber of Criminal Justice held Loskutkova's denial to be invalid, but she appealed to the Senate in 1863, arguing that she had not engaged in trade at all. The Senate ruled that Loskutkova was not to be held responsible because her husband admitted that she knew nothing about the loans, because she herself did not admit to anything, and because the bills of exchange were not properly registered with the municipal loan broker.[67] This case reveals the tension between formal law, which treated bills of exchange almost like cash, and regular civil law, which was more willing to accept outside evidence—and, surprisingly, the latter won.

The legal regime of separate marital property may have been instituted to protect noble families and especially noblewomen, but in the mid-nineteenth century, it served as yet another complex legal and business strategy deployed by property owners, one that was intimately connected with the culture and practice of debt. Court cases show that separating the spouses' property was rarely easy, even after the law of 1846 limited the kinds of property the spouse could legally hold to be his or her own. At the same time, the rule of separate property eliminated many other possible disputes, such as those that occurred in England because of the application of the law of necessaries.

In addition to using the regime of separate marital property to resist outside creditors, husbands and wives utilized the law to borrow from each other and to secure their interests at the other's expense. Such debt arrangements often provide insight into larger property disputes and the spouses' respective property-related strategies. One strategy was to contractually re-create the so-called dotal system, whereby the husband acquired the ability to use the wife's dowry in exchange for providing an equivalent amount of property as security in the event that he lost the dowry through bad investment or other circumstances.

This system, adopted in some mid-nineteenth century Continental legal systems, was not the default rule in Russia, where the dowry remained under the wife's complete control.[68] However, it could be arranged through a marriage contract. For example, in the 1850s, a lieutenant of the Imperial Guard, Prince Aleksandr Kol'tsov-Mosal'skii, issued loan letters for 7,500 rubles to his wife Elena (née Ghika, a well-known feminist and Romantic artist and writer who used the pen name Dora d'Istria).[69] According to the husband, this was done to enable him to repay his 5,000-ruble debt to a merchant's wife, Sofia Miller, for which debt Elena acted as a surety. When Elena sued her husband, he claimed that because he had already repaid Miller's debt, the loan letter should be nullified. However, the wife in her petition interpreted the story differently, arguing that her husband actually gave her the loan letter to guarantee the part of her dowry that she turned over to her husband to enable him to repay his other debts.

To support her claim, she sent to the Moscow Aulic Court from Florence, where she was living, carefully arranged and annotated extracts of her husband's letters that she had translated into Russian and had notarized by the Russian consul in Livorno. These letters showed that the prince had a habit of spending his wife's as well as his own property and was at least on paper feeling guilty about it. However, the court refused to accept copies of extracts of the letters as proof since the consul only certified the translations and not the original letters. Although Elena had no less a person working on her behalf than the future chief of the Third Section Aleksandr Potapov, she lost the first proceeding at Moscow Aulic Court, which held that her own petition admitted that the letter was "moneyless" because it was issued to guarantee her dowry. According to the court, Article 2017 of the Civil Code provided that loan letters "given in exchange for work performed, services, merchandise," etc. were still collectable. Incidentally, the legal scholar Konstantin Pobedonostsev in his treatise interpreted this rule as requiring that something of value be transferred—and here the husband clearly benefited by getting the money to pay this debt, which makes the decision appear incorrect. Unfortunately, the records from the rest of the case do not survive, so we do not know if this was its final chapter.[70]

Much more successful was another aristocratic woman, Anna Shevich, who held a "safekeeping note" from her estranged husband for 60,000 rubles. The couple exchanged arguments at the Aulic Court for over three years in 1863–1865. The husband recounted that Anna petitioned for divorce in 1862 in Kaluga, after an "unpleasantness" had manifested between them, and she moved to live with her father. The husband allegedly implored her to end the "unpleasantness," and the wife agreed but, knowing her father's dislike for her husband, suggested that the husband write a debt note in her name with the sole purpose of showing it to the father, thereby convincing him not to hinder the reconciliation. But having obtained the note, Anna remained with her father and stopped the proceedings in Kaluga, only to restart them in Moscow, and used the debt to persuade her husband not to hinder the divorce proceedings, by threatening him with a debt collection. The husband argued, rather convincingly to a modern reader, that his wife would hardly have loaned him 60,000 rubles while quarreling with him and engaging in divorce proceedings. The husband also submitted a letter from Anna, where, he claimed, she explicitly admitted that she was only using the debt to get the divorce:

> I cannot understand why you call [this note] moneyless. It is true, I did not give you the money precisely on the day you wrote the note, but it does state that the money was taken at different times. [*underlined in the original*] You should not think that I am tormented by the thought that I

want to proceed against you using a moneyless note, and I feel completely confident in this respect, because honestly I do not at all consider this note moneyless; this is not what I need, but rather [I am tormented by the fact that] I am compelled to employ such methods, which do not at all fit my character, and do not agree with my ways of thought. If there was not this other business between us, I would never even think to talk about this money, which I gave you not meaning to ever demand it back, and which I will never demand, if you will not hinder the divorce."[71]

Confronted with this letter, Anna claimed that it did not constitute a proof according to the Russian Civil Code and that, if anything, it showed that the debt was *not* moneyless. She was demonstrating a rather sophisticated understanding of the law, arguing that her statement that she did not in the future intend to ask for the money back was not a condition for the loan but simply an intention that could always change later. And even if the money did constitute a gift, she could demand it back according to Article 974 of the Civil Code because of her husband's "slander and clear disrespect." Whether or not the letter was a threat to her husband was completely irrelevant because it did not in any way suggest that the note was moneyless.

While it is not clear how the courts would eventually rule, the husband chose not to try his luck. As of March 1866, Anna Shevich was referred to as the wife of Titular Councilor Popov and was said to have gone abroad. Thus, the final resolution of the court was to close the case because the wife had "returned the note to her husband and thereby acknowledged that it did not require payment."[72] This case is perhaps illustrative of the pre-reform legal system in that it clearly shows some of the requirements for success in litigation: first, a certain amount of guile; second, access to qualified professional assistance; and third, recognition that the legal system was often more effectively used by threatening litigation than by an actual suit.

Another use of debt was to enable husbands to seize a portion of their wives' property that was officially off-limits to them. For example, another notable mid-nineteenth century female Romantic author, the major-general's wife Ekaterina Lachinova, signed a promise to her husband in 1837 to pay him 30,000 assignat rubles out of the 100,000-ruble dowry that her father was supposed to provide for her to pay for Lachinov's expenses during the first seven years of the marriage. The agreement was that if the father, Chamberlain Petr Shelashnikov (a wealthy tax farmer), did not pay this money, the husband could still recover this amount through the debt. In order to prevent "marital discord" between the spouses, the wife's mother acted as a surety. Lachinov sued his wife and her mother in 1847 but was unsuccessful.[73]

Another aristocrat who attempted to get his hands on his wife's property via debt was Prince Ivan Aleksandrovich Urusov, who in 1864 sued his wife, Yekaterina Ivanovna, pursuant to a loan letter for 10,000 rubles that had been issued in 1860. The wife presented as security an estate in Tver province but claimed the suit to be illegal, arguing that "the above-mentioned loan letter is moneyless, taken from me by trick during my difficult illness—in the last month of my pregnancy, and given by me with the sole purpose of providing for my husband's future in the event of my death, on the condition that he desist from collecting the debt while I am still alive."

Apparently, Urusova had allowed her husband to manage her property, and before a trip abroad in 1858 had issued a will under his persuasion, but seeing how he mismanaged her property and wishing to provide for her children, she nullified the will and instead issued the loan letter so as not to deprive him of a living in the event of her death. Urusova's petition reversed gender stereotypes:

> This current [debt] collection [proceeding] against me is even more unjust, because during the many years of our life together, my husband had no means of his own and all the maintenance of the house, children, and of himself was always effected, and is still effected, solely at my expense; my husband's capital, which he received after his father's death, was squandered by him before 1860, according to his assurances in order to improve my estate in Kaluga province and on various speculations; however, my estate not only was not improved, but rather was brought to a ruinous condition. But in October 1860 my husband did not have ten thousand rubles that he could loan me; otherwise, he should have been able to give exact directions as to when exactly and for what purpose I borrowed this kind of money from him, while being very ill and not leaving my room for several months, as well as where he kept this amount, in what kind of bills it was given to me and who else knew about this? Otherwise his suit is an abuse of my trust, with which he, not in any way helping me in bringing up five children and taking all of his maintenance from me, is using a document that was taken from me by deceit in the above-mentioned circumstances, to harm the entire family.[74]

At the end of this petition (composed by townsman Kusovnikov and presented to the court by Collegiate Assessor Zhuazel'), Urusova requested the police to investigate the "moneylessness" of the loan letter. The police forwarded the case to the Aulic Court without making any kind of determination or resolution, so the court sent it back, reporting to Urusova that once the police did make an official resolution, she could submit her petition to the appropriate court that had jurisdiction over her, in the event "she wished to begin a legal suit."[75]

It appears that dowries were often paid in debt documents, which is what Alexander Akakievich Demidov did when his daughter Anna married a former guard officer, Viacheslav Bolobonov. According to Anna, she gave her husband 15,000 rubles of her dowry and another 10,000 that she inherited from her mother to enable him to pay his debts and instead took debt documents that were not written up correctly. After their marriage failed, she continued to live on her husband's interest payments, and after he stopped making them, she petitioned the government in 1859 to make him issue her proper debt documents that would give her the same priority as her husband's other creditors.

The husband's version of the story could not have been more different: he insisted that he received not cash but his own debt documents for the money that he originally borrowed from his father-in-law. The weak spot in Bolobonov's claim was that he neglected to tear up these documents but instead kept them in his desk, and his wife managed to remove them. Bolobonov was compelled to continue his payments under the threat of having his estate taken over by a trustee, and in 1861, his property was going to be auctioned off because of his insolvency.[76]

A much easier solution for a spendthrift husband in need of money was to sell the wife's loan document to another person, which is what Gubernial Secretary Ivan Martynovskii did with the 10,000-ruble loan letter from his wife Avdotia. The husband sold the letter to merchant Andrei Eikhel', who in turn sold it to another merchant, Pavel Bronnikov. Once the demand for payment trickled back to Martynovskaia in 1853, she claimed that she had made the final payment to her husband, and she presented his receipt as well as witnesses who confirmed that she had to borrow money to pay off her husband, and that he had promised to tear up the letter. The receipt dated August 17, 1852, stated that the husband obligated himself to tear up the debt and was witnessed by Gubernial Secretary Timchenkov, the merchant's son Basarev, and State Councilor Kovalevskii. Merchant Novikov, hired to collect on behalf of Bronnikov, argued that the receipt did not indicate whether it referred to that same loan letter or some different one and did not contain the signature of the municipal loan broker *(makler)* or of Martynovskaia's sisters, who had signed the original letter as sureties. Eventually, Martynovskii was subjected to a criminal trial for forgery and "left under strong suspicion," which was the pre-reform equivalent of a suspended sentence. The trial did not determine whether Avdotia was responsible for the debt, and the creditors had to start their suit over again in a civil court.[77]

In addition to using debt notes in marriage, men used these notes to provide for women with whom they had illicit relationships. For example, Lidia Dmitrievna Telesheva, after a falling out with her husband, decided to buy a house in the name of her boyfriend, Prince Mikhail Mikhailovich Golitsyn, and in 1858 had him sign a loan letter for 120,000 rubles. They broke up shortly thereafter, but Telesheva never returned the debt document and instead sold it to a merchant who promptly sued Golitsyn.[78]

A similar story happened in the 1850s to Ensign Mikhail Ilyin, who had relations with a titular councilor's wife, Mrs. Rebi, who made him sign loan letters for 9,000 rubles. As Rebi transferred her affections to Mr. Schube, a riding-master at the imperial court, Ilyin's desperate wife petitioned the Third Section in 1857 to get the letters invalidated.[79]

Memoirist Dmitry Nikiforov, who was close to Count Asenii Zakrevskii, the notorious governor of Moscow under Nicholas I, recalled a scene when the governor was approached by a young merchant who inherited a fortune from his father and engaged in a life of carousing and drinking, which involved an infatuation with an "adventuress." In just a few days, the woman ended up holding debt notes for the merchant's entire fortune, and there was nothing to be done through legal channels to dispute the collection. Although the count was widely believed to despise Moscow's merchant class, he held a face-to-face meeting between the young man and his mistress, and having caught the latter in a lie, tore up the debt obligations.[80] For our purposes, it is important to note that the cultural attitudes at that time connected debt, especially moneyless debt, with sexual adventures.

This chapter contains the first systematic attempt to examine the links between credit relations and family and kinship structures in imperial Russia. While family members relied on each other to help cope with the burden of debt, they also used debt relations to assert their financial and other interests vis-à-vis each other. This applied to parents and children—who were required to bring their disputes to the special Equity Court—and also applied to spouses, who in Russia possessed separate legal personalities and readily took advantage of this legal regime. The legal rules deployed in such family conflicts and family strategies were likewise applied in a variety of ways. Most notably, the regime of separate marital property was used to fight off creditors' attempts to seize their debtors' property. But the law could also be deployed in strategies that were likely unintended by the legislator—for instance, by wives defending their interests or by husbands attempting to control their wives' separate property. In sum, the legal rules affecting debt and family structures appear primarily as instruments used to defend and promote property interests that were not necessarily the same ones that these rules were originally designed to protect.

Part **II**

_____

DEBT AND THE LAW

Figure 6.1a & Figure 6.1b. I. Alekseev, *A Group of Civil Servants* (1851)
Source: Kaluga State Regional Museum.

CHAPTER 6

Debtors and Bureaucrats

A LTHOUGH THE CULTURE of credit in Russia relied on the discretion and initiative of private persons, it was equally dependent on the machinery of the tsarist government. Unless a loan was completely undocumented and either repaid or forgiven without dispute, state institutions affected the transaction from the day it was registered and notarized to the day it was either repaid or resulted in a final judgment by a court of law. The preceding chapters of this book have explained how imperial laws regulating the culture of credit were applied in practice, from the prescribed forms for debt transactions to rules concerning individuals who could or could not participate in the credit network. This chapter, by contrast, focuses not on the legal rules themselves, but on the daily engagement of private debtors and creditors with government officials at all levels and on the interactions that took place after the procedure of incurring the debt but before the courts or bankruptcy boards became involved. This includes formal debt collection procedures carried out by regular police; semi-formal interactions in which higher officials such as provincial governors and gendarme officers used their police power to intervene in debt disputes; and examples of informal interactions including bribery and corruption, as well as out-of-court negotiations and settlements that were often carried out without any direct participation by officials but were motivated and guided by legal rules and the possibility of litigation or official sanctions.

Although Alexander Gerschenkron famously argued that the tsarist state generally exercised a positive influence on Russia's economic development in the nineteenth century, the more commonly accepted narrative is that of failure—that there was something fundamentally wrongheaded about the way Russia was governed. Many economic and institutional historians have argued that the Russian bureaucracy failed in its task to modernize imperial governance and introduce the rule of law.[1] One reason given for this failure is that the eighteenth-century police state, with its extensive administrative regulation of all aspects of life and an insufficient system of checks and balances, persisted into the nineteenth century when other major European nations began to rely increasingly on formally independent courts, public participation in politics, and civil society.[2]

Another line of reasoning emphasizes the persistence of the tsar's personal power, exercised at the expense of a bureaucratic apparatus that lacked a coherent structure and sufficient trained personnel.[3] Such talented statesmen as Mikhail Speranskii and the "enlightened bureaucrats" of the 1860s are seen as splendid but ephemeral and almost tragic figures who could not change the overall pattern.[4]

However, another line of inquiry takes advantage of the newly opened archives to focus on actual daily interactions between bureaucrats and ordinary individuals and considers such interactions on their own terms—that is, apart from Max Weber's model of formal rationality or Marx's model of the bourgeois state replacing a "feudal" one. For instance, Susanne Schattenberg and Richard Robbins show Russian provincial bureaucrats not as the traditional tyrants but as politicians and consensus builders who governed through personal influence and negotiating skills. While historians debate whether the Russian state was primarily an instrument protecting the nobility's interest, it is clear that the bureaucracy shared power with elites through various formal and informal channels, including elected offices, social interactions, and philanthropy, as Aleksandr Kupriianov shows in his study of pre-reform urban governance. Even ordinary townspeople and peasants were able to pursue their strategies and interests in their engagement with tsarist officials both individually and as members of their local communities, as Alison Smith has pointed out.[5]

In a similar vein, my contention is that the role of administrative and police officials in the daily running of the system of private credit was complex and brittle: it was neither a brutish imposition nor anarchy any more than it was an example of Weber's formal rationality. It is of course impossible to conceive of the tsarist administration as a neutral mechanism, but it is equally impossible to define it as unequivocally pro-debtor or pro-creditor. Whereas bureaucratic machinery operated in routine debt-related matters with reasonable efficiency, personal discretion and personal authority were an important counterbalance, whether in enforcing or resisting debt collections or negotiating private settlements.

It is not in itself striking to discover that the police and the bureaucracy were challenged by ordinary persons because this was routinely done even by members of the lowest orders of the Russian Empire.[6] However, the confidence, and even élan, with which supposedly downtrodden individuals picked fights suggests that the urban classes were prepared, culturally and mentally, to take an active role in political and social life. Contrary to the conventional wisdom that a politically conscious "middle class" was "missing" in Russia, urban Russians were able to deploy their wealth, their social status, and their knowledge of legal and other bureaucratic procedures to protect their property and to engage in a complex relationship with administrative authorities.[7]

Formal Channels: Debt Collection and the Police

Collecting debts was only one of the numerous tasks of the police in pre-reform Russia. In the mid-nineteenth century, Catherinian-era codes that set out provincial and municipal administration were still in force.[8] It is commonly pointed out that police officials in imperial Russia enjoyed exceptionally broad powers, especially compared with those of the pre-reform judiciary. At the same time, Russia was paradoxically underpoliced, even after the reorganization in the 1850s and 1860s. This was largely due to a very extensive list of responsibilities for policemen, combined with insufficient personnel, lack of training, and a low budget that encouraged corruption.[9]

The Petersburg and Moscow police were better trained than those in the rest of the country but were still spread thinly, largely reactive, and, I argue, completely dependent on the cooperation of other officials, on elected self-government, and on private individuals. Moscow, for example, was divided into seventeen precincts, headed by bailiffs and assisted by quarter overseers and quarter lieutenants. These officers were assisted by rank-and-file policemen who were conscripted soldiers without any special training in police work. Beneath them were the so-called "booth-men" *(budochniki)*, the beat cops who inhabited tiny huts spread throughout all the major streets and squares and were armed with medieval-looking halberds. In pre-reform Moscow, there were only four special "investigating bailiffs" who handled the more complex criminal investigations. Occasionally the governor general

Figure 6.2. The old court building on Resurrection Square, Moscow, 1870s

Source: N.A. Naidenov. *Vydy nekotorykh gorodskikh mestnostei, khramov, primechatel'nykh zdanii i drugikh sooruzhenii. Prilozhenie vtoroe* (Moscow, 1891).

delegated one of his "special aides" to help with the most important cases. Policemen were commonly retired military officers who obtained their positions through personal connections or as sinecures for distinguished service or bravery in battle; they had to learn their trade on the job. They tended to bring with them a military culture that during the reign of Nicholas I (1825–1855) emphasized drill and blind obedience to superiors.

Police debt collection involved three possible outcomes if the debtor refused or was unable to pay. The basic procedure was for the police to come to the debtor's home and to inventory and seize his or her property to pay the debt. Police officers were motivated to take this task seriously, because they could themselves be held liable for the amount of the debt if they allowed a debtor to escape.[10] A play by Ostrovskii, *Mad Money* (1869), depicts this process as routine, with a foppish character trying to raise the spirits of a profligate young noblewoman on the verge of insolvency: "What are you afraid of? Cheer up! Yesterday two of my friends got their furniture inventoried, today it's you, tomorrow it's me, and then your [friend] Kuchumov. This is the plague these days."[11] Nikolai Nekrasov, in a little-known 1840 semi-autobiographical prose piece, vividly described the matter-of-fact character of a routine debt collection in Petersburg: the landlord, the laundress, and the local shopkeeper came to the apartment of a penniless aspiring author with a policemen, seized all of his movable possessions, and threw him out without ceremony. They did show some regard for his potentially higher status by allowing him to change his clothes, and they did not see any advantage in placing him in debtors' prison, but there is nothing pro-debtor in that episode.[12]

The second option in the event that the debtor had no property or did not reveal its location was to arrest him or her, as long as the creditor paid the required prisoner maintenance fee. The third possible outcome was to transfer the case to the appropriate court if the debtor presented one of the enumerated defenses—for example, if the debt had already been repaid or the signature on the debt document had been forged. In such an event, the debtor still had to "secure" the case—that is, to post money or property in the amount under dispute, or, alternatively, present another property owner as a surety—or be arrested. The process was much more complex if the debtor was a wealthy person or if the property to be seized was a serf-populated village. Sometimes it was possible for the debtor to claim that he owned property higher in value than the amount of the debt and thus avoid imprisonment, but this was a tenuous argument, especially for individuals indebted to many lenders.

There were relatively few foolproof techniques for resisting lenders' demands. Unlike in the Anglo-American legal tradition, barricading oneself in one's house was not an option in Russia.[13] It was, however, possible to change one's residence without informing the creditors, albeit at the risk of being accused of fraudulent bankruptcy. Other strategies included getting help from family members or remaining in state service, because government officials were immune to personal arrest for debt as long as a portion of their wages went to satisfy their creditors.[14] Sometimes individuals served in a poorly paid or even preposterous capacity in order to evade their creditors. For example, the young spendthrift Count Dmitrii Tolstoy was serving at the Moscow Noble Assembly in the early 1860s solely for that purpose.[15]

It was a fairly common sentiment on the eve of the court reform of 1864 that the Russian justice system was in effect "geared to protect the debtor" by making debt collection overly difficult, so that some provincial nobles clamored for the reform in the hopes of making credit cheaper.[16] In practice, however, the efficiency of collection depended entirely on the parties' relative wealth, social standing, and connections, much as it did in any other legal system. After all, British aristocrats were widely criticized for being shielded from debt collection by their status, wealth, and privilege every bit as much as the Golitsyns, Naryshkins, and Yusupovs.[17]

Geographic proximity seems to have been a much more tangible factor than any arguable slant in the procedural rules: debtors with the means to do so could evade their creditors by moving to a different town. Memoirist, historian, and entrepreneur Dmitrii Nikiforov recalled how in the 1860s he was trying to collect a debt from Valerian Aleksandrovich Voeikov, who was something of a financial dealer despite his love of gambling, and who quickly moved from Petersburg to Moscow and back to evade the police.[18]

Russia's physical distances made debt collection difficult even for the most influential creditors. In 1847, long before the Great Reforms, a group of leading Petersburg merchants that included the banker to the imperial court, Baron Alexander von Stieglitz, obtained the tsar's personal permission to engage a Corps of Gendarmes officer, Staff Captain Kolomyitsev, to collect their debts in Moscow, Vladimir, Smolensk, Kaluga, and Nizhnii Novgorod provinces, arguing that they had trouble obtaining satisfaction from the local courts and police because of their debtors' relationships with police and legal officials. Kolomyitsev successfully bullied many of the debtors into paying or surrendering their concealed assets, and this appears to have been his special area of interest, but such a method of debt collection could obviously be used only by the best-connected creditors.[19]

The present study features numerous debtors, usually wealthy or at least propertied people, who lost their estates, shops, and factories, were declared insolvent, or were sometimes imprisoned despite their rank and reputation. Any pro-debtor slant is difficult to discern in Russia's actual legal practice apart from the fact that wealthy individuals indeed possessed more means to resist collection; yet, they were never collection-proof. Even in the eighteenth century, debt collection in Russia, while lenient toward aristocrats, was very harsh toward ordinary persons.[20]

Routine as it might seem at first glance, a police visit to a debtor's house or apartment, sometimes accompanied by the creditors, was inherently an exercise of power, involving searching, inventorying, and sometimes seizing such items as horses, carriages, merchandise, clothing, furniture, icons, silverware, books, and jewelry. In an age that discovered and placed great stock in the notion of privacy, the experience of having a despised moneylender rummage through one's bedroom and moneybox was humiliating indeed.[21] Debt collection could therefore easily lead to bitter personal and legal disputes. These were more complex and prolonged when debtors were either wealthy or influential, but altercations with police were not limited to the upper classes: even debtors from modest commercial and urban backgrounds were able and willing to resist collections through a combination of direct disobedience and official action. Suing a policeman directly was not permitted; any complaints went to the offending officer's superiors, who might not be inclined to pursue the matter. Nonetheless, at least some administrative complaints were effective, especially beginning in the 1860s, at the high point of Alexander II's liberal reforms. One such case began as a matter of routine debt collection but quickly turned into a conflict between a wealthy but otherwise ordinary Old Believer merchant and two noble-born police officers.[22]

On the evening of December 1, 1859, the recently appointed chief of the Prechistenka police precinct in central Moscow—a decorated veteran of the 1831 campaign in Lithuania with the unimposing surname Puzanov ("Potbelly")—received an order from the city's central police office to collect a debt from the younger son of a wealthy Old Believer merchant named Ivan Butikov.

In addition to owning a large textile factory, Butikov served as an elected judge on the Moscow Magistrate Court and was well acquainted with Moscow's bureaucratic world. Nonetheless, he chose not to enroll in the city's most prestigious first merchant guild and thus seems to have intentionally kept a lower profile than his wealth warranted. Moreover, at that particular historical period, in the late 1850s, Moscow's Old Believers were subjected to a particularly intense prosecution after the altars at their religious center at the Rogozhskoe Cemetery were sealed by the authorities in 1856.

The collection order against Butikov had to be executed by nine o'clock the next morning, and the chief handed the task over to a younger officer, a veteran of the 1849 Hungarian campaign named Shkinskii who had only recently been appointed to the force on the recommendation of the tsar's personal physician. Both policemen already knew Butikov well, only two weeks before having partaken of his hospitality at his wife's nameday celebration.

Shkinskii vigorously proceeded with his assignment. He assembled four policemen, a scribe, and two "good-faith witnesses," ordinary citizens delegated for the purpose, and marched to Butikov's house. In an operation that resembled a modern-day commando raid, Shkinskii posted policemen around the building and forced his way into the side entrance by waking up the doorman and "dragging him around by his arm" until he opened up the building to the police.

In the kitchen, Shkinskii found a cook and slapped him until he agreed to show the way upstairs with a candle. The entire company thundered up, meeting a chambermaid at the top of the narrow stairs. The "good-faith witnesses" just behind Shkinskii heard the chambermaid exclaim, "Why are you hitting me?" but did not actually see him do it. Butikov's eldest son, also named Ivan, appeared immediately on the landing and remarked that "this is a merchant's house and he [Shkinskii] was not allowed to rough-house here," upon which the policeman, according to his own testimony, pulled Ivan by his coat, and, according to Butikov's complaint, beat him up.

At this point, the senior Butikov woke up and came out of his room. With him Shkinskii adopted a different tone, claiming that he was merely delivering some important papers. To this Butikov—being no stranger to bureaucratic routines—replied that Shkinskii was free to come by whenever it was necessary but that "it is not proper to be noisy." Shkinskii then dispensed with the niceties and demanded point-blank either the money or his son, which Butikov promptly refused, further insulting the policeman by saying, "I will not give the money *to you*" and promising to resolve the issue later in the day at the police station. The policeman took offense that Butikov used the familiar *ty* to address him, but Butikov responded that *ty* was "God's word," and even the Savior was addressed this way.

According to Shkinskii's report, Butikov then gave a little speech to the "good faith witnesses" that, if true, revealed a familiarity with the political trends of the Great Reforms: "You demean yourselves [before the police], because in reality you are the superiors of the Quarter Overseer [Shkinskii], and not the other way around; the Sovereign does not trust the police, but instead trusts You, and therefore you should not listen to him (pointing at Shkinskii)." Butikov then said to the officer himself, "Don't you ever dare to visit either my factory or my house, otherwise I am going to see you off in a different way." This, no doubt, indicated that Shkinskii was no longer to partake of Butikov's customary hospitality to important local officials, which amounted to a form of bribery and patronage peddling. This would have been bad news for Shkinskii, whose financial well-being undoubtedly rested upon this kind of informal patronage.

While Shkinskii and the senior Butikov argued, the sought-after younger Butikov (Stepan), who was at first also present on the landing, quietly left the building, easily getting past the policemen stationed outside. Since Shkinskii's objective had clearly failed with Stepan's disappearance, the elder Butikov retired to his room, whereupon the policeman further humiliated himself by continuing to knock on Butikov's bedroom door, asking for Stepan and threatening to conduct a search and to write up a police report. In a verbal exchange that in its repetitious form resembles a folk tale, Butikov kept asking Shkinskii, "Why are you here, what do you want," as if he did not already know, and replied to the policeman's demands, just as confidently as before, that he simply would not allow the police to conduct a search, and as to the report, he was free to write two reports if he wanted, but he, Butikov, would provide neither ink nor pen for that purpose. Shkinskii was then induced to gather up his entourage and retreat to the police station to write his report there. It is remarkable that the household of a wealthy merchant, such as Butikov, could not be protected against a sudden police raid, but Butikov was able to rally and fend off the police after they had already penetrated all his defenses.

In the morning, Puzanov, the precinct bailiff, summoned Butikov in the hopes of persuading him to surrender his son. The old man was detained for several hours, during which time he had another verbal altercation with Shkinskii and then with Puzanov, who also became offended at Butikov's use of the familiar form of address, to which Butikov responded that he even addressed generals in this way, and that in any event, he had for many years "lived in concord with the police and even frequently patronized them." Obviously, Butikov's notions of living in concord with the police were different from those of the policemen themselves, and he was prepared to enforce his view. Notably, during his detention Butikov was not constrained or harmed in any way other than having his overcoat taken from him. Puzanov had to let him go when a procuracy official showed up at the police station and saw Butikov there.[23] However, policemen were stationed around Butikov's house day and night to seize Stepan if he returned home.

The old merchant hired the "well-known" Moscow lawyer Aristov and initiated a series of petitions to the city police chief, the governor general, and the head of the Third Section. Butikov's petitions adopted two lines of attack: the first was to point out that Stepan's debt was in dispute and that, in fact, the policemen were attempting to collect on a debt obligation that had already been determined to be bad by their own superiors. The second line of attack was to emphasize the rudeness and invasiveness of Shkinskii's visit, the harm to Butikov's business reputation, and the "dishonor" inflicted upon him "in the opinion of the public." All of the complaints were written in simple language, characteristic of the higher-level, better-educated bureaucrats of the time and entirely free of the convoluted legalese typical of Russian daily court practice well into the 1860s. The documents did not burden their high-profile audience with citations to any particular legal statutes, but made it perfectly clear exactly which of Butikov's legal rights had been violated.

Butikov's complaint went to the Moscow governor general, Pavel Tuchkov, and was assigned to his aide Shimanovskii, who outranked the bailiff Puzanov. Shimanovskii's investigation did not at first produce any satisfactory results. Shkinskii and the other policemen were protected by the Moscow police chief, Prince Kropotkin, and they did their best to avoid an interview with Shimanovskii, engaging instead in a vicious quarrel over control of bureaucratic language. The issue was that Butikov's testimony was initially recorded through a procuracy official who provided dictation for the record, no doubt to provide a smoother narrative. One of Shkinskii's fellow officers, Smirnov, who was also interrogated by Shimanovskii, thought that this way of doing things favored Butikov and refused to sign the protocol, provoking Shimanovskii's fury. Shimanovskii's interactions with the local policemen are notable as a collision between "high" and "low" bureaucratic cultures during the Great Reforms, the former represented by the highly educated governor's aide and the latter represented by boorish and not very literate ex-soldiers. Furthermore, this altercation points to an unlikely alliance forged in the course of the investigation between a schismatic merchant and the tsar's "enlightened" bureaucrats, who in only a few years were to carry out the reforms.

The policemen successfully stalled the investigation until April 1860, when Shimanovskii received another complaint against Puzanov, this time from a lowly police scribe named Nikolskii. The ostensible reason for this complaint was Nikolskii's fear of being implicated in the investigation because his boss Puzanov allegedly ordered him to tamper with the police report to show Butikov's behavior in an unfavorable light. Nikolskii also alleged (1) that Puzanov had illegally detained Butikov at the police station; (2) that Puzanov lost Nikolskii's service certificate; (3) that Puzanov searched Nikolskii's property without cause; (4) that Puzanov freed from arrest his brother's household serf, who was found to possess counterfeit banknotes; and (5) that Puzanov embezzled the money assigned for transporting prisoners.

These allegations conveniently provided Shimanovskii with a strategy to rid the Moscow police of Puzanov. In order to demonstrate his objectivity, he launched an inspection of all the police precincts, most of which, including Puzanov's, were found to have some required documentation missing and some trivial irregularities in their account books. When asked why he was unable to keep the books in proper order, Puzanov replied that he was new to his position and was overwhelmed by emergencies happening in the large city, such as fires, robberies, and dead bodies found on the street. When asked why he considered these ordinary events to be so overwhelming, he responded that he was new at his job and to him any incident seemed like a huge emergency.

Shimanovskii eventually achieved his goal. As of early 1861, the case had been closed due to the "discharge of the person against whom the complaint was brought, which turned out to have been substantiated in part." The term for "discharge" *(uvol'nenie)* did not necessarily mean dismissal for cause, as it does today—it could also refer to a voluntary departure—but it is hardly conceivable that Puzanov would voluntarily leave his lucrative position so early. In March 1861, Butikov's attorney certified that he would discontinue the case and had no further claims against Puzanov, who had been dismissed, or Shkinskii, who appears to have kept his job, possibly because of his court connections through the tsar's physician.

In sum, Puzanov absorbed the punishment for his subordinate's rudeness as well as for his own, and Butikov vindicated his honor in a rather round-about way. This much does not depart from the stereotype of Russian bureaucratic routine. It is, however, striking that Butikov thought himself superior and in a position to act condescendingly toward the city police. Police officers, still employing brute physical force, appear as more subaltern here than the schismatic merchant, who was not supposed by historians to have that kind of influence in the mid-nineteenth century. Butikov's wealth allowed him to overcome two noble-born and decorated, though uncouth, policemen not yet used to paying the proper respect to Moscow's merchant class. The policemen's superiors both in Moscow and in St. Petersburg—among Russia's most powerful statesmen—were perfectly capable of smoothing over the affair as a misunderstanding, but at the same time clearly believed it was important to placate Butikov in some way.

While Butikov was much wealthier and better connected than most Muscovites, his case was not an isolated incident. For example, the "foreigner" Viktor Rozetti, a 35-year-old Lutheran son of a French music teacher who worked as a traffic agent on a railroad, had a similar confrontation with the police in 1864.[24] When the police came to his house to inventory his property, he refused to cooperate, claiming that everything in the house belonged to his mother and sisters. Notably, the police did not simply break the moneybox after Rozetti refused to surrender its key. Moreover, when a policeman reminded him that he was acting on the orders of the police office *(Uprava)*, Rozetti said "with fervor" that "the *Uprava* means nothing to me, I want to shit on the *Uprava*, and you I can just kick out." The police did not beat or arrest the recalcitrant man but simply left, ordering him to be at home the next morning. The police ruling about the incident was that Rozetti's words were proven by two witnesses, and so he could be prosecuted, but it was not proven that the policemen could consider themselves under threat, and therefore Rozetti was to be merely placed under house arrest.

Rozetti, however, submitted his version of the story to the court, claiming that he was a "well-bred" person and never allowed himself insolent expressions about the police. He complained that the police showed up without warning and "charged together with some other persons into my sisters' bedrooms," adding that a "well-behaved person should not enter ladies' rooms without permission." Rozetti also accused the two police witnesses of having taken part in the mayhem. The court did not accept this accusation, which after all would have undermined the very purpose of employing public witnesses in police operations. Finally, Rozetti argued that his house arrest would prevent him from working. The police responded that it would not be possible to inventory Rozetti's property without going into the rooms and that Rozetti's sisters were not present. While the police officer admitted that he had not been endangered, he noted Rozetti's "excitement, disobedience to the Sovereign Authority, and insolence" and explained that he had refrained from his search so as not to increase this insolence.

The Aulic Court first freed Rozetti, pending trial, so he could continue with his job and then ruled that although Rozetti was clearly guilty of insulting the police, he had acted in a state of irritation that might have been induced by police actions, and so he should be given a talking-to *(vnushenie)*. This ruling, like many others of that period, had been prepared beforehand, with a blank left for the exact punishment, into which the word *vnushenie* was inscribed.

Rozetti perhaps could afford to be insolent because he was educated, but the state peasant Nikifor Semenov certainly was not.[25] He was an illiterate 40-year-old engaged in the gilding craft. In 1863, he was summoned to a police station, told that his property was to be inventoried to satisfy a debt claim by the peasant woman Alekseeva, and asked to accompany the police to his apartment and be present during the inventory. Semenov then pronounced unspecified "indecent and insulting" words about the police, for which a policeman was dispatched to take him back to his apartment. However, Semenov sat down on the pavement in the middle of the street and started to scream, "Help! The police are robbing me." It is likely Semenov knew that without him the police were not legally permitted to conduct the inventory. After the inventory finally started, he again began to curse, to push the public witness, and to threaten the policeman with a beating. When later interrogated about the incident, Semenov revealed some knowledge of legal procedures by challenging the police witnesses on the grounds that they served the officials who were complaining about his behavior. The case file is incomplete, but it is sufficiently clear that even a peasant in the 1860s was not afraid to enter into an altercation with the police and had some idea about its procedures.

While Butikov's experience and relations in the world of officialdom facilitated the successful outcome of his feud with the police, we should not exaggerate their impact.[26] It was not connections alone that helped him but rather his knowledge of bureaucratic practices, along with the acknowledgment by high-ranking state officials that protecting his honor—closely related to his business reputation—was a valid and important concern. A similar concern for protecting personal honor and financial interests is found in Rozetti's case; although his obvious culpability resulted in his acquiring a criminal record, there was no real punishment. Finally, Semenov was an uneducated bankrupt who nonetheless had a rudimentary sense of legal procedures and perhaps was even aware that the more open political climate of the mid-1860s made it acceptable for individuals to assert themselves against police actions. Of course, neither Rozetti nor Semenov had Butikov's money, which allowed him to purchase the services of a top lawyer, who, in turn, helped Butikov to access the policemen's superiors using their own "enlightened" language. In sum, the assertiveness of Moscow's urban and commercial groups in the mid-nineteenth century was based on a combination of factors: knowledge and manipulation of bureaucratic jargon and practices, the power of money that brought control of legal expertise, and links of patronage and acquaintance. Individuals' concerns for property interests were closely linked with concerns about honor and kinship, all of which were also shared by government officials of all ranks.

Governors and Gendarmes as Arbiters

One of the most common criticisms of the attempt to develop the rule of law and a rational bureaucracy in nineteenth-century Russia focuses on the prerogatives of provincial officials and especially provincial governors, who were given extensive powers by Catherine II's 1775 statute establishing a uniform system of local government.[27] Of all administrative officials, the provincial governors exercised the most direct daily influence upon the courts' operations, both formally and through their informal personal influence. Their powers steadily grew during the first half of the nineteenth century. The law of 1837 referred to governors as the "master of the province" and greatly increased their authority, especially by subordinating the provincial administrative board *(gubernskoe pravlenie)* that was originally established as a collective organ but then became little more than the governor's secretariat.[28] Governors controlled the police, and the police collected debts, imprisoned debtors, assessed and seized debtors' property, and could even remove undesirable individuals from the city. At the same time, the police could not directly cancel a debt; even if a lender was expelled from the city, the debt itself could still be sold or transferred to another person. This fact no doubt induced most borrowers to negotiate rather than go to the authorities.

In addition to their police powers, governors had extensive judicial functions, especially before the 1864 reform. The most important judicial role of the governors was to review and approve criminal sentences that involved the loss of estate-specific legal rights and penal exile. Criminal issues routinely came up in debt disputes, as in the cases of fraudulent bankruptcy or when a debtor alleged that the signature on the debt document had been forged. If a governor disagreed with the court's ruling, he could not change the sentence but only forward the case for further review by the Senate. Late imperial jurists and historians regarded this authority as exemplifying pre-reform courts' lack of independence from administrative officials, but post-Soviet scholars have shown that the extent of the governors' interference with criminal justice in practice was "insignificant."[29] Aside from these provisions, the law of 1825 explicitly prohibited governors from stopping the implementation of a court decision, much less vacating it or "allowing a digression from its precise meaning."[30]

Governors did however control pre-trial procedures and could, for example, order their aides to investigate a particularly important or complicated criminal case. Also influential was the governors' personal informal network of influence, which usually helped with their appointment in the first place and which often included a direct personal link with the tsar, as well as peers from prior military or civil service positions, friends from their home region, and relatives who were numerous indeed for most of Russia's old noble families. On some particularly notorious occasions, these networks of influence allowed corrupt governors to remain in their positions for decades. For example, Alexander Panchulidzev, who served as the governor of Penza from 1831 to 1859, was associated with organized criminal groups, took bribes, and embezzled with impunity, thanks to his connections both among local elites and back in Petersburg.[31]

The governor's authority was particularly noticeable in Moscow because of its geographical distance from the imperial court and the highest bureaucracy. Whereas in the eighteenth century governors had changed every few years, in the nineteenth they often ruled for extremely long terms, essentially as mini-tsars; for example, Prince Dmitrii Vladimirovich Golitsyn served from 1820 to 1843, Prince Vladimir Andreevich Dolgorukov from 1865 to 1891, and Grand Duke Sergei Aleksandrovich from 1891 to 1905. The most controversial long-term "master" of Moscow was Count Arsenii Andreevich Zakrevskii (1848–1859), a hero of the war of 1812, whom Muscovites referred to simply as "the Count" and remembered for his suspicion of any free thinking, for his arbitrariness, and for his dislike of merchants and moneylenders that eventually led to his downfall.[32] In short, after his dismissal he became a symbol of arbitrary and despotic rule associated with the Nicholaevan epoch.

To many observers, Zakrevskii's personal authority appeared to be above the law. The lawyer Nikolai Davydov recalled that he was the "true master of the capital" and that "the entire population submissively and quietly obeyed the decrees, customs, and commands that were not always justified by their contents, but to violate which seemed to be almost a mortal sin, and in any case an act of extraordinary bravery."[33] Ilya Selivanov, who headed the Moscow Chamber of Criminal Justice from 1855 to 1862, recalled that Zakrevskii believed that "the law was not written for him and that he was permitted anything" and that throughout his term of office, Zakrevskii "through various very transparent hints let everyone believe that he had carte blanche and that he could do anything he considered to be appropriate. Only after his removal from Moscow did it turn out that he did not have carte blanche and that he did not have any more power than any other governor general." As a result, Zakrevskii "created such fear in Muscovites that they did not dare to say a word even when he became involved in such circumstances of their family lives that were not any concern of his, and over which he did not have any legal authority."[34] In his memoirs, Selivanov hints at his own association with Herzen and other political exiles, and so his depiction of Muscovite submissiveness is clearly polemical, but the general sense of Zakrevskii's powerful personality and personal involvement in the city's daily life is unmistakable.

At the same time, it is clear that this general dislike of Zakrevskii stemmed not simply from his mandate from the tsar to maintain order in Moscow in the wake of the European revolutions of 1848; another important reason was that he was an outsider in Russia's networks of power and owed everything directly to the tsar. The real Zakrevskii was anything but a gruff simpleton, since in 1812 he had headed Russia's military intelligence service. However, he was poorly educated and came from a noble family that was neither wealthy nor well connected. His wife, Countess Agrafena Tolstaia, was a wealthy heiress and a famous beauty, but she was nonetheless shunned by Moscow's aristocratic circles. Boris Chicherin recalled that even at the height of Zakrevskii's power, Muscovites liked to attend his grand balls but avoided getting socially close to his family.[35]

This lack of social standing limited Zakrevskii's patronage network compared to that of the more aristocratic governors, and so his apologists were far fewer than his enemies. Memoirist Dmitrii Nikiforov was one of the few acquaintances who continued to visit Zakrevskii after his eventual disgrace and thought that he was fundamentally a "truthful" man who in extreme circumstances bent legal rules to achieve justice. Nikiforov thought it a positive thing that Zakrevskii "could not stand usurers." On one occasion, he personally tore up the bills of exchange issued by a profligate young merchant to an adventuress who had seduced him, and in another case he kept a moneylender waiting in his office, unable to intervene, while a noblewoman who asked for his help was busy executing and registering a sales agreement that was going to place her property out of that lender's reach.

These stories appear to be perfect examples of Zakrevskii's arbitrariness and contempt for the law, unless one realizes that in the former episode, the "adventuress" was given the opportunity to present her case in front of Zakrevskii himself and that in the second case Zakrevskii had to use a rather risky subterfuge rather than exercise his power in a more direct way.[36] Even in his dealings with lesser-ranking provincial officials, Zakrevskii preferred political maneuvering to open confrontations. For example, Zakrevskii's ill-wisher, Selivanov, the chief criminal judge in Moscow, noted that while the count ordered him placed under police surveillance, he did not have the authority or the power to simply get him removed and eventually had to use another official as a go-between to repair their relations.[37]

Restrictions on governors' powers included a senior Corps of Gendarmes officer posted in each province, whose task was unofficial oversight over the governors. The elected provincial marshals of the nobility came from distinguished and wealthy backgrounds at least as influential as those of the governors themselves. It was an unwritten custom for the governors and the marshals to be at loggerheads with each other. It appears to have been quite easy for a powerful marshal to use his Petersburg connections to induce the Senate to appoint an inspection that could recommend the governor's dismissal, which is what happened, for example, to the Kursk governor Andrian Ustimovich in 1850.[38] The key legal officials did not depend on the governor for their careers. This applies, most importantly, to the chairmen, assistant chairmen, assessors, and even secretaries of the provincial Chambers of Civil and Criminal Justice, all of whom were either appointed from Petersburg or elected by the local nobles or merchants. Even some of the most important police officials, at least in major cities, were appointed by the tsar personally. Finally, a governor was supposed to remain an outsider in his province, in which he was not supposed to own any landed estates.

Thus in debt disputes governors served as arbiters rather than as overwhelming authority figures and were themselves subjected to many checks and limitations, even when their mandate was unusually extensive. Although governors could and often did intervene in property disputes, they could not do so indiscriminately. I have not located any evidence of personal and direct intervention by Zakrevskii or by one of his immediate successors in debt disputes that had already entered the court system. The count could order a creditor to drop his claim on pain of administrative reprisals, but he could not directly order the judges of the Criminal or Civil Chamber to rule against this creditor. Needless to say, the governor could attempt to influence the proceedings secretly and informally, and Zakrevskii, for example, had a reputation for bribery.[39] However, even in criminal cases his authority could not be taken for granted: judges in Moscow courts had no qualms about disagreeing with his views on specific criminal law issues.

As a general rule, even in pre-reform Russia, administrative officials appear to have respected the integrity of the legal process and intervened directly only in a specific set of circumstances, such as a potentially criminal issue emerging from a disputed debt, especially one that affected a sufficiently large number of persons to threaten public order, or when pre-reform evidence laws did not permit any redress of a wrong that was abundantly and clearly established by circumstantial evidence. Moreover, officials intervened not by contacting courts directly but rather operated outside the judicial process by exerting their personal influence, as well as by using their considerable police powers. It is remarkable, though, that in many cases one or more sides to a dispute openly resisted a governor's or the gendarmes' persuasions and insisted on continuing their lawsuits and even imprisoning their debtors while themselves being threatened with financial ruin.

One example from 1857 illustrates the nature and the extent of a governor's personal direct intervention to sanction an individual who could not be disciplined through legal channels. A Class 12 official, Aleksandr DeMazer, was subjected to a criminal trial for embezzling from a wealthy female serf owned by Count Sheremetev, who wanted to purchase a house in DeMazer's name.[40] There were several witnesses to confirm the transaction, but only one agreed to testify under oath, and under Russia's system of formal proofs, this evidence was not sufficient to convict DeMazer. The judges of the Criminal Chamber left him under the "strongest suspicion" and recommended that the governor order his expulsion from the city. Shortly after this ruling, Count Zakrevskii ordered DeMazer to be removed from Moscow as "unreliable" and "harmful to the capital city." However, DeMazer remained the legal owner of the property he embezzled. This case thus shows both the governor's power and its limitations: while neither he nor the judges were able to help DeMazer's victim, they allowed the legal proceeding to run its course and then acted to the extent of their authority to prevent DeMazer from continuing his dishonest practices, as long as his property rights were not openly violated.[41] Ironically, the case also shows that courts were not too averse to leaning upon the governor to achieve their goals, as opposed to the opposite situation that is usually assumed. Another example of such cooperation was recalled by Selivanov, who talked Zakrevskii's more liberal and law-abiding successor, Pavel Tuchkov, into approving an obviously incorrect criminal sentence to avoid the mandatory review by the Senate in order to save two Old Believer youths from being sent to Siberia for blasphemy.[42]

In cases when no criminal proceedings were initiated, the governor's ability to influence the outcomes was even more limited. Consider the previously mentioned case of Ivan Butikov, who complained of misconduct by police officers when they broke into his house in an attempt to arrest his son for debt.[43] Simultaneously with the governor's investigation of the police's actions, his office was also investigating the usurious activities of the junior Butikov's lenders. Governor Tuchkov chose to intervene as directly as he ever did by summoning Butikov's creditors to his office and "urging" them to settle their claims against Butikov out of court. Two of the creditors, merchant Sabanin and a civil servant Ivanov, made a "good-faith settlement" with Butikov, but the third creditor, Gubernial Secretary Logotini, despite all the "urgings," refused the settlement and petitioned to proceed through "legal channels." Then in June 1860 Tuchkov and the chief of gendarmes, Prince Dolgorukov, agreed that because it was not "possible to compel Lagatini [sic] with administrative measures to end the case," it was necessary to continue the legal proceedings but on the condition that Logotini, as a "reprehensible usurer," be expelled from Moscow.[44]

If it were true that Russia's administrative officials disdained the law and legal procedures, how can we explain the fact that Tuchkov and Dolgorukov could not simply prevail upon the police or the courts to stop the proceedings against Butikov, which contined in the prescribed fashion? Even more remarkable is Logotini's steadfast refusal to accommodate the officials; perhaps it can be explained by his hopes of greater liberalization in the early 1860s, but in any case it suggests that his property was more important to him than official favor.

On some occasions the governor's interference could have even less effect. In a case similar to the previous two, moneylender Semen Briukhatov was put on criminal trial for defrauding the nobleman Abramov, whose loan was secured by a landed estate with serfs.[45] This was only part of an extensive investigation by the governor's office of Briukhatov's predatory lending practices with respect to approximately ten other young men of property. The special commission established by the governor's decree on March 16, 1865, included Colonel Sochinskii (from the procurator's office), a procuracy official, Pavlovskii, Colonel Voeikov from the Corps of Gendarmes, and Mr. Saveliev, the special aide to the governor general. Despite all this pressure against him, Briukhatov continued to keep Abramov imprisoned for his debt and even induced him to come to a settlement, which Abramov later managed to rescind.

A similar situation beset the insolvent Count Dmitrii Tolstoy, whose father notified the Gendarmes that one of the creditors, a "baptized Jew" named Gorodetskii, took advantage of Tolstoy's youth and took debt notes for twice the amount actually borrowed. In response, gendarme Colonel

Voeikov wrote that Gorodetskii had on "many occasions" evoked "critical comments" for engaging in illegal usury and that he had gone as far as to take the young count's personal clothing. While the anti-usury sentiment of the Moscow upper classes and of the authorities is not surprising, it is remarkable that the collection and insolvency proceedings against Tolstoi continued despite the involvement of the gendarmes and only stopped when the father reached a settlement with his son's creditors.[46]

While in most of these examples the governor's intervention was directed against an alleged predatory lender, authorities were by no means always pro-debtor. In fact, the Moscow governor's archive—although ravaged by Soviet-era "systematizations" and "expert evaluations"—contains numerous petitions by individuals complaining that their debtors were maliciously evading payment and asking for his special intervention.[47] What could the governor do for such persons? Consider the case of retired private Leiba-Srulevich Sumgalter, who had served in the Moscow police force for twenty-eight years and retired to Zhitomir province.[48] In December 1859 he traveled back to Moscow to collect a 118.50-ruble debt from townsman Krasil'nikov and spent several months trying to negotiate with Krasil'nikov and then going through police collection and the courts. Eventually Sumgalter petitioned governor Tuchkov to summon Krasil'nikov to his office and induce him to pay Sumgalter's traveling expenses. Interestingly, this is exactly what Tuchkov did on January 19, 1861; even more interestingly, Tuchkov's personal interview with Krasil'nikov seems to have had very little effect upon Sumgalter's ability to collect because Krasil'nikov proceeded to hide his property with relatives and then was declared insolvent. And of course, the governor's most potent power of expelling the debtor from the city in this situation would not have been very helpful. Sumgalter was only able to collect a portion of the amount owed to him several years later by placing Krasil'nikov in debtors' prison, from which he was ransomed by the Imperial Prison Committee.

In addition to pleading with the governor and his subordinates, individuals could turn to other officials of comparable rank, such as the minister of justice and the minister of the interior, and to the Third Section, whose officers were frequently called to intervene in debt disputes. As noted earlier, the Third Section functioned as an alternative system of last-resort justice by investigating particularly important criminal cases, as well as civil-law disputes when one of the sides petitioned for its intervention. Its directors could be approached by individuals in difficult legal circumstances, both by wealthy and sophisticated ones, and those clearly from middling ranks. However, the gendarmes' involvement in debt cases could not be taken for granted even in high-profile cases, and achieved mixed success. For example, in the 1845 case of Lieutenant Rakhmanov in Petersburg, the creditors agreed to cut their claim by 85 percent after the gendarmes' invervention.[49] In 1859, Lieutenant General Sergei Sergeyevich Golitsyn, a highly decorated war hero imprisoned for debt in Petersburg, petitioned the Third Section to be released in order to earn money and repay his debt. Initially his five creditors would have none of it, but the gendarme Colonel Rakeev started an investigation into their lending practices, which quickly persuaded them to change their minds and to assert that they had never had any idea of inflicting inconvenience on the good general.[50] In the fraud case of Princess Ekaterina Cherkasskaia, a Commercial Bank official named Zaborovskii—who supplemented his income by lending money—was convicted wrongfully and swiftly, most likely because of the intervention of a gendarme, a Colonel Tolstoy. Eventually Cherkasskaia's embezzling estate manager Konovalov repented and sent written confessions both to the Moscow governor and to the minister of justice, Count Panin. Perhaps because of these high personages' special attention, Zaborovskii's initial conviction was quickly invalidated.[51]

However, in the course of the previously discussed 1859 investigation of alleged usurers by the Third Section, the gendarmes made no effort to broker a settlement between General Buturlin and Vasily Chestnokov. The Third Section could also limit its involvement to notifying the local authorities that the case enjoyed its special attention. For example, merchant Butikov in the course of his vendetta against the Moscow police petitioned the chief of gendarmes, Count Shuvalov, who wrote to Governor Tuchkov asking him to give his protection to Butikov if his allegations proved to be true. No separate investigation was initiated, however.

Earlier in the nineteenth century, before the Third Section was established, such complaints were addressed directly to the tsar, such as in the 1805 case of a wealthy Moscow merchant, Goriunov.[52] Although Goriunov's retail buildings next to the Kremlin wall were sufficient to cover his debt, he was declared a "bankrupt" under the 1800 Bankruptcy Code. He was kept imprisoned for long periods of time, made several deals with his creditors, was allowed to continue to manage his property, but was then imprisoned again. Much as in the Butikov case sixty years later, Goriunov's complaint was forwarded to the Moscow authorities without any specific and direct command or instructions that could predictably affect the outcome. It seems that the value of these petitions was not in producing a specific governmental action but rather in showing local officials that their actions were being monitored by their superiors.

The grandees of Nicholas I's reign, such as Count Zakrevskii and Count Benckendorf (the first chief of gendarmes), were obviously unable and unwilling to help every person who petitioned them. In a case involving a less prominent petitioner with no significant properties or any possible threats to public order, a high official could simply forward the case to one of his subordinates, who might not choose to expend his efforts. This is what happened in another fraud case involving a civil servant, Dmitriev, who had served as an agent for the wealthy Glebov brothers and continued to borrow in their name long after being dismissed from their service.[53] In that case, one of the victims, no novice in the world of Moscow officialdom, complained to Count Benckendorf, who transferred the matter to his subordinate, Major General Perfiliev, who did not seem particularly sympathetic to her case: his questions to the woman suggest that he was somehow more suspicious of her than of the perpetrator of the crime. From this and other similar cases it is clear that the tsar's governors and ministers did not seem to think that they had to personally affect the outcome of every case in which their assistance was summoned.

Much like the governors' interventions, those of the gendarmes could fail. State Councilor Alexander Varentsov, married to the daughter of Collegiate Assessor Prince Fedor Andreevich Golitsyn, had a debt dispute with his father-in-law in 1863. The gendarmes in the town of Tver, where Golitsyn resided, staged what they called "mediation proceedings" and urged Golitsyn and his attorney to settle the dispute amicably. However, the old prince positively refused to budge, stating to the gendarmes that he could not drop the case as a matter of principle. Moreover, his response to the letter from the Third Section was rather cheeky: "I cannot fail to inquire, why an exception was made for my son-in-law from the general Law under which all of us Russians live and which requires that every dispute and every suit must be initiated in a Judiciary institution, before which I stand as a direct and obedient respondent." In their internal correspondence, the gendarmes referred to Golitsyn's "unscrupulous stubbornness" and noticed "a shade of irony" in his communications with the Petersburg military governor, General Prince Suvorov, suggesting that the gendarmes were getting involved in a matter that was of little concern to them. Although Prince Golitsyn was obviously a usurer, perhaps because of his family name there was not even a hint of exiling or otherwise harassing him in the manner in which less well-connected lenders were sometimes treated by the Third Section.[54]

Even individuals who lacked a prestigious surname and lived in far less favorable financial circumstances could reject the gendarmes' mediation. For example, a former guard officer, Viacheslav Bolobonov, a spendthrift without any wealth or particularly helpful connections, flat-out refused the attempt by a gendarme officer, Colonel Koptev, to get him to provide for his estranged wife.[55]

It thus appears that government officials, most importantly provincial governors and officers of the Third Section, had at their disposal significant means to influence court proceedings, both through their legally mandated authority and through their personal informal influence and prestige. However, a set of practical considerations limited excessive exercise of this authority. They tended to intervene in debt-related cases only under a predictable and defined set of circumstances—for example, when public order was at stake or when unusual criminal proceedings were involved. Officials were clearly unable and unwilling to personally intervene in every case in which a litigant requested their patronage. In cases in which bureaucrats did intervene, their influence affected the proceedings but did not necessarily determine the outcome, mostly because they were unable or unwilling to directly subvert court proceedings but rather chose, or felt compelled, to respect established legal procedures and especially the legally established property rights of the litigants, even those who engaged in behavior that was condemned by society, such as predatory lending.

In other words, officials could harass lenders or borrowers, but they could not simply void the debt or seize the debtor's property without following the required procedures. A danger of denunciation and bureaucratic rivalries, as well as the practical inability to intervene in all important cases, limited even informal influence to a very circumscribed set of facts. Neither Count Zakrevskii nor Leontii Dubelt nor Prince Vasilii Dolgorukov appear to have had any special kind of respect for the courts of law. Rather, a routine bureaucratic demarcation of power was most likely the chief motive for their relative moderation. Nonetheless, the effect of this demarcation was to provide pre-reform courts with considerable space in which to exercise their function.[56]

Corruption and Bribery

From what has been discussed so far, it is clear that the criticism of Russia's pre-reform legal system as being informal in the Weberian sense—that is, basing its decisions upon some outside non-legal criteria such as the political will of the sovereign or the interests of a particular legal estate or population group—should not be exaggerated. Such influences were significant but not automatic or necessarily determinative of the outcome. Obvious follow-up questions concern the effects of bribery and other forms of corruption, as well as the influence of kinship and personal friendships, which, as we already know, were central to the operations of Russia's network of private debt.

Of course, direct evidence of corruption is always difficult to identify and evaluate. However, researchers are aided by the fact that Russian pre-reform legal procedure was almost entirely written, courtroom rhetoric was nonexistent, court petitions were frequently prepared by individuals without formal legal training, and the petitions tended to focus on technical legal argumentation, making the subtext easier to identify than is often the case with post-1864 court proceedings. Recent studies on the practices of reciprocity in Russia that are based on archival evidence persuasively argue that bribery must not be regarded as inherent in Russian mentalities or culture, that it could serve an important social objective of leveling power relations between government officials and private individuals, and that official corruption was greatly reduced by the turn of the twentieth century.[57]

As part of Russia's culture of credit, extra-legal intervention appears not as a dichotomy between corruption and honesty but rather as a continuum, one end of which was akin to lobbying and the other end consisting of outright bribery. For example, calling upon a powerful relative in a difficult situation was an obvious strategy. When the elderly Princess Ekaterina Cherkasskaia became a victim of fraud, her first action was to "invite the assistance" of her nephew Colonel Begichev and of the gendarme Colonel Tolstoy. These two officers helped her to contact the police and presumably kept an eye on the investigation. Wealthy Muscovites strove to make friends with police officers, inviting them to their houses for meals and giving them gifts. In the Butikov case, the wealthy Old Believer merchant cultivated a good relationship with local policemen and even "patronized" them (*pokrovitel'stroval*—a striking word to apply to one's relationship with police), thus making his abuse at the hands of a local police officer particularly outrageous in his eyes.[58]

Court cases routinely contain allegations of one of the sides being friendly with a judge, reflecting the fact that judges from first-tier courts were elected from the same social milieu as the litigants, as well as the common recognition that personal connections could affect outcomes. For example, in the debt collection case of Colonel Nikitin in the early 1850s—distinguished only by the wealth and sophisticated knowledge of the law of both litigants—the defendant, Actual State Councilor Surovshchikov (equivalent to a major general in the army), claimed that his creditor had "acquaintance and friendship" with one of the judges on the County Court, Vinogradov, and had him replaced by a judge delegated from the Aulic Court.[59] More than ten years later, at the beginning of the reform period, Collegiate Secretary Vasilii Gruzdev complained that the Moscow Aulic Court ordered a criminal investigation against him solely out of its collusion with his debtor. Gruzdev complained to the Criminal Chamber that the lower-level Aulic Court appeared to consider itself entitled to do "everything on its whim" and that it was concerned more with expanding, rather than reducing, its caseload. As a busy civil servant, he was irritated at losing time and energy by being implicated in a completely baseless criminal investigation. The Criminal Chamber agreed and immediately closed the case.[60]

Outright bribery was also rampant, and even the highest officials, such as the Petersburg governor Peter Pahlen or Minister of Justice Viktor Panin, famously had to bribe lowly court clerks.[61] However, many such bribes, while illegal, in effect functioned as fees for the clerks' services, compensating for their extremely low official salaries. For example, Pahlen had to pay only 100 rubles as a bribe to speed up the sale of his house, not an exorbitant amount, considering that the sale had to be completed in three days, the time period given him by the tsar to wind up his affairs and leave St. Petersburg.[62] Many memoirists made this distinction explicitly: Feliks Luchinskii, serving as a petty police official in the 1850s and 1860s, recalled that the important distinction was not how large the bribe was but where it came from. Thus, in Kiev and its environs, bribes essentially served to supplement a policeman's meager salary and were sometimes levied by local property owners to prevent the more predatory type of bribe taking.

By contrast, in nearby Kherson province, bribery was far more widespread because police officials were under much weaker control by the local governor.[63] Bribery was similarly institutionalized in Riazan province in the early 1860s, according to Peter Kostyliov, who served as the court investigator in the small town of Rannenburg.[64] Even in the Senate, Russia's highest appeals court, the over-secretaries tasked with reporting cases sometimes owned nice brick houses, and, according to Ivan Bocharov, charged a contingency fee for reporting a case in a favorable way, promising to refund the money if the senators failed to heed their persuasions.[65]

Selivanov's account of criminal justice in Moscow in the late 1850s suggests that bribery was strictly regulated within each department or institution: for instance, secretaries to the aides to the Moscow governor not only did not "dare" to take bribes but "simply could not . . . take one step" without their bosses' permission.[66] Surprisingly, Nikolai Kolmakov, a reform-minded jurist and memoirist, argued that the bad reputation of the old courts for bribery was based on the fact that the Civil Chambers included a records office that was overworked and required relatively small payments to speed the process of registering sales, loans, wills, and other contracts. Post-reform notaries charged that fee openly, whereas in pre-reform courts, an "immature" public opinion considered these to be bribes and impugned all court personnel.[67]

Individuals who could not rely on powerful friends and relatives had more limited options. For instance, the former Commercial Bank employee Aleksei Zaborovskii was wrongfully convicted of defrauding old Princess Cherkasskaia but was eventually cleared after the true criminal, Konovalov, repented and confessed. However, during the investigation that eventually cleared him, Zaborovskii was indicted for destroying evidence that he may have persuaded Konovalov to change his story, for having his brother bring presents to the police investigator, and for coaching his serf and his fellow prisoners to testify in his favor. Although in the end Zaborovskii was only sentenced to a church penance, this case shows in detail the methods available to an average Muscovite from the "middling" classes who did not have any special leverage to influence the police and court officials.[68] In another case, a townswoman, Ekaterina Bulasheva, seeking revenge against a pawnbroker, collegiate registrar's wife Elizaveta Pereshivkina, apparently bribed several individuals with criminal records to falsely testify on her behalf. Bulasheva's stratagem was discovered, and she came close to serving time in the Moscow Workhouse.[69]

Failure to follow the informal rules of bribery could lead to unpleasant consequences. Several years after Zaborovskii's case, the Aulic Court judged Collegiate Councilor Lebedev, who seemed to be completely inexperienced in that art.[70] Lebedev was an elderly professional "mechanic," from the family of a junior officer. Lebedev's rank corresponded to that of an army colonel but, unlike its military equivalent, only conferred "personal" noble status as opposed to hereditary nobility; however, he married a noblewoman who owned 48 serfs. Despite his poor health and lack of children, Lebedev had a good position at the Moscow Palace Office and a good pension of 571.84 rubles. In his old age, Lebedev decided to become a serfowner himself by purchasing the estate of Titular Councilor Kologrivov at an auction that was to be held on September 25, 1862.

However, Lebedev was intimidated by the bureaucratic procedures involved and in particular was intelligent enough to fear that the officials would contrive to sell the estate without its accumulated stocks of rye, hay, and straw, which constituted much of its liquid value. Lebedev wrote a letter to the secretary responsible for the auction, named Mikhail Tsvetkov, asking him for assistance with the sale and promising twenty-five rubles for his labors. Either this letter was read by the wrong person or the amount was too small, but this proved to be Tsvetkov's chance to show his probity by reporting Lebedev. During the auction itself, in the presence of all the officials and potential buyers, Moscow's civil governor asked Lebedev whether it was he who had written the letter. Lebedev admitted he had and his case was sent to the Moscow Aulic Court.

During his interrogation, Lebedev testified that there were many legal problems with the estate he was trying to buy and that it was only natural for him to offer Tsvetkov a compensation for his labors, which he was not otherwise obligated to perform for Lebedev, and complained that Tsvetkov's denunciation *(donos)* was a grave moral insult to him and his family, considering that he had spent thirty years in government service.

At the same time, Lebedev did not hesitate to write a letter asking for help from his old acquaintance and neighbor, whose name, unfortunately, was not mentioned, in "providing protection against the hostile actions of Mr. Tsvetkov, which inflicted great sorrow on me and my family, about which I am induced to ask you more in order to sooth my family." Lebedev maintained that he wrote the letter to Tsvetkov "without thinking" and "offered gratitude out of kindness of my soul and not doubting the Christian kindness of Mr. Tsvetkov's soul, as well as because of my inexperience in such matters," which he could not acquire by working in a technical field.

Lebedev also claimed that he did not offer the bribe forcefully or persistently, but only "in the event this would be allowed, and not with the intention of gaining anything for my profit." Whether it was the intervention of the old friend, or the Aulic Court's good judgment, the court gave Lebedev a warning for "merely asking for permission to offer a gratuity to a public official, even if for his official labors [as opposed to in exchange for doing something illegal]."[71]

Compared to the sporadic interventions of highly ranked bureaucrats, personal informal connections and influence that ranged in character from outright bribery to the exercise of political patronage were clearly more widely used in debt-related legal proceedings. However, I found that these attempts were neither universally available nor invariably effective, especially once a case was transferred from the lower-level courts, with their links with local society, to more professional intermediate-level provincial chambers and the Senate. When the opposing sides were relatively evenly matched, they did not hesitate to challenge each other on the grounds of having some special unfair advantage, such as a relationship or acquaintance with one of the judges.

It is precisely such evenly matched disputes of prosperous property owners that remained beneath the notice of the critics of pre-reform courts who mostly wrote at the end of the nineteenth century. Notwithstanding contemporary critics' rhetorical abuse, corruption and the influence of patronage and political connections complemented formal legal rules and procedures but do not seem to have fundamentally undermined or compromised them. Moreover, if corruption were all-powerful and determined the outcome of every case, as some extreme critics of Russian law would have it, such a level of corruption would have made legal rules and institutions meaningless, thus making it pointless for individuals to try to subvert them.

Bargaining in the Shadow of the Tsar

The practice of civil law before and during the Great Reforms involved intense interpersonal communication and negotiation, both within and outside the court system. High-stakes litigation was time-consuming, unpredictable, and expensive, and so it is not surprising that the legal process involved informal negotiation and that cases could be resolved without ever reaching judgment. Out-of-court settlements were by no means always fair, but they were an additional mechanism for asserting individual interests and resolving disputes when a formal trial was not desirable. In the United States today, even non-lawyers are aware that an overwhelming majority of cases are settled out of court. This is, of course, far from a recent phenomenon, as one article on a seventeenth-century local court in England has shown.[72] Robert Mnookin and Lewis Kornhauser, in their landmark paper focusing on U.S. divorce law, emphasized the continuity between formal legal adjudication and the social processes of negotiation, viewing law "not as imposing order from above, but rather as providing a framework ... [to] determine ... rights and responsibilities." The court's function in some cases examined by Mnookin and Kornhauser could legitimately be limited to merely approving—even rubber-stamping—private negotiations.[73]

Despite the advantage of reducing costs by settling out of court, some cases are still litigated for a variety of reasons, such as the desire to punish the other party rather than increase one's net worth, a distaste for negotiation or distrust of the opponent, calling the bluff on a party that makes excessive threats, overestimating one's chances of winning, or the impossibility of dividing up the object of dispute.

Other modern-day legal scholars have also noted that legal considerations, in turn, affect private negotiations; for example, Herbert Jacob has argued that the practical effect of a legal rule depends on the way a claim is framed— that is, whether people initially articulate their problems in legal terms, the involvement of lawyers or other intermediaries, and the use of informational networks, that is, whether one's friends and relatives encourage legalistic thinking. For example, Jacob found that debtors in the United States who knew other individuals who had gone through bankruptcy were more likely to avail themselves of that procedure.[74]

Imperial Russian law explicitly promoted informal dispute settlement both before and after the 1864 reform. Pre-reform civil procedure included detailed provisions for out-of-court settlements *(mirovaia sdelka)*, arbitration *(treteiskii sud)*, and arbitration commissions that could be established for indebted gentry landowners *(posrednicheskaia komissia)*.[75] The pre-reform legal system, in other words, was structured similarly to the system described by Mnookin and Kornhauser—as a framework for individuals to resolve disputes that could not be solved through negotiation and arbitration.[76]

Anecdotal evidence suggests that bargaining typically began long before the commencement of legal proceedings. Alexander Miliukov narrated the story of a bankrupt merchant in Moscow who held a dinner party for all of his creditors, during which he kneeled in front of them and offered to settle his debts for 25 percent. The cleverness of this strategy was that all the creditors had to make their decision in each other's presence and risk ruining their reputations—and, consequently, credit—if their behavior was not approved by their peers.[77] More commonly, it was the creditor who commenced the bargaining by visiting the debtor and demanding payment. Nikolai Makarov recalled that in 1860 he was trying to collect a debt from one "Excellency" (presumably a high-ranking civil or military official) who was refusing to repay his debt of 1,400 rubles. Makarov wrote with satisfaction and even glee that he "stormed" the debtor's dwelling, created "fright" in his office, and recovered the debt, "which, without my speed and energy, would have only smiled at me and remained forever in the bottomless pocket of the Excellency."[78]

It was also routine to settle debts after beginning litigation. One very typical example is the debt case against Collegiate Registrar Nikolai Dolbinin that was begun in 1856 by the Moscow townsman Lev Spiridonov, who wanted to collect 4,950 rubles in bills of exchange issued by the Vladimir townsman Kornil Medvedkin, who claimed that he had never issued them.[79] The rather confusing investigation of who owed what to whom continued for almost ten years, until in 1864 Spiridonov petitioned the court that he wanted to discontinue the claim because he had had a "reckoning" with Dolbinin. The Criminal Chamber closed the case in 1867 because of the mutual reconciliation. Another similar case began in January 1859, when a Moscow merchant (in her own right), Irina Vorobiova, submitted a debt claim for 1,112 rubles against another Moscow merchant, Ivan Isaev.[80] A literate 48-year-old who "knew the laws of the Russian state," Isaev claimed that he did not know or have any dealings with Vorobiova but did borrow 400 rubles from her sons. Then, on March 30, Vorobiova and Isaev submitted a joint petition to close the case because, upon a mutual accounting, this debt ended up being "void." The chamber was happy to oblige, although it took until 1867 to issue the final ruling, as it was obviously not high on the court's priority list. In these and other similar cases in which a debtor denied signing the bill of exchange, the courts did have the option of continuing proceedings despite the parties' reconciliation—thereby earning extra income from fees and bribes—but they chose not to exercise it.[81] However, there were cases when a settlement could be reversed, as in the case of Sumgalter discussed above, in which the creditor was offered a partial payment by the debtor's father-in-law but apparently was unwilling to forgive the remainder of the debt, for which reason the payment was revoked and the litigation continued.[82]

It is clear that court action could be only incidental to the process of mutual negotiation and accounting among the parties to a dispute. Settlements could be worked out even after many years of litigation, as, for example, in the Tvorogova case, which involved a debt claim against the highly ranked Prince Dolgorukov, who for many years successfully delayed Tvorogova's claim. In 1859, seventeen years after the suit began, Tvorogova's property was taken under trusteeship, and her son, no doubt realizing that he was unlikely to win in court against one of the most important bureaucrats of the empire at the time, reached an agreement with Dolgorukov to discontinue their suit: Tvorogova's son would not demand payment of the debt, and Dolgorukov would not ask for the damages, fees, and penalties that would be due to him had he won the case. However, Tvorogova's trustee, a civil servant named Kuzmin, would not agree to stop the suit but petitioned the court that his case was "righteous" *(pravoe)* and that he could not see what kind of damages Dolgorukov might have suffered in the case. Both the Noble Trusteeship Board and the courts agreed, and as of 1863, the case was still ongoing.[83]

In addition to mutual accounting and negotiation, another important aspect of settlement involved debt forgiveness. The tsars were known to pay the debts of their favored servitors, although sometimes a servitor refused the gift.[84] In 1805, Alexander I offered to pay the debts of Petersburg governor Count Peter Tolstoy as he was leaving his post to join the army. The tsar noted that others in similar positions retired with fortunes, but Tolstoy instead had came to ruin. However, Tolstoy refused the favor, ostensibly not wanting to be an example to spendthrifts.[85] Vasilii Gettun, the memoirist who narrated this anecdote, had himself both benefitted from debt forgiveness and extended it to others, such as when he destroyed the debt documents received from the Engelgardt family, whose court case he lost as their representative.[86]

While cases of debt forgiveness by private persons commonly involved debtors from humble ranks, one notable exception was the 1871 case of Colonel Nikolia.[87] A well-off engineer and entrepreneur, he became insolvent, but his creditors, impressed by his new patent for using old rails to construct bridges and other buildings, were willing to free him from "all consequences of insolvency" in exchange for a payment of 3,000 rubles over the course of five years, 40 percent profit from the patent, and the eventual 100 percent payment of all debts. One of the creditors, however, protested, citing Nikolia's previous business failures, and proposed to continue the operations of his bankruptcy board. Apparently it could be a bad idea to be the last creditor to hold out; in 1865 old Count Tolstoy bought up his son Dmitrii's debt and had his insolvency case closed, although some of the Moscow moneylenders resisted. The last creditor to hold out had to eventually settle with the count instead of selling his claim.[88]

The more common kind of debt forgiveness cases involved impoverished debtors who clearly had no hope of repaying. The peasant Voronov forgave the debt of one of his workmen, townsman Viktor Lebedev, "because of his poverty."[89] A "trading" peasant woman Mavra Bubentsova, who made her living selling fish, became insolvent, and her daughter offered to pay one percent of her debt as a settlement. However, the creditors "condescended" to her "ruined and impoverished condition" and discontinued "all collection" against her.[90] A 52-year-old Moscow merchant, Sofia Tepfer, was indicted for selling off her late husband's movable property instead of turning it over to his creditors.[91] She claimed to have done it out of necessity to feed her children and because of her "extreme poverty." She submitted a special certificate of her poverty from the senior Lutheran pastor in Moscow. The Moscow Magistrate Court sentenced her to a year in the workhouse but ruled "to pass no judgment on this matter" because the creditors had discontinued their claims against her. In another case, townswoman Maria Lebedeva, who claimed to be a music teacher, rented pianos from various Moscow music shops, and then proceeded to pawn them, but was absolved from criminal responsibility by one of the pawnbrokers because of his consideration for her repentance and because she had small children.[92]

Despite these cases, it would not be accurate to conclude that "settlement" usually meant that a debtor was able to avoid paying the full amount or that Russian courts were slanted in the debtor's favor. The opposite kind of situation was also common, with a creditor having considerable leverage vis-à-vis his debtor and forcing him to enter into a clearly disadvantageous settlement. For example, Collegiate Secretary Semen Briukhatov, a prominent Moscow usurer, was indicted in criminal court for defrauding nobleman Nikolai Avramov from Tiraspol'.[93] Briukhatov apparently purchased the estate of Avramov's uncle without paying the promised amount. In revenge, Briukhatov had Avramov placed in the debtors' prison in Moscow for his 15,000-ruble debt. After about six months, in March 1866, Avramov and Briukhatov submitted a joint petition to the Moscow governor general, asking him to discontinue all prosecution of Briukhatov. Avramov emphasized that the case was basically civil in character and that "a peaceable settlement is permitted not only in civil cases, but also in criminal ones." He asked that all the relevant documents be returned to Briukhatov, that the interdiction be removed from his property, and that he be allowed to go abroad for medical treatment.

However, only six days later, Avramov submitted another petition to Governor Dolgorukov, claiming that "being deprived of freedom, which is extremely necessary to me because of my other affairs, devastated morally by my misery, with my health completely ruined, I was in desperate circumstances and hardly in possession of my reason. . . . Briukhatov, having learned that the investigation of his actions was taking an unfavorable turn, suggested to me to stop the case by settlement. Excited simply by the thought of freedom ... , I gladly accepted Briukhatov's offer." In exchange for dropping his claims, Avramov would be freed from prison and get back the purchase agreement for the land Avramov was selling, as well as the moneyless bill of exchange that was in Briukhatov's possession. However, Briukhatov did none of these things, for which reason Avramov asked the authorities to consider the settlement void.

A similar impasse occurred in the case of nobleman Vladislav Khlopetskii, who was trying to collect money from the university student Ivan Chulkov.[94] The debtor turned out to have been a minor, thus making the debt void. However, Chulkov himself was going to be prosecuted for fraudulently misrepresenting his age, and in the end it was worthwhile for the two of them to settle; in the end, Chulkov paid the debt, and both parties petitioned the court to close the case because it was all a "misunderstanding which cleared up at our personal meeting." The police and the Aulic Court accepted this story and closed the case.

Pressure to settle a lawsuit could also occur completely outside the legal framework and involve "peer" influence. One memorable example is the case of the young Prince Nikolai Obolenskii, who owed 14,500 silver rubles to a major general's wife, Anna von Bussau, possibly as part of a complicated inheritance arrangement.[95] The case record includes the following curious document:

> Certificate:
> We, the signatories below, certify, according to our conscience and honor, that Lieutenant Prince Nikolai Obolenskii, at the apartment of Anna Pavlova, Major General's widow von Bussau, on the sixteenth day of this August, 1863, in our presence, brought his apology for still not paying her his debt pursuant to the loan letter for 15,000 rubles, and, inviting us to be witnesses to his words, offered her to pay in the beginning of this September, 1863, nine thousand rubles, promising on his honor to pay the other six thousand rubles at the first opportunity. In certification of which we issue this certificate which includes our seal and our signature. Saint Petersburg, August 20, 1862 *[sic]*. Signed: Major-General Maleev, Gubernial Secretary A. Kametetskii, Major De Galet[96]

Von Bussau clearly enrolled the help of her kinship and acquaintance network to tie down her reluctant debtor. It is also virtually certain that her late husband was Major-General Wilhelm von Bussau, who was killed in battle on the Malakhov redoubt in Sevastopol in 1855, which would explain the special attention shown to his widow by other members of Russia's service elite.[97] However, the solemn ritual seems to have had little influence on Obolenskii's determination not to pay that debt. On November 22, von Bussau petitioned the Aulic Court, claiming that Obolenskii had visited her, asked to finish this affair "peaceably," and offered settlement conditions, which she rejected because she no longer believed his promises. She attached the draft settlement agreement brought to her by Obolenskii:

> We below-mentioned have concluded between us a peaceful resolution in regard to the property division between me and my sister . . . , according to which my part is to include ___ [serf] souls in the Beltsy County of Tver province, which souls with their apportioned land have been already submitted for redemption. The redemption certificates that are to be received I will turn over to von Bussau to satisfy [my debt] . . . the rest of the money will come from a "merchant's bill of exchange" for ten years.[98]

This note suggests that Obolenskii intended to take advantage of the impending liberation of the serfs and pay with the redemption certificates issued by the government to serfowners as payment for the serfs they were losing. Von Bussau's reluctance no doubt stemmed from the fact that redemption certificates were to be redeemed by the government only in the remote future, and in the near term, if she wanted to benefit from Obolenskii's payment, she would have to sell them at a considerable discount.

In sum, it appears that out-of-court settlements could be used by individuals from all property-owning groups and involve a variety of strategies and arrangements. They could favor either creditor, debtor, or both. A settlement could involve a commercial arrangement or a charitable debt forgiveness; it could reveal either a legal stalemate, or, to the contrary, a realization by one of the parties that he or she could not win the dispute. Settlements therefore reveal another, less formal aspect of pre-reform legal practice, showing that the organizational structure introduced by Catherine II in 1775, which delegated an important role to the less formal dispute resolution mechanisms, found its manifestation in actual court practice and that pre-reform civil law, in this important sense, could serve as a mere background framework for private negotiation and debt restructuring.

The tsarist bureaucracy is often interpreted as powerful yet archaic and brittle and thus unable to deploy the empire's resources with the same efficiency as Russia's Western European competitors. But on the level of daily practical interactions, the culture of personal credit and, by extension, of private property depended on negotiation and compromise between property owners and government officials of all ranks. Private individuals, even those who were not particularly wealthy, routinely bribed, made friends with, and on occasion openly challenged the police or even such mighty figures as Moscow's governor general, all in order to protect their property or their reputation. Court procedures were available and readily deployed, but so were out-of-court settlements designed to avoid prolonged legal battles.

Officials' ability to manipulate and even subvert the law was real, and so were daily bribery and influence peddling. However, both statutory law and governmental practice maintained the courts' relative autonomy from other officials, even though provincial authorities did exercise certain limited judicial functions. Even the highest-ranking officials who had the power to circumvent the law could not expect to openly violate it without jeopardizing their careers. The written character of court procedure and the relative accessibility of appeals ensured that bribery and corruption could not by themselves determine litigation success. At the same time, the power of such emperors as Nicholas I or Alexander II was inconceivable apart from a robust regime of private property protected by a bureaucratic and legal system but also dependent upon individual discretion and initiative. Daily corruption in the context of this system therefore appears as just another stratagem in debt disputes and not a factor that would have made the law unworkable or unpredictable.

CHAPTER 7

In the Pit with Debtors

THE DEBTORS' SECTION of the Moscow Provisional Prison, known colloquially as the "Debtor's Pit" *(Dolgovaia Yama),* was a major part of the city's culture of debt, despite its complete neglect in historiography.[1] Although the number of its inmates was small compared to its English counterparts or even to Petersburg's debtors' prison, the Debtor's Pit and its legends left their mark on the city's cultural memory, figuring prominently in popular guidebooks and descriptions of the city, as well as in the famous sketches of Moscow life by Vladimir Giliarovsky.[2] More importantly, debt imprisonment illustrates several key aspects of the daily interactions between private individuals and the tsarist state.

First, the process of debt imprisonment illustrates that imperial Russia's authoritarian political regime, especially before the reforms of the 1860s, relied on private discretion and initiative for many of its everyday functions. Debtors were arrested at the request of individual creditors and imprisoned at their expense, a surprising concession of what we today view as a major prerogative of the centralized modern state. At the same time, private discretion was limited in scope because the government refused to privatize prison operations. Moreover, the fact that creditors had to pay for prisoner upkeep limited their discretion to cases when imprisonment was either economically profitable or at least emotionally satisfying.

Second, what we know about the conditions of the imprisoned debtors shows that they occupied a peculiar position between free persons and the mass of Russia's prison population, thus bringing into question the extent of the rights granted to the tsar's subjects, and especially the meaning of individual freedom and of its deprivation.

Third, imprisoned debtors were regularly set free when their debts were paid by anonymous private donations, including those from members of the imperial family, usually on important religious and dynastic occasions. These rituals of redemption thus forged emotional and symbolic connections within propertied groups, as well as links with the imperial family and with their Orthodox faith.

History and the Law of Debt Imprisonment

As was the case with all other legal rules related to property ownership and control, the ability to imprison one's debtors was used by individuals as a strategic and negotiating tool, with much of the bargaining power favoring creditors. Debt imprisonment raised complex legal issues concerning the legal remedies that should be available to private persons, the nature of punishment, and the distinction between civil and criminal law. Lawyers and statesmen queried whether private law remedies could properly include effectively holding one's debtors hostage for ransom or, conversely, punishing them with prison for not being able to repay, or whether there was a way to view imprisonment as somehow nonpunitive. The logical implications of such inquiries, as well as the evolving understanding of debt from a moral to an economic failure, led most Western legal systems, including Russia's, to reform and gradually abolish debt imprisonment in the second half of the nineteenth century. In England, as Margot Finn has shown, debtors' prisons, despite their often-abusive practices, could serve as shelters for their inmates, protecting them from their creditors' arbitrary authority. Inmates themselves exercised considerable autonomy in their affairs. In the course of the mid-Victorian reforms, wealthier debtors were gradually freed from the menace of the debtors' prisons, whereas the poorer ones began to be subjected to an increasingly punitive regime that assumed and enforced their moral defectiveness.[3]

Debt imprisonment in Russia was significantly influenced by the English model in the early nineteenth century and developed along a similar trajectory—but with some rather telling deviations. In early modern Russia, debt collection had typically involved measures against a debtor's person, especially when the debt was commercial in nature and the debtor did not possess any property that could be easily sold. The procedure known as *praviozh* (also used to collect tax arrears) at least theoretically involved daily beatings of the debtor until he paid up or the mandated time period had lapsed, in which case the collection was then directed against the debtor's property.[4] Considering that commercial debts typically required cosigners, failure to pay would expose the debtor's partners or friends to beatings as well. Indentured service for debt was also available: under the Law Code of 1649, creditors could claim the debtor's labor at the rate of 5 rubles per year, a considerable sum; lesser amounts were counted for women's and children's labor.[5]

In 1700 Peter the Great reaffirmed the *praviozh* system and required that if it failed to produce results, the debtor was to be beaten with a knout and sent to penal labor in the southern fortress of Azov for three years, where, in the unlikely event of survival, he was to be subsequently resettled. If there were several creditors, one of them could pay off the debt and acquire the debtor as his permanent indentured laborer. The decree also suggested that the way this harsh law was evaded in practice was by use of a front man in whose name the debt obligation was issued and who would be the person beaten and exiled in the event of nonpayment.

Consequently, it is not surprising that in 1718 another decree abolished *praviozh* and instead granted delinquent debtors a six-month grace period, as long as they could provide a guarantor; if no payment was made, both the debtor and the guarantor—and if the debtor had died, then his wife and children—were required to be employed on the galley fleet as rowers or, if unfit, then on other state projects or—for women—in the Petersburg Spinning House for life or until they worked off the debt. Creditors were paid one ruble per month for each person, but debtors' wives were apparently not counted.[6] Yet debt collection during the early eighteenth century often continued to be a violent procedure, and the violence could go either way; for example, in 1714, one creditor arriving with witnesses and a police bailiff was beaten by the debtor and his friends with clubs and a rifle butt.[7]

A more durable alternative to pure debt slavery was to bind debtors not to their creditors but to third parties. In the eighteenth century, indentured service for debt became common and was known as *partikuliar*. This term, officially decreed in 1736, referred to the remedy's "private" character. The rate according to the 1736 decree was at least 24 rubles per year.[8] Although this system would have been reasonably efficient for smaller debts, the legally mandated fees could not possibly repay larger loans. A 1795 memorandum from the Moscow city police chief to the city governor argued that the arrangement whereby someone with multi-thousand-ruble debts went to work for 24 rubles per year in effect allowed spendthrifts and "bankrupts" to escape their obligations, considering that even an unskilled laborer at that time received at least 60 rubles per year. The proposed correction in the police memorandum was to indenture those debtors who became insolvent through no fault of their own to the highest bidder and to sentence the more blame-worthy bankrupts to penal exile.[9] Apparently the city authorities followed this recommendation at least in part because a later page from the same document contains a list of debtors indentured to work for as much as 100 rubles a year, although most were still fetching between 24 and 30 rubles. At the same time, the Moscow magistrate compiled a list of fifty-one debtors who wished to enter indentured service, including four women.[10] The fact that the debtors' wages were not officially adjusted suggests that *partikuliar* was not in practice used to effect repayment or to punish debtors but rather served as a form of bankruptcy discharge, if the debt was large, and as a set-tlement between debtors and creditors, if the debt was moderate. Indentured labor seems to have fallen out of use by the first half of the nineteenth cen-tury and was abolished in 1834.[11]

Debt imprisonment per se was also commonly used by the end of the eighteenth century, especially after Russia began to acquire an organized prison system under Catherine II. A 1793 list of imprisoned debtors from Moscow province included very small numbers of individuals who agreed to serve as indentured laborers. For example, in Kolomna there were only two such individuals out of eighty prisoners in the town jail. It is unclear, how-ever, how many of these eighty were debtors and how many were ordinary prisoners.[12] In Moscow itself, imprisoned debtors were numerous enough by the beginning of Paul's reign to participate in an elaborate redemption ritual in 1797.[13] Although provinces without large cities did not have specialized debtors' prisons, debtors could still be arrested. For example, memoirist Feliks Luchinskii (Luczynski) recalled that in the Ukrainian town of Cherkasy in the 1840s, "if a debtor did not pay . . . he would be locked up [by the police] in a cold room and kept there until he paid up."[14]

Like many other Russian laws relating to debt, debt imprisonment was for the first time regularized by Tsar Paul's Bankruptcy Statute of 1800. One key innovation was that individuals could no longer be arrested for debt if they had sufficient property to cover what was owed.[15] Debtors who were unable to repay and had no property could be subjected to arrest. Officially insolvent debtors who were subject to bankruptcy proceedings could also be arrested at their creditors' discretion while their case was being processed, and they could be held for up to five years if they were found to be "reckless" bankrupts. Finally, individuals could be imprisoned in lieu of "securing" civil lawsuits against them if they could not post property sufficient to cover the amount of the suit or find a friend or a relative who had enough property to guarantee the suit. In the English and American systems in the eighteenth and early nineteenth centuries, in some notorious cases, debtors grew old in prison. In contrast, in the French and Russian systems officials were not eager to increase their prison population; in Russia the length of imprisonment for any one claim was limited to five years. However, until the reform of 1864, a debtor who had served this time continued to be liable for the debt if he or she later managed to acquire any property. Moreover, there were several categories of persons who could not be arrested, including government officials and individuals holding elected office.[16]

Another important reform, introduced in 1828, required creditors to provide debtors' monthly "maintenance fees," which were set to one and a half times the amount provided by the state to imprisoned criminals; debtors whose creditors failed to pay within one week were then freed and could not be rearrested for the same debt.[17] This rule followed the French practice and was very much unlike the English practice of requiring imprisoned debtors to pay their own way.[18] In the 1840s and 1850s, this law prompted debate within the bureaucracy as to whether charging prisoner upkeep to creditors was the best policy choice. In 1841 Count Benckendorff, the director of the Third Section, who as president of the Imperial Prison Society oversaw prisoners' living conditions, argued that increasing the maintenance fee would not only make imprisonment less onerous for individuals who had not been convicted or even suspected of any crime, but also to some extent prevent collusion between creditors and debtors who were known to imprison each other solely in order to benefit from charitable donations. Higher charges would at the same time discourage "avaricious speculators" who bought up debt documents for a tiny fraction of their cost and then imprisoned debtors to extort the entire amount.

The response by Minister of Justice Viktor Panin belies the view that the Russian legal and administrative system at the time was geared toward protecting debtors and instead reveals an attempt to reach some kind of balance. Panin wrote that neither the Senate nor he himself wanted to increase the amount charged to creditors because he found that "any concession to a debtor already in a way violates the rights of the creditor, who, failing to recover his property, has the right to expect from the Government, not concessions to [the debtor], but rather aid through all legal measures and a just recovery of his loss." Displaying a curious mixture of reliance upon private initiative and paternalistic regulation that was so characteristic of Nicholas I's regime, Panin concluded that he wished to avoid any measure that would look like a concession to debtors and that "imprisoning debtors constitutes a measure of preserving private credit in the State[, w]hich must be brought under the protection and care of the Government, and therefore there are insufficient grounds to free it completely from all expenses that may occur in this regard and to demand that all expenses be carried by private persons." Panin and the Senate thought that although collusions and fraud would decrease if the maintenance fee were raised, the measure would damage or even ruin the less wealthy creditors who could not afford the higher charge.[19]

Debt Imprisonment in Practice

In practice, the decision to imprison one's debtor was merely one of several strategic negotiation choices available to creditors. The maintenance fee was obviously an important factor, since creditors were reluctant to pay yet more money after already losing their investment, although this consideration could be outweighed by the desire for retribution. However, several creditors could split the fee among themselves and make imprisonment much more affordable. But on the whole it appears that only a minority of creditors who had the option to have their debtor imprisoned were actually willing to pay their fees. In a typical case, a bankrupt Moscow merchant Vasilii Prokhorov remained free in 1859 because none of his creditors was willing to pay for his upkeep.[20] It seems that when creditors did pay the maintenance fee, they first of all wanted to demonstrate their resoluteness and thereby induce their debtors to pay. Resoluteness was demonstrated because creditors had to pay the nonrefundable maintenance fee for the entire month even if the debtor paid up and was freed within a few days. Initial court petitions to collect debt were often submitted together with the prison maintenance fee to minimize delay and no doubt also as an additional threat. Even when the threat was actually carried out, approximately half of all prisoners were freed within one month for one reason or another.[21]

In addition to the expense of the fee, creditors could be disinclined to imprison debtors for a number of other reasons. Between 1864 and 1879 imprisonment wiped away a debtor's liability, and creditors were motivated not to imprison debtors whenever there was any chance for future repayment. Creditors could also choose to allow debtors to retain their freedom or free them after a brief confinement so that they could continue their employment or trade and earn the money for repayment. For example, in the case of the bankrupt engineer and entrepreneur Colonel Nikolia, his creditors left him free "to give him opportunities to engage in activities suitable to his profession."[22] In 1858, the creditors of Collegiate Assessor Semen Yesaulov wanted to free him to earn some money for repayment, but the Moscow Aulic Court denied the request because Yesaulov was accused of fraudulent bankruptcy and had to remain in prison at the state's expense if the maintenance money was not paid.[23]

In 1859, Lieutenant General Sergei Golitsyn, a highly decorated war veteran imprisoned for debt in Petersburg, successfully petitioned the Third Section to help him persuade his creditors to accept a negotiated settlement that would allow him to be free and able to find the money for repayment. Golitsyn argued that even the Commercial Bank—not particularly known for charity—made these kinds of deals with its debtors.[24] Incidentally, this case also shows that in Petersburg, with its large population of civil servants and military officers, Golitsyn's high rank did not prevent him from being imprisoned. This study found no evidence of anyone similarly highly ranked being imprisoned in Moscow, although wealthy merchants did occasionally end up in the Pit.

Creditors could also choose not to imprison their debtors because of their pitiable condition, such as illness or responsibility for a large family, or they could otherwise be prevented from exercising their discretion by the authorities. For example, Anna Bestozheva, the fifty-five-year-old insolvent widow of a guard captain, was in bed when the police came to arrest her and she refused to come along because of her illness. She was then examined by a police doctor on February 7, 1868, and found to have an inborn heart defect and a developing paralysis. One of the creditors demanded that she be placed in the prison hospital, but the doctor determined that she could be neither sent to the hospital nor brought to the police station.[25]

Thus, there were numerous reasons not to imprison one's debtors; however, sometimes it was the only practicable way to obtain repayment, whether because the creditor knew of some hidden property or because of the high probability of a redemption by charitable persons or the Moscow Prison Committee. For example, the ex-policeman Leiba-Srulevich Sumgalter traveled to Moscow to collect his 118.50-ruble debt from townsman Krasil'nikov and won every court proceeding but was still unable to get his money because the debtor managed to hide his property with relatives. Finally, Sumgalter had Krasil'nikov imprisoned despite the small amount of his debt, and in March 1863, he was redeemed by the Prison Committee.[26] Other creditors were apparently not so desperate but merely wished to take advantage of popular— as well as official—charitable sentiment: one official report in 1856 mirrored Minister Panin's earlier observation and suggested that "at least half" of the unusually large prison population on the eve of Alexander II's coronation that year were confined for fake debts just to take advantage of the charity, as apparently had happened frequently in the past.[27] Another police report to the governor included the following anonymous denunciation:

> Having learned that Your Excellency will be redeeming debtors from the Provisional Prison before Easter, I resolved to notify You that the debtors being redeemed only imprison themselves for the purpose of being ransomed; in particular I must point out townswomen Kalinina and Uskova, who each year before each holiday imprison more than ten people, who they claim owe them large amounts of money, for the purpose of collecting the ransom. I take the liberty to bring this to your attention.[28]

Even genuine creditors apparently waited to imprison their debtors until just before Easter and Christmas, in the hopes of a charitable redemption.[29]

The effectiveness of using debt imprisonment as a way to obtain repayment can be judged by the various reasons imprisoned debtors were released in Petersburg and in Moscow in 1862, summarized in Table 7.1.

While the number of debt prisoners listed for Moscow was somewhat low for the 1860s, it is notable that every one of Moscow's prisoners was freed through the charity administered by the Imperial Prison Society. In Petersburg, almost 50 percent of all creditors initially chose to imprison their debtors but gave up before receiving any repayment. However, almost 29 percent were rewarded for their perseverance and were repaid either by debtors or by charitable donations. Even this number is rather high and suggests that debt imprisonment was an effective strategy both in Moscow and in Petersburg.

The number of imprisoned debtors in Moscow, as shown in the statistics of the Imperial Prison Society, was much smaller than in Petersburg and was only a tiny fraction of the huge English debtor inmate population, but it was roughly comparable to the number in France, where the debtors' prison in Paris held 125 prisoners in 1851.[30] Several statistical snapshots of the Moscow Debtor's Pit show that the numbers of prisoners gradually increased from the early nineteenth century. In 1808, there were 60 debtors, including

Table 7.1 Released Debtors in St. Petersburg and Moscow, 1862

	Prison Committee		Private Donations		Debtor or Relatives Paid the Debt		Creditors Dropped Claims or Failed to Pay Prison Fees		Total No. of Debtors Released
	No. of Debtors	Amt.	No. of Debtors	Amt.	No. of Debtors	Amt.	No. of Debtors	Amt.	
St. Petersburg	70	385 / 101[a]	61	215 / 78	31	166 / 134	280	837	442 / 564[b]
Moscow	96	307 / 98	n/a[c]	n/a	0	0	0	0	96 / 96

a. The numerator represents the average debt, and the denominator represents the average sum paid to secure the release.
b. The numerator represents the number of debtors released, and the denominator represents the number of debtors imprisoned during the year.
c. In Moscow, private donations were administered through the Prison Committee.
Data source: GARF 123.1.322.

11 nobles and 49 merchants,[31] whereas in 1817 there were already 125, including 10 nobles.[32] During the second half of the century this number varied from 100 to 150 and began to include more poor debtors; at one period in 1865, for example, the Pit held 143 persons, including 19 nobles, 54 merchants, 53 townspeople, 7 peasants, and 10 others.[33]

During major state celebrations that included mass redemption operations, the numbers of prisoners could skyrocket. For example, in 1856, on the eve of Alexander II's coronation, the Pit held 400 debtors, suggesting that there was some truth in reports that many Muscovites were imprisoned with the express expectation of charitable redemption.[34] None of these numbers included debtors who were detained for tax arrears at the Moscow Workhouse or who were briefly detained at police precincts for either private debts or tax arrears.

Earlier, in 1841, a Senate report cited a much smaller number of imprisoned debtors: only 12 persons in Petersburg at the end of 1841, between 20 and 35 at any one time in Moscow, and no more than 58 in Odessa during the entire year.[35] Given that the Senate was justifying its refusal to increase debtors' maintenance fees, these numbers are obviously too low: most debtors were redeemed or otherwise set free before Christmas, and so their number was as a matter of course low at that time of year.[36] In addition to Christmas and Easter donations, the Prison Committee also redeemed debtors on November 19, the anniversary of the death of its founder Alexander I.

The overall numbers of persons imprisoned for debt in Moscow during a particular year can be surmised from the statistics of the Imperial Prison Committee, which for some years include numbers for the Workhouse and police precincts, as shown in Table 7.2.

Table 7.2 Imprisoned Debtors in Moscow by Year

1830[a]	1850[b]	1851[c]	1852[d]	1855[e]	1861[f]	1862[g]	1868[h]	1869[i]
281m, 35f	944	429	982	884	616	96 (1054)	(1223)	(1149)

Note: In parentheses—number for all of Russia without police arrests.

Data sources: a. V. Androsov, *Statisticheskaia zapiska o Moskve* (Moscow, 1832), 143; b. GARF 123.2.155 (322 in Provisional Prison, 49 in the Workhouse, 573 in police precincts); c. GARF 123.2.606, l. 68 ob.; d. GARF 123.2.208 (257 in Provisional Prison, 374 in the Workhouse, 350 in police precincts); e. GARF 123.2.302 (240 in Provisional Prison, 472 in the Workhouse, and 172 in police precincts); f. GARF 123.2.510 (9 in Provincial Prison, 325 in Provisional Prison, 185 in the Workhouse, 97 in police precincts); g. GARF 123.1.322 (Provisional Prison only); h. GARF, f. 123, op. 1, d. 446; i. GA RF, f. 123, op. 1, d. 446.

These are at first sight not large numbers, but they should be compared to Russia's overall prison population, which in the mid-nineteenth century was superficially large but consisted overwhelmingly of persons detained briefly for petty theft, passport violations, brawling, and drunkenness. For example, the 573 debtors held at Moscow's police precincts—not including the Debtor's Pit—in 1850 should be compared to 1,430 thieves, 21 murderers, 12 robbers and 10 rapists also detained there. The rest of the police detainees (altogether 16,590 males and 4,706 females) were arrested for petty crime, with the largest category by far (7,327 arrests) being accused of "drunkenness and a dissolute life."

During 1850, 196 male and 48 female Muscovites were exiled to hard labor in Siberia, and 946 males and 246 females were sentenced to the milder penal settlement.[37] In 1855, there were 168 murderers and murder suspects held at the provincial transit prison and 12 at police precincts and elsewhere in the city.[38] In 1862, there were 2,573 persons altogether held on suspicion of murder, robbery, and arson in the entire Russian empire, 58 held for bribery, and 55 for blasphemy, as compared to 1,054 debtors.[39]

In 1868, the total number of prisoners in the state's custody in Russia was 153,828, which included 2,372 debtors, as compared to 1,410 murderers and murder suspects, 420 arsonists, 89 smugglers, and 637 counterfeiters, whereas almost 50,000 persons were held for theft and vagrancy.[40]

While the overall numbers of imprisoned debtors was small compared to those of thieves and tramps, it was quite considerable compared to the number of persons held for serious crimes like murder and arson. Moreover, official reports only occasionally included the hundreds of debtors detained at police stations; these numbers make debt imprisonment—at least in Moscow—into much more of a routine practice than is suggested by the occupancy of the specialized debtors' prisons in Moscow and Petersburg.

The nineteenth-century system of debt imprisonment existed without much change until the judicial reform of 1864, when the new civil procedure statute prohibited its use with respect to minors, persons over 70 years old, women who were pregnant or had recently given birth, clerics, and parents of children who would otherwise be left without means. Arrest for debt was also prohibited among direct relatives or siblings. Interestingly, arrest for debt also could not be applied for debts of less than 100 rubles. Finally, the traditional five-year limit for debt imprisonment was now reduced for amounts less than the astronomical 100,000 rubles. Thus, imprisonment for the most common amount of debt—from 100 to 2,000 rubles—was limited to six months. Once a debtor was freed, any remaining debt was canceled.

The law of debt imprisonment thus became so mild that it is no surprise that an 1879 decree purported to abolish personal arrest for debt. The exceptions included bankruptcy proceedings, which were only available for debts over 1,500 rubles—that is, to wealthier debtors; in *veksel* (bill of exchange) claims as a brief preliminary arrest; and in those borderland provinces of the Russian Empire that had not yet adopted the court reform of 1864.[41]

This measure was in line with other European countries that abolished debt imprisonment in the late 1860s, but it was different from the English development. In Victorian England, according to the general legal trend to introduce greater protections for entrepreneurs viewed as legitimate risk takers, debt imprisonment was abolished for the wealthier debtors but was retained in a different guise as a measure imposed by small claims courts against poorer debtors, who were seen as undisciplined and requiring correction rather than protection.[42] By contrast, in Russia debt-related imprisonment after 1864 was employed primarily against wealthy individuals.

Debt imprisonment in Russia as it was institutionalized in the nineteenth century was also more regulated than the better-known English model. This regulation must have contributed to the relatively limited use of the institution, but it never threatened its essentially private-law character, thus manifesting the mixture of governmental paternalism and reliance on private discretion and initiative in financial and economic matters that was typical of Nicholas I's epoch. However, debt imprisonment also shows how even a relatively limited legal institution was utilized by private persons striving to protect their interests and to accomplish their strategies, sometimes in a manner that was entirely unanticipated by the government. Only after 1879 did the imperial Russian state manage to largely rid itself of this anomalous practice and strengthen its prerogative to imprison its subjects.

Life at the Debtor's Pit

The Debtor's Pit in Moscow was anomalous among Russia's prisons because of its conditions and the social composition of its inmates. Because it was run by the Moscow police and because lengthy terms of imprisonment for debt were uncommon, it did not possess a distinct internal social structure and rituals, nor was it in any sense a haven for distressed debtors in the manner of the unreformed English gaols and sponging houses. However, the Pit curiously intermingled repression and privilege, and, much like the other tsarist institutions that regulated Russia's culture of debt, it was a place where private individuals strove to protect their interests against the administration and their fellow inmates, as well as to affirm their understandings of personal identity and autonomy.

In the late eighteenth century, imprisoned debtors in Moscow were kept in the regular city prison originally located near the quarters of the venerable Butyrskii Regiment and therefore colloquially known as Butyrka.[43] However, the idea that debtors should be kept separately from other prisoners already existed in the eighteenth century. Soviet historian Mikhail Gernet reproduced a 1791 model floor plan for a province-level prison building in his landmark study of tsarist prisons. However, he did not remark on the fact that no less than one-quarter of the entire building and the adjacent courtyard was to be allocated to debtors, just as other smaller subdivisions were to house women and minor offenders.[44] In 1800, the new Bankruptcy Statute mandated that debtors be kept separately from criminals with minimum restrictions, and it became clear that separate facilities were needed in the larger cities.[45]

Unlike in Petersburg, where debtors were housed in a separate building for much of the nineteenth century, the Debtor's Pit in Moscow was placed at the heart of the city's bureaucratic landscape, in the provincial court building on Resurrection Square, just outside the Kremlin (Figure 6.2). A portion of the court building was allocated to the Provisional Prison, whose primary purpose was to house criminal defendants on the days when they were needed in courtrooms. The courts occupied the building—originally constructed in 1733–1740 to house the Imperial Mint—after 1783, but it is unclear when exactly the Provisional Prison also began to house debtors.[46] It seems that the move took place during the first years of the nineteenth century. At least a local administrative report from 1803 suggests that the prison was still used for its primary purpose, since there is no mention of debtors.[47] However, another government report from 1808 treated the Pit as mainly a debtors' prison; moreover, the clerk who wrote up the report apparently thought this to be its primary function from the beginning.[48] But criminals on trial still continued to be kept there, though separately from the debtors.

The section of the court building occupied by the Pit was in the wing closest to Red Square, and it consisted of two levels with vaulted chambers surrounding the open internal courtyard. This courtyard was sunk one floor beneath street level, thus giving the prison its colloquial name. An urban legend traced the Pit's curious topography to its use as a zoo during the reign of Boris Godunov in the early seventeenth century.[49] However, there is no actual evidence for that, and the likely origin of the indentation was the mint facilities that required easy access to running water from the nearby Neglinnaia River that today is confined to an underground pipe.

There seems to have been a marked distinction in the quality of the basement chambers, which were damp, poorly lit, and reserved for the poorer debtors, and the better rooms on the upper floor, which were reserved for nobles and wealthier merchants, as well as for the prison chapel (Figures 7.1 and 7.2).[50] In 1861, a reform-minded official in Moscow wrote with some exaggeration that "fresh air and sunlight almost never reach the prison, in the winter the entire courtyard is covered in snow, and in the spring and summer flooded with water, and for that reason the prison is constantly damp, which acts very ruinously upon the health of the inmates, and one can positively state that one can hardly find a prison building in Russia that would combine so many inconveniences and hardships for the inmates as the Moscow Provisional Prison."[51]

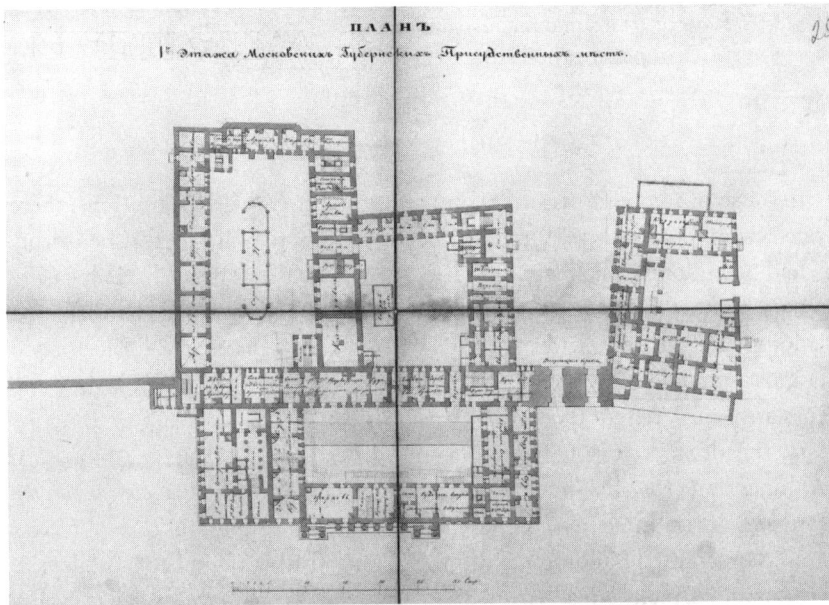

Figure 7.1 The floor plan of the old court building in Moscow, first floor. The Debtors' Pit is on the bottom right, with the merchants' chambers facing the colonnaded portico.

Source: TsIAM 54.182.602, l. 25.

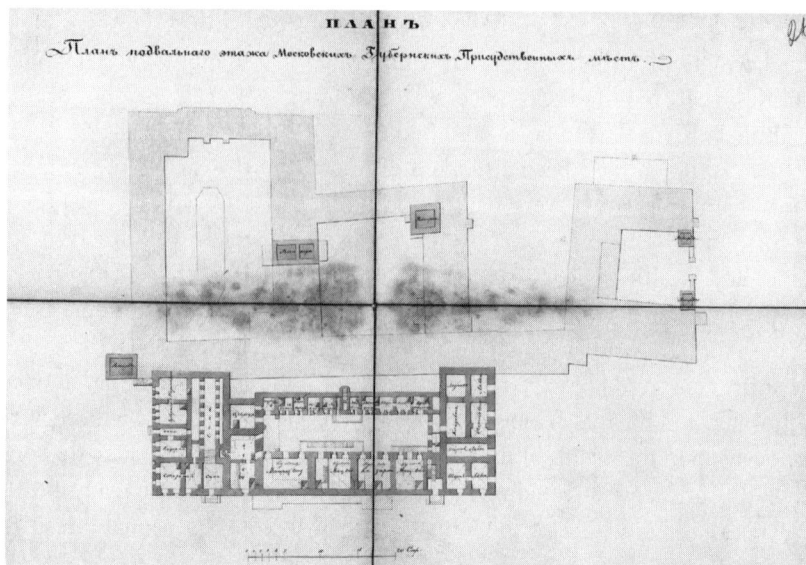

Figure 7.2 The floor plan of the old court building in Moscow, basement floor. The sunken courtyard in the center is framed by the chambers of the Debtors' Pit.

Sources: TsIAM 54.182.602, l. 26.

Because of frequent prisoner complaints about crowded conditions, there were several proposals to purchase or rent a separate building for the prison, as had been done in Petersburg.[52] The tsar personally approved this measure in 1862, but just at that moment the Moscow City Duma moved to a separate building and the authorities used the extra space to improve the Pit. It shed its most dilapidated features but never acquired the palatial look that one Russian visitor noted about the Parisian debtors' prison in 1851.[53] By contrast, the debtors' prison in Petersburg, officially known as the House of Confinement for Delinquent Debtors *(Dom soderzhaniia neispravnykh dolzhnikov)*, acquired a separate building in 1844, and until 1876 it was housed in a rented building next to the Trinity Cathedral in the Izmailovsky Regiment barracks area. After that, most likely to save money, it was moved to the quarters of the Rozhdestvenskaia police precinct on the opposite side of the city, not far from Znamenskaia Square.[54] Both locations were relatively close to the city center but not in any sense prestigious. Interestingly, the prison in Petersburg was only closed in 1889, ten years after personal arrest was abolished for defendants in civil-law disputes and for non-commercial debtors. Bankrupt merchants and several other categories of debtors continued to be subject to imprisonment until the end of the tsarist period. Moscow's Debtors' Pit was closed in 1882, and debtors were kept in a jailhouse located in the former textile factory compound of the Titov family. According to Giliarovsky, from there the debtors' prison moved to the building of the Prechistenskaia police precinct.[55]

The Moscow Debtors' Pit was originally officially structured to reflect the empire's system of legal estates. An early description of the prison listed six rooms: for noble debtors, for merchants and townspeople, for criminal defendants, for women, for sick persons (with six beds), and for persons temporarily arrested for petty crime.[56] However, by the mid-nineteenth century, the estate-based system was no longer operational in the prison. Ostrovsky observed this when a character from his 1870 play, *Mad Money,* a vain and profligate young noblewoman, exclaimed: "I can suffer cruelly. I am all-around in debt, they will throw me into the Moscow Pit together with townswomen."[57] One of the reasons for this leveling quality of the Pit was probably that all debtors, even peasants and townspeople, were entitled to the higher daily maintenance amount that among ordinary prisoners was allotted only to nobles and civil servants.[58]

In 1841, Petersburg police specifically noted that imprisoned debtors were provisioned "without any division into estates."[59] In Moscow, the issue came up during the great renovation project of the court building and the Provisional Prison in the early 1860s. Governor Tuchkov sent his aide, Count Konovnitsyn, to determine how the expanded space should be apportioned among the various categories of debtors. Konovnitsyn was reacting to complaints from the humbler type of debtors, who had been housed in inferior rooms, while the better chambers went to those "who asked most persistently," without there being any definite rule. Thus, he wanted "to destroy the lack of certainty, the existing arbitrariness in accommodating debtors, which, like any arbitrariness, can bring harm."

Konovnitsyn's proposed solution was to house debtors based on the amount of their debt, rather than based on their legal estate. He reasoned that debtors who owed larger amounts had to be confined longer and thus deserved better space, but also that larger debtors must have had "larger business, had more money, and therefore were used to a better life." Thus, two rooms were to be reserved for debtors owing up to 150 rubles, two rooms for those owing up to 300 rubles, and two rooms for those owing over 300 rubles. Four more rooms were given to the wealthy bankrupts, who could be confined for up to five years. Finally, there were to be ten single rooms for foreigners, nobles, and elderly persons of all estates, as well as a special chamber for "unruly persons rejected by the [debtors'] community." Thus debtors could house themselves according to their "personalities" *(kharaktery)*, although the dining room was common to all.[60] Yet another proposal was to adopt the rule used in Petersburg and house debtors "according to their position in society."[61]

It appears that this proposal was never officially introduced. But it is clear that in practice there was no clear segregation by social estate. For example, as of June 15, 1865, the Noble Section of the Debtor's Pit held 14 prisoners, of whom 9 were nobles and 5 were merchants. The First Merchants' Section held 13 merchants, 2 civil servants, and 3 others. The Second Merchants' Section held 15 merchants, 15 townspeople, 4 officers and civil servants, and 6 others. Other sections, while mostly occupied by merchants and townspeople, also included a few nobles and civil servants; interestingly, the First Townspeople Section did house mostly townspeople and was clearly intended for the poorer type of debtors, whereas the Second Townspeople Section housed 8 merchants, one civil servant, 2 peasants, and only 4 townsmen.[62] Thus, the real distribution of debtors was clearly based on either their wealth or the amount of their debt, but definitely not on the prisoners' official legal rank.

Although the Pit held a scattering of nobles and an occasional truly wealthy merchant, the bulk of its inmates consisted of reasonably well-to-do merchants and townspeople who were still far removed from the rich bankrupts who could owe hundreds of thousands of rubles, but at the same time were far above poor debtors who were imprisoned in the Moscow Workhouse for small tax arrears. For example, the average debt on the list of 66 debtors prepared by the governor's officials in 1826 was 2,060 rubles, with a median of 1,250.[63] Since even 200 rubles—the smallest debt on the list—was a sizable sum amounting to a petty clerk's or a skilled workman's annual wages, there were no truly poor persons on the list, nor were there any truly large debts except for one person.

The internal rules governing everyday life in the Debtor's Pit had nothing of the easygoing chaos of unreformed English debtors' gaols, where prisoners could often leave the premises during the day, have family members live with them, and enjoy outside food, drinks, and smokes.[64] However, there was also none of the harshness of regular Russian prisons, where inmates often had their heads shaved, were placed in irons and subjected to arbitrary corporal punishment, and had to dress in disfiguring and uncomfortable prison clothes.

Although the law required special rules for debtors' prisons to be issued by the Ministry of the Interior, the authorities found out in the early 1860s that no such instruction existed even for Petersburg, where debtors were kept based on a set of rules that had "solidified over time" but apparently were not issued by any higher authorities.[65] In Moscow, the instructions to the watch officer at the Pit were identical to those for Butyrka Prison, among other things prohibiting debtors from having ink, quills, and paper. The instructions also prohibited prisoners from begging for alms, possessing knives and other weapons, playing cards, having alcohol, singing songs, or making music. In 1860 the military authorities also instructed the watch officer to prevent alcohol from being brought into the prison unless accompanied by a note from the caretaker; another order prohibited the soldiers from searching female visitors "indecently and impudently."[66]

The duties of the military guard were limited to preventing debtors from physically escaping the building, conducting a daily roll-call, and stopping any disturbances among the prisoners, but only at the caretaker's request.[67] Entering prisoners were to be examined by a doctor and were deprived of sharp weapons, large amounts of money, and any alcoholic beverages. Debtors could keep their own clothes and underwear, but if they had no bedding or linen of their own, they were to be issued a bed with a mattress, a sheet, a blanket, and a cover; a small cupboard; and a stool. Debtors in Moscow were not obligated to perform any labor other than keeping their rooms clean and tidy.

With respect to dining, the rules in Moscow and Petersburg differed considerably. In Petersburg food was prepared for everyone at once and consumed in the dining hall during set hours. In Moscow, individual debtors received their own maintenance money to use as they saw fit, usually by forming an eating group with several other prisoners or buying food from the outside. Debtors were allowed not only food from outside but also small sums of money to buy tea, sugar, and other necessary supplies. The menu in Petersburg consisted of beef soup (*shchi,* a cabbage base, or *borshch,* with beets added), millet or buckwheat kasha with butter, and on holidays roast beef with sauce and potatoes or cucumbers. During fast days, soup was made with sturgeon or *snetki* (small dried salted fish), white mushrooms, and peas, and served with *kasha* prepared with sunflower oil or replaced by potato *kisel'* (a savory pudding-like suspension), supplemented on Sundays by fried fish. During high holidays prisoners were to receive *pirogi* (savory filled pastries); on the last three days before Easter, they ate pancakes; and on Easter itself, they received eggs, *kulichi,* and *paskha* (Easter cakes), and then, for dinner, roasted veal and ham. In addition, prisoners were to receive bread and salt at all times without limit. While simple, this fare corresponded to what could be had in a simple eatery in the city for a very small sum; it also seems to be better and cheaper than what was offered in unreformed English debtors' gaols.[68] Petersburg rules that were almost certainly not followed in Moscow also required that prisoners be quiet during dinner and not be allowed to cook by themselves.

Debtors were to be housed in such a way as to fit each other's personalities and in the event of a quarrel were to be moved to different rooms to ensure "quiet, peace, and concord." They were to have complete freedom inside the prison, their rooms were not locked, and there were no guards inside the prison. The outside gate was to be unlocked during the day, with a doorman posted at the entrance. Prisoners could engage in crafts and read books and journals in their rooms. Debtors could write letters and petitions concerning their cases, although official court submissions had to go through the caretaker. Whereas in Petersburg visitors were only allowed in the special visitors' room, in Moscow visiting was allowed from eight in the morning to four in the afternoon in the debtors' rooms. Neither drinking nor gambling was permitted. No quarreling, swearing, songs, or excessive noise were to be tolerated, and offenders could be placed in the "jail room" for one hour to three days. Otherwise, the prison staff was to treat inmates "as politely and meekly as possible, through which they would be persuaded to be polite and respectful to each other."[69]

Female debtors were also imprisoned but in smaller numbers than men. The Workhouse (a separate building) held up to 100 women imprisoned for tax arrears. The Provisional Prison also included a separate women's section. The number of female debtors imprisoned throughout the year seems to have been between 20 and 40, though the women's section only had 22 beds. According to an 1853 report, female debtors were housed separately from non-debtors in a "rather comfortable and large room, supplied with the necessary furniture, beds, bed supplies, and linen." Non-debtor female prisoners, by contrast, slept on bunk beds on felt mattresses and pillows stuffed with hay, and were subjected to constant supervision by a female overseer who treated them to "spiritual books."

Nonetheless, female debtors were subjected to far greater scrutiny than were male debtors, since the Ladies' Committee of the Prison Society appointed one of its members to gather "the most precise information about social position *[sostoianie]*, conduct, way of life, and the morality of female prisoners, and about the reasons for which they fell into insolvency, at the same time inquiring into the social position of the creditors themselves and into the nature of their debt."[70] The inspector of the women's section in the late 1840s was Anna Pichugina, the wife of a fourteenth-class civil servant. She was hired in 1844 and paid 85.7 rubles directly by the committee, as well as provided with a two-room apartment, three Dutch ovens, and firewood for them.[71]

Although Prison Committee officials were frequently concerned about maintaining the morality of female prisoners throughout Russia, only in 1861 were women's quarters required to be entirely separated from the rest of the prison and the door to be locked at all times. Thus, female debtors' freedom was significantly restricted compared to that of their male counterparts. This was in line with the French practice, reported in 1851 by a Russian visitor, to allow male debtors to receive their wives and children in their rooms during visiting hours or take walks together in the prison's flower garden but not allowing the same privilege to imprisoned married women, who were only allowed to see their husbands in the common visitors' room, for the avowed purpose of preventing pregnancies.[72] But in Moscow, keeping male and female debtors in the same building was still deemed to be inappropriate, and a female member of the Prison Committee, Novikova, donated 1,500 rubles in 1862 to establish a separate women's debtors' prison at the Prechistenka police station, where, the committee boasted, the women's section became "most comfortable" and could "stand among the best establishments of this kind."[73] The report suggests that the new facility separated women by their rank, which was not done in the Provisional Prison.

Prison Conflicts

Despite their relatively relaxed living conditions, imprisoned debtors frequently challenged the authorities and attempted to circumvent the rules. For example, in 1856 the numbers of prisoners increased approximately four-fold because creditors were expecting massive charitable redemption on the occasion of the upcoming coronation of Alexander II. State Councilor Gastev reported to the city's governor general that ever since the debtors' bathing facilities were converted to living space to house their swelling numbers and visits to outside baths had been allowed, debtors used these visits mainly as a chance to walk through the city and obtain drink, which was not permitted in the prison.[74] Debtors also skillfully explored the lack of coordination between different bureaucratic structures; for example, they would first petition the city police chief to be allowed to leave prison for various private reasons and, if refused, they would petition the provincial procurator, who was more generous.[75] Furthermore, they managed to evade the restrictions against drinking by consuming vodka not only when visiting their relatives or the baths but even on visits to the police offices or the courts that were all located in the same building as the prison. Debtors also managed to smuggle alcohol into the prison, in violation of the rules; for example, in 1847, the city police chief inspected the Pit and noticed the smell of vodka in one of the rooms. Investigation revealed that the drink had been brought in by retired sergeant Boitsov, who had been hired by the Prison Committee as a servant and was immediately fired after the incident.[76]

Quarreling and disorders of various sorts also seem to have been common in the Pit. For example, in 1830 Collegiate Secretary Aleksei Komarov, who was not a debtor but was placed in the Provisional Prison during a criminal investigation, inflicted knife wounds on another civil servant, Botashev, apparently because Komarov asked Botashev to bring him vodka, but he brought a carafe of water as a joke and then took a small whip that was for some reason found in their room and started jokingly hitting Komarov, who eventually lost his patience. Botashev, however, claimed that Komarov was hitting him with his pipe and that he was using the whip in self-defense. Komarov was at first sentenced to be conscripted to the army, but the Senate overruled this and sentenced him to one month's arrest instead.[77]

A much more disruptive episode occurred in June 1865, when a sixty-four-year-old moneylender, the merchant Andrei Lukin, visited one of his imprisoned debtors and was beaten by a group of inmates in the presence of a police officer who was for some reason unable or unwilling to intervene.[78] The pretext for the beating was that Lukin had "unjustly" imprisoned the Armenian nobleman and wine merchant Serebriakov. Lukin complained to the police, and after a preliminary investigation, the governor assigned the case to a special high-ranking aide, Prince Chagataev, a colonel. Given the subversive character of the incident, the colonel was zealous in his efforts.

However, the prisoners refused to implicate any of their number, and none of the young male merchants and townsmen accused by Lukin confessed, whereas Serebriakov, who allegedly was the cause of the incident, soon paid his debt, was freed, and immediately took a train to Nizhnii Novgorod before Chagataev had a chance to question him. The police officer, who was eventually dismissed from his position, was likewise either unable or unwilling to recognize any of the culprits. Lukin himself changed his story and became lost in details, and apparently was greatly disliked by the police.

Strikingly, the investigation made progress only when the elderman of the room where Lukin was beaten, a Jewish merchant from Berdichev named Natanzon, agreed to testify and identify three men who were the most active perpetrators of the beating. Chagataev had managed to locate the one prisoner who was most likely to cooperate, since he was harassed by prisoners and by the authorities alike and was probably all too happy to be rid of his tormentors. But one witness was not enough for conviction under the Russian law of evidence, and Lukin assisted the investigation by getting another imprisoned Jewish debtor, Matvei Shmuller, to testify as well. Subsequently three non-Jewish debtors also agreed to testify and confirmed Natanzon's and Schmuller's account of the incident.

Although the case file is not complete, we can be certain that with so many witnesses, Chagataev was going to get the convictions he sought.[79] An indirect confirmation of this is presented by a different incident that occurred a couple months into the investigation, around eleven o'clock in the evening on August 11, 1865, when eight imprisoned debtors pummeled Natanzon and three other debtors, threw out Natanzon's furniture and belongings from his room, and insulted the caretaker and the police officer on duty. Apparently the cause of the riot was that several debtors had decided that a police officer, Voznesenskii, wanted to free Jewish debtors. However, every eyewitness to the incident gave a different version of the story, and the newly established post-reform District Court closed the case.[80]

Lukin's story suggests that Moscow's authorities were deeply conflicted about their approach to the trade of moneylending and to the practice of debt imprisonment. To begin with, the police guards warned Lukin not to go inside by himself but were unwilling or unable to prevent or to stop the beating and unwilling to cooperate with the investigation. This might indicate either a personal dislike of Lukin or a more systemic distaste for professional predatory moneylending. But once the investigation had been launched, Prince Chagataev located the culprits quickly and efficiently after finding a way to break through the prisoners' code of silence. His efficiency was prompted, no doubt, by the governor's motivation to suppress and punish any prison riot in such a central location as the city's court building.

However, the wealthy and literate Lukin himself does not appear in this story as a downtrodden type of moneylender who—if the stereotype about the universal hatred of moneylenders were true—should have been afraid to remind the authorities about his very existence. Instead, he took an active part in the investigation, meeting with witnesses and constantly petitioning Chagataev, the police, and the governor. The case, in fact, closely resembles that of the elderly Old Believer merchant Butikov, who complained against police misbehavior in 1859 and eventually saw the offending officer dismissed; both cases suggest that higher-level city authorities were reluctant to antagonize Moscow's influential and wealthy commercial strata, whatever they may have thought about the morality of usury.[81] Lukin's case also shows that the times had changed: Alexander II's liberal reforms were in full swing, and thus there is no indication of any police abuse toward the accused individuals, who fifteen or twenty years earlier would probably have been placed in solitary confinement and pressured to confess.

In sum, although the Provisional Prison was located in the city's bureaucratic hub, and although it was unmistakably a prison locked up for the night under military guard, its everyday conditions were comparatively relaxed and permissive, in some aspects—such as in the general level of supervision and surveillance—surprisingly more so than in the semi-privatized debtors' prison in Petersburg. Even more important, the prisoners were not segregated according to the empire's system of legal estates but rather housed according to their wealth and social status; while most of them were townsmen, they mingled freely with merchants, civil servants, military officers, and even wealthier peasants. Interestingly, none of the imprisoned debtors were destitute, nor were any but a few exceptional cases truly rich, with most prisoners owing only a few hundred rubles. While inmates regularly challenged the authorities in various ways, this misbehavior was not harshly punished, and even serious violations like the beating of Lukin were investigated energetically but carefully.

The Debtor's Pit's operations thus question, or at least complicate, the meaning of authority and punishment in microcosm just as these concepts were being reworked within the larger cultural context by the Great Reforms. Although the stereotypical view of Nicholas I's reign emphasizes its paternalism and authoritarianism, the Debtor's Pit, as well as many other elements of the pre-reform legal and administrative system, relied upon private action and discretion. As long as the prison was filled up on behalf of private individuals with debtors who were not considered real prisoners, the Pit could not be fully subjected to bureaucratic control. While the partial abolition of debt imprisonment in 1879 appears to have mostly followed the trend in all major legal systems, it should perhaps be also understood as delineating more sharply between the government and the public and asserting the former's power to control the penal system.

Redemption Rituals and Official Nationality

The Debtor's Pit, in addition to being a place of conflict and cooperation among creditors, debtors, and government officials, also attracted the charitable sentiment both of ordinary Muscovites and of some of the most influential persons in the empire. Twice a year, on Easter and Christmas, most imprisoned debtors were redeemed with money from private donations. On other occasions throughout the year, tied to the memory of important dynastic events and to religious holidays, smaller numbers were set free as well. These ceremonies were supervised by important government officials, ostensibly in their private capacity as members of the philanthropic Moscow Prison Committee. Often involving complex negotiations with creditors, as well as assessments of the debtors' moral character and behavior, redemption procedures demonstrate the curious way in which public and private elements intertwined in Russian life before and during the Great Reforms of the 1860s.[82]

Official tutelage encouraged private charitable sentiment, while directing it along desired lines. In the late eighteenth century, charity and debtor redemption contributed to the imperial social project that attempted to create a Western-style urban bourgeois culture, as argued by Alexander Martin.[83] In the first half of the nineteenth century, redemption rituals transcended this original meaning to forge a symbolic link between Moscow's propertied populace, who provided most of the money; the imperial family, whose members donated their influence, some of the funds, and the use of the bureaucracy to administer the charity; and the Orthodox faith. During the reign of Nicholas I (1825–1855), these three elements coincided with the government-designed doctrine of "Official Nationality," first formulated in 1832 by Count Sergei Uvarov and other conservative intellectuals inspired by German Romantic philosophy.

The doctrine centered on the triad of "Orthodoxy, Autocracy, and Nationality." It represented the tsar's response to the growing challenge of nationalism and liberalism and was designed to fuse Russian national sentiment with the monarchy's fundamentally Western European character. Earlier historians have tended to dismiss the extent to which the doctrine was successful in taking root in Russia's society and culture, although

Nicholas Riasanovsky argued that the doctrine was directly influential at least as far as the daily operations of the higher bureaucracy were concerned. He concluded that this influence was ultimately harmful, alienating Russia's educated society from the government.[84]

However, John Randolph, in his microhistory of the aristocratic and intellectual Bakunin family, argued that its members were not quite as alienated from the government as had been previously assumed. As to the middling provincial nobility, Katherine Pickering Antonova has shown that the conservative themes encapsulated in the triad were interpreted, shared, and put into practice in a world far removed from the capitals and their aristocratic salons. Finally, Alexander Martin has argued that patriotic literary and journalistic discourse under Nicholas I turned Moscow into a key symbolic element of Official Nationality, thanks to the way it "admirably combined Russian tradition and enlightened modernity": "had Moscow not existed, the spokesmen of Official Nationality would have had to invent it."[85]

Debtor redemption rituals were an integral part of Official Nationality as it was practiced in Nicholaevan Moscow. Originating from a different philanthropic discourse, redemption predated the triad by over thirty years and quickly became integrated both into public patriotic discourse and into the wider system of charitable practices and institutions. Yet there was a special intensity in the way debt redemption reflected, captured, and expressed the same popular sentiment that was coopted by Uvarov and other tsarist ideologues and propagandists. A citizen could doubt whether Moscow was actually as modern or as prosperous as they represented it to be, but there was very little doubt that real debtors were really set free from a real prison, aside from the fact that Muscovites sometimes imprisoned their debtors or even their friends for the sole purpose of benefiting from charitable donations.

During most of the nineteenth century, redemption operations were administered by the local committees of the Imperial Prison Society, which was established by the English philanthropist John Venning, who came to Russia in 1817 to propagate the ideas of the Bible society and the English Prison Society.[86] Alexander I took the project under his patronage, and its operations were launched in 1819, with branches eventually opening in all sizable cities and towns. It is also possible that earlier redemption rituals involved Empress Maria Fedorovna, well known for her charitable work. She was commemorated by the Prison Society along with Catherine II and Alexander I, but I have not found any evidence of her involvement in any redemption rituals.[87]

Society operations had from the start a semi-official character: while technically a private charitable society, the Imperial Prison Society was headed by the minister of the interior and staffed by bishops, governors, and other local dignitaries. Not surprisingly, by 1879 the Society lost most of its philanthropic character and morphed into the Chief Directorate of Prisons within the Ministry of the Interior.[88] The second important aspect of the Prison Society was the way it combined practical efforts to improve the prisoners' physical condition with a concern for their spiritual well-being, as well as with the introduction of "prison discipline," such as strict visitation hours, a combination of work and rest periods, and in general various restrictions and regimentation.[89]

The rules of the Petersburg debtors' prison required clerks processing new prisoners to find out as much information as possible about the circumstances that caused these people to default on their debts, which was to be verified at each debtor's home address by interviewing his (or her) acquaintances and combining it with "detailed information about his way of life." In Moscow this duty was delegated to the Prison Committee, whose members made regular visits and investigated any inmates who were particularly worthy of compassion, although they seem to have been prying only with female debtors. Another member was appointed as an intermediary *(khodatai)* on behalf of debtors who were detained at police precincts throughout the city.

Yet another interesting impact of Prison Society ideas was that both in Moscow and in Petersburg, the prison's caretaker was charged with negotiating with creditors to persuade them to free debtors from arrest altogether or to forgive part of their debt. Even more importantly, the Committee set aside some of its funds, in addition to private donations, to redeem prisoners. In addition, Dr. Fedor Gaaz (Friedrich-Joseph Haass), the famous nineteenth-century philanthropist, received 100 rubles once a month to help the families of poor imprisoned debtors, and each December he received another 200 rubles to redeem Workhouse inmates detained for city tax arrears. When redeeming the Workhouse inmates, Dr. Gaaz also distributed religious literature that he had purchased with his own money, as well as Russian and Church Slavonic grammars.[90]

Large-scale redemptions were already taking place during the reign of Catherine II, but this study did not reveal evidence of any accompanying rituals or celebrations. For example, Catherine ordered a redemption in 1765, and the merchants of Moscow redeemed 150 poor and middling debtors in

1796 on the occasion of Grand Duke Konstantin Pavlovich's wedding.[91] The earliest redemption ritual whose detailed description I was able to locate took place in 1797, on the occasion of Emperor Paul's birthday, long before the Prison Society was founded, but it established the scenario: the philanthropic subjects of the tsar donated money, and then the city's top officials arrived at the prison and rescued grateful debtors. As the city's governor general reported to the tsar: "For the Most happy day of your Imperial Majesty's Supreme birth, the inhabitants of this capital as a sign of their feelings toward Your Majesty's most Supreme favors toward them, donated a sum of money . . . in order to redeem individuals imprisoned pursuant to *veksels* and other collections, with which on that day 51 persons were redeemed and freed. The joy of those receiving their freedom was so touching that many creditors . . . conceded 50 to 60 percent of their claims."[92]

The newspaper account of this event noted an ethnic Greek merchant, Konstantin Bakcheev, who contributed over 5,000 rubles and described the collective visit to the prison by the military and civil governors, the ober-procurator of the Senate, the vice governor, the Moscow provincial procurator, and other officials, who administered the redemption and inspired such joy among the prisoners that many creditors were then induced to forgive additional sums. One just-released debtor hurried to find his own debtor, who was still imprisoned, and set him free. This description suggests that the ceremony—although not strictly a public one like a coronation—took place in the confined but crowded and emotionally charged environment of the Provisional Prison, with its church, its courtyard, its broad corridors and staircases, and its numerous chambers. Inmates, creditors, and government officials appear to have been able to directly observe each other's bargaining and its results, much in contravention of the usual practice. After the ransoming was completed, all the debtors and the officials also went to the prison church together and prayed for the tsar's health.[93]

A similar ceremony took place on the occasion of Nicholas I's coronation in 1826, when the dowager Empress Maria Fedorovna donated 5,000 silver rubles for redeeming those debtors who were "worthy of compassion."[94] On Coronation Day (August 22), 17 persons were redeemed for the amount of 2,880 rubles, exactly 25 percent of their original debt. Creditors had to issue signed receipts agreeing to discontinue their claims. The anniversary of Alexander I's death, on November 19, was also a popular occasion for charitable works, given that he was the august founder of the Prison Society.[95] After Nicholas I died in 1855, four Moscow merchants donated 10,000 silver rubles to redeem debtors in memory of the anniversary of his death.[96] This was enough to redeem 15 persons from the Provisional Prison and 92 persons who were kept in the Workhouse for tax arrears.

The imperial family also redeemed debtors during regular holidays. As noted above, Catherine II seems to have set the example in 1765 by redeeming 93 debtors for the amount of 3,796 rubles (apparently emptying the prison because there was money left over). This tradition continued into the nineteenth century. For example, before Easter in 1847, the Prison Committee received 572 rubles for redeeming "debtors who are more worthy than others of compassion and aid" from "two Persons who wished to remain anonymous" but used the Hofmarshal of the heir to the throne to transfer the money.[97] In 1850, Nicholas I donated 10,000 rubles to redeem debtors owing no more than 100 rubles.[98] In 1855 he donated 6,329.03 rubles.[99]

Private citizens also actively contributed to the redemption rituals. For this they certainly had the means, given that Petersburg and especially Moscow had a powerful and prosperous merchantry. In fact, unless a given year happened to include a major dynastic event, most donations to redeem debtors came from private persons; for example, in 1850 the imperial family gave 572 rubles to redeem debtors in Moscow, and various private donors gave 6,598 rubles.[100] Some specific collective donations were quite large for their time. At the wedding of the Grand Duke Konstantin Pavlovich in 1796, the merchants of Moscow redeemed 150 people with debts of up to 300 rubles.[101] The sum of the donation is not given, but the potential commitment was 45,000 rubles, vastly exceeding the usual amounts of a few thousand rubles. For example, in 1807, on the occasion of the peace treaty with France, a group of Moscow's liquor tax farmers donated 5,000 rubles to redeem debtors who owed between 100 and 500 rubles, which curiously excluded the poorest and the richest debtors alike and benefited Moscow's middling groups.[102]

In 1817, debtors at the Pit received private donations for 2,500 rubles and large quantities of bread, fish, eggs, salt, and other supplies.[103] In 1847, to mark the 700th anniversary of Moscow's foundation, the elders of its Old Believer communities and a group of tax farmers sent 1,000 silver rubles to the city governor to redeem debtors "who deserve it." The governor forwarded the money to the Committee and directed its particular attention to the unfortunate condition of lieutenant's wife Princess Kastrova, who was at the time hospitalized but was to be imprisoned upon discharge for her debt of 750 paper rubles to the wife of a Class 14 civil servant, Rombakh.

During the second half of that year, charitable donations for redeeming debtors amounted to 1,149.82 rubles.[104] In 1856, Count Zakrevskii personally donated 825 rubles; twelve other people, —including merchants, civil servants, and a priest—donated between 2.5 and 145 rubles; and "various unknown donors" gave 3,420.36 rubles.[105] It seems that Muscovites were far more charitable than Petersburgers. For example, in 1862, new private donations in St. Petersburg amounted to only 755.40 rubles. In Moscow, private donations were over ten times that amount: 7,848 rubles.[106]

In addition to giving money directly, private donors set aside certain sums in their wills to be deposited at a bank to be used for redeeming debtors, usually on a holiday like Good Friday. For example, in 1810, the famous Princess Ekaterina Dashkova willed 500 rubles, enough to redeem eight persons. In 1811 there was a set of bequests including state councilor's wife Alfimova (600 silver rubles), *hegoumenos* (abbot) Simonovskii (5,000 paper rubles), an unmarried noblewoman Bileva (400 paper rubles), cavalry Lieutenant Tarelkin (200 paper rubles), and state councilor's wife Baskakova (100 rubles). The income from this amount (310 rubles) was sufficient to redeem six Moscow townspeople during Easter.[107] Their creditors—who had to make a considerable concession of the original total debt of 1,155 rubles—included an army non-commissioned officer, a craftsman, a merchant, a soldier's wife, and a servant. Grigorii Potemkin's favorite niece, Aleksandra Branicka (née Engelgardt), before her death in 1838 bequeathed 200,000 rubles for redeeming imprisoned debtors.[108] Other donations were not self-advertising and not timed for some festive occasion. For example, in 1823 townsman Ivan Kholshchovnikov was freed when "an unknown philanthropic person" paid his debt of 184.50 rubles.[109] Thus the redemption ritual symbolically connected the donors with the middling stratum of Moscow's propertied classes that made up the overwhelming majority of the imprisoned debtors.

Creditors who received redemption money could only hope to recover a fraction of the original debt. As of 1826, the number could be as little as twenty percent, which was of course better than not receiving any payment at all.[110] However, complex negotiations often took place. It seems as though creditors who sensed that a particular debtor attracted the authorities' sympathy were more likely to hold out. In 1859, the creditors who imprisoned Lieutenant-General Sergei Golitsyn, imprisoned in Petersburg, initially refused to negotiate, apparently because they knew that the old general attracted the tsar's personal attention and sympathy. Instead, the creditors attracted the attentions of the Third Section, which regarded these lenders as suspected harmful usurers and threatened to shut down their operations. Although Russian tsars were jealous of their autocratic prerogatives and Alexander II did have sympathy for the old warrior, as it turned out this did not prevent him from explicitly refusing to circumvent or undermine the legal procedures.[111]

Earlier, in 1826, Moscow officials were unable to persuade sergeant's wife Ezhevskaia to accept anything but the full amount owed to her by collegiate registrar's wife Maria Aleeva, who incurred her debt because of a complicated lawsuit. Despite the high amount of her debt, officials were sympathetic to her situation because she had been nursemaid to Prince Paul of Württemberg, father-in-law of the tsar's brother Grand Duke Mikhail Pavlovich. Only several months later did her creditor agree to take 1,300 rubles in cash and to take over Aleeva's own lawsuit against townsman Dolgov for 25,000 rubles.

Whereas a connection to the imperial family automatically entitled Aleeva to special consideration, redemption procedures typically involved assessments of debtors' behavior and moral qualities. One 1826 redemption created the most detailed record of such a procedure that I was able to locate. One of the governor's special aides, Aulic Councilor Nechaev, drew up a list of all prisoners and selected those who deserved preference in light of the length of their confinement, the large size of their families, and the small size of their debt, which "condemn them to a useless lack of activity and distract them from their families and their ordinary commercial or craft activities." Even then, the amount of their debt was four times what was available as ransom, and Nechaev had to hope for concessions from the creditors.[112]

Nechaev's short list included 29 persons, of whom three were women. This is a rather small number, considering that Russian women frequently engaged in commerce and typically there were at least a dozen imprisoned female debtors at any one time. Altogether, there were 20 townspeople, 1 civil servant, 3 foreigners, and 5 craftsmen. The first on the list was townswoman Katerina Prakhova, who was also the subject of a separate memo, detailing that she had absorbed her late husband's debt of 2,800 rubles, originally borrowed from a county treasurer in connection with his liquor tax farming operation in the town of Makariev. It turned out that the treasurer had stolen the money in the first place, and so the Prakhovs were left responsible for the debt to the Treasury. Next to each name Nechaev made notes about each debtor's character and reasons for indebtedness. When the debtor's references were good, the notation was simply "outstanding," "good," or "decent." Sober behavior was definitely a plus, as was having a spouse and children, although drunkenness was not automatically a minus. It is noteworthy that the debtors' acquaintances' vouching for them made further elaboration into a debtor's qualities unnecessary, as far as Nechaev was concerned.

Bad or ambivalent references were more varied: for example, Collegiate Registrar Tselevich was "unsober," and his wife had a small amount of property; the "way of behavior" of Gubernial Secretary Naryshkin was "well-known," soldier's wife Fomina was "an idle woman of mediocre behavior," and craftsman Rodionov was "not completely sober, but otherwise ha[d] good qualities"; townsman Gavrilov was "not always temperate but deserves compassion because of her poverty and a large family." Other sample notations were "owns a house"; "decent man but poor; son keeps a drinking establishment"; and "went into debt because of illness." To summarize, people with a weakness for drink were not automatically out of luck, while keepers of drinking establishments definitely were, even when their debt was not large; also out of luck were merchants with relatively large debts. The reasons for indebtedness varied but seemed to have little bearing on whether someone made it onto the short list, unless it was one of only a few accidental insolvencies caused by fire, flood, or illness.[113]

Although the 1826 list was unusually detailed, the practice of bureaucratically evaluating debtors' characters persisted into the 1850s. For example, when in 1855 four Moscow merchants donated 10,000 silver rubles to redeem debtors in memory of Nicholas I's death, authorities redeemed 15 debtors from the Pit and emptied out the Workhouse of its 92 inmates. Officials assessed the debtors' moral qualities and even compiled a list of 22 persons who were not to be redeemed under any circumstances. This included a handful of "thieves and frauds," one debtor who had already been redeemed in the past, and several men who were involved in the business of furnishing substitute recruits to clients who wished to avoid military conscription.[114]

No inquiries were ever made about Workhouse inmates kept for tax arrears and routinely redeemed *en masse* without any extra ceremony: Muscovites seemed to show a rather more unconditional charity toward the poorest debtors, as compared to the contemporary English trend of treating poor debtors as blameworthy delinquents. Indeed, the assumption seems to have been just the opposite: many donations were explicitly limited to the poorer debtors who owed very small amounts. This was the case not only in the nineteenth-century cases but also earlier, under Catherine II. In 1765, she redeemed 25 Muscovites for tax arrears averaging 43.6 rubles and 68 private debtors averaging 39.8 rubles—that is, members of the lower middle class. The redemption in 1796 was limited to Muscovites owing under 300 rubles.[115]

Redemption rituals curiously mingled official and private behavior and symbolically linked the people of Moscow, who were both the donors and the recipients of charity, with the Orthodox faith, given that redemption was often carried out during a holiday and tapped into popular religious sentiment; with the imperial family through the donations of its members and the tying of many ceremonies to important dynastic events; and with the bureaucracy, which actually presided over the rituals. Redemption rituals thus began to apply the underlying sentiments of Official Nationality in practice even before the doctrine itself was officially enunciated.

Finally, the procedure of evaluating debtors' characters and behavior reflected—and perhaps even helped partly to form—the identity of Moscow's middling classes. Categories of wealth, commercial success, and official rank were secondary compared to the debtor's reputation with his or her acquaintances, the size of the debtor's family, and any personal connections with the imperial family. Redemption rituals thus show an interesting example of how existing popular charitable sentiment was blended with—and clearly triumphed over—foreign-derived ideas of Protestant prison reform and moral discipline.

There were only a few places in imperial Russia where imprisoned debtors were kept in large numbers, but the inmate population, while small compared to its English counterparts or to the vast mass of Russia's vagrants and petty thieves, was significant compared to the small numbers of persons arrested or convicted for serious crimes. Moreover, the rituals and practices of debt imprisonment challenged and renegotiated some of the key understandings of the tsarist political system relating to punishment, authority, and personal autonomy. Debt imprisonment relied upon the cooperation, and even initiative, of private persons, as did police collection procedures and bankruptcy and civil-law proceedings.

Similarly to other mid-century institutions, the debtors' prison had its peculiar dynamic of cooperation and confrontation between individuals and authorities, showing that the relationship between the overt political and police power of the government and the more subdued "exercise of gentle violence" (to use Bourdieu's words) represented by creditors when they forgave their debtors was less of a dichotomy and more of a symbiosis.[116] The Debtor's Pit existed because private persons were imprisoned at the discretion of other private persons and were treated differently from Russia's generally miserable regular prison population. The corollary was that the authorities could not control the Pit any more efficiently than they could bankruptcy boards or the regular courts, with their often drawn-out proceedings. Finally, the history of debt imprisonment, as part of Russia's culture of debt, reveals the formation of a single "middling" class that was supplanting Russia's official legal hierarchy of estates. Materially, this process is revealed in the make-up of the imprisoned debtor population, which excluded truly rich and truly poor persons, and in the prison rules and regulations that had little regard for their legal estate as opposed to their wealth. Symbolically and mentally, this process is revealed in the debtor redemption rituals, which emphasized the middling classes' identity as propertied Orthodox Muscovites and linked them with the upper classes and the imperial family.

CHAPTER 8

Intermediaries, Lawyers, and Scriveners

NETWORKS OF FRIENDSHIP and acquaintance, which defined the cultural boundaries of creditworthiness and respectability, depended—in an economy and society as large as imperial Russia—on credit intermediaries who brought together borrowers and lenders. As in any other early-industrial culture of credit, more loans involved business partners, fellow servitors, employers, servants, social acquaintances, and of course relatives, compared to what was still customary in the late twentieth century. In most situations, debt routinely exploited or cemented already existing social connections. But because of Russia's size and the policies that delayed the development of private banks and other elements of a formal credit infrastructure, its nineteenth-century culture of debt increasingly involved transactions that were the only identifiable link between the participants.

By the 1850s, credit networks centered on the key commercial and financial centers, especially Moscow and Petersburg, were large and often impersonal. More and more lenders and borrowers who were unable or unwilling to go to friends and relatives had to find each other through word of mouth, newspaper ads, and loan brokers of varying skill and reliability. The parties would meet for the first time when the borrower came to the lender's house to sign the documents, and it was possible that the intermediary would do all the work. The nineteenth century was a heyday of intermediaries and brokers of all types (referred to in Russian usage of the time as *poverennye, posredniki, komissionery, khodatayi, maklery,* or, less flatteringly, *svodchiki*), who helped to bridge spatial and social divisions within the culture of credit and also provided advice on negotiating the world of bureaucracy and the law. In their role and their diversity these intermediaries closely resemble late imperial Chinese litigation masters—discussed in an illuminating study by Melissa Macauley—who acted to link local interests and the imperial state, mostly in the interests of the elites but also of a surprising number of subordinate actors.[1]

The Pre-Reform Legal Profession

Arguably the most important division negotiated by intermediaries was that between ordinary individuals and Russia's legal system. Among the most commonly praised achievements of the judicial reform of 1864 was its establishment of an organized bar that strove to regulate and discipline its members and that was filled by individuals with university law degrees. After all, several Russian tsars had been quoted as expressing their disgust with the very word "lawyer" (*advokat*, which could be distorted as *ablakat* or *abvokat*) and their firm belief that in their lifetime an organized bar would not appear in the empire.[2] According to Nikolai Kolmakov, memoirist, Ministry of Justice official, and one of the drafters of the reform legislation, there were only a handful of lawyers in Petersburg on the eve of the reform who openly called themselves "advocates." Some of them appear to have been harassed by the Third Section.[3]

The introduction of Western-style lawyers, with their university education, their practices of public speaking, and their knowledge of the bureaucratic apparatus, was threatening to a monarchy that sought to instill legality in Russia while avoiding the political upheavals often associated with politically conscious jurists.[4] Nonetheless, legally savvy individuals, legal advice, and legal representation existed in Russia for centuries before the 1864 reform, and under Nicholas I there was even a small, organized body of lawyers known as *prisiazhnye striapchie* (sworn representatives), who practiced before the commercial courts. Moreover, Poland, Lithuania, and the Baltic provinces of the empire had had a German-style organized bar for a long time.[5] Given that these territories' loyalty was of considerable concern to the tsars, it is noteworthy that an organized bar was tolerated there but not permitted in the core Russian provinces, whereas the opposite might be expected. It therefore appears that an equally important reason why the legal profession in most of the Russian Empire was left unregulated was that Nicholas I's regime, so heavy-handed in some areas, left most economy-related activities largely or completely unregulated and unstructured.

Despite Nicholas I's reputation, his government was criticized later for not promoting capitalist development in Russia through direct intervention and investment. Nicholas's hands-off approach to economically-relevant matters is evidenced throughout this study, such as by the fact that private individuals were allowed to imprison their debtors and to control civil litigation, or that private lenders were completely unregulated apart from ineffective interest rate restrictions. In light of these tendencies, it should not be too surprising that regulating legal representatives in private law cases was not considered to be an important priority. If anything, the government was apparently concerned not so much about individual advocates' possible disloyalty as about the idea of an organization of legally trained individuals as such.

It is ironic that the 1864 reform restricted, rather than liberalized, access to legal advice, creating a small body of elite attorneys to service the wealthier clients and rebranding other practitioners as inferior "private" or even illegal "underground" ones.[6] Although the reform resulted in more supervision over lawyers' conduct—both from the government and from their own professional bodies—it did not ensure the quality of their services or eliminate conflicts of interest, embezzlement, and other ethical violations, to say nothing of uncivil behavior.[7] While readily conceding the political and ideological significance of an organized elite legal profession and its crucial impact on post-reform public criminal and political trials, it is important not to exaggerate its impact on Russia's everyday legal practice, especially in the less politically charged property and debt disputes.

By contrast, before 1864 there were very few restrictions on who could serve as a legal representative. The basic rule permitted it to anyone competent to sue or be sued in court, thereby excluding minors, all clergy, convicted criminals, and several other less important categories. Civil servants could compose petitions and other legal documents unless they had been fired for misconduct, and they could serve as full legal representatives with a power of attorney unless they were employed at the Governing Senate or the proceedings were taking place at their own court or office.[8] Otherwise, individuals could be prohibited from practicing only by a court-imposed sentence.[9] The government also reserved a broad power to prosecute representatives "inciting out of avarice the composition of false petitions" by peasants and other commoners; punishment varied from arrest or lashes to military conscription or penal exile for repeat offenders.[10]

An organized legal profession is usually seen as one of the essential elements of a modern legal system that were absent in pre-reform Russia.[11]

However, the one overlooked advantage of the old system was that a wide range of legal practitioners was available to serve different classes of the population. Much maligned by the jurists of the post-reform era, these practitioners varied widely in their ability, education, and social standing, which ranged from trusted household serfs to educated lawyers who handled appellate litigation in the Senate. They were crucial for the functioning of Russia's culture of debt, as lawyers usually are in any legal system, although only some of the lawyers also acted as credit and business brokers and intermediaries.

Critical accounts of pre-reform lawyers are easy to find. One modern historian has argued that it was more efficient in pre-reform courts to spend resources bribing a chancellery clerk than on hiring an "attorney."[12] Memoirs and fictional accounts have been marshaled to "attest to the disdain" and "suspicion" for pre-reform legal practitioners, as if disdain or suspicion of lawyers were somehow peculiar to pre-reform Russia.[13] Modern critiques are traceable to the writings of pre-Soviet scholars, such as Iosif Gessen, the liberal author of the first comprehensive study of Russian lawyers, who listed the most scathing memoir criticisms of *striapchestvo* (a colloquial term for low-brow legal and other official representation).[14] The disparagement is aided by a common—and misleading—use of the term *striapchii* as the general name for pre-reform lawyers.[15] While *striapchii* was a colloquial, even folksy, way of referring to private legal representatives, the term used in pre-reform law-related documents and correspondence was *poverennyi,* which emphasizes trust and, moreover, suggests much greater continuity with the post-reform barrister (*prisiazhnyi poverennyi;* the word *prisiazhnyi* used by itself was short for a juror, *prisiazhnyi zasedatel'*).

What is most fascinating about Gessen's examples is the catalogue of pre-reform lawyers' misdeeds. The most concrete allegation was conflict of interest—that is, representation of both parties in the same lawsuit. As today's Western legal practice shows, this open violation of legal ethics is perhaps the easiest to eradicate. The bulk of Gessen's criticisms, however, were more abstract—for example, alleging that pre-reform lawyers perpetuated legal disputes rather than helped to solve them. Interestingly, this allegation is not limited to pre-reform Russian lawyers but is current in today's Western legal systems, especially in the United States. Many American jurists today agree that lawyers "may make negotiations more rational, minimize the number of disputes, discover outcomes preferable to both parties, increase the opportunities for resolution out of court and ensure that the outcomes reflect the applicable legal norms."[16] Others, however, claim that the positive impact of the legal profession is far from obvious—for instance, when lawyers deprive judges of discretion by "forum shopping" (selecting a court in which to sue as part of a litigation strategy), prevent cases from reaching decision, or cause cases to be decided on technical issues instead of their merits.[17] Lawyers may be more likely to use improper threats and misrepresentation, and their participation may lead to more disputes and higher costs without improving the fairness of outcomes, the situation referred to as "iatrogenic disease."[18]

Gessen and other post-reform jurists and memoirists were of course not so unsubtle in their analysis as to simply claim that pre-reform lawyers caused disputes whereas modern ones invariably helped to resolve them. At stake was not so much pre-reform lawyers' lack of effectiveness or uniformly low qualifications but rather their varying quality and lack of professional regulation and discipline. Gessen's own evidence, collected to defend the achievements of the judicial reform, shows that there was a gradation among pre-reform legal practitioners in terms of their education and honesty.[19]

Moreover, memoirs and legal cases are not as uniformly critical as late-imperial jurists might lead us to believe. For instance, memoirs by Mikhail Dmitriev and Elizaveta Vodovozova, or, for the 1780s to the 1810s, by Prince Ivan Dolgorukov, do contain occasional criticisms but nothing that can be interpreted as "disdain" or "suspicion."[20] Or consider the Third Section's 1828 investigation of Petersburg lawyers Lerkh and Grek, who operated in a partnership, apparently unusually for Russia, where solo practice was the norm.[21] The two of them were accused of various types of chicanery and conflicts of interest, but even the Third Section's senior officers noted that the original file had not indicated how these alleged abuses might be uncovered, had not mentioned a single specific court case in which they represented both sides at the same time, and had not named a single legal official who assisted them.[22]

It is also important to keep in mind the comparative dimension: while an organized bar is a venerable institution in Western law, effective legal advice and legal representation available at trials as a rule rather than as an exception applying only to the wealthy is a relatively recent innovation that even in England only took firm roots in the mid-nineteenth century. In the United States, the Sixth Amendment was only applied to the states in fits and starts after 1932. The fact that most American or Western European litigants and defendants could not expect to have access to effective legal advice until well into the twentieth century makes Russia's lack of an organized bar not quite as glaring a failure as it might appear from the reformers' perspective.[23]

It is true that criminal defendants in Russia were not permitted to hire attorneys during the preliminary investigation—both before *and* after the 1864 reform. Before the reform, the task of protecting their interests was officially vested, first of all, in the local procuracy official, and second, in special deputies assigned to defendants who belonged to the clergy, to the military, merchants, townspeople, state peasants, retired soldiers, or those from any other particular "department" *(vedomstvo)*. Serfs could be represented by their masters.[24]

However, on closer examination, it turns out that defendants could hire their own attorneys for the most important stage of the pre-reform criminal trial—namely, reading, commenting on, and signing the case extract on the basis of which the judges rendered their decision. A leading late imperial jurist who wrote an important reform-minded study of the Russian bar, Evgenii Vas'kovskii, misrepresented the facts rather crudely by claiming that attorneys were allowed to review the case extract only during the unimportant lower-tier criminal proceedings that were not going to move to the next tier, concluding that criminal defendants were in effect denied legal representation.[25] Had he looked through several more pages of the Digest of the Laws, he would have noticed that representatives were explicitly permitted to review criminal case extracts both in the second-tier Chamber of Criminal Justice and in the Senate after 1828.[26]

The term "representative" *(poverennyi)* often referred to individuals who provided legal advice or facilitated access to the court system. However, it was much broader than that, technically including anyone with a power of attorney *(veriushchee pis'mo)* from another person. Table 8.1 and Appendixes D.1 and D.2 summarize the information for powers of attorney registered at the Moscow Civil Chamber in 1852, 1857, 1861, and 1867, noting the range of activities that involved the services of a *poverennyi*.

Table 8.1 Legal Practice by Type of Matter (Based on Registered Powers of Attorney)

Type	1852	1857	1861	1867
Real estate	136	101	110	33
Commercial	44	44	54	21
Litigation	54	47	84	80
Other[a]	8	5	4	2
Total	**241**[b]	**197**	**252**	**136**

a. Mainly receipt of money and mail; b. Some powers of attorney had multiple purposes.
Data sources: See Appendix D.1.

Powers of attorney show that despite the lack of a formal legal profession, litigation-related matters were in practice distinguished from other tasks, such as property management and routine one-time visits to government offices to sign or obtain documents. Court registers show that debt collection represented between 10 and 27 percent of all matters for which representatives were hired. Moreover, registration books show that many more individuals were already being hired as court representatives from the late 1850s onward—that is, long before the new courts were in the works. It is also noteworthy that women were actively involved in court representation before the reform of 1864, but not more so than the principals' close relatives, such as parents, children, siblings, and spouses.

Other evidence suggests that even those *poverennye* who did specialize in providing legal services could supplement their income with other types of assignments. Katherine Pickering Antonova's study of a middling gentry family from Vladimir province, northeast of Moscow, identified correspondence between the noble landowner, Andrei Chikhachev, and his Moscow attorney, Ivan Gruzinov, who was mainly employed to deal with Chikhachev's loans to the Board of Trustees in the 1830s and 1840s. However, he also volunteered to help him purchase tea, coffee, and sugar, undertaking to get a better price as a bulk buyer.[27] In his 1859 investigation of St. Petersburg "usurers," the Corps of Gendarmes officer Fedor Rakeev noted that many of them doubled up as legal representatives, accepting debt documents in lieu of legal fees.[28]

Whereas the boundary between legal and non-legal work was obviously porous, it is important to remember that it continued to be so long after the reform, and Russian lawyers continued to be engaged in various less glamorous activities, such as collecting debt, even after the most successful of them became barristers after 1866.[29] We have already met one prominent Moscow barrister, Aleksandr Saltykov, who for decades embezzled his clients' money and eventually, in 1891, fled the city and staged his own suicide. Aside from his successful legal practice, he assisted his highly placed clients by investing their money in loans and mortgages, taking advantage of the prestige granted to the legal profession in post-reform Russia.[30] He found out that it was much easier to "invest" in fraudulent mortgages than in real ones, although it took his clients many years to become suspicious because he paid them off with the proceeds of his new "investments." The connection between legal representation and commercial and financial activity was not unique to Russia: in the Anglo-American legal world, attorneys managed property, collected debt, and performed other paid functions.[31]

Those pre-reform *poverennye* who focused on actual legal work usually had some background or connection with government service. It could be someone with a very low official status. For example, a wealthy and legally knowledgeable owner of one of the largest public baths in Moscow, when sued by an equally wealthy Colonel Nikitin for a debt of 110,000 rubles, hired a police copyist, Nikolai Semenov, to prepare his court petitions.[32] Many more debt litigants were represented by a *poverennyi* who held a junior commissioned rank either in the military or in the civil service. For example, merchant Marshchev was imprisoned for his debt to the treasury related to a liquor concession, and his illiterate wife petitioned for his release with her as a surety with the help of the Second Lieutenant Mogilevich.[33] In the forgery case of Moscow merchant Stepan Tikhomirov, the alleged fraud victim, another merchant named Iakov Chistiakov, was represented by Gubernial Secretary Konstantin Lozhkin, who in March 1867 requested the Chamber to be allowed to review the case and "give explanations" to the court; he was told that the case had been already reported to the court but that he could still give his comments *(poiasneniia).*[34] Incidentally, this case shows how a criminal defendant in pre-reform courts could be served by an attorney in the absence of a public jury trial.

In yet another debt case, collegiate councilor's wife Strekalova hired Collegiate Assessor Mikhail Rakhmaninov to defend her against a lawsuit by her creditor, nobleman Faleev.[35] Lozhkin and Rakhmaninov seem to have been mid-range lawyers, equally removed from the ranks of the lowly scriveners and from the highly successful *poverennye* with university degrees.

The latter group were employed by the wealthiest and most influential clients, such as the wealthy Old Believer merchant and textile factory owner Ivan Butikov, who in the early 1860s waged a bitter feud with Moscow police over a debt collection against his son. Because of his wealth, Butikov could afford the services of Titular Councilor Mikhail Aristov, who was referred to in a police document as the "well-known Moscow *advokat.*"[36] Aristov seems to have specialized in representing wealthy merchants in complex commercial and bankruptcy matters, including appeals to the Senate.[37] In 1866 he became one of Moscow's first sworn barristers.[38]

In the case of the young spendthrift Count Dmitrii Tolstoy, his father's representative Shimanovskii negotiated with creditors and ended up buying up the majority of the son's debt, so that the father controlled the disposition of the bankruptcy proceedings.[39] In defending her debt case in the early 1850s, the noblewoman Anna Faleeva mentioned in her petitions to the court that she spent a large sum of money on hiring *poverennye* to pursue appellate litigation in St. Petersburg.[40]

At the same time, some lawyers had a reputation for cheating their clients and attracted the attention of the Third Section, whose reports do, however, indicate that these lawyers' chicaneries were exceptional and violated all accepted standards of conduct, even in Russia's largely unregulated pre-reform legal profession. For example, Titular Councilor Aleksandr Alekseevich Bilbasov practiced in Petersburg from the 1850s to the 1870s. In 1858 he assisted noblewoman Lidia Telesheva, who defrauded her lover, Prince Mikhail Mikhailovich Golitsyn. In 1866, he was accused of forging a receipt for the money owed to his client, Praskovia Zasetskaia, the widow of a colonel. Finally, in the early 1870s, he became tangentially involved in the massive fraud case known as the Jacks of Hearts Club, allegedly assuring some lenders that a penniless noble, Dmitriev-Mamonov, was about to get a large sum of money by winning a legal case against two other aristocratic families. The Corps of Gendarmes was well aware of Bilbasov's reputation and filed away the matters in which he took part. Interestingly, the well-known critic of the old courts, Kolmakov, listed Bilbasov as one of Petersburg's openly established *(glasnye)* "advocates," representing them as victims of the Third Section.[41]

Another similarly negative figure was Collegiate Assessor Ivan Davydenko, who was described in a secret police memo as obstinate in character, stubborn, and insolent; a pettifogger *(kliauznik)*; a false denouncer; and always extremely mendacious with his clients.[42] Before engaging in private practice in the 1830s he had served at the Spiritual Consistory and at the Petersburg provincial administrative office, at the police in the Ukrainian town of Nikopol, at the Fifth Department of the Senate, and then as the chief of police in the Russian town of Kashin. He had been placed on trial and fired for making false denunciations, fraud, and rudeness toward the investigating officials. To be completely fair, none of these accusations sound particularly horrible: ungrounded denunciations were—and are—pretty common in all parts of the world, regardless of the tradition of the rule of law; forged receipts in the petty cash register were no doubt routine practice, and drunken threats against the same man he had earlier falsely denounced suggest a personal conflict rather than some fundamental flaw of character. Eventually he was able to secure a position at the central police office in Petersburg.

The Third Section accumulated an impressive list of cases in which Davydenko allegedly cheated his clients. For example, in 1863, he promised one of them to take her case on a contingency basis but in the written agreement he was to be paid 5,000 rubles unless the case was lost because of his negligence or mistake. This particular dispute was taken to the Gendarmes, but Davydenko managed to deceive them by signing a settlement agreement but still submitting his claim to the police for collection. In several other cases, he was accused of taking his clients' fees but doing nothing to work on their cases; he was also accused of the defloration of a young girl in 1856 and of falsely denouncing his own estranged wife, accusing her of becoming pregnant with someone else's child. Finally, he was known to take money from criminal defendants whose cases were hopeless, as in the prosecution of a serfowner Svirskaia, accused of torturing and murdering her serfs and most certainly about to be exiled to Siberia. Davydenko promised her that he would get her sentence reduced or overturned on appeal, in which case she would pay him between 300 and 600 rubles, and if he did not, he would give her 3,000 rubles, on the premise that Svirskaia would be unable to enforce this agreement while performing hard labor in Siberia.

The Gendarmes noted that no conscientious attorney could undertake such a reckless obligation, suggesting that Davydenko's conduct, while outrageous by any standards, was regarded by the Third Section—which was not known to harbor any special affection for private legal practitioners—as standing apart from the generally accepted standards of conduct. When confronted by the Gendarmes Davydenko told them that he was not afraid of them, or of their superiors at the Third Section, or the Petersburg governor, and that none of them could "prohibit him from conducting cases the way he wants to do it." This interview took place in October 1864: the landmark court reform was to be enacted in only a month, and Davydenko no doubt felt emboldened by the spirit of reforms.[43] The Gendarmes had clearly assumed that lawyers valued their good reputation; in the 1863 debt-related dispute between the old Prince Fedor Andreevich Golitsyn and his son-in-law, the Gendarmes urged Golitsyn's attorney, Yefremovskii, to help reach an amicable settlement, arguing that if the case proceeded to court and he lost, he would "incite an unfavorable opinion of himself as a lawyer among the public."[44]

On the lowest end of the scale were the Russian counterparts of British pettifoggers who for a small fee prepared court petitions and were commonly criticized for engaging in legal—or illegal—trickery.[45] Merchant and memoirist Ivan Slonov remembered:

Near the Resurrection Gate, next to the building of the provincial administration, from time immemorial there was a litigious exchange of scriveners, chancery clerks, and fired former civil servants, who engaged in the writing of all kinds of denunciations, complaints, and petitions for illiterate, ignorant folk. Among the common folk such persons are known as the "Iberian Lawyers" [referring to the nearby Chapel of the Iberian Mother of God]. All of them to a man are alcoholics, with puffy faces and red-purplish noses. Such a "lawyer," having found his client on the street, invited [that client] to follow him to a tavern[, where], in exchange for a glass of vodka, he would wrote him such an elaborate petition that not only an unrelated person, but often even the author himself could not understand it.[46]

Slonov made it clear that only poor and ignorant clients hired such attorneys. In one of Ostrovsky's plays, a pettifogger *(abvokat)* named Petrovich, who supplemented his income by forging passports, provided his teenage neighbor advice about possible trouble with the police after he kissed a merchant's daughter; the important legal point was that he had not climbed the fence into the merchant's garden because his feet were still located on the street, and only his lips were technically in the garden.[47]

As legal historian William Pomeranz has shown, such bottom-level legal practitioners continued to be important long after the reform of 1864 and evoked concern from authorities and officially recognized attorneys.[48] Sometimes these "underground" *(podpol'nye)* lawyers were former chancellery clerks, but on occasion they had no clearly discernible prior connection to the official world. Lower-end legal representatives could find employment even with wealthy gentry, such as titular councilor's wife Aleksandra Vasilievna Kupriianova, who in the late 1840s was fighting her late cousin's creditors for his inheritance and delaying accepting the property to avoid it being sold for debt.[49] Kupriianova engaged an illiterate Moscow townswoman Stepanida Matveeva and later another Moscow townswoman, Elizaveta Diushkova, to help her with the busy work at the courts. While it is unclear whether Kupriianova prepared her petitions herself or hired someone else, her case was masterfully defended, so either the townswomen were efficient or their apparent vulnerability was part of Kupriianova's litigation strategy.

A particularly memorable "lawyer" with no observable qualifications for his occupation was the twenty-nine-year-old former peasant Boris Korotkov, who was arrested in 1865 for pawning fake gold watches.[50] Because the police seized and inventoried his belongings, we now have a unique insight into the world of an "underground lawyer" on the threshold of two epochs in Russia's legal and social development. While Korotkov had no background in the law and made his living as a low-level intermediary in credit and employment matters, the police also found among his possessions a written agreement to open a law office in partnership with a man who was most likely the actual source of the fake watches. This fascinating and unique document is fully reproduced in Appendix E, preserving as much of the original as possible in translation. Despite its clumsy style, the agreement is surprisingly well crafted. It required each partner to provide 400 rubles for start-up expenses, stated that Korotkov would hire a clerk to deal with paperwork and accounting, and provided for a 50-ruble penalty in the event of an early termination, as well as arbitration for any disputes that might arise.

Korotkov's law business either failed or did not get a chance to take off before Korotkov's arrest because his papers contained only several commissions to provide domestic servants and governesses. At the same time, he had some advantages: although he was semi-literate at best, this was still a period when the overwhelming majority of Russian peasants and many townspeople were not literate at all. Moreover, Korotkov's handwriting was quite good, which was an extremely useful skill, although he made many spelling and punctuation errors. Despite his low status and young age, the agreement mentions significant amounts of cash (400 rubles was the annual salary of a midlevel civil servant) that the partners either possessed or expected to possess. The agreement itself, despite its awkward style, is sophisticated and even contains an arbitration clause. Even Korotkov's intellectual outlook was not as limited as we may presume; included in his papers was the following poem:

> Mr. Bribes! You
> have Mastered the Learning
> . . . tell us Why We are given
> hands—is it Truly So
> that we can take bribes
> and smack people
> on the head.[51]

The poem suggests that Korotkov was even somewhat familiar with the then-fashionable rhetoric of legal reform. But above all, what is most fascinating about Korotkov is the very fact that this young semi-literate peasant was hoping to make a living as a "lawyer" in Moscow, no doubt perceiving the demand for legal services and aware of the profession's desirability, profitability, and perhaps even prestige. In other words, it was a desirable thing for Korotkov to open specifically an *advokatnaia* office rather than simply be a busy go-between like many other enterprising peasants.

More commonly, lower-status individuals employed as *poverennye* were not "underground" lawyers like Korotkov but rather privileged household servants, either serfs or freedmen, who sometimes handled complicated cases with large amounts of money at stake. For example, Natalia Naryshkina, the daughter of a privy councilor, engaged her freedman Petrov in her litigation with her wastrel brother for her mother's inheritance.[52] Although Natalia seems to have eventually lost, Petrov's petitions were literate and clearly written, albeit without great legal subtlety or energy.

Legal representation by one's serf could also be both competent and energetic, as in the debt case of Lieutenant Nikolai Tolstoy.[53] Tolstoy mortgaged his landed estate populated by nineteen serfs to Lieutenant Beklemishev for 9,000 rubles. Beklemishev acted through his serf, who prepared and filed complaints when Tolstoy avoided payment by constantly moving his residence and continued to get into still more debt. Beklemishev's serf also represented another creditor, named Goffard, and showed considerable energy in pursuing Tolstoy and locating his other estate in Orel province, which Tolstoy was trying to hide from his creditors.

A serf could even engage in what appeared to be a fully-fledged paralegal-style practice, as did Count Zakrevskii's serf Matvei Toropov. He was commissioned by a merchant named Vorontsov from Vyborg to collect debts pursuant to a large number of debt documents, which Vorontsov transferred to Toropov in exchange for an advance payment, often of thousands of rubles.[54]

While it is clear that even persons of moderate means could access some kind of legal representation and that wealthy individuals could access the services of higher-end lawyers who functioned similarly to post-reform barristers and who in some cases did join the bar after 1866, the related question of how easily information about the law was accessed is less clear. This question is important because, as contemporary research shows, the individual's ability to conceive his or her circumstances in legal—as opposed to moral, cultural, social, religious, or other—terms is one of the key factors determining the decision to litigate.[55] Evidence on how well informed Russians were about the law before the reform is conflicting. For example, Michelle Lamarche Marrese, in her study of female property ownership and control in Russia, tends to be pessimistic, emphasizing the difficulties.[56]

Some of my research is in the same vein. Individuals of considerable means and social standing made mistakes in negotiation and litigation and either used bad legal advice or none at all. For example, an exceedingly wealthy noblewoman, Anna Shevich, whose debt suit against her husband was closely related to her divorce proceedings, lost because she admitted in writing that no money exchanged hands when the debt note was signed.[57] We have already encountered the case of an elderly civil servant and aspiring landowner, Lebedev, who was naïve enough to write a letter offering a bribe to a court official.[58] Moneylender and civil servant Aleksandr Zaborovskii, whose case is discussed throughout this book, was employed by the Commercial Bank, but he was unable to devise a legal strategy to fight off allegations of fraud by his borrower's attorney, a much lower-status, uneducated townsman, Konovalov. Thus, even comparatively sophisticated and educated individuals could be so helpless in the world of courts and government offices as to fail to obtain basic legal information or legal advice of any quality.

At the same time, in other cases, individual Russians displayed a remarkable command of legal issues related to their proceedings. Particularly interesting are situations when individuals initially made mistakes but later managed to obtain helpful advice, whether from a legal representative or from well-informed friends or acquaintances. For example, in the fraud case of the twelfth-class official Aleksandr DeMazer, a wealthy serf woman named Mashkina gave money to DeMazer so that he could purchase a house in her name in order to avoid getting her master's permission. However, she then suspected that DeMazer was swindling her, "consulted with other people," and asked DeMazer for an accounting and the original purchase agreement for the house; she eventually complained to the police.[59]

Similarly, an illiterate Moscow merchant woman, Daria Kartasheva, initially admitted a debt to the police, but two weeks later changed her mind and contested the collection, claiming that her son issued the debt note in excess of the amount allotted on his power of attorney.[60] Kartasheva's petition to the Commercial Court stated the reasons the debt was not valid in a clear and professional way that sounds very much like a document that could be written today, suggesting that Kartasheva was able to secure the services of a competent lawyer.

In another fraud case, discussed below in greater detail, the defendant Dmitriev allegedly used a forged blank sheet of paper with his former employers' signatures to borrow money in their names. After accumulating significant debt, Dmitriev surrendered this sheet to one of his creditors, who, in turn, was advised by his *poverennyi* that the sheet was most likely fraudulent because Dmitriev's employers would have used a standard power of attorney if they had really authorized him to borrow money.

Finally, a remarkable example of a sudden and dramatic change in an individual's legal circumstances is found, again, in the Zaborovskii case. The defendant originally confessed to a fraud he never committed, but at the end of the proceeding he obtained accurate information about the laws governing confessions and persuaded the court to dismiss his initial confession as wrongfully obtained.[61]

Individual cases thus suggest a more nuanced view of the availability of legal information: while wealthy and sophisticated litigants could make egregious mistakes, many members of Moscow's middling administrative and commercial classes had access to legal advice and information that made a considerable difference in the outcome of their cases, even after initial mistakes. In short, access to legal knowledge was not a given, but it was by no means rare, and, most importantly, it was not limited to persons of wealth and privilege. Most likely, it depended—much as it does today in Russia or in the United States—on the quality of one's social and kinship network and whether it included individuals with legal experience or helpful connections.

Credit Intermediaries

The variety of activities of the *poverennye* corresponded to their widely different social ranks and relations with their employers. The *poverennye* whose powers of attorney were registered in Moscow can be divided into three groups. The largest one consisted of individuals who held either a civil or military officer's rank included in the Table of Ranks (either active or retired). The second group consisted of merchants and townspeople, which is not surprising given Moscow's commercial significance. Finally, another group included serfs, peasants, and domestic servants, who were typically engaged to manage an estate or to furnish a conscript to the military authorities and also frequently employed to pursue debt-related matters, most notably obtaining a certificate required to remortgage an estate, or even for court appearances, especially for the rather mechanical procedure of hearing the lower-court decision and signing the intention to appeal. It is also notable that the practice of engaging women, servants, or close relatives—very common in the 1850s—deteriorated rapidly in the 1860s, as summarized in Table 8.1 and Appendixes D.1 and D.2.

A freelancing loan broker *(svodchik)* was a familiar figure in Moscow. A *svodchik* was typically hired by the borrower and accompanied him or her both during the preliminary negotiations of the terms of the loan and during the final signing. A flamboyant example of this kind of broker was Boris Korotkov, who, as already mentioned, attempted to become a legal representative and was eventually arrested for pawning fake gold watches. His other occupations were to work as a clerk for a merchant Sudakov, as well as a pawnbroker in a loose partnership network with other individuals, including his victim, Emma Flik, whom he assisted with finding clients. When Korotkov was arrested, the police prepared a detailed inventory of all papers and objects seized from him, which, in addition to a remarkable agreement to provide legal services, included three passports that apparently had been pawned by Korotkov's clients, two bronze watches, a silver watch case, a leather wallet, a leather-bound notebook, and thirteen notes *(zapiski)* of unspecified character.

Korotkov also acted as a domestic servant-finding broker, as evidenced by a reference letter from one aspiring servant and by several sheets of paper containing information about individuals available as servants or needing servants. Finally, Korotkov possessed several cheat-sheets for his loan brokering business. One of them listed the colors of different banknote denominations. The other sheet was titled "At what amount to receive collateral for a 100-ruble nominal price," and it specified, for example, that Finnish public debt went for 70 percent of its nominal value, and 1 pound sterling went for 6.3 rubles, while one share of the Riga–Dünaburg Railroad sold for 100 rubles. Altogether the list included nineteen various types of currencies and commercial paper that were commonly circulating in Moscow in the 1860s.[62]

Engaging a broker of Korotkov's variety was of course risky: not only could these brokers be dishonest, but they could turn out to be incompetent. For instance, the serf girl Praskovia Gavrilova was arrested for fraud when she attempted to sell to a merchant's brother, Lintsov, a loan letter that belonged to her brother-in-law, using the go-between services of chancery clerk Nikolai Pokhorskii, who himself somehow managed to avoid a closer look by the police.[63]

Similarly, the retired chancery clerk Dmitrii Zaitsev, who was engaged to find money for aulic councilor's wife Maria Skrebkova, may or may not have known that she was attempting to cheat the lender, Staff Captain Georgii Balakan, but he was arrested and put on trial together with Skrebkova; he claimed in his defense that he was tricked by her as to who exactly was supposed to act as the borrower, and he successfully asserted that during the key moment when Skrebkova and her accomplice signed a fraudulent loan letter, he was standing in a different room and so did not know what was happening.[64]

Another *svodchik*, Tikhon Nikolaev, helped Collegiate Registrar Sheremetievskii in 1855 to borrow 100 rubles from *meshchanin* Ivanov, but could not prevent a misunderstanding when the debt document was actually written out for 200 rubles; Sheremetievskii initiated a criminal investigation for fraud and usury. Ivanov saw Nikolaev at the court building and loudly blamed Nikolaev for finding him a client who refused to understand the rules of the game and for testifying against him. Nikolaev called him a "usurer" *(rostovsh-chik)*, and Ivanov replied with "idiot" *(durak)*. This is the only indication in the sources that this kind of *svodchik* may have had any implied responsibility for vetting potential parties to a transaction as opposed to simply introducing them to each other.[65]

Wealthier borrowers who could afford a hired property manager *(upravli-aiushchii)* could entrust him with finding loans, either in specified amounts or to borrow whenever it was possible or expedient to carry out their responsibilities. Only rarely were their powers of attorney issued to collect or to borrow from a specific person on a specific occasion; typically, the principal issued a blanket permission to borrow on his or her behalf.[66] The common practice was for the principal to note the credit limit he or she was granting to the agent on the power of attorney, where all the debts incurred on the principal's behalf had to be recorded as well.[67] Those nobles who did not have a hired property manager, or did not sufficiently trust him, employed a relative, a trusted serf, or a freedman who continued to associate with his former masters.

For example, the brothers Aleksandr and Dmitrii Glebov, from a line of important tsarist bureaucrats and both holding the rank of state councilor, employed Titular Councilor (equivalent to army captain) Nikolai Dmitriev, the son of their emancipated former serf who had himself reached the civil service rank of collegiate assessor (Class 8 on the Table of Ranks) and thus acquired hereditary noble status.[68] Nikolai's rank was the more junior

Class 9, although his official job was at Moscow's Board of Trustees. Dmitriev's duties included obtaining loans from various private persons, none of whom had the Glebovs' social standing. Dmitriev had decades-long relationships with some of these lenders. When meeting potential creditors, Dmitriev would show them a blank sheet of paper with the Glebovs' signatures and claim that if his patrons refused to honor the debt incurred by Dmitriev on their behalf, he would convert this sheet into a promissory note and collect from them in court. Seeing such apparent trust from the Glebovs, creditors quickly came up with the money, without ever asking themselves why the brothers did not simply give Dmitriev a regular power of attorney.

Although Dmitriev's family had served the Glebovs for decades, in 1835 they allegedly had a falling out, and Dmitriev was fired. However, he continued to borrow money in the Glebovs' name until 1839, when the brothers finally thought to announce Dmitriev's dismissal in newspapers, and several creditors complained to the police and the gendarmes. However, the best they could do at that point was to try to collect from the penniless Dmitriev. We can only speculate whether it was Dmitriev's ambition or—if the Glebovs were involved in the scheme—loyalty to his patrons that caused him to embezzle, but all of his creditors, one of whom had known him and his father for decades, noted that he had always made timely payments and thus earned their trust.

What is most interesting about this case is the extent of the Glebovs' involvement after the case came to court, and the authorities' hesitation to pry into their affairs. The police made no attempt to ascertain whether the Glebovs actually received any of the money borrowed by Dmitriev in their name or why they failed to notify creditors about his dismissal in a timely fashion. The brothers, in turn, claimed that their signatures on the blank sheet were forged but made this claim impossible to verify by buying the sheet for 10,000 rubles and destroying it. For the destruction of a key piece of evidence in a large-scale criminal fraud case, they were indicted but received only a mild reprimand that was cleared under the tsar's 1841 amnesty.

The brothers also indirectly admitted their responsibility by offering and in some cases reaching settlements with Dmitriev's creditors for a fraction of the original amounts. Of course, bribery and personal connections must have played some role here, and the case record also mentions the Glebovs' financial complications, suggesting that their ability to pay must have been limited. In any case, the convenience of placing all the blame on Dmitriev— who died before his case went on trial in 1846—must have been as obvious to the court as it was to the Glebovs. It appears that the authorities may have considered the risks and ultimately chose not to pursue the inconvenient, embarrassing, and no doubt ultimately futile investigation of the Glebovs' possible culpability. The police and the courts may also have considered their willingness to repay some of the creditors, for whom this was the only chance to recoup at least a portion of their losses.

Even individuals much less wealthy than the Glebovs employed property managers who could be tasked with finding loans. For example, Princess Ekaterina Cherkasskaia, who came from a prominent family but owned only seventy-two serfs in Iaroslavl' province in addition to a house in Moscow, employed a young Moscow townsman and former merchant Sergei Konovalov as her estate manager and agent *(poverennyi i upravliaiushchii),* as he styled himself. Apparently not aware of his less than stellar past—he was expelled from his home by his own parents for dissolute behavior—Cherkasskaia asked him in 1842 to find a loan of 10,000 rubles. The lender that Konovalov found, the previously mentioned Zaborovskii, was none too naïve himself, insisting on getting a receipt signed by Cherkasskaia, whom he never met in person, even though the loan letter was executed at the Second Department of the Moscow Chamber and so, legally speaking, Cherkasskaia would not be permitted to claim that she never received the money.[69]

Konovalov received the money, embezzled it, and then complained to the princess that Zaborovskii never paid him. Cherkasskaia complained to the gendarmes, and Zaborovskii was summoned to Police Chief Lev Tsynskii, famous for his heavy-handed investigation methods; according to the authorities, Zaborovskii confessed during the interrogation, after which he was convicted of fraud in court. However, in 1845, Konovalov repented and confessed everything, in part because he interpreted his unspecified but serious venereal disease as a punishment from above. While in prison, Konovalov bragged to another inmate, a "tramp" and army deserter Diakov, that he used the money to rent a sizable apartment in Moscow and stage "evenings in Paradise, where dancers of both sexes represented the first humans before the Fall" for as much as 1,000 rubles per night.

The type of agent represented by Dmitriev or Konovalov must have been a familiar presence in all types of credit or sale transactions. Their networks of acquaintance were firmly rooted in Moscow's middling classes, consisting of civil servants and nobles of modest means as well as merchants and entrepreneurs. Their ambition could lead them to violate their principals' trust, but typical lenders seem to have thought that the agent's reputation and social connections would prevent fraud. For example, in the case of the Senate Registrar Petr Veselkin, which involved a complex mortgage fraud conspiracy, only one of his many victims became suspicious at all, and even then he waited several weeks after handing over his money to a "representative" of a nonexistent Prince Kropotkin from Vladimir province.[70]

It was also possible for a less highly ranked principal to hire a more highly ranked agent. For example, the victim of the Class 12 civil servant Aleksandr Demazer was a wealthy female serf of Count Sheremetev, Akulina Mikhailovna Mashkina, with whom he was "acquainted."[71] Demazer suggested to Mashkina that she could live more comfortably in her own house and proposed to buy one for her in his own name because as a serf, she could not effect the purchase in her own name or in her landlord's (this last claim was false), but in practice the house would belong to her. She agreed and gave Demazer 6,573 silver rubles, which he used to buy a house that he promptly began to claim as his.

While in her court papers Mashkina claimed that she was illiterate and inexperienced, this case is not so simple: Mashkina was certainly sophisticated enough because she kept her money deposited in a bank, and once she became suspicious of Demazer, she quickly obtained advice on how to proceed and went on to complain to the police. In addition to claiming "inexperience," it is also possible that Mashkina simply did not want to buy a house through her landlord, thinking Demazer to be more reliable.

In addition to using a *poverennyi* to find loans or serve as a legal front man, it was common for individuals of all levels of wealth to hire an intermediary to assist them in dealing with the Board of Trustees. We have already mentioned Ivan Gruzinov, hired by a middling landowner from another province. Whereas there are no indications that Gruzinov himself was in any way dishonest, it is also clear that the Board's operations created many opportunities for fraud and embezzlement. For example, in 1861, a peasant from Novgorod province, Konon Osipov, needed to deposit 354 rubles with the Board. He hired a townsman from the town of Valdai, Ivan Stoliarov, to help him with the task. Stoliarov deposited the money, took the receipt, and promptly appropriated it as his own. There was nothing Osipov could do to prove his ownership of the money.[72]

A more circumspect investor than Stoliarov would have preferred to hire an actual Board employee, but this was not a foolproof strategy either, judging from the case of one such employee, twenty-four-year old Collegiate Registrar (the lowest fourteenth class) Aleksandr Shtibing (Stibing).[73] His victims, the Board's borrowers, must have thought it a smart precautionary measure to engage him when receiving or depositing money to help them with the paperwork. Most of these victims were serving or retired junior officers and civil servants, their wives, mothers, and sisters, a "noble-born maiden," a townsman, and a wealthy serf, but also Actual State Councilor (equivalent to major general) Petr Divov and actual state councilor's wife Princess Elizaveta Dolgorukova. In other words, all ranks and estates of Russian society, from serf to aristocrat, were represented. Incidentally, many of them admitted that they knew they were not legally allowed to pay a Board employee to help them. Shtibing took his clients' money and issued them bogus receipts with forged signatures of senior Board officials.

For years nobody noticed anything, until in 1854 one out-of-town merchant asked for verification of two such receipts that came to him from one of Shtibing's victims, a physician's wife, Ekaterina Bove. The clerks checked the Board's journal and found that no payment was recorded under the numbers of those receipts. When questioned about the receipts, Shtibing confessed to embezzling Bove's money, and when his apartment was searched, the Board officials found evidence of about a dozen other similar episodes. It seemed that he made no effort to conceal his activities and had no explanation prepared in case he was discovered. It is also notable that the Board did not have any procedure in place to catch this kind of embezzlement.

Although Shtibing's victims appear rather foolish, considering how easy it was to catch Shtibing once he came under suspicion, it would have been reasonable to expect the Board to have some kind of audit mechanism to detect this kind of embezzlement, and it actually may have been more reasonable to engage him rather than hire someone completely unrelated.

Shtibing's superiors were understandably reluctant to get the police involved immediately because any official investigation could damage the Board's reputation and thus its otherwise highly profitable operations. In Russia, as well as in Victorian England, employers often preferred to deal with embezzlers in private.[74] However, Board officials also failed to detain Shtibing or otherwise prevent his flight. He slipped away as soon as his questioners left, and so we cannot find out much more about his motivations. He left behind a letter, which claimed that he was about to drown himself in the Moscow River and that he alone was to blame for his crimes. Two weeks later, a dead body was found floating in the river; it was sufficiently decomposed that the police could not determine the precise cause of death, but there were no obvious signs of beatings or injuries. Shtibing's relatives recognized the clothes found on the corpse as belonging to him.

However, they were never shown the body itself, and so we can only guess whether he did actually kill himself or managed to stage his suicide. Interestingly, the clothes on the corpse did belong to Shtibing but did not fit the description of what he wore when he was last seen; furthermore, the police report gave the corpse's age as approximately forty-five, whereas Shtibing was only twenty-four. In any event, the Criminal Chamber was not convinced and ruled "not to enter a judgment" about the dead body or about Shtibing until he was found. Whoever that corpse really was, once Shtibing was revealed to have abused the trust inherent in his position in Russia's credit system, his only escape, in his mind at least, was either his own literal death or a metaphorical death in which he had to commit further frauds and begin his career completely new with a fresh identity—as if his old identity, having lost its respectability, had lost all its value.

Although traditional credit ties between acquaintances and relatives remained strong in imperial Russia until the end, the use of intermediaries who might or might not be acquainted with both participants to the transaction was a routine practice in Moscow long before the Great Reforms, considering that even such individuals as Korotkov managed or at least attempted to make a living from this activity. No less common was the use of an agent who would substitute for one of the parties. Activities of credit brokers blended into those of legal practitioners. While imperial-era writers such as Gessen emphasized the striking novelty of the emergent organized bar in terms of personnel, the first twenty-seven barristers sworn in during 1866 included individuals who had been practicing law for some time, such as Nikolai Aristov and Adam Fal'kovskii, as well as some lawyers who had been practicing before the Moscow Commercial Court.[75]

Stories of actual pre-reform legal practitioners suggest that, although they could have benefitted from greater social status and professional self-regulation, they were not the dysfunctional and pathetic group depicted by late-imperial-era publicists committed to preserving the achievements of the Great Reforms. Rather, pre-reform lawyers as a group performed real services for their clients and for the legal system. While educated *advokaty* were available for complicated cases, such as appellate proceedings in the Senate or to serve wealthy and prominent clients such as the merchant Butikov, middling-level lawyers were available and adequate for the variety of matters that required practical acumen and experience but not necessarily a university education or a persuasive pen. This business must have been profitable enough to leave room for such lower-level "lawyers" as Korotkov. It is, moreover, important to note that the gradation in the quality and character of legal services in Russia before the reform of 1864 also persisted after the reform, according to William Pomeranz. In sum, the real shortcomings of pre-reform legal practitioners should not be exaggerated or taken to support the case for Russian legal exceptionalism.

CHAPTER 9

Creditors and Debtors
in Pre-Reform Courts

ISPUTES ABOUT DEBT were the bread and
butter of any Western legal system. In pre-reform
Russia, most provincial Chambers of Civil Justice had two departments—
one for disputes about landed estates and especially inheritance, and the
other for lawsuits about contracts and especially debt—in addition to the
Records Office, which registered sales, loans, and other private agreements.
This court system was widely used, with approximately half a million cases
on its docket in a given year, split roughly equally between first- and second-tier courts and between civil and criminal matters; after the reform, the
courts became even busier.[1]

But one of the most persistent beliefs about Russian law is that—in any
historical period—it has lacked a legal tradition comparable to those of
Western and Central Europe and especially that the law has lacked a firm
foundation in either political or popular culture. This general argument is
made particularly forcefully about pre-1864 law. In addition to the lack of
institutional autonomy or a regulated legal profession—which I have already
argued to be greatly exaggerated—other specific criticisms focus on court
structure and procedures, alleging that the courts were fragmented according
to the estate system, that they deployed inferior "inquisitorial" rules of procedure, as well as a system of evidence based on "formal proofs," which deprived
individual litigants and judges alike of flexibility and discretion.

This chapter explores whether and in what ways these features of pre-
reform justice affected actual cases involving property and debt, and especially

the interests and strategies of property owners who used the courts. First recall that in any legal system, even a very elaborate set of procedural rules cannot foresee all possible facts and circumstances and so is inevitably modified in practice. In actual cases litigated in pre-reform courts, practical considerations undermined the principle of estate-based justice as soon as it was established; inquisitorial procedure surprisingly left civil law proceedings to private individuals' discretion; and the requirements of expert evaluation of debt documents undermined the system of formal proofs.

None of this is to deny that pre-reform procedures did not conform to the model featuring public trials, juries, and elite barristers that was becoming predominant elsewhere in Europe. But my research contradicts the myth that pre-reform law was dysfunctional to the point of not deserving to be called law at all and that Russians possessed no culture of using the courts in a rational and efficient way to promote and protect their property interests. To the contrary, the pre-reform legal system was reasonably efficient in protecting the system of private credit and of private property more generally. It therefore should be seen as a logical precursor of late imperial law rather than a dead branch on the tree of Russian legal development.

Interpretations of Pre-Reform Courts

There is little doubt that the reform of 1864, with all its limitations and disappointments, was a momentous achievement, and the 1860s are rightly seen as a watershed in Russia's legal development. Numerous accounts by memoirists and legal scholars contrasted the new courts with the legal reign of darkness that allegedly preceded it. This consensus owes much to fiction and memoirs by Gogol, Ostrovskii, Sukhovo-Kobylin, Saltykov-Shchedrin, Herzen, and Aksakov. Their arguments were then marshaled by late imperial jurists to defend the reformed justice system against conservative attacks. Jurists Anatolii Koni, Iosif Gessen, Ivan Blinov, or Grigorii Dzhanshiev used the old court system as a rhetorical backdrop to better highlight the reform's achievements.[2] But while this literature's polemical framework is very clear, its specific claims are neither as accurate nor as unambiguously critical as they first appear.

To give just a few typical examples, Gessen supported his claim of pre-reform corruption and inefficiency by discussing a single low-profile, out-of-court commercial arbitration case while revealing nothing about actual court procedures.[3] His stories about officials falsifying legal documents refer to the police rather than the courts, and his claim that pre-reform judges did not write their decisions themselves but employed clerks and secretaries does not sound very shocking.[4] Gessen also quoted the well-known post-reform barrister Vladimir Spasovich as claiming that judges in the old courts were "only concerned with conducting the case mechanically according to the law, rather than according to their conscience."[5] Even if we do for a moment agree that judging a case according to the law is actually a shortcoming, Gessen later in his book noted that this criticism could be directed at the new courts as well.[6] Blinov thought that judicial corruption in Russia could be studied on the basis of literary works, press articles, and Herzen's émigré publications, with "original cases" *(podlinnye dela)* only useful for providing additional examples, which he deemed to be unnecessary.[7] By contrast, my study maintains that the evidence of "original cases" is essential for studying any country's legal practice and legal culture.

Even those accounts that are grounded in personal experience are still polemical; an example is one of the best-known memoirs about pre-reform law by Nikolai Kolmakov, who had extensive experience with pre-reform justice and was personally involved in drafting the reform legislation. At the same time, he never served on an actual trial court; as a Ministry of Justice official, he formed his opinions by working in Petersburg, conducting appellate procedures or the inspections of provincial courts and administration that were specifically tasked with rooting out local corruption.[8] Kolmakov's condemnation of pre-reform courts was indeed scathing: "old courts . . . in their composition and circumstances, and in their procedural forms . . . and above all in their dependence on the provincial authority and other officials . . . were pathetic institutions, which did not at all fulfill the great responsibility of the state—that of administering justice!"[9]

However, Kolmakov's criticisms can be reduced to only a few specific issues. One was that the provincial nobility did not take seriously their responsibility to participate in the administration of justice, most importantly by electing chairmen of provincial Judicial Chambers. But Kolmakov's evidence showed exactly the opposite: that the nobles were capable of acting in concert to vote down candidates who were approved by the authorities but were thought to be detrimental to the nobles' interests, although competent professionally.

Second, Kolmakov argued that the Ministry of Justice and the judiciary as a whole were not sufficiently powerful as compared to the Ministry of the Interior and the police, which admittedly had a very extensive range of responsibilities. But, once again, Kolmakov's horror stories all concerned police misconduct and did not reveal anything about the courts. Other representative critical accounts include those by Ivan Bocharov, who had extensive—and highly negative—experience as a court secretary at the Senate in Petersburg, which, as he himself acknowledged, occurred before the codification of 1832 had transformed Russia's legal landscape. Another account is provided by Piotr Kostylev, who began his career as a court investigator in the early 1860s and had some experience with pre-reform justice but did not provide any detailed examples aside from general incantations about "the sinister labyrinth of . . . written procedure."[10]

Although imperial-era lawyers and memoirists clearly did not set out to objectively analyze pre-reform justice, even taken at face value their accounts show that the condemnation was not unequivocal, and they also provided considerable evidence of fairness and professionalism. For example, Aksakov, in his frequently quoted tirade from 1884 about his younger years spent as a court clerk, admitted that second-tier all-estate courts were staffed by individuals trained in law "who could not be fooled by a *zapiska* [a case summary prepared by court secretaries who could theoretically falsify the facts]."[11]

Vasilii Gettun, whose memoirs contain rich information on patronage, bribery, and all types of official malfeasance in the early nineteenth century, first made his career in Petersburg as an unpaid judiciary volunteer, by taking the initiative to investigate the case of a minor civil servant in the far-away Urals who was wrongly convicted and sentenced to hard labor. When much later the Grand Duchess Ekaterina Pavlovna asked him in a social setting how a judge should rule in a civil law case that could be resolved in favor of either side, he said that the rule of thumb was to rule in favor of the poorer side. Even taking into account Gettun's hypocrisy, it is important to note the general sentiment he was trying to exploit.[12]

At the end of his sharp analysis of the courts' shortcomings even Kolmakov asked himself, "Were these and other similar phenomena general and ubiquitous? I would say no. There were also such Chambers [province-level courts], especially those where chairmen were appointed by the government[and] assisted by useful deputies, [that] conducted cases expeditiously and decided them correctly. But these were the exceptions." Kolmakov thought that the main issue reducing the Chambers' effectiveness was their Records Office, which performed non-judicial, notarial functions and crowded out actual court proceedings, imparting to the courts a reputation for bribery. Kolmakov clearly implied that the Records Office's reputation for regularized petty bribery was not shared by the regular court personnel.[13]

Ilya Selivanov, in his bitterly humorous account of the elderly judges of the Senate's Moscow departments, at the same time added that some of the senators did not share their colleagues' senility and incompetence. Once again, he was referring to the period before 1832.[14] In his work on the history of the Russian bar, Gessen admitted that some pre-reform lawyers were good; his claim that some were bad does not seem all that surprising or shocking, or for that matter necessarily rectifiable by the creation of an organized bar.[15] Blinov, after mentioning the horrors of pre-reform criminal procedure, noted that they did not apply to "privileged" offenders.[16] Journalist Yekaterina Kozlinina wrote an uncommonly subtle account of pre-reform justice, once again mainly describing police procedures and not the courts themselves. While condemning their moral and intellectual underpinnings, she argued that actual institutions and proceedings had positive aspects; for example, criminal trials included the possibility of a suspended sentence—known as being "left under suspicion"—that was absent in post-reform criminal procedure. Even the infamously rough police investigations that relied on beatings and freely doled out corporal punishment were speedy and—Kozlinina implied—fundamentally reliable. Despite her reform-minded rhetoric, Kozlinina's account creates the impression of a faulty but vibrant and viable legal and administrative apparatus.[17]

The reform-centered rhetoric of imperial-era writers also migrated into more recent scholarship, most notably through the groundbreaking book of the U.S.-trained historian Samuel Kucherov, who originally studied law in imperial Russia.[18] The most detailed modern analysis of the early imperial court system, by John LeDonne, stops at 1825 but has clear implications for Nicholas I's reign, which did not introduce any significant procedural innovations. LeDonne convincingly emphasizes the influence of patronage and social networks upon the legal process, as well as the court system's responsiveness to political pressure—none of which were (or are), however, unique to Russia. The English ideal of the rule of law that is taken as a given in LeDonne's analysis not only never existed in actual practice, but was itself still in the initial stages of being formulated during the time period covered by his study.[19] For example, how can one—partially accurately—criticize Russia's legislative procedure for being haphazard and casuistic and—inaccurately—for not containing clear procedural rules, when the very idea of codification was under sharp attack throughout Europe in the first quarter of the nineteenth century because of its association with Napoleon's dominance?

Although no comprehensive, archival-based study of Russia's pre-1864 courts has existed until now, some historians have departed from the reform-driven narrative to illuminate various aspects of Russian legal culture before the 1850s.[20] The most ambitious of them is Boris Mironov's sweeping social history of imperial Russia, which argues rather sanguinely that pre-reform courts already manifested a progression of legality and individual rights, and even employed some adversarial procedures. A much more convincing and empirically grounded depiction of the pre-1864 legal universe is found in Michelle Lamarche Marrese's study of female property ownership and control, which has implications far beyond her stated topic, showing that pre-reform Russia had a vigorous culture of private property, intimately linked to imperial legislation and to a legal practice that served to protect property interests in court. Marrese's approach is close to studies of pre-Petrine courts by Nancy Shields Kollmann and George Weickhardt, who establish the existence of a vibrant, sophisticated, and widely used legal structure with well-developed procedural rules. Without attempting to whitewash the problems, all these works question the divergence of Russia's legal universe from the Western "norm."[21] My study similarly focuses on the stories of individual litigants and interprets any legal system as a venue where multiple interests and influences intersect and where political ideas often determine the outcome.[22]

Estate-Based Court Structure

As has been mentioned above, the degree to which Russia was divided into a strict system of predominantly closed legal estates has been questioned by recent scholarship showing estate boundaries to be porous and contested. However, other scholars argue for the continued relevance and importance of estate-based social identities until the end of the imperial period.[23] One factor that has been seen to unequivocally support the estate structure was the pre-reform legal system, which is commonly labeled as estate-based in its entirety. It is true that Catherine's 1775 Provincial Statute established a system of first-tier trial courts that was based on her notion of peer-administered justice and therefore divided into County Courts for nobles and, later, free peasants; Magistrate Courts for merchants and townspeople; and Aulic Courts in Moscow and Petersburg primarily for government officials.

Scholars of Russian law for the past 150 years have interpreted this structure as evidence of the fractured and unreliable character of the Russian legal system. One historian, for example, has argued that the courts were "disjointed and separated" and that "there was no unified system of national courts to apply a common law."[24] Any lawyer would object that all legal systems are fragmented in some way, but historians of imperial Russia have extrapolated the first-tier court structure onto the legal system in general, ignoring the elements of the court system that were common to all estates. Most importantly, province-level courts included noble and urban assessors, who were explicitly required to take part in deciding all cases, "regardless of the estate of the litigants."[25] Estate-based first-tier courts were closely supervised and reviewed by the Chambers. In reality Russia's pre-reform legal system was unified to a remarkable degree even compared to the late imperial period, when the new courts were established only gradually outside the core Russian provinces. Moreover, no previous scholar has attempted to find out how estate-based pre-reform courts actually functioned in practice.

It turns out that the estate principle built into the 1775 system had to be eroded in practice, most importantly because the system inevitably raised the issue of jurisdiction in cases involving members of different estates. The basic principle of Russian law that the suit was to be brought to the court that had jurisdiction over the defendant obviously gave advantage to the latter. In the United States today, such cases are transferred from state to federal courts. In imperial Russia, all-estate provincial courts (Civil and Criminal Chambers) were overburdened by having to review virtually all serious first-tier decisions. The problem became even more complicated for cases involving multiple defendants from different legal estates. Theoretically, such cases could be split into separate proceedings. However, such splitting would violate the principle of "procedural indivisibility," also known in Western European law, which prohibited the break-up of large cases with multiple defendants.[26]

The solution adopted by the 1775 Provincial Statute mandated joint trials in cases when more than one court was "involved" in a case.[27] Even in the early years, the government viewed local court judges as interchangeable despite their estate affiliation; for example, when one of the two elected County Court assessors was not available, he was to be replaced by a member from the lower court for peasants.[28]

Subsequent legislation and court reorganization only furthered the erosion of the estate principle. Catherine's successor, Paul I (1796–1801), abolished the original second tier of the court system, which was also estate-based.[29] This change undermined the estate principle severely because from then on, only the lowest and least important county- or city-level courts were estate-based.

Alexander I ascended the throne in 1801 but did not reverse Paul's reform. Rather, he continued to erode the estate principle by eliminating special courts for peasants and placing state peasants under the jurisdiction of County Courts, thus eliminating these courts' all-noble character.[30] State peasants, relatively few in number in the eighteenth century, multiplied enormously in the first half of the nineteenth until they made up almost two-thirds of the empire's peasantry on the eve of the emancipation of 1861. The court structure was therefore adapted to account for the participation of peasant representatives in County Courts by strengthening the nobles' role and by prohibiting the peasants from judging cases that involved only nobles.[31] This legislative activity reflects the government's desire to strengthen the nobility's tutelage over other estates, but it also undermined the original compartmentalization of the courts and the principle of peer justice.

The fact that lawsuits frequently involved members of different estates caused pre-reform courts to function in practice as one single unit, as one little-known imperial-era jurist noted.[32] Joint sessions of estate-based courts prescribed in the Provincial Statute were actively practiced in the nineteenth century. An 1848 law elaborated the rules on the joint sessions of County Courts and Magistrate Courts. These sessions were to be chaired by the crown-appointed County Court judge and consist of three or five members of each court, depending on whether peasant members were involved.[33] In Moscow, the practice of joint sessions became common at least by midcentury, in criminal as well as civil cases. Virtually every significant case discussed in this study involved a joint court session.

Exact statistics would take years to compile from thousand-page annual "journals" of each court, but notes from 1860 of occasions when the Moscow magistrate invited County Court members to a joint hearing of various civil cases do provide some indication (see Table 9.1).[34] The fact that this list is not hugely long should be explained by the fact that the Magistrate did not process "commercial" cases in which merchants were likely to be involved; they were litigated at the Commercial Court.[35] Nor does this list include criminal cases or instances of other courts inviting each other's or the Magistrate's members to *their* joint sessions. What is important is the fact that this list was compiled at all, which provides additional confirmation that at least in the minds of court officials, joint sessions were a regular practice, and lower-level courts in Moscow tended to operate as a single unit.

Table 9.1 Joint Hearings at the Moscow Magistrate Court with Members of the Moscow County Court, 1860

Date	Litigants	Type of Case
Apr. 26	Coachmen (iamshchiki) N. Sharov and S. Bezport(ill). v. townswoman M. Shchukina	Unlawful building by Shchukina on plaintiff's children's land.
May 10	Guard Colonel V. B. and Staff Captain D. D. Kazakovs v. late merchant N. N. Kraiushkin	Collection of a debt (38,000 and 9,000 rubles) incurred by Kraiushkin's father.
May 8 & 24	Townsman A. Dmitriev	Exercise of the redemption right to Dmitriev's patrimonial house, on sale by a nephew.
June 15	Kraiushkin (see above)	Kraiushkin's wife demands her share of her husband's inheritance.
July 20	Household serf of Count Sheremetev A. Mashkina v. retired twelfth-class official A. DeMazer	Contested ownership of a house, income money and insurance expenses.
Aug. 31	Kraiushkin (see above)	See above.
Oct. 18	Collegiate Registrar's wife A. Gukova	Contested will. One judge removed because of his legal claim against Gukova's husband.
Oct. 17	Moscow Merchant A. F. Bovastro v. Collegiate Councilor V. F. Mit'kov	Contested ownership of a "chocolate machine."
Nov. 29	Gukov and Mit'kov (see above)	See above.

Data source: TsIAM 92.9.1092.

Yet another factor promoting a single legal system in the core provinces of the empire actually resulted from what is commonly thought of as a defect—namely, the notorious Nicholaevan over-centralization, which concentrated key decision-making authority in the non-estate provincial Judicial Chambers and in the Governing Senate.[36] This is not to suggest that lower-court proceedings were always a mere formality; in many cases, the most interesting action took place precisely there (for example, in the Blaginin debt-related inheritance case, where the parties were a clerk from Orenburg province and a Moscow townswoman).[37] As noted by Ilya Selivanov, the head criminal judge in Moscow in the 1850s, the function of the County Court was to impose comparatively severe sentences that would be reduced after further review.[38] But, higher-tier courts could also simply rule to affirm the lower court decision.

Nevertheless, numerous other examples suggest that province-level Civil and Criminal Chambers had the real authority, responsibility, and legal expertise, compared to the estate-based first tier, and that the lower courts functioned as the Chamber's subdivisions, essentially doing its busy work.[39] In criminal cases, the Chamber was required to review all but the most minor convictions, and in civil ones, all disputes involving more than 30 rubles could be—and virtually invariably were—appealed by the losing side to the Chamber.[40]

One of the most illustrative cases is the debt proceedings of a widow of a *kamer-lakei* (servant at the imperial court) Nastasia Chizhikova, in which the court ordered a sale of the house that belonged to a woman who signed Chizhikova's debt as a surety.[41] From this routine and uncomplicated debt case, one gathers that the County Court was not a judiciary organ in its own right because the Chamber oversaw, reviewed, and second-guessed every step of the litigation, no matter how minor. Chambers of Criminal and Civil Justice reviewed every case of any consequence, sometimes in excruciating detail, and thus largely obviated the already eroded estate-based court structure.

In sum, the alleged fragmentation of the court system on the basis of the empire's estate structure existed more on paper than in real legal practice. Court cases, as well as legislation, show that the estate-based court organization was eroded almost from the moment it was introduced, in part because of practical considerations of judging cases with multiple plaintiffs and defendants and in part because of the early-nineteenth century drive for centralization, so that the all-estate provincial courts, applying the same laws and staffed by professional judges, quickly became the key locus of Russian legal practice and thus should be seen as precursors of the post-reform trial courts.

Pre-Reform Civil Procedure

Memoirist and legal official Vasilii Gettun quipped that civil cases were more complicated than criminal ones because they presented two extreme positions, and officials therefore needed considerable caution and perceptiveness to avoid making judicial mistakes. By contrast, criminal cases were difficult to review only in cases of blatant misconduct.[42] A pre-reform civil case began when a plaintiff submitted a petition to the appropriate lower-level court or when the debtor raised a legal objection during the police collection procedure.[43] The proper lower-level court was the one that had jurisdiction over the defendant's legal estate in the locale where the defendant resided or owned property.[44] Unless a debtor raised one of the enumerated objections, the police collection against him continued even after the case was transferred to a court.[45] This meant that he or she was required to "secure" the suit by posting the contested amount of money or by being arrested.[46]

Once the suit was initiated, parties exchanged written petitions responding to each other's claims and presenting evidence. This exchange was the longest part of the proceedings. The 1716 rule allowing only two rounds of petitions was obviously not feasible, and already in the eighteenth century, many suits involved more than thirty rounds. Rather than try to require another, more practicable number, the law was left in suspense, without any set limit.[47] The law permitted one month for the first round of petitions and from two to six months for the second round, thus making it easy for the parties to delay the proceedings.[48] In addition, the court could make information requests of its own; for example, in an inheritance case, it could require the heir to produce documents confirming his relation to the deceased, or if a litigant referred to a document without producing it, the court could demand to see it. Interlocutory appeals were permitted and could further delay a case.[49] The parties could reach a settlement *(mirovaia sdelka),* which the court had to review to ensure that it was truly voluntary.[50] Actual cases show that individual litigants controlled the pace of a lawsuit in practice, as well as in theory.

The open-ended procedural framework in pre-reform courts allowed even persons of moderate means, connections, and education to formulate a litigation strategy and to pursue it with minimal expense. This is illustrated by the litigation regarding the inheritance left by Lieutenant-Colonel Andrei Blaginin, a typical Nicholaevan soldier of serf origins who became commissioned at age thirty-one and thus gained hereditary nobility.[51] After retiring in 1839 at only age forty-one, he lived in a small wooden house in Moscow on his pension of 666 rubles per year, never marrying and keeping no servants. Instead, he met Anna Gavrilova Antonova, an illiterate daughter of a household serf from the backwater Zaraisk County who had managed to move to Moscow and enroll as a townswoman. Blaginin visited Antonova, ten years his junior, twice a day at her apartment, and boarded with her until in June 1849 he became ill with chest pain and heart palpitations aggravated by his love for "hot" (i.e., alcoholic) beverages. On June 9, Antonova went to check on him and found him dead in his bed. She summoned the police, who sealed up the house and inventoried all the property inside.

Typically, the next step would be for Blaginin's heirs, if any, to take over his property; however, Antonova immediately submitted for collection a debt note for 600 silver rubles issued by Blaginin two years previously. Her petitions did not anticipate any challenge to the collection and requested that the house be rented out until the case was resolved. However, the County Court ruled to wait until the legal heirs had been notified. In July, the court heard back from Andrei's brother Petr, a retired non-commissioned officer serving as a petty clerk in his native Troitsk in the south Urals. Petr claimed the inheritance for himself and for his two married sisters, although he had no money to come to Moscow himself. At first he did not know about the house, but he asked the police to send him any property or cash left from his brother's estate. He also asked the police to investigate the validity of any debt claims against the estate—that is, whether they were properly witnessed and notarized.

Petr's petitions to the court are remarkable for their clear style, good handwriting, and extreme attention to detail. Petr asked why there was only one witness to the property inventory, why the house was located on someone else's plot of land, and why it was—in his opinion—undervalued, whether Andrei had received his last pension installment, whether the police had checked if Andrei's acquaintances or his—nonexistent—servants stole his property, and whether Andrei's creditors had at any point lived in his house and whether they had somehow been able to take advantage of him. He was also unsure about his brother's actual social standing, writing about completely fantastical "teams of horses" and "fur garments." Petr's petitions sound as if he had an absolute and indisputable right to know about all of these things and that some large-scale conspiracy to defraud him might have been brewing, perhaps even with police participation. However, he skillfully managed to avoid making his claims sound offensive or target specific legal officials or institutions.

It is unclear whether Petr's paranoid style benefited his case by persuading court personnel in Moscow that he was more trouble than he was worth, but at least they did not harm him, considering the outcome of the case. When he demanded to see the original debt documents so that he could decide whether to contest them, they were mailed to him, and in July 1850 he wrote to the court, arguing that they were invalid because they were written on the wrong variety of stamped paper and not witnessed. He did not stop there but listed other reasons he thought Antonova's claim was suspicious—for example, that a 600-ruble loan was secured by a house that was worth only 100. Petr also claimed that Antonova had lived with Andrei for several years, that she forged the note, and that her "enterprising" character was proved by the fact "that she dared, without any permission from the local police and contrary to existing laws to spend a significant sum on the funeral and the wake." Petr could not be more specific on what kind of self-interest induced Antonova to pay these expenses.

This exchange continued for most of 1850 and 1851, until the parties were finally summoned to court. There is no indication that Petr ever made it to Moscow in person, and there is no mention of any other person who helped him prepare or submit his petitions. It seems that he conducted the entire litigation by mail from Troitsk. The joint session of the County Court and the Magistrate Court acknowledged Petr as Andrei's heir on February 27, 1852 and ordered payment of Antonova's funeral expenses out of his estate but ruled that Antonova could not collect her debt because the note was written on the wrong kind of paper and even fined her for "incorrectly bringing the suit." The court also ignored the ambiguous result of the hand-writing analysis and ruled that Andrei's signature was not genuine. Interestingly, Antonova appealed the case to the Civil Chamber, lost her appeal, and decided not to pursue the case to the Senate.

This uncommonly well-detailed case record raises several key questions about pre-reform legal culture and legal practice. First, we see that central and local officials, litigants, and institutions could interact perfectly seamlessly, showing that the law under Nicholas I could operate as a single fairly efficient system despite the empire's estate system and size. Second, the case shows that pre-reform legal culture, while clearly appearing as somewhat amateurish compared to post-reform law, could be effective in enabling individuals to identify and pursue their interests in court and that legal cases that did not involve strong incentives for corruption or delay could be conducted efficiently and inexpensively. Finally, it is remarkable that Petr Blaginin managed to maintain an extremely proactive and even aggressive stance during the proceedings, despite being somewhat irrational and living very far away. Antonova, in turn, was herself a remarkably active participant in the legal culture, despite her humble origins. Compared to the two litigants, the court itself appears reactive, even aloof, and its only "inquisitorial" action was the obvious step of asking Petr to confirm his relation to his late brother.

Wealthier litigants who could afford good legal advice were more likely to cite sophisticated legal concepts in their petitions, although they could at the same time supplement them with the kind of speculative and circumstantial arguments used by Petr Blaginin. The case of Colonel Nikolai Nikitin was litigated in the same County Court at the same time as the Blaginin case, and, similarly, it involved parties with equal social and economic status.[52] The difference was that Nikitin was a wealthy moneylender and the family of his debtor, State Councilor Surovishchikov, had for decades owned hugely profitable public baths in Moscow.[53] This case shows even more confidence by the litigants in their dealings with the court. Nikitin had loaned the staggering sum of 100,000 rubles to Surovshchikov's wife, on the condition that the debtor, Surovshchikov, was to pay a 15,000-ruble penalty if he failed to repay the loan on the due date. Surovshchikov missed the deadline but was unwilling to pay the penalty and started a lawsuit.

The legal contest regarding the validity of the penalty clause took the familiar shape of a seesaw-like exchange of petitions. Surovshchikov's position strikingly combined legally sophisticated arguments with arguments bordering on the ridiculous. He claimed that he did not authorize his wife to borrow money on such unfavorable conditions and at the same time accused Nikitin of usury and of showing insufficient respect by not addressing Surovshchikov by his name and patronymic. Surovshchikov also had one of the judges removed from the panel on the grounds that he was Nikitin's friend. Nikitin objected that the whole point of the clause was that Surovshchikov agreed to pay 15,000 rubles in the event of default, without any contest, and that his wife was authorized to borrow money on any conditions. The court's only attempt to be proactive was in denying one of Surovshchikov's information requests, which was reversed by the Senate after an interlocutory appeal, showing the court to be largely powerless to direct the proceedings.

The ruling by two of the three judges held on June 1, 1853, was that Surovshchikov had to pay only 100,000 rubles. One judge ruled that his wife was only authorized to mortgage the baths for 100,000, and the other held that under Russia's civil code, penalty clauses were prohibited for mortgages of real estate and that here the clause was part of the debt document and not a separate contract.[54] The dissenting judge argued that the clause was a separate agreement motivating Surovshchikov to repay on time and compensating Nikitin for his possible loss, since he otherwise might not have lent such a large sum of money. This ruling shows the County Court, despite its insufficient force to channel the proceedings and despite the Chamber's oversight, was still being independent-minded enough to find it necessary to list all these arguments.

Even more importantly, the judges were well oriented in the legal issues, despite the stereotype about lower-level court judges being untrained in the law and completely dependent on their secretaries. Or should we imagine that this court's secretary prepared different opinions for different judges?

While in this instance the debtor won the case, it is important to note that the entire litigation only contested the penalty clause: as to the baths themselves, Nikitin quickly seized them. This case clearly contradicts the commonly made observation that the pre-reform legal system was geared against the creditor; rather, the effect of this ruling seems to have been to prevent Nikitin's unjust enrichment and to emphasize the fact that the entire point of a mortgage is that it is secured by real property and nothing else.

The exchange of petitions ended when "all the evidence had been presented," after which neither party was permitted to submit any additional petitions or claims. Who made this determination was left unclear. The secretary of the court then compiled a summary of all the pleadings *(zapiska)*, prepared according to specified rules. The parties reviewed the summary for accuracy, made additions they thought were necessary, and signed at the end. The secretary then listed applicable statutes, which was a much easier task after the Digest of the Laws was published in 1832.

Once the case was ready for trial, a hearing was held, during which the *zapiska* was read out to the judges. Although these hearings were by no means "public," they were not "secret" either: the small courtrooms—more closely resembling offices—and adjacent corridors and stairways seem to have been crowded by staff and visitors. The parties and their lawyers could be present during the hearing and were allowed to give oral "explanations" but not to present any new evidence, claims, or arguments.[55]

Many writers on Russian law have claimed that these all-important case summaries were "unreliable" and placed undue power in the hands of the court secretary, who could slant the case in favor of one of the parties.[56] Vasilii Gettun recalled that his boss, Field Marshal Count Kamenskii, did not trust these extracts but preferred to read the original.[57] However, I found exactly the opposite to be the case. Most cases that I reviewed contain pencil marks on the petitions showing the alterations made during the preparation of the digest. I have not been able to locate any material alterations in any of the summaries. At most, secretaries slightly improved the summaries by removing superfluous verbiage and misspellings, but even this happened only rarely. Typically, secretaries merely changed all first-person pronouns to third-person and kept the text of each petition intact. For example, in the case of collegiate councilor's wife Strekalova, the secretary simply changed the pronouns, dropped some of the most extreme verbiage, and changed Strekalova's lawyer's misspelling of the word *sekverst* (sequester) to the standard *sekvestr*.[58]

Even if a secretary did misrepresent one side's arguments, the litigants were required by the law to review the digest, note anything they did not agree with, sign it, and, if they felt necessary, make oral explanations in person in front of the judges. This right was not a mere formality but was widely deployed in actual cases. For example, in the Nikitin case mentioned above, the colonel examined the digest and noted his objection to the fact that it incorrectly named Surovshchikov, rather than his wife, as the borrower.

This right was exercised even in criminal cases in which defendants' rights were much less protected. For example, merchant Mokhov's case started as a debt collection against a merchant woman named Levi, who was able to leave Moscow without having to "secure" the claim against her.[59] The litigation turned against him, and he was subjected to a criminal accusation of not proving a denunciation *(izvet)*[60] and of including in his court papers an improper *(neprilichnoe)* expression about the actions of the joint session of Moscow County Court and the magistrate, as well as "irrelevant" language in his receipt relating to his complaint against the police. After the summary of these criminal charges was prepared, he was able to add two large pages of very small handwriting, which in his view must have better stated his position than his own prior petitions, since these had been accurately summarized by the secretary. After successfully arguing that the type of denunciation that he made was not punishable, nor were "irrelevant" expressions, he was only given a warning for his choice of words.

As another example, the case of Moscow merchant Stepan Tikhomirov began as a regular debt collection but was transferred to the criminal court when the debtor, merchant Iakov Chistiakov, denied having signed the bill of exchange.[61] In 1867 Chistiakov decided to hire a new-style barrister to represent him in the Criminal Chamber; the barrister was allowed to "comment" on the case even after it had already been presented to the judges.

Finally, even in the previously discussed fraud case of Gubernial Secretary Aleksei Zaborovskii, who was rather roughly treated by the police, he was allowed in 1846 to review the case summary and did not hesitate to petition the Criminal Chamber to be allowed to appear before it in person when he felt that the written record was not sufficient to properly present his defense.[62]

None of this is, of course, to deny that Russian pre-reform civil and criminal procedure was written rather than oral. What is surprising is the fact that the parties often seemed to have preferred it that way. The procedure that, since the days of Peter the Great, had provided for simplified oral pleadings *(sud po forme)* as an alternative to the usual lengthy procedure was only rarely used, as shown by my own research and by one other legal historian.

In the cases considered in this study there were only a handful of references to litigants using this procedure, but even in such instances, they preferred to exchange written pleadings whenever the court would allow it. For example, *sud po forme* was the required procedure at the Moscow Equity Court, which had jurisdiction over all money suits between parents and children, and this is where a wealthy merchant Savinov sued his daughter for 200,000 rubles.[63] Although the parties were required to meet in court to present their arguments, at every court date, either only one party showed up or none at all. The daughter's husband, who represented her, even argued that he was not required to have face-to-face meetings with his father-in-law, according to the Provincial Statute of 1775 and according to the Civil Code. Savinov's representative, the chancery clerk Nechaev, pursued the case through the customary exchange of written statements, despite the court's repeated attempts to have both parties face each other. In the end, the court decided the case not on the basis of a face-to-face oral trial but on the basis of the documents that the parties submitted.

The decision itself was a multi-stage process: after hearing the case, the judges recorded and signed their decision *(rezoluitsiia)* in the court's journal. The next step was to combine the *zapiska* with the decision and produce the official case record *(protokol)*, until which point an individual judge could still change his mind and record his new opinion in the journal. After the *protokol* had been signed, no more changes were permitted. The parties were then notified in writing and assigned a date to appear in court, review the decision, and sign off, whether they were satisfied with the decision or intended to appeal. The decision was considered to acquire its legal force when the *protokol* was signed, even though it was not yet announced to the parties. This was different from "final legal force" when it was the kind of case that could not be appealed or the party that intended to appeal missed the deadline for filing it. In its decision, the court had to list the ways it was to be executed and forward it directly to the applicable police authorities for execution.

Debt cases show that claims that pre-reform law "rejected" adversarial proceedings in favor of the inquisitorial system are exaggerated.[64] The term "inquisitorial procedure" refers to the judges' overall control over the proceedings and the balance of power in criminal prosecutions significantly favoring the state.[65] The judge is supposed to take an active part in questioning the parties and their witnesses. Inquisitorial procedure is associated with the Continental legal systems from which Russian law borrowed freely in the eighteenth century, in contrast with the "adversarial" common law systems, in which the famous English Court of Chancery was an important exception, employing written non-public proceedings. However, the distinction of inquisitorial and adversarial procedure was most directly observable in criminal cases and is much less relevant to civil ones, in which "the determination of what issues to raise, what evidence to introduce, and what arguments to make is left almost entirely to the parties" by either of the two Western legal traditions.[66] These differences were present in Russian procedures as well, contradicting John LeDonne's claim that Russian "judicial procedure so lacked autonomy and recognition that it was not even clear whether a distinction existed between civil and criminal procedure."[67]

Moreover, while lawyers trained in the common law tradition are accustomed to thinking that the adversarial system is the best type of procedure, recent European and American legal practice has tended to merge the two types of procedures in order to mitigate their worst features.[68] In civil cases in particular, English procedure has recently witnessed "an erosion of the adversary and orality principles, marked by increasing intervention by the court ... and ... a greater reliance on the use of written materials."[69] Jurist Cyril Glasser has noted that this tendency could improve the "inchoate" English discovery system.[70]

In the United States, many federal judges have long abandoned their traditionally dispassionate attitude in the famous movement "to adopt a more active, 'managerial' stance."[71] More active involvement by judges is thought to be more suitable for complex cases with large numbers of witnesses and a voluminous documentary record.[72] Legal scholars have noted that in actual legal practice, a purely adversarial civil trial is no more possible than a purely inquisitorial one, given that the judge must exercise his discretion and that it is therefore impossible to determine the winning side objectively.[73]

It is thus more correct to discuss adversarial or inquisitorial *elements* in civil procedure. In other words, procedural rules can be placed on a sliding scale, and while the Russian rules were firmly located on the inquisitorial end of the spectrum, this does not mean that Russian litigants did not have an opportunity to match wits against their opposing side. Thus, I suggest that when discussing Russian civil procedure on the eve of the judicial reform of 1864, the ideal model should be an effective form of merger between the two types of procedure, not a triumphant progress of the common law archetype. Depending on the individual case, what I have discussed here can be characterized as an adversarial element within the inquisitorial model or, conversely, as lax case management by the courts. In any event, these cases suggest that the major problem with pre-reform courts was not that they employed inquisitorial procedure but rather the fact that it was not inquisitorial enough.

"Formal Proofs" in Practice: Handwriting Experts and Forgery

Another often-criticized feature of pre-reform law was its rules of evidence—namely, its reliance on so-called formal proofs long after they were abandoned by other Western legal systems. Formal proofs reflected the attempt to achieve rational legal certainty and predictability by depriving judges of discretion in evaluating evidence.[74] The various types of proofs were ranked according to their evidentiary force: a personal confession was preferred, followed by the testimony of two sworn witnesses, documentary proof, and a judicial oath.[75] Debt cases sometimes involved witnesses or confessions, but the analysis of written documents was far more important than oral testimony. Pre-reform evidence rules were widely criticized by later writers for requiring judges to ignore much pertinent evidence and for placing excessive value upon confessions.[76] Critics correctly point out that formal proofs ensured less, rather than more, certainty in courts' rulings.

More recent work, however, shows that such broad generalizations do not exhaust the subject. For instance, Elisa Becker has argued that the quest for legal certainty embodied in the system of formal proofs actually promoted the rise of forensic expertise, particularly forensic medicine.[77] Becker discovered that medical expertise was privileged second only to confession and was thus legally insulated from "legal evaluation, challenge, or criticism," although she did not examine legal practice to determine how medical testimony was used in real cases.[78] According to Becker, "ironically, the inquisitorial system that reformers such as [A. F.] Koni disparaged, in fact, granted the physician the legal status, probative weight, and unfettered discretion that such reformers would seek for medical experts in the postreform period ... the limitation on judicial discretion (imposed by the rules of proof) entailed the displacement of that discretion to the physician ... the physician and his form of knowledge—in theory and practice—enjoyed basically unconstrained discretion, autonomy, and immunity from external attack."[79] By contrast, I argue that the use of document analysis in debt cases actually served to undermine rather than reinforce the system of formal proofs—not because handwriting experts were challenged in court but because the way the analysis was conducted led to ambiguous results and forced judges to exercise their discretion.

Handwriting identification, as Jennifer Mnookin has pointed out, is "an unusual form of expert evidence because it was the first kind of expertise that was primarily *forensic*, invented specifically for use in the legal arena."[80] Unlike doctors, professional handwriting experts generally do not exercise their skills outside the courtroom in a sizable community of other professionals. In Anglo-American law, this accounts in part for lawyers' uneasiness about handwriting identification.

Until 1854, English courts prohibited any handwriting comparison, especially by handwriting experts, as did most U.S. courts until the first half of the nineteenth century.[81] The four-fold rationale for this prohibition was so curious and logically indefensible that it reminds us how contingent is the very notion of legal rationality: (1) the party introducing a writing sample would in turn also need to prove its authenticity (the rejoinder to this is why not do so if the document is important to the case?); (2) the sample could misrepresent the individual's handwriting (but any other type of evidence also can potentially be misleading); (3) illiterate jury members would not be able to evaluate the analysis (which was originally a key issue in English practice but became irrelevant as literacy spread in the nineteenth century); and (4) the professional expert could be unreliable (but so can any witness testimony).[82] Thus, instead of the expert handwriting comparison, Anglo-American law relied on the procedure of handwriting *recognition* by someone personally acquainted with the writer and with his hand. In the nineteenth century, this practice began to change as credit networks became more reticulated and impersonal and personal connections between the writer and the witness became less common, so that handwriting experts were gradually allowed to testify, although they were not securely established in the United States until late in the century.[83]

In Russia the development of handwriting identification followed Western European patterns, experimenting with a variety of arrangements before "scientific" handwriting experts appeared in the second half of the nineteenth century.[84] The earliest court cases involving handwriting identification date from the sixteenth century. As in early modern Western Europe, these cases involved disputed wills rather than debt instruments; they were carried out by senior court staff *(diaki)*.[85]

Subsequently, Russian law followed the Continental model in allowing handwriting expertise to be used as evidence.[86] The experts were engaged by the court and not by the parties to the case. In the mid-nineteenth century, Russian courts experimented with two kinds of experts: one method was to poll large numbers of court clerks.[87] The alternative, parallel to developments in Anglo-American law, was to employ respectable calligraphy and drawing teachers.[88] The Russian case was peculiar because instead of employing only one expert, courts used a panel of four or five teachers from different schools. I have not located any cases from pre-reform courts when individual experts were used instead of a panel. Not surprisingly, panels rarely reached full consensus, thus leaving it to the court to interpret their usually rather intricate findings and thereby to exercise the very discretion that was supposed to be eliminated by the system of "formal proofs."

The most notable feature of handwriting comparison by court clerks is the large number of individual clerks invited from those courts that were equal in rank to the one in which the comparison was performed. One example of how the procedure operated is supplied by the inheritance case of Andrei Blaginin, used throughout this study to illustrate various features of the pre-reform legal system.[89] After Andrei's brother, Petr, contested the validity of the debt note issued to Andrei's caretaker, Anna Antonova, the Moscow Aulic Court ordered a handwriting comparison with the account books of the city treasury, which Andrei signed each month to get his pension. The comparison was conducted by court clerks, and the results were sharply divided: the officials from the first and second departments of the Moscow Magistrate Court and the second and third departments of the Aulic Court concluded that the signature on the debt note "had resemblance" to Blaginin's undisputed signature. The officials from the first department of the County Court judged that the signature "in the character of some letters has small resemblance, but complete resemblance cannot be observed." Finally, the officials from the Orphan Court thought that "the handwriting had no resemblance." The results were obviously far from certain, and the "experts" themselves were far from clear, limiting themselves to a rather weak "has resemblance"; had they been really sure, they would have said "has strong resemblance" or "has perfect resemblance." Strangely, the judges interpreted these findings to mean that the writing on the note was not Blaginin's and noted this in its decision, ruling against Antonova.

In the Blaginin case, the size of the panel was not specified, but the forgery case of a merchant's son, Klavdii Rudnev, appears to have been fairly typical. Rudnev confessed to forging bills of exchange in his father's name. However, rather inconveniently for the investigation, fifteen court secretaries from "the courts equal in rank to the Moscow Magistrate" found that the allegedly forged signatures were "similar" to the senior Rudnev's genuine ones, thus implicating Klavdii's father in the case.[90]

A slightly different approach to handwriting identification by court clerks can be found at the same County Court at the same time. In the case of major general's wife Tvorogova, a grand-niece sued her great-aunt's heirs for debt pursuant to a note that the old lady allegedly issued shortly before her death.[91] The defendant, Prince Sergei Dolgorukov, was an ambitious young bureaucrat in the beginning of the suit, and at its end he was one of the empire's highest-ranking civil servants; not surprisingly, he was able to delay the proceedings for several years by not finding the right kind of document for handwriting comparison. After the court carried out a handwriting analysis anyway, using only the plaintiff's papers, Dolgorukov had this comparison overturned through a collateral appeal but had to finally provide his own papers. Altogether there were three comparisons, the first two conducted at the Moscow Criminal Chamber, which compared the debt note to a registered power of attorney and to a receipt relating to a property sale; the third was conducted at the Civil Chamber and used all available documents.

The first expertise involved 180 officials, of whom 22 judged the documents to be "completely similar," 6 to "have small similarity," 146 as "not having any similarity," and another 6 "gave a conclusion that did not contain a positive definiteness." The second expertise involved 182 officials, of whom 164 found that the signatures were "similar," and 18 found that they were "similar in some letters." Finally, the third expertise involved 124 officials, of whom 98 found "similarity," 18 found "some similarity," and 6 found "no similarity." Taken together, of these 486 persons, 283 affirmed similarity, 152 denied it, and 51 gave an indeterminate conclusion. With these results, first the Moscow County Court and then, on appeal, the Moscow Civil Chamber and the Seventh Department of the Senate ruled in Tvorogova's favor. However, Dolgorukov appealed further, and the joint session of Moscow Senate departments held that 283 officials did not constitute a proper majority because that number included 146 officials who had originally denied any resemblance during the first comparison. Another comparison was ordered, whose results we do not know, although the case dragged on into the 1870s.

The strategy of using a large number of "experts" was clearly not very reliable in practice, nor was the practice of taking a vote of each individual expert any more helpful than recording their collective opinion. Pre-reform courts also experimented with other solutions, such as using a smaller number of clerks or using a combined panel of experts; for example, in a debt-related case of witness bribery in the mid-1860s, the panel consisted of a secretary of the local magistrate, two teachers, a court investigator, and an official "for special assignments."[92] In another case that originated outside the city of Moscow, involving the merchant's son Aleksandr Prokofiev, only four local court secretaries conducted the first identification and found that the signature on the debt instrument "did not resemble" the debtor's actual signature. The second identification, conducted by nineteen secretaries, had the same result. Chiefly based on this evidence, Prokofiev was convicted of forgery and sentenced by a joint session of the Moscow Aulic Court and the Magistrate Court to be stripped of his estate privileges, branded, punished with ninety lashes, and exiled to Siberia.[93]

Another method of handwriting identification that became particularly popular in the 1860s was to invite four or five teachers of calligraphy and drawing. The use of the calligraphy and art communities as a "breeding ground" for handwriting experts, as Mnookin has pointed out, was also the norm in nineteenth-century Anglo-American law.[94] In Russian legal practice, as Krylov could not have known without studying archival materials, there developed a group of calligraphy and drawing teachers who were invited to serve as handwriting experts over and over throughout the 1860s.

The service list of one of these teachers, who served as an expert in many of the cases in this study, was fortunately preserved.[95] Aleksandr Trofimovich Skino was born in 1826 in a Greek family settled in the town of Nezhin and had no landed property. He studied at the Second Moscow Drawing School, and in 1847 he joined the First Moscow County School as a drawing and calligraphy teacher. In 1849 he was hired by the First Moscow Gymnazium. Throughout the 1850s he moved through the ranks, becoming a collegiate secretary in 1856 and two years later receiving from the "Gracious Sovereign Emperor" a diamond ring with a ruby as a reward for presenting the tsar with a model of one of the Kremlin towers cut out of wood. He also received occasional rewards of money from his superiors for excellent service, as well as "gratitudes" in 1864 and 1870. In 1866 he was promoted to titular councilor. His annual salary in the 1860s was approximately 400 rubles, which was comparable to the salary of a midlevel retail clerk. All this detail is important to show that Skino was not a stereotypical radicalized intelligentsia member but rather a reliable civil servant, highly valued and promoted by his superiors—a good indication for the courts of his reliability as an expert witness.

The cases I have reviewed that involved identifications by Skino and his colleagues involved much more sophisticated conclusions than identifications performed by court secretaries. For example, in the forgery case of Moscow merchant Aleksandr Smirnov, the debtor challenged signatures on several of his debt documents.[96] However, the calligraphy teachers not only confirmed his handwriting on these documents but also determined that he intentionally modified his handwriting when signing papers at the police station. On the basis of this identification, the Criminal Chamber held the debt notes to be genuine and returned them to the police for collection.

However, even calligraphy teachers could fail to agree, forcing courts to consider other evidence, which is what happened in the case of Moscow merchant Ilia Shatov.[97] Together with a partner, another Moscow merchant, Taras Kalinin, Shatov contracted with the government to transport wool cloth to Nikolaev for the Black Sea fleet. Kalinin presented as collateral to the government his stone house, valued at 10,400 silver rubles, while Shatov presented two deposit tickets, one to the Deposit Treasury and the second to the Loan Bank, totaling 2,755.75 rubles. Subsequently, Shatov claimed that he discharged all of his obligations to Kalinin by presenting a receipt, but Kalinin claimed that the signature on it was not his. A handwriting identification conducted largely by the same teachers mentioned above was only able to establish "some resemblance" to Kalinin's handwriting. The court interpreted these ambiguous results to mean that the receipt was forged. However, Shatov did not confess to anything, and the only other evidence in the case was testimony by one witness, which was not enough to convict him, and he was only "left under suspicion" of knowingly presenting a forged document.

In another similar case, that of Moscow merchant Stepan Tikhomirov, the court conducted two identifications of the writing on a bill of exchange.[98] The first one, by secretaries of the Provincial Office *(Gubernskoe pravlenie)*, the Provincial Treasury, and the Commercial Court ("official places," equal in rank to the Criminal Chamber), found that the debtor's writing "had resemblance" to the signature on the note, whereas the defendant's did not. However, the second comparison, carried out by calligraphy teachers Sabinin,

Kondyrev, and Skino, determined that the debtor's handwriting "did not have resemblance" to that on the debt note. The debtor must have been confident of his ability to change his signature and dismissive of the experts' ability to detect his forgery because two witnesses later testified that the debtor asked for a postponement on his debt, threatening otherwise to deny his signature.

Although it has been used widely in many different legal systems, handwriting identification has often been criticized as unreliable. The solution that pre-reform Russian courts eventually adopted was very similar to that of U.S. courts—namely, to use a small group of experts well known to judges for their professional ability and reliability. Identifications by a handful of calligraphy teachers were certainly more manageable than those by crowds of court secretaries, but as individual debt cases show, they still came far short of the rational certainty demanded by the doctrine of formal proofs. When no other proofs, such as confession or sworn witnesses, were available, courts had to exercise their own judgment about the debt documents' authenticity. Thus, from the perspective of the law of evidence, debt cases represent yet another direction from which pre-reform legal system was being undermined and even dismantled long before 1864.

This chapter has argued that some of the most commonly criticized features of pre-reform justice operated quite differently than expected in actual practice. Estate-based justice could not be fully implemented because all important decisions were reviewed by the all-estate provincial courts and because many cases involved individuals from different estates, causing even the first-tier courts to operate as a single unit. Moreover, the exchange of written petitions that was at the heart of pre-reform civil procedure was largely left to individual parties' discretion. While Russian law was inquisitorial in many important respects, in practice it retained some important adversarial features. Finally, debt cases highlight the fact that Russia's archaic evidence system could not in practice eliminate judicial discretion because the techniques of handwriting identification necessary to analyze debt documents necessarily involved a discretionary and even arbitrary element.

For all its peculiarities, pre-reform court procedure was more viable and dynamic than has previously been recognized. It depended heavily upon individual discretion and initiative, much like Russia's culture of private credit, to which it was closely linked. One may therefore argue that the biggest weakness of pre-reform justice was its complete reliance on an institutional and procedural framework that left too much discretion to private individuals with their own interests and strategies. In other words, pre-1864 courts represented an alternative disciplinary regime to the one that appeared in late imperial Russia and featured posh lawyers, journalists, and eventually parliamentary politicians who appropriated and flexibly interpreted the language of power and the meaning of legal norms, serving as mediators between the public and the autonomous system of legal rules. By contrast, the law in pre-reform Russia depended only on a combination of strict legal forms internal to the system and the innumerable individual relationships, interests, and strategies whose disciplinary powers lay largely outside the world of the law.[99] While today we are accustomed to the former model, we can't conclusively establish that the latter was as "archaic" as it has often been represented or even that it was necessarily weak and inefficient.

Conclusion

THIS BOOK HAS engaged with two longstanding
stereotypes about Russia that to this day continue to
shape both academic analyses and popular views. The first stereotype is that
there is something fundamentally wrong with the way Russians have historically dealt with challenges and anxieties related to wealth, money, and capitalism. Russians were either unable to get wealthy or else did not want to. The
reasons usually given for this deviance range from unfavorable natural and
economic conditions to cultural backwardness and the harmful influence of
the autocratic state. Each of these arguments has been either questioned or
undermined individually, but well-rounded histories of money and capitalism that use a variety of historiographical perspectives and that are so
common to students of English or U.S. history are still absent in the case of
Russia. This book, therefore, has sought to revive the debate about the role of
money and property in Russian history and culture by examining private
credit: that is, practices, beliefs, and relationships going far beyond the con-
fines of economics or economic history to affect virtually every aspect of
culture, society, and government.

The period of social and political innovation and unrest in the 1860s and
1870s that accompanied the Great Reforms involved a transformation of
Russia's financial structure, but large new banks only complemented the
existing network of informal personal credit without supplanting it. Often
assumed to be expensive or even predatory, this credit was not any more
abusive than today's "capitalist" consumer loans. Debt certainly did reflect
hierarchies of power and sometimes involved ruthless exploitation, but taken

as a whole, it operated through mutual cooperation and existing links of kinship, service, and personal acquaintance.

The network of private credit linked individuals of all social and legal categories, men and women, into a large and amorphous stratum of property owners who—despite their often-observed political conservatism—actively defined, protected, and promoted their economic and personal interests. This was accomplished in part through interpersonal negotiation and cooperation and in part through the use of legal and administrative channels, including legal formalities, litigation, and interaction with various officials. But above all, the network of debt was driven by a set of shared cultural attitudes and practices. In order for credit to function, most participants had to believe that borrowing was unavoidable and even desirable, that debts had to be repaid, that charging interest was permissible, and many other things. They also had to engage in a set of rituals to find a lender, ask for a loan, determine the borrower's creditworthiness, and ensure repayment. These attitudes and practices changed slowly, but they did change, as I argue, in the same direction that was common to other major economic and legal systems that in the late eighteenth and nineteenth centuries gradually limited debt imprisonment, partially lifted interest rate restrictions, and introduced bankruptcy discharge at least for the wealthier classes.

I have not romanticized the informal credit network based on personal connections; most people today try to avoid loan sharks and would rather use a credit card than borrow from their boss or their neighbors. But the question of the role of credit in our society and especially of its alternative sources and structures is as important as ever, and it is instructive to investigate how these were regarded and addressed in the past. Specifically, the role of personal acquaintance, family, and local community may easily become far more important when the capitalist market becomes less accessible even to the propertied and educated classes.

Just as in the case of the law, these concerns are conveniently illustrated by the example of Russia, where post-Soviet developments closely parallel the financial revolution of the 1860s: newer capitalist structures such as mortgage banks and credit cards became widely available, and there are even more pawnshop signs on the streets now than there were in Dostoevsky's Russia. However, indebtedness and consumer credit are still an outstanding development problem that is not being adequately addressed, and it is likely to intensify as a result of the post-2014 Western economic sanctions. Therefore, drawing lessons from imperial Russia no longer means romanticizing it as

was customary in the 1990s but rather should mean drawing practical conclusions and inspiring specific solutions. Above all, it is important to avoid
the two pitfalls that infect many historical studies of imperial Russia: first,
the temptation to assume a blank slate, dismissing or demonizing preceding
models and experiences and, second, forgetting that individual agency and
discretion, as well as kinship and community ties, are essential for private
property to function.

The second myth about Russia concerns Russia's norms, institutions, practices, and attitudes related to the law. The longstanding assumption is that all
these components were fundamentally defective or even absent in Russia.
Partial exception is sometimes made for the courts established by the judicial
reform of 1864, but many scholars have argued that the reformers' achievements were limited not simply by the autocratic tradition of personal rule but
also by an insufficiently developed legal tradition—that is, the lack of appreciation of, and a need for, European-style rule of law in the mass of Russia's
population. Moreover, pre-1864 courts are assumed to be not simply flawed
but so fundamentally defective as to place Russia outside the framework of
the Western ideal of law.

This study is of course mindful of that ideal but recognizes the difficulty of
even formulating it precisely, much less applying it to actual rather than idealized legal systems, including Russia's. Instead, I focus on specific features
of the courts and procedures that were criticized particularly often, and I
found that their harmful effects were exaggerated and that even pre-1864
courts, with all their flaws, provided a reasonably efficient machinery for
resolving property disputes. This study therefore argues against a "revolutionary" approach to Russia's development, especially to that of its law,
focusing instead on incremental and often little-noticed steps that, for
example, reformulated the framework of credit and property ownership in
the eighteenth century, created a working bankruptcy procedure in 1800, and
prepared the legal framework for the "emancipation of capital" that neither
began nor ended in the 1860s. In this book, I have discussed the most
important changes in the law of debt in imperial Russia, but my objective has
been to remove the reform-centered rhetoric from my narrative and instead
to explain what it was like to borrow, lend, and own property, and argue
about it, in nineteenth-century Russia.

None of this is to deny that the old courts had serious problems and that
the new ones were much easier to use, at least for wealthier litigants. However,
I propose that we continue looking closely at Russia's culture of bureaucratic

legality, which peaked during the reign of Nicholas I and appears to have successfully weathered all the reforms and revolutions of our own day and is now coexisting with carefully circumscribed attempts to reinstitute the ideals of 1864 in post-Soviet Russia. It has by now become clear that Russia will not attempt to fully replicate nineteenth-century European values and institutions, which are indeed beleaguered elsewhere as well. Although judges will not rule Russia, it is crucial to understand and to develop ordinary legal institutions, norms, and procedures and especially to understand their role in securing individual property rights. Nineteenth-century law, which even after the reform of 1864 operated in a much more restrictive political and intellectual sphere than is the case today, in this respect can prove relevant and instructive.

APPENDIX A

APPENDIX B

APPENDIX C

APPENDIX D.1

APPENDIX D.2

APPENDIX E

ABBREVIATIONS

NOTES

ACKNOWLEDGMENTS

INDEX

APPENDIX A

Glossary

Aulic Court *(Nadvornyi sud)* First-tier pre-1864 court in St. Petersburg and Moscow for civil servants and military officers who did not own property in those cities.

Bankruptcy Board *(konkurs or konkursnoe upravlenie)* In commercial bankruptcies, a subunit of the Commercial Court, consisting of a court-appointed official and a committee of creditors. Ruled on whether to grant a bankruptcy discharge, subject to court approval.

Bill of exchange *(veksel')* A debt document operating under a separate statute and intended to be used by merchants.

Board of Trustees of the Imperial Orphanage *(Opekunskii Sovet)* Administered a "Deposit Treasury" *(Sokhrannaia kazna)* in St. Petersburg and Moscow. These opened in 1772 and served as the principal mortgage banks for the nobility until 1859.

Chambers of Civil and Criminal Justice *(Palaty Grazhdanskogo i Ugolovnogo suda)* Province-level, second-tier, all-estate courts before the reform of 1864.

Commercial Court *(Kommercheskii sud)* Equal in status to provincial chambers, courts that processed commercial disputes and especially bankruptcies. First established in Odessa in 1808; opened in Petersburg in 1832 and in Moscow in 1833. Survived the reform of 1864.

Complete Collection of the Laws *(Polnoe Sobranie Zakonov Rossiiskoi imperii)* A chronological collection of the laws issued after 1649. Used mostly for reference.

Corps of Gendarmes *(Zhandarmy, Otdel'nyi korpus zhandarmov)* A special military formation in imperial Russia, whose officers staffed the Third Section.

County Court *(Uyezdnyi sud)* A first-tier pre-1864 court established in each county *(uezd, often translated as "District")* for nobles and free peasants.

Digest of the Laws *(Svod Zakonov Rossiiskoi imperii)* A 15- (later 16-) volume thematic compilation of the laws in force at the time of its issue in 1832. Went into effect January 1, 1835 and updated in 1842 and 1857. Technically not a code because it was not supposed to alter the substance of the legal norms that it contained; nonetheless, it had full legal force and was referenced in judicial decisions.

District Court *(Okruzhnoi sud)* A first-tier trial court after the reform of 1864, usually serving several counties *(uyezdy)*.

Equity Court *(Sovestnyi sud)*, literally "court of conscience" A pre-reform court, equal in status to provincial chambers, with jurisdiction over crimes committed by minors, cases of witchcraft, and disputes between parents and children (although not between husbands and wives). Less populous provinces had an equity judge instead of a separate court.

Loan letter *(zaiomnoe pis'mo)* A promissory note used primarily for noncommercial debt.

Magistrate Court *(Magistrat)* A first-tier pre-reform municipal court with jurisdiction over townspeople and other urban groups.

Merchant *(kupets, f. kupchikha)* A legal status with three subdivisions ("guilds"), acquired by paying a special fee. Enjoyed a variety of commercial and personal privileges. The top two guilds were exempt from military conscription and corporal punishment.

Safekeeping receipt *(sokhrannaia raspiska)* A "safekeeping deposit receipt" used as a debt document.

Senate *(Pravitel'stvuiushchii Senat)* An appellate court divided into Moscow, Petersburg, and Warsaw departments.

Third Section *(Tretie Otdelenie)* Russia's political police in 1826–1879.

Townsman / townswoman *(meshchanin, f. meshchanka)* The lowest category of urban inhabitants; had its own local self-government. Unlike that of a merchant, this status was inheritable.

Table of Ranks *(Tabel' o rangakh)* A system of military, civil, and court service ranks, divided into fourteen classes.

The Table of Ranks (as of 1850)[a]

Class	Civil Service	Army
1	Chancellor	General-field marshal
2	Actual privy councilor	General
3	Privy councilor	Lieutenant-general
4	Actual state councilor	Major-general
5	State councilor	(abolished)
6	Collegiate councilor	Colonel
7	Aulic councilor	Lieutenant-colonel
8	Collegiate assessor	Major
9	Titular councilor	Captain
10	Collegiate secretary	Staff captain
11	(abolished)	(abolished)
12	Gubernial secretary	Lieutenant
13	Senate registrar	Second lieutenant
14	Collegiate registrar	Subaltern *(praporshchik)*

a. Between 1845 and 1856, the rights of hereditary nobility were attained by reaching Class 8 in the military and the Class 5 in civil service; personal nobility was attained at Class 14 in the military and Class 9 in civil service. After 1856, the threshold for hereditary nobility was raised to the Class 6 in the military and the Class 4 in the civil service. Classes 1 through 4 were referred to as *generalitet* (generals); Class 5 was an in-between category; Classes 6 through 8 were referred to as *shtab-ofitsery* (senior officers); Classes 9 through 14 were referred to as *ober-ofitsery* (junior officers).

St. Petersburg Pawnbrokers, 1866

Name	Rank	Loan per 35-ruble watch	% per Mo.	Grace Mo.	Notes
Sokolov, Feofan	Ret. official	7	10	2	Issues receipt
Yakovlev, Petr	Merchant	10	10	1	Issues printed receipt
Yefremov, Dmitrii	"Penniless swindler"	15	10	0	
Altukhova, Varvara	Widow	18	6	2	
Zakharov, Boris	Merchant, former lawyer	10	12	0	Lives with a mistress
Yakobson (male)	Jew	10	12	2	Issues receipt
Floriani, Berhard	n/a	12	10	1	Issues printed receipt
Pavlov, Andrei	Ret. officer	8	12	3	Purchase receipt; piano swindle
Mrs. Rozenberg	Gentlewoman	10	12	1	Purchases pawn
Karpovich, Vladimir	Pole	8	11	0	Issues receipt; sells to his own customers; operates with others' money
Ellenreis, Zabella	Polish woman	8–9	10	0	
Miller	Merchant	12	10	0	Sells items at his discretion; has family
Karpovich, Yuri	n/a	n/a	7–12	2	Only sells items to insiders

(*Continued*)

Name	Rank	Loan per 35-ruble watch	% per Mo.	Grace Mo.	Notes
Karpov	Ret. police lieutenant	same as Zakharov (above); likely his agent			
Matveeva	Baptized Jewess	10	12	2	Only sells items to insiders
Shtein & Kuzmin	Ret. officials	n / a	12	n / a	Nice furnishings but bad business reputation. Operate with others' money
Kon	Merchant	7	10	n / a	Married
Frint, Osip	n / a	18	11	4	
Sokolov	Ret. sapper NCO	20	5	none	Purchase
Cherepakhina Yekat.	officer's wife	10	10	0	
Adandi	Greek	20	10	3	Others' money
Saveliev	Ret. sapper NCO	n / a	5	none	Cream dealer keeps cows
Kirilovich	Noblewoman	10	8	6	Milk vendor
Vasiliev	Police private	10	5	none	
Bormand	Merchant	n / a	8	3	
Falk, Karl	Goldsmith	n / a	10		
Tokarev	Gerchant	n / a	10		

Data source: GARF 109.3a.1610.

Objectives of Legal Representation, Based on the Powers of Attorney Registered at the Moscow Chamber of Civil Justice

Type of Matter	1852	1857	1861	1867
Register document	22	20	17	5
Property transactions[a]	29	31	24	14
Property divisions	9	8	8	1
Property management	49	21	64	17
Render army recruit	8	6	1	0
Borrow money (unsecured)	0	0	3	0
Mortgage operations	26	12	8	2
Government contracts	6	8	14	6
Customhouse representation	17	29	14	1
Debt collection	23	22	34	36
Court representation	27	25	48	46
Court appearance to hear decision	6	2	5	0
Collect and issue money, merchandise, mail	22	13	9	4
Serf redemption matters	0	0	3	4
Total	**241**[b]	**197**	**252**	**136**

a. Purchase, sale, lease of real estate and serfs, borrowing money; b. Some powers of attorney had multiple purposes. *Data sources:* TsIAM f. 50, op. 14, dd. 4 and 5 (1852); TsIAM f. 50, op. 14, d. 108a (1857); TsIAM f. 50, op. 14, d. 220 and 221 (1861); TsIAM f. 50, op. 14, d. 387 (1867, February only)

Legal Representatives Registered at the Moscow Chamber of Civil Justice

Rank[a]	1852	1857	1861	1867
Generals (class 1–4)	0	3	4	0
Sr. officer (class 5–8)	40	30	43	17
Jr. officer (class 9–14)	63	40	81	45
Noble without rank	3	3	6	7
Civil servant w / o rank	5	2	8	3
Lawyer[b]	0	0	3	7
Soldier (not officer)	3	1	1	1
Merchant	47	56	45	24
Townsperson	14	14	19	10
Craftsperson	0	1	3	0
Foreigner	7	10	4	1
Serf, peasant, servant	53	34	21	10
Other	6	3	14	11
Total	**241**	**197**	**252**	**136**
of these				
Female	16	12	16	4
Male	225	185	236	132
Relatives to principal	46	35	49	15
Serfs of principal	36	21	11	n / a

a. Civil and military ranked servitors are shown together; b. *Prisiazhnyi poverennyi, kandidat prav* or *kandidat na sudebnye dolzhnosti.*

Data sources: See Appendix D.1.

Agreement to Provide
Legal Services, 1865

Agreement.

I, Korotkov, proprietor of a legal and brokerage company *[advakatnuiu i kamision-erskuiu kompaniiu (sic)]* in Moscow with the capital of 400 silver rubles, have accepted as a companion Mr. Maliutin with the capital of 400 silver rubles, which I received from him in cash.

2nd. Maliutin, as Korotkov's companion, has accepted the obligation, having given 100 silver rubles to secure *[v obespechenie]* his activities, to be engaged in those activities constantly, with a profit, and not concealing anything from Korotkov, in whichever litigation *["iskovymi i tiazhebnymi"]* matters will be taken up by either of them on commission from private persons, as well as to be engaged together, as diligent companions, in sale and purchase in general of movable and immovable property on commission received at our office.

3rd. Accounting and paperwork, pursuant to the account books, are to be carried out in a proper order by a clerk *[kontorshchik]* provided by Korotkov; we both have a full right with the agreement of the other to account and examine them on any day, entering into these books all credits and debits, both in the accounts *[po kasse]*, as well as in the contested cases, sales, purchases, and mortgages of movable and immovable property, according to pure conscience and complete truth.

4th. All expenses relating to the office, such as travel in the city, office upkeep, renting apartments for employees, furniture, heating and lighting and other items I Maliutin and I Korotkov accept in equal amounts amongst ourselves pursuant to the inventory and to our mutual agreement.

5th. If either of us leaves the companionship before its term expires, he must announce it three months in advance and pay 50 silver rubles for violating its terms, after which no legal proceedings will be possible.

6th. If either one of us will be caught in an injustice or negligence or concealment from each other of cases accepted by us for commission, then we will elect two persons by our mutual agreement and resolve the matter without any legal proceedings and he who will be shown to commit a wrongdoing will be removed from the office's affairs completely, and will pay a penalty of one hundred silver rubles. Our partnership will then be permanently terminated.

7th. Pursuant to everything written above we, companions Mssrs. Maliutin and Korotkov, shall divide equally all amounts of money received by us as commissions from private persons pursuant to our partnership for litigated court *[iskovym, tiazhebnym striapcheskim]* cases, sales, purchases, mortgages, re-mortgages of movable and immovable property and recommendations of all kinds of domestic servants, and shall account to each other monthly.

8th. To our clerk we undertake to pay the salary of 10 *kopeek* from all our income from every ruble, which for each of us will be 5 *kopeek* from every ruble.

9th. The expenses related to the signing of this agreement we agree to share equally;

10th [We undertake] to keep this agreement sacred and unbreakable *[sviato i nerushimo]*. The original signed by Maliutin and I Korotkov [ill.]

11th. The cash that we have we shall spend with each other's agreement as good companions.

Source: TsIAM 50.4.8945.

Notes

Abbreviations

GARF   *Gosudarstvennyi Arkhiv Rossiiskoi Federatsii* (The State Archive of the Russian Federation)

  PSS   *Polnoe sobranie sochinenii* (Complete Collection of Works)

  PSZ   *Polnoe Sobranie Zakonov Rossiiskoi imperii* (The Complete Collection of the Laws of Russian Empire)

  RA   *Russkii Arkhiv* (Russian Archive)

  RS   *Russkaia Starina* (Russian Antiquities)

  SZ   *Svod Zakonov Rossiiskoi imperii* (The Digest of Laws of the Russian Empire)

TsIAM   *Tsentral'nyi Istoricheskii Arkhiv Moskvy* (Central Historical Archive of Moscow)

Note on Citation

This book cites archival materials in the following format: *"Fond.opis.delo, list* (if given)*"* Full case titles are omitted due to their length but are available upon request. Citations to PSZ are given as *"Volume:number (year), page* (if given).*"* Citations to SZ are given as *"Volume/part:Article, note or appendix (year of edition)."*

Introduction

1. Leo Tolstoy, *Anna Karenina,* translated by Richard Pevear and Larissa Volokhonsky (New York: Penguin Group, 2004), 302–304. I am grateful to Nathaniel Knight, who many years ago reminded me of this passage.

2. P. F. Vistengof, *Ocherki Moskovskoi zhizni* (Moscow, 1842), 113; V. V. Shevtsov, *Kartochnaia igra v Rossii: konets XIV—nachalo XX v.* (Tomsk, 2005); Ian Helfant, *The High Stakes of Identity: Gambling in the Life and Literature of Nineteenth-Century Russia* (Evanston: Northwestern University Press, 2001). Even Tsar Nicholas I paid his card debts promptly; see M. A. Korf, *Zapiski* (Moscow, 2003), 254.

3. GARF 109.91.113, l. 23.

4. The English Club in St. Petersburg was known for its "black board," which listed the names of nonpaying debtors. S. S. Komissarenko, *Kulturnye traditsii russkogo obshchestva* (St. Petersburg, 2003), 101–103.

5. V. N. Gettun, *"Zapiski," Istorichskii vestnik* 1 (1880), 280; see also, e.g., TsIAM 50.5.13156.

6. Some existing work denies the existence of such a shared identity among Russia's propertied groups. Edith Clowes, Samuel Kassow, and James West, eds., *Between Tsar and People: Educated Society and the Quest for Public Identity in Late Imperial Russia* (Princeton: Princeton University Press, 1991); Harley Balzer, ed., *Russia's Missing Middle Class: The Professions in Russian History* (Armonk, NY: M.E. Sharpe, 1996).

7. On the Great Reforms, see, e.g., Ben Eklof, John Bushnell, and Larissa Zakharova, ed. *Russia's Great Reforms* (Bloomington: Indiana University Press, 1994); Richard Wortman, *The Development of a Russian Legal Consciousness* (Chicago: University of Chicago Press, 1976); I. V. Gessen and A. I. Kaminka, ed., *Velikie reformy shestidesiatykh godov v ikh proshlom i nastoiashchem* (St. Petersburg, 1905); and G. A. Dzhanshiev, *Epokha velikikh reform*, 2 vols. (St. Petersburg, 1905). On the financial aspects, see B. V. Ananich, *Bankirskie doma v Rossii, 1860–1914 gg* (Leningrad, 1991); Ananich et al., *Kredit i banki v Rossii do nachala XX veka: Sankt-Peterburg i Moskva* (St. Petersburg, 2005), 244; A. V. Bugrov, *Ocherki po istorii kazennykh bankov v Rossii* (Moscow, 2003), 7; I. I. Kaufman, *"Gosudarstvennye dolgi Rossii," Vestnik Evropy* 20/1 (1885): 572–618, esp. 584; Thomas Owen, *The Corporation under Russian Law, 1800–1917: A Study in Tsarist Economic Policy* (Cambridge: Cambridge University Press, 1991); Yanni Kotnonis, *States of Obligation: Taxes and Citizenship in the Russian Empire and Early Soviet Republic* (Toronto: University of Toronto Press, 2014).

8. Richard Pipes, *Russia under the Old Regime* (New York: Charles Scribner's Sons, 1974); Olga Crisp and Linda Edmondson, eds., *Civil Rights in Imperial Russia* (Oxford: Oxford University Press, 1989); Arcadius Kahan, *The Plow, the Hammer, and the Knout: An Economic History of Eighteenth-Century Russia* (Chicago: University of Chicago Press, 1985); Lee Farrow, *Between Clan and Crown: The Struggle to Define Noble Property Rights in Imperial Russia* (Newark: University of Delaware Press, 2004); William Wagner, *Marriage, Property, and Law in Late Imperial Russia* (Oxford: Oxford University Press, 1994); Alfred Rieber, *Merchants and Entrepreneurs in Imperial Russia* (Chapel Hill: University of North Carolina Press, 1991); Thomas Owen, *Capitalism and Politics in Russia: A Social History of the Moscow Merchants, 1855–1905* (Cambridge: Cambridge

University Press, 1981); Walter Pintner, *Russian Economic Policy under Nicholas I* (Ithaca: Cornell University Press, 1967); Jörg Baberowski, *Autokratie und Justiz: Zum Verhältnis von Rechtsstaatlichkeit und Rückständigkeit im ausgehenden Zarenreich 1864–1914* (Frankfurt am Main, 1996); for somewhat more optimistic accounts, see Paul Gregory, *Before Command: An Economic History of Russia From Emancipation to the First Five-Year Plan* (Princeton: Princeton University Press, 1994) and Martin Malia, *Russia under Western Eyes: From the Bronze Horseman to the Lenin Mausoleum* (Belknap Press, 1999); see also Christopher Read, "In Search of Liberal Tsarism: The Historiography of Autocratic Decline," *Historical Journal* 45 (2002): 195–210.

9. Ekaterina Pravilova, *A Public Empire: Property and the Quest for the Common Good in Imperial Russia* (Princeton: Princeton University Press, 2014), 292, n. 5.

10. Eklof, *Russia's Great Reforms;* Rieber, *Merchants and Entrepreneurs;* Owen, *Capitalism and Politics;* William Blackwell, *The Beginnings of Russian Industrialization, 1800–1860* (Princeton, Princeton University Press, 1968).

11. S. Ia. Borovoi, *Kredit i banki Rossii (seredina XVII v.—1861 g.)* (Moscow, 1958); I. F. Gindin, *Banki i ekonomicheskaia politika v Rossii (xix-nachalo xx v.)* (Moscow, 1997); Ananich, *Kredit i banki; Ocherki;* V. V. Morozan, *Istoriia bankovskogo dela v Rossii: vtoraia polovina XVIII—pervaia polovina XIX v.* (St. Petersburg, 2001); S. A. Salomatina, *Kommercheskie banki v Rossii: dinamika i struktura operatsii, 1864–1917* (Moscow, 2004).

12. See, e.g., Alison Smith, *For the Common Good and Their Own Well-Being: Social Estates in Imperial Russia* (Oxford: Oxford University Press, 2014); Alexander Martin, *Enlightened Metropolis: Constructing Imperial Moscow, 1762–1855* (Oxford: Oxford University Press, 2013); Katherine Pickering Antonova, *An Ordinary Marriage: The World of a Gentry Family in Provincial Russia* (Oxford: Oxford University Press, 2013); Vera Bokova, *Povsednevnaia zhizn Moskvy v XIX veke* (Moscow, 2009); David Ransel, *A Russian Merchant's Tale: The Life and Adventures of Ivan Alekseevich Tolchënov,* Based on His Diary (Bloomington: Indiana University Press, 2008); Mary Cavender, *Nests of the Gentry: Family, Estate, and Local Loyalties in Provincial Russia* (Newark: University of Delaware Press), 2007; John Randolph, *The House in the Garden: The Bakunin Family and the Romance of Russian Idealism* (Ithaca: Cornell University Press, 2007).

13. David Graeber, *Debt: The First 5,000 Years* (New York: Melville House, 2011); Charles Geisst, *Beggar Thy Neighbor: A History of Usury and Debt* (Philadelphia: University of Pennsylvania Press, 2013).

14. A. I. Delvig, *Moi vospominaniia,* vol. 2 (Moscow, 1913), 116.

15. For Britain, see Craig Muldrew, *The Economy of Obligation: The Culture of Credit and Social Relations in Early Modern England* (Palgrave Macmillan, 1998); Margot Finn, *The Character of Credit: Personal Debt in English Culture, 1740–1914* (Cambridge: Cambridge University Press, 2003); Paul Johnson, *Making the Market: Victorian Origins of Corporate Capitalism,* (Cambridge: Cambridge University Press, 2010); Catherine Ingrassia, *Authorship, Commerce, and Gender in Early Eighteenth-Century England: A Culture of Paper Credit* (Cambridge:

Cambridge University Press, 1998). For the U.S., see Bruce H. Mann, *The Republic of Debtors: Bankruptcy in the Age of American Independence* (Cambridge: Harvard University Press, 2002); T. H. Breen, *Tobacco Culture: The Mentality of the Great Tidewater Planters on the Eve of Revolution* (Princeton: Princeton University Press, 1985); Herbert Sloane, *Principle and Interest: Thomas Jefferson and the Problem of Debt* (Charlottesville: University of Virginia Press, 1995); Edward Balleisen, *Navigating Failure: Bankruptcy and Commercial Society in Antebellum America* (Chapel Hill: University of North Carolina Press, 2001); Lendol Calder, *Financing the American Dream: A Cultural History of Consumer Credit* (Princeton: Princeton University Press, 2001); Louis Hyman, *Debtor Nation: The History of America in Red Ink* (Princeton: Princeton University Press, 2011). For France, see Clare Crowston, *Credit, Fashion, Sex: Economies of Regard in Old Regime France* (Durham: Duke University Press, 2013); Laurence Fontaine, *The Moral Economy: Poverty, Credit, and Trust in Early Modern Europe* (Cambridge: Cambridge University Press, 2014); Amalia Kessler, *A Revolution in Commerce: The Parisian Merchant Court and the Rise of Commercial Society in Eighteenth-Century France* (New Haven: Yale University Press, 2007); Erika Vause, "In the Red and in the Black: Bankruptcy, Debt Imprisonment, and the Culture of Credit in Post-Revolutionary France" (Ph.D. diss., University of Chicago, 2012). For Germany, see Jonathan Sperber, *Property and Civil Society in South-Western Germany, 1820–1914* (Oxford: Oxford University Press, 2005). See also Daniel Lord Smail, *Legal Plunder: Households and Debt Collection in Late Medieval Europe* (Cambridge: Harvard University Press, 2016).

16. John Smail, "Credit, Risk, and Honor in Eighteenth-Century Commerce," *Journal of British Studies* 44 (2005): 439–456; Muldrew, "Interpreting the Market: The Ethics of Credit and Community Relations in Early Modern England," *Social History* 18 (1993): 163–183.

17. N. Kh. Bunge, *Teoriia kredita* (Kiev, 1852), 20.

18. Fontaine, *The Moral Economy,* 6; Karl Marx, *Capital,* vol. 3, ch. 36; V. O. Kliuchevskii, *"Proiskhozhdenie krepostnogo prava v Rossii,"* in *Sochinenia,* vol. 8 (Moscow, 1990), 120–193.

19. Borovoi, *Kredit i banki;* Bugrov, *Ocherki.*

20. Rieber, *Merchants and Entrepreneurs;* Owen, *Capitalism and Politics;* Blackwell, *The Beginnings;* Kahan, *The Plow;* Jerome Blum, *Lord and Peasant in Russia: From the Ninth to the Nineteenth Century* (Princeton, 1961), 379–385.

21. Borovoi, *Kredit i banki,* 9–38; Ananich, *Kredit i banki,* 11–70; Daniel H. Kaiser, "'Forgive Us Our Debts': Debts and Debtors in Early Modern Russia," *Forschungen zur osteuropäeischen Geschichte* 50 (1995): 155–193; M. N. Tikhomirov and A. A. Zimin: *Kniga kliuchei i Dolgovaia kniga Iosifo-Volokolamskogo monastyria XVI veka* (Moscow, 1948); Bugrov, *Ocherki,* 14–32; V. N. Zakharov, *Zapadnoevropeiskie kuptsy v rossiiskoi torgovle XVIII veka* (Moscow, 2005); N. B. Golikova, *"Rostovshchichestvo v Rossii nachala XVIII v. i ego nekotorye osobennosti,"* in *Problemy genezisa kapitalizma* (Moscow, 1970), 242–290; and Golikova, *"Kredit i ego rol' v deiatel'nosti russkogo kupechestva v nachale XVIII v."* in *Russkii gorod, vyp. 2* (Moscow, 1979), 161–197; Tracy Dennison, *The*

Institutional Framework of Russian Serfdom (Cambridge: Cambridge University Press, 2011), 181–198.

22. Muldrew, *The Economy of Obligation;* Mann, *The Republic of Debtors;* Finn, *The Character of Credit;* Jay Cohen, "The History of Imprisonment for Debt and Its Relation to the Discharge in Bankruptcy," *The Journal of Legal History* 2 (1982): 153–171.

23. Finn, *The Character of Credit;* Calder, *Financing the American Dream,* 28; Vause, "In the Red and in the Black"; Sperber, *Property and Civil Society,* 127.

24. Yuri Lotman, *Roman A. S. Pushkina "Evgenii Onegin": kommentarii* (Leningrad, 1983), 36–42; Kahan, *The Plow,* 311–318; Blum, *Lord and Peasant,* 379–385; these arguments are reiterated in Farrow, *Between Clan and Crown,* 179, 195-201; for commercial credit, see Owen, *Capitalism and Politics,* 10–15; Rieber, *Merchants and Entrepreneurs,* 27, 35, 191–195; Blackwell, *The Beginnings of Russian Industrialization,* 88–95.

25. Gindin, *Banki,* 465–467, 505–507; Borovoi, *Kredit,* 181–213; B. G. Litvak, *Russkaia derevnia v reforme 1861 goda: Chernozemnyi tsentr, 1861–1865 gg.* (Moscow, 1972), 379–384; Seymour Becker, *Nobility and Privilege in Late Imperial Russia* (DeKalb: Northern Illinois University Press, 1986), 47–51; S. A. Nefedov, *Demograficheski-strukturnyi analiz sotsialno-ekonomicheskoi istorii Rossii: konets xv—nachalo xx veka* (Ekaterinburg, 2005), 220–221; Evsey D. Domar and Mark J. Machina, "On the Profitability of Russian Serfdom," *The Journal of Economic History* 44 (1984): 919–955; Peter Gatrell, "The Meaning of the Great Reforms in Russian Economic History," in Eklof, *Russia's Great Reforms,* 84–101. See also Daniel Field, *The End of Serfdom* (Cambridge: Harvard University Press, 1976), 31; Terence Emmons, *The Russian Landed Gentry and the Peasant Emancipation of 1861* (Cambridge: Cambridge University Press, 1968), 30; Blum, *Lord and Peasant in Russia,* 379–385. On England, see David Cannadine, *Aspects of Aristocracy: Grandeur and Decline in Modern Britain* (New Haven: Yale University Press, 1994), 37–54.

26. A. A. Vvedensky, *Dom Stroganovykh v XVI–XVII vekakh* (Moscow, 1962), 36.

27. Zakharov, *Zapadnoievropeiskie kuptsy.*

28. A. N. Ostrovsky, *PSS,* vol. 1 (Moscow, 1973), 85–152. See also V. Ya. Lakshin, *Aleksandr Nikolaevich Ostrovsky* (Moscow, 1982); Marjorie Hoover, *Alexander Ostrovsky* (Boston: G. K. Hall and Co., 1981); Jules Patouillet, *Ostrovski et son Théatre de Moeurs Russes* (Paris: Plon-Nourrit et Cie, 1912), 108-120.

29. D. N. Mamin-Sibiriak, *Sobranie sochinenii,* vol. 9 (Moscow, 1958), 7–362.

30. Johnson, *Making the Market,* 24.

31. G. R. Searle, *Morality and the Market in Victorian Britain* (Clarendon Press, 1998), 77–106; Timothy Alborn, *Conceiving Companies: Joint Stock Politics in Victorian England* (Abington: Routledge, 1998); James Taylor, *Boardroom Scandal: The Criminalization of Company Fraud in Nineteenth-Century Britain* (Oxford: Oxford University Press, 2013); George Robb, *White-Collar Crime in Modern England: Financial Fraud and Business Morality, 1845–1929* (Cambridge: Cambridge University Press, 1992); Nancy Henry and Cannon Schmitt, eds., *Victorian Investments: New Perspectives on Finance and Culture* (Bloomington:

Indiana University Press, 2009); Sarah Maza, *The Myth of the French Bourgeoisie: An Essay on the Social Imaginary, 1750–1850* (Cambridge: Harvard University Press, 2003), 203.

32. Pravilova, *A Public Empire*, 4; Walter Johnson, *River of Dark Dreams: Slavery and Empire in the Cotton Kingdom* (Belknap Press, 2013); Edward Baptist, *The Half Has Never Been Told: Slavery and the Making of American Capitalism* (Basic Books, 2014); Sven Beckert, *Empire of Cotton: A Global History* (Knopf, 2014); Stephen Mihm, *A Nation of Counterfeiters: Capitalists, Con Men, and the Making of the United States* (Cambridge: Harvard University Press, 2007); Mike Davis, *Late Victorian Holocausts: El Niño Famines and the Making of the Third World* (Verso, 2001); Smail, *Legal Plunder*, 14; for the critique of North's theory, see Robert Allen, *The British Industrial Revolution in Global Perspective* (Cambridge: Cambridge University Press, 2009), 5.

33. Farrow, *Between Clan and Crown*, 21-22. Farrow's conception of private property is based on popular-culture notions of absolute and exclusive ownership, which have never existed in any legal regime, whether normatively or in practice. For a historiographical overview of "optimistic" literature, see Read, "In Search of Liberal Tsarism."

34. Alison Smith, *For the Common Good*; Catriona Kelly, *Refining Russia: Advice Literature, Polite Culture, and Gender from Catherine to Yeltsin* (Oxford: Oxford University Press, 2001), 99; Michael Confino, "The *Soslovie* (Estate) Paradigm: Reflections on Some Open Questions," *Cahiers du monde russe* 49 (2008): 681–704; Gregory L. Freeze, "The *Soslovie* (Estate) Paradigm and Russian Social History," *The American Historical Review* 91 (1986), 11–36; Elise Kimerling Wirtschafter, *Structures of Society: Imperial Russia's "People of Various Ranks"* (DeKalb: Northern Illinois University Press, 1994); N. A. Ivanova and V. P. Zheltova, *Soslovnoe obshchestvo Rossiiskoi imperii* (Moscow, 2010); Boris Mironov, *A Social History of Imperial Russia*, 2 vols. (Westview Press, 1999); see also Amanda Vickery, *The Gentleman's Daughter: Women's Lives in Georgian England* (New Haven: Yale University Press, 1998).

35. For early modern England, see Muldrew, *The Economy of Obligation*.

36. David Moon, *The Russian Peasantry 1600–1930* (Reading: Addison Wesley Longman, 1999); Jane Burbank, *Russian Peasants Go to Court: Legal Culture in the Countryside, 1905-1917* (Bloomington: Indiana University Press, 2004); Dennison, *The Institutional Framework*; Alessandro Stanziani, *Bondage: Labor and Rights in Eurasia from the Sixteenth to the Early Twentieth Centuries* (New York: Berghahn Books, 2014); see also Stephen Hoch, *Serfdom and Social Control in Russia* (Chicago: University of Chicago Press, 1989). An important earlier English-language work on the peasants is Blum, *Lord and Peasant*.

37. Blum, *Lord and Peasant*, 379–385.

38. Becker, *Nobility and Privilege*; Michelle Lamarche Marrese, *A Woman's Kingdom: Noblewomen and the Control of Property in Russia, 1700–1861* (Ithaca: Cornell University Press, 2002); Valerie Kivelson, "The Effects of Partible Inheritance: Gentry Families and the State in Muscovy," *Russian Review* 53 (1994): 197–212; Cavender, *Nests of the Gentry*; Susan Smith-Peter, "The Russian Provincial

Newspaper and Its Public, 1788–1864," *The Carl Beck Papers in Russian and East European Studies* 1908 (Pittsburgh: University of Pittsburgh Press, 2008); Catherine Evtuhov, *Portrait of a Russian Province: Economy, Society, and Civilization in Nineteenth-Century Nizhnii Novgorod* (Pittsburgh: University of Pittsburgh Press, 2011); Antonova, *An Ordinary Marriage.*

39. Lee Farrow, *Between Clan and Crown: The Struggle to Define Noble Property Rights in Imperial Russia* (Newark: University of Delaware Press, 2004); William Wagner, *Marriage, Property, and Law in Late Imperial Russia* (Oxford: Oxford University Press, 1994).

40. See, e.g., Rieber, *Merchants and Entrepreneurs;* Owen, *Capitalism and Politics;* Pintner, *Russian Economic Policy.*

41. Alison Smith, "Trading in Tsarist Russia," Review of Ransel, *A Merchant's Tale, H-HistGeog* (November 2009), https://www.h-net.org/reviews/showrev.php ?id=25651; Blackwell, *The Beginnings of Russian Industrialization;* A. I. Kupriianov, *Kul'tura gorodskogo samoupravleniia russkoi provintsii, 1780–1860-e gody* (Moscow, 2009); Martin, *Enlightened Metropolis.* See also A. B. Kamenskii, *Povsednevnost' russkikh gorodskikh obyvatelei: istoricheskie anekdoty iz provintsial'noi zhizni XVIII veka* (Moscow, 2006); and O. Ie. Kosheleva, *Liudi Sankt-Peterburgskogo ostrova Petrovskogo vremeni* (Moscow, 2004).

42. Muldrew, *The Economy of Obligation.*

43. V. M. Zhivov, *Razyskaniia v oblasti istorii i predystorii russkoi kul'tury* (Moscow, 2002), 256–270.

44. For critical general accounts of legality in Russia, see Pipes, *Russia under the Old Regime,* 287–297; John LeDonne, *Absolutism and Ruling Class: The Formation of the Russian Political Order, 1700–1825* (New York: Oxford University Press, 1991), 179–235; Baberowski, *Autokratie und Justiz;* Elise Kimerling Wirtschafter, "Russian Legal Culture and the Rule of Law," *Kritika* 7 (2006): 61–70; Laura Engelstein, "Combined Underdevelopment: Discipline and the Law in Imperial and Soviet Russia," *The American Historical Review* 98 (1993): 338–353; Uriel Proccacia, *Russian Culture, Property Rights, and the Market Economy* (Cambridge: Cambridge University Press, 2007), 95–143; for a historiographical overview of such literature, see Richard Wortman, "Russian Monarchy and the Rule of Law," *Kritika* 6 (2005): 145–170.

45. V. B. Kobrin, *Vlast' i sobstvennost' v srednevekovoi Rossii* (Moscow, 1985); Nancy Shields Kollmann, *Crime and Punishment in Early Modern Russia* (Cambridge: Cambridge University Press, 2012) and *By Honor Bound: State and Society in Early Modern Russia* (Ithaca: Cornell University Press, 1999); George G. Weickhardt, "The Pre-Petrine Law of Property," *Slavic Review* 52 (1993): 663–679, and "Due Process and Equal Justice in the Muscovite Codes," *Russian Review* 51 (1992): 463–480; Richard Hellie, *Slavery in Russia, 1450–1725* (Chicago: University of Chicago Press, 1982). See also Ananich, *Kredit i banki,* 11–70; Tikhomirov, *Kniga kliuchei.*

46. Kamenskii, *Povsednevnost';* Zakharov, *Zapadnoevropeiskie kuptsy;* Kosheleva, *Liudi Sankt-Peterburgskogo ostrova;* George Munro, "Finance and Credit in the Eighteenth-Century Russian Economy," *Jahrbücher für Geschichte Osteuropas,*

Neue Folge 45 (1997): 552–560, and "The Role of the *Veksel'* in Russian Capital Formation: A Preliminary Inquiry," in *Russia and the World of the Eighteenth Century,* ed. by R. P. Bartlett (Slavica Publishers, 1988), 551–564.

47. Marrese, *A Woman's Kingdom;* Burbank, *Russian Peasants Go to Court.* See also a detailed bibliography in Wirtschafter, "Legal Identity and the Possession of Serfs in Imperial Russia," *The Journal of Modern History* 70 (1998): 561–587.

48. On the 1864 reform, see Wortman, *The Development;* M. G. Korotkikh, *Sudebnaia reforma 1864 goda v Rossii: Sushchnost' i sotsial'no-pravovoi mekhanizm formirovaniia* (Voronezh, 1994); Baberowski, *Autokratie und Justiz;* Friedhelm Berthold Kaiser, *Die Russische Justizreform von 1864: Zur Geschichte der Russischen Justiz von Katharina II bis 1917* (Leiden, 1972); A. D. Popova, *"Pravda i milost' da tsarstvuiut v sudakh" (iz istorii realizatsii sudebnoi reformy 1864 g.)* (Riazan, 2005).

49. On the transition to the Catherinian legal system, see F. M. Dmitriev, *Istoriia sudebnykh instantsii i grazhdanskogo apelliatsionnogo sudoproizvodstva ot Sudebnika do Uchrezhdeniia o guberniiakh* (Moscow, 1859); V. A. Voropanov, *Regional'nyi factor stanovleniia sudebnoi sistemy Rossiiskoi imperii na Urale i v Zapadnoi Sibiri (posledniaia tret' XVIII—pervaia polovina XIX vv.)* (Cheliabinsk, 2011); on medical experts in pre-reform courts, see Elisa Becker, *Medicine, Law and the State in Imperial Russia* (Budapest: Central European University Press, 2011); on the emergence of bureaucratic legality, see Marc Raeff, *The Well-Ordered Police State: Social and Institutional Change Through Law in the Germanies and Russia, 1600–1800* (New Haven: Yale University Press, 1983) and LeDonne, *Absolutism and Ruling Class;* on Peter the Great's legal reforms, see D.O. Serov, *Sudebnaia reforma Petra I* (Moscow, 2009). On the pre-reform legal bureaucracy, see Richard Wortman, *The Development;* on Speransky, see V. A. Tomsinov, *Speransky* (Moscow, 2006); A. N. Fateev, *Speransky i ego vremia* (Moscow, 2012); and Marc Raeff, *Michael Speransky, Statesman of Imperial Russia, 1772–1839* (The Hague: Martinus Nijhoff, 1957).

50. *"Staryi sud! Pri odnom vospominaniia o niom volosy vstaiut dybom, moroz deret po kozhe!"* I. S. Aksakov, *"O starykh sudakh,"* in *Sochineniia,* vol. 4 (Moscow, 1886), 652–666, esp. 655. Another concise account is N. M. Kolmakov, *"Staryi sud," RS* 52 (1886): 511–544.

51. Pipes, *Russia under the Old Regime;* Baberowski, *Autokratie und Justiz.*

52. Pietro Costa and Danilo Zolo, eds. *The Rule of Law: History, Theory and Criticism* (Dordrecht: Springer, 2007), esp. 7–13. For a classic statement of the English doctrine, see A.V. Dicey, *Introduction to the Study of the Law of the Constitution,* 8th ed. (London: Macmillan, 1915); for the reception of the German concept of *Rechsstaat* in Russia, see Hiroshi Oda, "The Emergence of *Pravovoe Gosudarstvo (Rechtsstaat)* in Russia," *Review of Central and East European Law* 25 (1999): 373-434, esp. 378–379; see also Jeffrey D. Sachs and Katharina Pistor, ed., *The Rule of Law and Economic Reform in Russia* (Boulder: Westview Press, 1997); Max Weber, *Economy and Society,* ed. by Guenther Roth and Claus Wittich, vol. 2 (Berkeley: University of California Press, 1968), esp. 654-658.

53. For an application of Weber's ideas about politics and society to imperial Russia, without, however, a detailed analysis of law and legality, see Pipes, *Russia under the Old Regime.*

54. See, for example, Finn, The Character of Credit; Johnson, *Making the Market* and Johnson, "Class Law in Victorian England," *Past & Present* 141 (1993): 147-169; Lucas Powe, *The Supreme Court and the American Elite, 1789-2008* (Cambridge: Harvard University Press, 2009); Charles Lofgren, *The Plessy Case: A Legal-Historical Interpretation* (Oxford: Oxford University Press, 1987); Morton Horwitz, *The Transformation of American Law, 1780-1860* (Cambridge: Harvard University Press, 1977); Suzanne Desan, *The Family on Trial in Revolutionary France* (Berkeley: University of California Press, 2004); Kollmann, *Crime and Punishment*, 5.

55. Stephen Feldman, "An Interpretation of Max Weber's Theory of Law: Metaphysics, Economics, and the Iron Cage of Constitutional Law," *Law & Social Inquiry* 16 (1991): 205-248; David Trubek, "Reconstructing Max Weber's Sociology of Law," *Stanford Law Review* 37 (1985): 919-936. Anthony Kronman commented on Weber's concern that modern law's excessive bureaucratization and reliance on legal specialists leads to a loss of individual autonomy (the "iron cage" of modernity). See Kronman, *Weber* (Stanford: Stanford University Press, 1983), 174-5.

56. Paul W. Kahn, "Freedom, Autonomy, and the Cultural Study of Law," *Yale Journal of Law & the Humanities* 13 (2001): 149-150 and *The Cultural Study of Law: Reconstructing Legal Scholarship* (Chicago: University of Chicago Press, 1999); Sally Falk Moore, *Law as Process: An Anthropological Approach* (Abington: Routledge, 1978); Michael Breen, *Law, City, and King: Legal Culture, Municipal Politics, and State Formation in Early Modern Dijon* (Rochester: University of Rochester Press, 2007); see also the works cited in Burbank, *Russian peasants*, 5-10. For use of the law to initiate and maintain social conflicts, see also Austin T. Turk, "Law as a Weapon in Social Conflict," *Social Problems* 23 (1976): 276-291 and Daniel Lord Smail, *The Consumption of Justice: Emotions, Publicity, and Legal Culture in Marseille, 1264-1423* (Ithaca: Cornell University Press, 2003).

57. E.P. Thompson, *Whig and Hunters: The Origin of the Black Act* (London: Penguin, 1975), 258-269, esp. 263; see also Daniel H. Cole, "An Unqualified Human Good': E.P. Thompson and the Rule of Law," *Journal of Law and Society* 28 (2001): 177-203; Peter King, *Crime, Justice and Discretion in England, 1740-1820* (Oxford: Oxford University Press, 2000).

58. In 1889 it was replaced with the present Russian Revival building of the Moscow City Duma, which after 1917 became the Lenin Museum. P.V. Sytin, *Iz istorii moskovskikh ulits* (Moscow, 1958), 159.

59. *Moskva ili istoricheskii putevoditel' po znamenitoi stolitse Gosudarstva Rossiiskogo,* vol. 2 (Moscow, 1827), 330–332. I am grateful to N.S. Datieva for the reference.

60. Pintner and Don Karl Rowney, eds., *Russian Officialdom: The Bureaucratization of Russian Society from the Seventeenth to the Twentieth Century* (Chapel Hill: The University of North Carolina Press, 1980).

61. Richard Robbins, *Tsar's Viceroys: Russian Provincial Governors in the Last Years of the Empire* (Ithaca: Cornell University Press, 1987); Susanne Schattenberg, *Die korrupte Provinz? Russische Beamte im 19. Jahrhundert* (Frankfurt: Campus Verlag, 2008); Evtuhov, *Portrait.*

62. Konstantin Trotsina, *Istoriia sudebnykh uchrezhdenii v Rossii* (St. Petersburg, 1851); SZ 2/1:2376 and 2434 (1857).

63. On nineteenth-century bureaucracy, see Pintner, *Russian Officialdom;* P.A. Zaionchkovskii, *Pravitel'stvennyi apparat samoderzhavnoi Rossii v XIX v.* (Moscow, 1978); N.P. Yeroshkin, *Istoriia gosudarstvennykh uchrezhdenii dorevoliutsionnoi Rossii* (Moscow, 1983).

64. A.G. Chukarev, *Tainaia politsiia Rossii, 1825–1855* (Moscow, 2005); I.M. Trotskii, *Tret'ie otdelenie pri Nikolae I* (Moscow, 1930); Sidney Monas, *The Third Section: Police and Society in Russia under Nicholas I* (Cambridge: Harvard University Press, 1961); P. S. Squire, *The Third Department: The Political Police in the Russia of Nicholas I* (Cambridge: Cambridge University Press, 1968).

65. Desan, *The Family on Trial,* 283-310.

66. Burbank, *Russian Peasants Go to Court.*

67. Fontaine, *The Moral Economy,* xiii, 6; Cohen, "The History of Imprisonment," 160; T. Ye. Novitskaia, *Pravovoie regulirovaniie imushchestvennykh otnoshenii v Rossii vo vtoroi polovine XVIII veka* (Moscow, 2005), 386–387.

68. Zakharov, *Zapadnoevropeiskie kuptsy,* 206.

69. The Russian term is used in this section, and the English one is mostly used in the rest of the book.

70. G. F. Shershenevich, *Kurs torgovogo prava,* vol. 3 (Moscow, 2003; original 1909), 24–172; D. I. Meier, *"Ocherk russkogo vekselnogo prava,"* in *Izbrannye proizvedenia po grazhdanskomu pravu* (Moscow, 2003; original 1857), 296–379.

71. PSZ.II 7:5462 (The *Veksel* Statute of 1832, Article 442).

72. PSZ 26:19692 (1800); Meier, *"Ocherk."*

73. S. M. Baratz, *Kurs veksel'nogo prava* (St. Petersburg, 1893), 676.

74. PSZ 8:5410 (1729). Baratz, *Kurs.*

75. Zakharov, *Zapadnoevropeiskie kuptsy,* 204–207.

76. Munro, "The Role of the *Veksel'*."

77. Meier, *"Ocherk,"* 311.

78. Shershenevich, *Kurs,* vol. 3, 36.

79. Novitskaia, *Pravovoie,* 385–387; Ye.P. Karnovich, *Zamechatel'nye bogatstva chatsnykh lits v Rossii* (St. Petersburg, 1874), 353–354.

80. PSZ 15:11204 (1761).

81. SZ 11/2:546, Note (1857) *(Ustav Vekselnyi).*

82. Ya. V. Abramov, *Zaiom, zaklad i zalog* (St. Petersburg, 1898), 33–34.

83. For example, loan letters distinguished from mortgage notes in PSZ 22:16460 (1786).

84. PSZ 26:19692 (1800). These rules were broken up in 1832 into the various provisions of Volumes 10 and 11 of the Digest of the Laws, but substantively remained in force (with some alterations) until the end of the imperial period.

85. Novitskaia, *Pravovoie,* 438–439.

86. Meier, *"Ocherk,"* 312. See also PSZ 23:16851 (1790). Senators disagreed, and Catherine II ordered that debts pursuant to "moneyless" veksels not be collected. In that case, both the holder of the veksel and the original lenders admitted that no money was actually issued.

87. PSZ.II 37:38993.

88. Abramov, *Zaiom, zaklad i zalog,* 13.

89. Shershenevich, *Kurs,* vol. 3, 61–64.

90. Bugrov, *Ocherki* 50–51, 140–141; PSZ 15:11581 (1762).

91. D. Filimonov, *"Kreditnye uchrezhdeniia Moskovskogo vospitatel'nogo doma,"* RA 14 (1876), 265–275. I refer to this institution as the "Board of Trustees" or the "Board" to follow contemporary usage.

92. Filimonov, *"Kreditnye uchrezhdenia,"* 269–270.

93. Aleksandr Skrebitskii, *Krestianskoe delo v tsarstvovanie imperatora Aleksandra II,* vol. 4 (Bonn, 1868), 1244–1249; Nikolai Troinitskii, *Krepostnoe naselenie Rossii po 10-i narodnoi perepisi* (St. Petersburg, 1861). Troinitskii's figures for the Loan Bank do not include unsecured loans (335 million rubles in 1855). See I. I. Kaufman, *Statistika russkikh bankov,* part 1 *(Statisticheskii vremennik Rossiiskoi Imperii. Ser. 2. Vyp. 9)* (St. Petersburg, 1872), 3. See also Blum, *Lord and Peasant,* 379–385. B. G. Litvak argued that Russian landowners often exaggerated their indebtedness in their reports to the statisticians. See *Russkaia derevnia,* 380–383.

94. Borovoi, *Kredit i banki,* 197–198 (from 90 million rubles in 1823 to 425 million in 1859).

95. *Sobranie pravil Sokhrannoi i Ssudnoi kazny pri Moskovskom i S. Peterburgskom Imperatorskikh vospitaltelnykh domakh* (St. Petersburg, 1847).

96. Bugrov, *Ocherki,* 135.

97. *Materialy dlia geografii and statistiki Rossii, Simbirskaia guberniia,* part I (St. Petersburg, 1868), 502.

98. *Materialy dlia geografii and statistiki Rossii, Riazanskaia guberniia* (St. Petersburg, 1860), 235.

99. TsIAM 92.6.746 (Zubov).

100. A. I. Chikhachev, "O dolgakh," *Zemledelcheskaia Gazeta* (Sept. 6, 1846). I am grateful to Katherine Pickering Antonova for the reference. A. D. Galakhov, *Zapiski cheloveka* (Moscow: NLO, 1999), 25.

101. Gindin, *Banki,* 505–507.

102. Ibid., 465–467.

103. I. V. Pushechnikov, *"Zametki starozhila Yeletskogo uezda. S 1842 po 1872 g.,"* RA, 117 (1905): 599.

104. Kaufman, *"Gosudarstvennye dolgi Rossii,"* Vestnik Evropy 20 (1885), No. 1, 184–218 and No. 2, 572–618; Bugrov, *Ocherki,* 32.

105. Over 88% of state loans were issued to landowners with more than 100 serfs. Litvak, *Russkaia derevnia,* 383.

106. Borovoi, *Kredit i banki,* esp. 206–207 and 235–240.

107. Hoch, "The Banking Crisis, Peasant Reform, and Economic Development in Russia, 1857–1861," *The American Historical Review* 96 (1991): 795–820; Bugrov, *Ocherki;* Morozan, *Istoriia bankovskogo dela.*

108. I.V. Pushechnikov, *"Zametki,"* 599.

109. D.I. Nikiforov, *Moskva v tsarstvovaniie imperatora Aleksandra II* (Moscow, 1904), 48–49 and 127.

110. Becker, *Nobility and Privilege,* 78–79.

1. Usurers' Tales

1. F. M. Dostoevsky, *Prestuplenie i nakazanie [Crime and Punishment]* (Moscow, 1970), 10. Passage translated by the author.

2. *Prestuplenie i nakazanie,* 54.

3. It is unclear whether Dostoevsky was aware that early modern Russian monasteries acted as large-scale lenders.

4. Translation adapted from Richard Pevear and Larissa Volokhonsky (New York: Macmillan, 2002), 344; see also p. 695 (Fedor Karamazov was "above all a usurer").

5. V. O. Mikhnevich, *Yazvy Peterburga* (St. Petersburg, 1886), 282.

6. R. E. Tsimmerman, *Kulachestvo-rostovshchichestvo* (St. Petersburg, 1898); G. P. Sazonov, *Rostovshchichestvo-kulachestvo* (St. Petersburg, 1894). Even Charles Geisst's book about usury is written from the abstract perspective of intellectual critiques and government policies. Geisst, *Beggar Thy Neighbor.*

7. N. I. Pavlenko, *"O rostovshchichestve dvorian v XVIII v. (k postanovke voprosa)* in N. I. Pavlenko, ed., *Dvorianstvo i krepostnoi stroi v Rossii XVI–XVIII vv.* (Moscow, 1975), 265–272; N. B. Golikova, *"Rostovshchichestvo v Rossii;* V. R. Tarlovskaia, *"Rostovshchicheskie operatsii moskovskikh kuptsov i torgovykh krest'ian v nachale XVIII v.," Vestnik MGU, Seriia 8. Istoriia* 3 (1977): 44–55; Bugrov, *Ocherki,* 27, 31; Kaiser, "Forgive Us Our Debts"; Borovoi, *Kredit i banki,* esp. 206–207 and 235–240.

8. Fontaine, "Antonio and Shylock: Credit and Trust in France, c. 1680–1780," *Economic History Review* 54 (2001): 39–57 ("Despite the shift in thinking, the law remained impervious to credit.").

9. For a similar discussion in the context of imperial Russia's system of taxation, see Kotsonis, *States of Obligation.*

10. Searle, *Morality and the Market.*

11. Geisst, *Beggar Thy Neighbor,* esp. 19; David Hawkes, *The Culture of Usury in Renaissance England* (New York: Palgrave Macmillan, 2010). One the role of anti-Semitism, see Helmut Walser Smith, "The Discourse of Usury: Relations Between Christians and Jews in the German Countryside, 1880-1914," *Central European History* 32 (1999): 255-276.

12. See, e.g., TsIAM 50.4.7229 (Ivanov). Other common slurs were *protsentshchik, kulak,* and *likhoimets.* The positive term was *kapitalist.*

13. *"Povest' o nekoem kuptse likhoimtse," Russkaia bytovaia povest XV–XVII vv.,* ed. by A. N. Uzhankov (Moscow, 1991), 380–384. Cited in Bugrov, *Ocherki,* 30. Bugrov does not note the resemblance.

14. N. A. Nekrasov, *"Rostovshchik,"* in *PSS,* vol. 7 (Leningrad, 1983), 127–145.

15. Sidney Homer and Richard Sylla, *A History of Interest Rates,* 4th ed. (Wiley, 2005), 2. The authors are cautiously skeptical of this view.

16. Ostrovskii, *"Ne bylo ni grosha, da vdrug altyn"* ["There Was Not a Single Penny, and Suddenly There Was a Dime"], *PSS,* vol. 3 (Moscow, 1974), 431.

17. A. F. Koni, *Otsy i deti sudebnoi reformy* (Moscow, 1914), 278.

18. V. M. Doroshevich, *Sakhalin,* vol. 2 (Moscow, 1903), 77; Koni, *"Landsberg (Iz predsedatel'skoi praktiki),"* in *Sobranie sochinenii,* vol. 1 (Moscow, 1966), 148–166.

19. TsIAM 50.4.8044.

20. GARF 109.178.195.

21. Ananich, *Kredit i banki,* 18–37; Geisst, *Beggar Thy Neighbor,* 14–15; Hawkes, *The Culture of Usury.*

22. D. Blagovo, *Rasskazy babushki* (Moscow, 1989), 222.

23. D. M. Kalikhman, *"Zabytye imena: dve sud'by v razlome russkoi revoliutsii," Prilozhenie k gazete "Novosti Akademii navigatsii i upravleniia dvizheniem"* 1 (2009).

24. GARF 109.89.693/3, l. 8.

25. TsIAM 81.16.1642. This passage sounds just as awkward in the original Russian.

26. GARF 109.91.113.

27. GARF 109.89.693/2.

28. Ibid., l. 23–23 ob.

29. M. I. Pyliaev, *Zamechate'nye chudaki i originaly* (St. Petersburg, 1898), 294.

30. GARF 109.89.693/3.

31. GARF 109.3a.1620.

32. GARF 109.3a.1610.

33. See also Judith Spicksley, "'Fly With a Duck in Thy Mouth': Single Women as Sources of Credit in Seventeenth-Century England," *Social History* 32 (2007): 187–207.

34. GARF 109.89.693/2, l. 1 ob.

35. Ibid.

36. Ibid.

37. GARF 109.3a.1610.

38. Attempts to calculate actual interest rates in the eighteenth century are based on guesswork. For example, see Golikova, *"Rostovshchichestvo v Rossii."*

39. For loansharking in New York City in the late nineteenth and early twentieth centuries, see Anne Fleming, "The Borrower's Tale: A History of Poor Debtors in *Lochner* Era New York City," *Law and History Review* 30 (2012): 1053–1098.

40. TsIAM 50.14.2363; 50.14.2366; 50.14.2380 (registered loan letters for 1852, 1854, and 1864, respectively).

41. TsIAM 50.11.95 (Arbenov) (1854–1856).

42. TsIAM 50.14.1597; 50.14.1621 (urban mortgages for 1855 and 1860, respectively); 50.14.1629 (rural mortgages for 1862).

43. Pavlenko, *"O rostovshchichestve dvorian";* Golikova, *"Rostovshchichestvo v Rossii";* V. R. Tarlovskaia, *"Rostovshchicheskie operatsii."*

44. GARF 109.3a.1610 (1866).

45. The Usury Act of 1571 set the ceiling at 10 percent, which was reduced to 5 percent by 1713. Geisst, *Beggar Thy Neighbor,* 81 and 102.

46. Vause, "In the Red and in the Black," 37, 89; Fabien Valente "Usury in France in the Nineteenth Century," in *Private Law and Social Inequality in the Industrial Age: Comparing Legal Cultures in Britain, France, Germany and the United States,* ed. Willibald Steimetz (London: Oxford University Press, 2000), 437–455.

47. Geisst, *Beggar Thy Neighbor,* 166–167; Fleming, "The Borrower's Tale"; James M. Ackerman, "Interest Rates and the Law: A History of Usury," *Arizona State Law Journal* (1981), 61–110; Horwitz, *The Transformation of American Law,* 241–245.

48. PSZ.II, 7:5462 (1852), section 120. For the rules under the 1649 law code, see PSZ 1:112 (ch. 10, art. 255, 258.). For the interest accrual rule, see PSZ 21:15379 (1781–1783).

49. PSZ.II 9:6775 (1834); 24:23112 (1849); and 29:28398 (1854).

50. PSZ 14:10235 (1754), 87; PSZ 22:16407 (1786); PSZ 30:23317 (1808); PSZ.II, 20:19283 (1845) (art. 2220).

51. Owen, *The Corporation.*

52. I refer to the senior Buturlin as "General Buturlin," otherwise referring to his son.

53. GARF 109.89.693/1, l. 2–50b.

54. Ibid., l. 10.

55. Ibid., l. 38 ob.

56. On the Third Section, see Chukarev, *Tainaia politsiia;* Monas, *The Third Section;* and Squire, *The Third Department.* On equity in England, see Dennis Klinck, *Conscience, Equity and the Court of Chancery in Early Modern England* (Ashgate, 2013) and J. H. Baker, *An Introduction to English Legal History* (London: Butterworths, 1990), 112–134.

57. GARF 109.89.693/1, l. 10. See also SZ 15/1:1186–1195 (1857).

58. See, e.g., 109.96.54 (Bilbasov).

59. TsIAM 50.5.13.

60. TsIAM 50.4. 5294(a).

61. GARF 109.3a.1610.

62. On the use of such brokers, see Ye. I. Lamanskii, *"Iz vospominanii Yevgeniia Ivanovicha Lamanskogo,"* RS 162 (1915): 340–341.

63. On Yusupov, see P. V. Dolgorukov, *Zapiski kniazia Petra Dolgorukova* (St. Petersburg, 2007), 604; On Zlobin, see Karnovich, *Zamechatel'nye bogatstva,* 353–354; see also Nikolai Mikhailovich, *Russkie portrety XVIII–XIX stoletii,* vol. 2, No. 3 (St. Petersburg, 1906), 122; P. G. Ryndziunskii, *"Gorodskoe naselenie,"* in *Ocherki ekonomicheskoi istorii Rossii pervoi poloviny XIX veka,* ed. by M. K. Rozhkova (Moscow, 1959), 308.

64. See, e.g., TsIAM 142.2.154 (Saltykov) (1897–1916).

65. Ostrovskyy, "Ne bylo ni grosha," 450–451; Nekrasov, "Rostovshchik"; Pyliaev, *Zamechate'nye chudaki,* 183–191; Jilian Porter, "Mad Ambition: Economies of Russian Literature 1830–1850" (Ph.D. diss., University of California–Berkeley, 2011).

66. See, e.g., PSZ 22:16300 (1785), 502; GARF 109.89.693 / 1, l.55.

67. N.N.Z., *Klub chervonnykh valetov: ugolovnyi protsess* (Moscow, 1877); Sergei Antonov, "Swindlers and Forgers of Moscow: the Jacks of Hearts and the Birth of a Show Trial" (article in progress)

68. GARF 109.89.693/1, l.210–210 ob.

69. M.Ye. Saltykov-Shchedrin, *Sobranie Sochinenii v dvadtsati tomakh,* vol. 13 (Moscow, 1972).

70. M. Gurenok, *"Pomeshchiki Poltoratskie,"* in *Pamiatniki Otechestva,* 34 (1995): 33–143.

71. See D. I. Patrikeev, *Krupnoe krepostnoe khoziaistvo xvii v.* (Leningrad, 1967), 133; Kaiser, "'Forgive Us Our Debts,'" 158–159; Borovoi, *"Rostovshchichestvo, kazennye ssudy i gosudarstvennyi dolg v protsesse pervonachal'nogo nakoplenia v Rossii,"* in *K voprosu o pervonachal'nom nakoplenii v Rossii (xvii—xviii vv.). Sbornik statei* (Moscow, 1958), 500.

72. Vvedensky, *Dom Stroganovykh,* 36.

73. Pavlenko, *"O rostovshchichestve,"* 270.

74. V. V. Ogarkov, *Demidovy: ikh zhizn' i deiatel'nost'* (St. Petersburg, 1891), 76–79.

75. Dolgorukov, *Zapiski,* 604.

76. GARF 109.93.538.

77. John LeDonne, "Ruling Families in the Russian Political Order, 1689–1825," *Cahiers du Monde russe et soviétique* 28 (1987): 233–293.

78. GARF 109.89.693/1, l. 180 ob.

79. TsIAM 50.14.2366 and 50.14.1621.

80. GARF 109.89.693/1, l. 120. On Rakeev, see A. V. Baranovskii, *Vyritsa pri tsare— dachnyi Peterburg* (St. Petersburg, 2005). He owned the village of Vyritsa, a summer rest spot just outside Petersburg.

81. GARF 109.89.693/1, l. 111—116.

82. GARF 109.89.693/1, l. 208.

83. For example, in the 1849 case of Lieutenant Rakhmanov that was also investigated by the gendarmes, his creditors agreed to cut their demand by 85 percent. GARF 109.89.693/1, l. 6–7.

84. For the gendarmes' analysis, see GARF 109.89.693/1, l. 111—116.

85. Ibid., l. 169–170.

86. Ibid., l. 179.

87. GARF 109.91.113.

88. Nekrasov, *"Rostovshchik."*

89. D. I. Meier, *Russkoe grazhdanskoe pravo,* 4th ed. (St. Petersburg, 1868), 632–633; SZ 10/1:2104–2111 (1857).

90. For the statute of limitations in Russia, see PSZ 22:16651 (1787).

91. Mikhnevich, *Yazvy Peterburga* 532.

92. This was recognized in Catherine's decree of 1764. PSZ 16:12124.

93. TsIAM 81.18.1259, l. 22 (Tolstoy) (1863–65).

94. TsIAM 50.4.7229 (Ivanov) (1863–65). Another instance of this practice may have occurred in the case of a young landowner from Kherson province, Nikolai Abramov, who issued a "moneyless" bill of exchange for 15,000 rubles to the Moscow usurer Collegiate Secretary Semen Briukhatov. See TsIAM 50.3.8323 (1865–1866).

95. Tsimmerman, *Kulachestvo.*

96. GARF 109.91.113, l. 18–18 ob.

97. TsIAM 50.4.8264 (Ulitin) (1865–1866).

98. TsIAM 50.4.8960 (1866–1869) (Riazanov). See also 109.89.369 (Golitsyn). Debt registers often contain pairs of debt documents, one being approximately 1 / 10 of the other and clearly representing the interest. GARF 109.89.693 / 1.

99. TsIAM 50.4.7229 (Ivanov) (1863–1865).

100. TsIAM 50.4.6234 (Durkina) (1861–1863).

101. TsIAM 50.4.3926 (Alekseev) (1851–1852).

102. TsIAM 50.4.4732 (Pereshivkina) (1856–1857).

103. V. M. Gessen, *Iskliuchitelnoe polozhenie* (St. Petersburg, 1908), 163 ff. Jonathan Daly, "On the Significance of Emergency Legislation in Late Imperial Russia," *Slavic Review* 54 (1995): 602–629.

104. GARF 109.89.693/1, l. 117–18

105. TsIAM 16.69.209 (1879–1882).

106. Ibid, l. 1—10b.

107. For another case of an extended Jewish family of artisans and traders first being allowed to settle in Moscow and then being expelled for allegedly engaging in usury and receiving stolen property, see TsIAM 16.69.454 (1879).

108. GARF 109.3a.1621 (1868).

109. PSZ.II 54:59370 (1879). Soviet scholar Iosif Gindin suggested that the legal limitation on the permissible interest rate did have the effect of lowering the rates of private moneylenders. See *Banki*, p. 491. Usually scholars simply state that private lenders charged much higher rates than the state.

110. Pobedonostsev, *Kurs grazhdanskogo prava*, vol. 3 (Moscow, 2003; original 1880), 96–99.

111. PSZ.III 13:9654 (1893).

112. G. O. Rozenzweig, *Iz zaly suda. Sudebnye ocherki i kartinki* (St. Petersburg, 1900), 456–569.

113. Although in the United States organized banking developed earlier than in imperial Russia, consumer loans, especially unsecure ones, were not easily available even in the early twentieth century, resulting in a thriving loan-sharking industry. See Fleming, "The Borrower's Tale"; Calder, *Financing the American Dream*.

114. Hawkes, *The Culture of Usury*, esp. 167–168.

115. Marx, *Capital*, vol. 3, ch. 36.

116. N. Goremykin, *O torgovle i kredite: prakticheskie zametki i nabliudenia* (Moscow, 1875), 5–9.

117. Tsimmerman, *Kulachestvo-rostovshchichestvo*, 147–160.

2. Nobles and Merchants

1. A. T. Bolotov, *Zhizn' i prikliucheniia Andreia Bolotova, 1738–1793*, vol. 2 (St. Petersburg, 1871), 46, 139, 178, 332–333.

2. Fontaine, *The Moral Economy*, 4.

3. Gindin, *Banki*; Borovoi, *Kredit i banki*.

4. Blum, *Lord and Peasant*, 381.

5. Evsey Domar and Mark Machina, "On the Profitability of Russian Serfdom," *Journal of Economic History* 44 (1984): 919–955.

6. Pavlenko, *"O rostovshchichestve dvorian."*

7. TsIAM 50.14.2360 (1850); 50.14.2363 (1852); 50.14.2366 (1854); 50.14.2380 (1864) (partial list).

8. TsIAM 50.14.2358 (partial list).

9. TsIAM 50.14.1629 (1862).

10. TsIAM 50.14.1581 (vol. 1).

11. TsIAM 50.14.1597.

12. Tarlovskaia, *"Rostovshchicheskie operatsii,"* 50.

13. Kaufman, *Statistika*, 4–5; Borovoi, *Kredit i banki*, 221–222; for slightly different figures, see Morozan, *Istoriia*, 383–386.

14. V. P. Bezobrazov, *Narodnoe khoziaistvo Rossii*, part 1 (St. Petersburg, 1882), 234.

15. P. I. Melnikov, *Nizhegorodskaia yarmarka v 1843, 1844 i 1845 godakh* (Nizhnii Novgorod, 1846), 120. Some types of merchandise were traded for cash, such as fashion goods, sugar, and sometimes tea and textiles. Ibid., 120, 203, 240.

16. Melnikov, *Nizhegorodskaia yarmarka*, 120, 286. The latter figure quoted in I.Ya. Gorlov, *Obozrenie ekonomicheskoi statistiki Rossii* (St. Petersburg, 1849), 273–274; Thomas C. Owen read this passage as indicating that credit was not widely used by Russian merchants, whereas Melnikov argued exactly the opposite. See Owen, *Capitalism and Politics in Russia*, 13.

17. V. O. Mikhnevich, *Peterburg ves' na ladoni* (St. Petersburg, 1874), 532.

18. Melnikov, *Nizhegorodskaia yarmarka*, 286. This estimate also includes barter transactions.

19. Bugrov, *Ocherki*, 198.

20. Yu.N. Karpinskaia, *"Iz semeinoi khroniki,"* *Istoricheskii vestnik* 70 (1897): 867.

21. GARF 109.89.195 (1859) (Bolobonova).

22. TsIAM 78.4.275 (1869–1870).

23. TsIAM 78.3.44 (1859).

24. TsIAM 50.4.8960 (1866–1869).

25. TsIAM 142.3.264.

26. Skrebitskii, *Krestianskoe delo*, vol. 4, 1244–46.

27. Golikova, *"Rostovshchichestvo,"* 246. These data are incomplete.

28. *Voenno-statisticheskoe obozrenie Rossiiskoi imperii*, vol. 6, part 1 (St. Petersburg, 1853), 173–174.

29. Bezobrazov, *Narodnoe khoziaistvo*, 37–38.

30. TsIAM 50.14.1629 (1862).

31. GARF 109.22.108 (1847).

32. Golikova, *"Rostovshchichestvo."*

33. Ananich, *Bankirskie doma*, 8–11.

34. *Materialy dlia geografii i statistiki Rossii, Khersonskaia guberniia*, part 1 (St. Petersburg, 1863), 566.

35. Ibid., 543–544, 564–566.

36. Ibid., 566–568. The 1853 figure is for wheat only.

37. Ibid., 628.

38. *Voenno-statisticheskoe obozrenie Rossiiskoi imperii*, vol. 10, part 1 (St. Petersburg, 1848), 169, 174. See also *"Mirovoi sud v Podolii,"* RS 89 (1897): 281.

39. Dennison, *The Institutional Framework*, 181–198; Rodney Bohac, "Family, Property, and Socioeconomic Mobility: Russian Peasants on Manuilovskoe Estate, 1810–1861." (Ph.D. Diss., University of Illinois at Urbana-Champaign, 1982), 64; TsIAM, 50.11.95 (Arbenov) (1854–1856) (1820 debtors' list from Temnikovo).

40. Borovoi, *Kredit i banki*, 206–207, 235–240.

41. Bugrov, *Ocherki*, 27. See also Kliuchevskii, *"Proiskhozhdenie,"* 134–135.

42. Kahan, *The Plow*, 311–318; Blum, *Lord and Peasant*, 379–385; Owen, *Capitalism and Politics*, 10–15; Rieber, *Merchants and Entrepreneurs*, 27, 35, 191–195.

43. Dennison, *The Institutional Framework*.

44. Kahan, "The Costs of "Westernization" in Russia: The Gentry and the Economy in the Eighteenth Century," *Slavic Review* 25 (1966): 40–66. Half of these costs were incurred to pay for sugar, whereas the expenses for silks, wines, and other similar luxuries were modest in comparison (requiring, using Kahan's methodology, only seven extra serfs per noble to pay for them).

45. Karnovich, *Zamechatel'nye bogatstva*; A. V. Romanovich-Slavatinskii, *Dvorian-stvo v Rossii ot nachala XVIII veka do otmeny krepostnogo prava* (St. Petersburg, 1870); Lotman, *Roman A. S. Pushkina*.

46. Bugrov, *Ocherki*, 144; Pavlenko, *"O rostovshchichestve,"* 271. Pavlenko noted that there was not a single merchant on the loan letter ledgers that he studied. However, this is to be expected because for non-secured loans, merchants used much more convenient bills of exchange not recorded in the ledgers he used.

47. Mamin-Sibiriak, *Sobraniie sochinenii*, 168.

48. Tsimmerman, *Kulachestvo*; Sazonov, *Rostovshchichestvo*.

49. Chukarev, *Tainaia politsiia*, 150.

50. Thomas Newlin, *The Voice in the Garden: Andrei Bolotov and the Anxieties of Russian Pastoral 1738–1833* (Chicago: Northwestern University Press, 2001).

51. A. I. Chikhachev, "O dolgakh," *Zemledel'cheskaia Gazeta*, Sept. 6, 1846.

52. Antonova, *An Ordinary Marriage*.

53. N. P. Makarov, *Izvlecheniia i vyderzhki iz moikh semidesiatiletnikh vospominanii* (St. Petersburg, 1881), 21, 31–33.

54. E. N. Vodovozova, *Na zare zhizni*, vol. 1 (Moscow, 1987), 86.

55. Vodovozova, *Na zare zhizni*, 100, 116–120, 153.

56. TsIAM 50.5.12064.

57. TsIAM 50.5.12253 (townsman Fedorov) (1852–1861) (inheritance worth 30.53 rubles); 50.5.12255 (merchant Sobolev) (1851–1862) (2,430 rubles); 50.5.12252 (merchantwoman Samsonova) (515 rubles); 50.5.12251 (townsman Aleksandrov) (17.20 rubles); 50.5.12068 (merchant's wife Andreeva) (1851–1864) (8,300 rubles).

58. A. T. Bolotov, *Pamiatnik pretekshikh vremen, ili kratkie istoricheskie zapiski o byvshikh proisshestviiakh i o nosivshikhsia v narode slukhakh* (Moscow, 1875), 59.

59. TsIAM 78.4.275 (Bubentsova) (1869–1870).

60. N.N.Z., *Klub chervonnykh valetov*, 57.

61. Lotman, *Roman A. S. Pushkina*, 37. Lotman suggested that middling gentry did not need to be quite as heavily indebted as the higher nobility.

62. GARF 109.85.456 (Urusov).

63. TsIAM 50.5.12256; 50.5.12332.

64. TsIAM 49.3.889.

65. TsIAM 50.5.12258.

66. TsIAM 142.5.1307.

67. TsIAM 92.9.803.

68. TsIAM 50.5.13156.

69. Gettun, "Zapiski," 279–280.

70. Blum, *Lord and Peasant*, 379–385; Nefedov, *Demografcheski-strukturnyi analiz*, 221.

71. Emmons and Field suggest that the emancipation bailed out serfowners from a debt burden that they would not have otherwise been able to bear. Field, *The End of Serfdom*, 31; Emmons, *The Russian Landed Gentry*, 30

72. Iosif Gindin has shown that the Russian state under Nicholas I extensively used the enormous private deposits accumulated in government-run banks to cover its budget deficit, thus avoiding the necessity of either borrowing from abroad or issuing official public debt. See *Banki i ekonomicheskaia politika*, 468.

73. Ananich, *Kredit i banki*, 122.

74. TsIAM 424.1.2081 (1852); 424.1.2083 (1854); 424.1.2085 (1856); 424.1.2087 (1858).

75. Morozan, *Istoriia*, 334, 383–386.

76. Becker, *Nobility and Privilege*.

77. Gindin, *Banki*, 505–507 (originally published in 1961 and 1968).

78. Ibid., 468.

79. Borovoi, *Kredit i banki*, 198.

80. Gindin, *Banki*, 485, 505–507; Litvak, *Russkaia derevnia*, 379–384; Becker, *Nobility and Privilege*, 47–51; Domar Machina, "On the Profitability of Russian Serfdom," Gatrell, "The Meaning of the Great Reforms."

81. I. V. Pushechnikov, *"Zametki starozhila Yeletskogo uezda. S 1842 po 1872 g.,"* *RA* 117 (1905): 537–646, esp. 599, 603.

82. Borovoi, *Kredit i banki*, 204.

83. Calder, *Financing the American Dream*, 28.

84. SZ 10/2:2225–2231 (1857).

85. Pyliaev, *Zamechate'nye chudaki*, 316–319.

86. Smith, *For the Common Good*; Confino, "The *Soslovie* (Estate) Paradigm"; Freeze, "The *Soslovie* (Estate) Paradigm"; Wirtschafter, *Structures of Society*.

87. Alfred Rieber, "Review of Elise Kimerling Wirtschafter, *Structures of Society*," *Russian Review* 55 (1996): 125.

88. Mark Granovetter, "The Strength of Weak Ties," *American Journal of Sociology* 78 (1973), 1360–1380, esp. 1361, 1373.

89. Kaiser, "'Forgive Us Our Debts.'"

90. Golikova, *"Rostovshchichestvo v Rossii."*

91. Tarlovskaia, *Rostovshchicheskiie operatskii*.

92. Golikova, *"Kredit i ego rol',"* 182–188; Pavlenko, *O rostovshchichestve*, 269, 271. Pavlenko insisted on the "primarily intra-estate functioning of usurious capital," although his numbers suggest exactly the opposite.

93. Fontaine, *The Moral Economy*, 293.

94. Nikiforov, *Moskva . . . Aleksandra II*, 101–102.

95. Sperber, *Property and Civil Society*, 119.

96. Ryndziunskii, *"Gorodskoe naselenie,"* 351.
97. Troinitsky, *Krepostnoe naselenie,* 45.
98. See, e.g., TsIAM 50.5.12256 (Trubetskoi); 49.3.889 (Golitsyn); 50.5.12073 (Muraviova); 50.5.12258 (Rakhmanova) (had no private debt).
99. TsIAM 92.6.746.
100. TsIAM 50.5.12260 (Nilus); 92.6.741 (Pevnitskaia).
101. Marrese, *A Woman's Kingdom,* 216–218; LeDonne, *Absolutism and Ruling Class;* I. M. Dolgorukov, *Povest' o rozhdenii moiom, proiskhozhdenii i vsei zhizni,* 2 vols. (St. Petersburg, 2004).
102. TsIAM 50.5.12073. I omit several loans that seem to have reflected self-dealing by the trustees appointed over Muraviov's estate after his death.
103. TsIAM 91.10.611.
104. TsIAM 142.5.1307.
105. TsIAM 50.5.11976, vol. 1.
106. TsIAM 50.5.12256.
107. TsIAM 50.5.11967.
108. TsIAM 142.4.81.
109. TsIAM 92.6.746.
110. TsIAM 142.5.1316.
111. TsIAM 81.18.1259.
112. TsIAM 50.5.13156.
113. M. M. Bogoslovsky, *"Moskva v 1870–1890-kh godakh,"* in *Moskovskaia starina,* ed. by Yu.N. Aleksandrov (Moscow, 1989), 387–390.
114. A. P. Miliukov, *Dobroie staroie vremia* (St. Petersburg, 1872), 170–190.
115. TsIAM 50.4.8960.
116. TsIAM 50.5.12271.
117. TsIAM 50.4.8434.
118. TsIAM 78.4.275.
119. Wirtschafter emphasizes the porousness and plasticity of social categories and argues for the existence of a "middle estate, which possessed all the cultural and socioeconomic ingredients of a European middle class." *Structures of Society,* 136.
120. TsIAM 142.4.64.
121. TsIAM 142.5.1281.
122. A.A. Polovtsov, *Russkii biograficheskii slovar,* vol. 7 (Moscow, 1994–2000), 270(reprint). Golubkov spent much of his fortune on the church, philanthropy, and the "sciences" and also published books and promoted Russian commercial expansion in Asia.
123. TsIAM 92.6.698.
124. TsIAM 142.4.1446.
125. TsIAM 142.5.1266.
126. TsIAM 142.4. 71.
127. TsIAM 50.5.12260.
128. TsIAM 50.4.5294(a).
129. Graeber, *Debt,* 106–108, 119–120.

3. The Boundaries of Risk

1. On discipline in imperial Russia, see Abby Schrader, *Languages of the Lash: Corporal Punishment and Identity in Imperial Russia* (Dekalb: University of Illinois Press, 2003); Laura Engelstein, *The Keys to Happiness: Sex and the Search for Modernity in Fin-de-Siecle Russia* (Ithaca: Cornell University Press, 1994); Jane Burbank, "Discipline and Punish in the Moscow Bar Association," *Russian Review* 54 (1995): 44–64.

2. Vause, "In the Red"; Julian Hoppit, *Risk and Failure in English Business, 1700–1800* (Cambridge: Cambridge University Press, 1987), 27–28.

3. N. P. Makarov, *Istoriia sozdaniia slovarei N. Makarova. Prilozhenie k "Moim semidesiatiletnim vospominaniiam"* (St. Petersburg, 1881), 10–11 and 15–16.

4. G. F. Shershenevich, *Konkursnoe pravo* (Kazan, 1898), 66.

5. Henry and Schmitt, *Victorian Investments.*

6. F. V. Bulgarin, *Ivan Vyzhigin* (St. Petersburg, 1829); Leo Tolstoy, *War and Peace*, tr. by Richard Pavear and Larissa Volokhonsky (New York: Vintage Books, 2008), 336–338.

7. TsIAM 81.18.1259. (Tolstoy); GARF 109.98.662 (Verigin).

8. TsIAM 142.4.758.

9. TsIAM 50.5.13, esp. l. 7 ob.

10. N.N.Z., *Klub chervonnykh valetov*, 56–69.

11. TsIAM 81.16.1998.

12. TsIAM 50.4.8264.

13. GARF 109.88.262.

14. Bolotov, *Zhizn' i prikliucheniia.*

15. I. M. Dolgorukov, *Povest'*, vol. 1, 110.

16. TsIAM 81.18.1277 (Bussau); 16.4.2607 (Vlasov).

17. "*Izobrazhenie i kharakteristika lits, zanimaiushchikh pervye i glavnye mesta pri Peterburgskom dvore*," RA 27 (1875): 120.

18. Suzanne Desan, *The Family on Trial in Revolutionary France* (Berkeley: University of California Press, 2004), 283–310. On England, see Finn, *The Character of Credit*, 274–275.

19. Pobedonostsev, *Kurs*, vol. 3, 38.

20. Trusteeship also could be appointed over all or part of one's property, in which case a person did not become legally incompetent but merely lost control of that property. Trusteeship over one's person, however, made one legally incompetent.

21. Novitskaia, *Pravovoie*, 220.

22. PSZ 5:2789 (1714), 91; 13:10021 (1752), 693; 37:28760 (1821), 857; PSZ.II, 1:752 (1826), 1,309; PSZ.II, 5/2:4160 (1830), 452; 5/2:4187 (1830), 491; SZ 10/1:211–218 (1842) (art. 217–224 in the 1857 edition). In 1817 the Council of State in a sharply contested appellate case involving the debts of Countess Sheremeteva (from Russia's wealthiest private family) specified the conditions for a collection against a minor to be held valid: Sheremeteva was not assigned a guardian, she received a large annual maintenance and was in charge of her own finances, and

so her creditors "could not know that she was a minor." PSZ 34:27033 (1817), 753. This case never evolved into a generally applicable exception to the law.

23. PSZ 22:16300 (1785), 502.

24. TsIAM 50.4.5362.

25. Pobedonostsev, *Kurs*, vol. 3, 37.

26. *Zakony grazhdanskie* (St. Petersburg, 1869), 41; Pobedonostsev, *Kurs*, vol. 3, 39.

27. TsIAM 81.16.1998.

28. TsIAM 50.4.5362.

29. SZ 10/1:6,534 (1857).

30. SZ 15/2:344 (1857).

31. TsIAM 68.2.172 *(Perepiska po prosheniiam arestantov)*.

32. TsIAM 91.2.704 (Savinov).

33. While there was no statutory law directly on this point, the Senate had ruled in similar cases that guardianship was incompatible with entering into a legal transaction with one's ward. Pobedonostsev, *Kurs*, vol. 2, 211.

34. TsIAM 50.4.8960.

35. GARF 109.89.693

36. H. Campbell Black, "Spendthrifts (Note)," *American Law Review* 28 (1894): 230–243; David Johnston, *Roman Law in Context* (Cambridge: Cambridge University Press, 2004), 41; French Civil Code of 1804, art. 513.

37. Novitskaia, *Pravovoie*, 230–231.

38. PSZ 26:19873 (1801), 639, 644 (art. 23 and 49).

39. PSZ 20:14392 (1775) (art. 84).

40. PSZ 34:26766 (1817). Victims could complain to the Senate after 1829. PSZ.II 4:2650. Governors were given the authority in 1825. PSZ 40:30297 (1825).

41. D. M. Gol'denov, *Opeka nad rastochiteliami* (St. Petersburg, 1904), 24, 51.

42. PSZ.II 34:34021 (1859).

43. Gol'denov, *Opeka*, 43–47.

44. PSZ.II 3:1662 (1828) (confirming the decree of 1803, PSZ 27:21059). Another 1828 law prohibited all transactions with mortgaged estates without the Board's permission. PSZ.II 3:2470.

45. TsIAM 49.3.889.

46. GARF 109.85.456.

47. TsIAM 78.3.38; 78.3.39.

48. Ostrovsky, *PSS*, vol. 1, 85–152. See also P. A. Plavil'shchikov, *Sobranie dramaticheskikh sochinenii* (St. Petersburg, 2002); and novels by P. D. Boborykin, such as *Del'tsy*, in *Sochineniia*, vol. 7 and 8 (St. Petersburg and Moscow, 1885–1886).

49. *O bankrotstvakh v torgovom soslovii* (St. Petersburg, 1848), 14.

50. In nineteenth-century German bankruptcy proceedings, the recovery rate for unsecured debt was very low, often 10 percent or less, despite the existence of credit-rating agencies. Sperber, *Property and Civil Society*, 109.

51. For American law, see Donald R. Korobkin, "Bankruptcy Law, Ritual, and Performance," *Columbia Law Review* 103 (2003): 2124–2159.

52. Mann, *The Republic of Debtors*.

53. Cohen, "The History of Imprisonment for Debt"; Hoppit, *Risk and Failure*.

54. See, e.g., Vause, "In the Red," esp. 202.

55. Finn, *The Character of Credit*. In Russia bankruptcy was only available for debt exceeding 1,500 rubles. Shershenevich, *Konkursnyi protsess* (Moscow, 2000; original 1899), 170.

56. *Sobornoe ulozhenie tsaria Alekseia Mikhailovicha 1649 goda* (Moscow, 1907), 62–63 (10:203–206).

57. PSZ 11:8300 (1740), 310–321.

58. PSZ 18:13001; 22:16062. See also Shershenevich, *Konkursnoe pravo*, 61–75.

59. PSZ.II 2:1206 (1827), 573–75.

60. Novitskaia, *Pravovoie*, 426–427; William Blackstone, *Commentaries on the Laws of England* (St. Paul: West Publishing Co., 1897), 384–385.

61. Shershenevich 71, 102–107. For the English context, see Hoppit, *Risk and Failure*, 24–25. (The distinction was not adopted in the American colonies.)

62. PSZ.I, 26:19692 (1800), art. 132; Novitskaia, *Pravovoie*, 425–427; Shershenevich, *Konkursnoe pravo*, 442–447; for France, see Vause, "In the Red," 205.

63. TsIAM 142.4.64.

64. For other sample large bankruptcies, see TsIAM 142.1.862 (Solodovnikov) (1881–1892); 81.21.302 (Golitsyn).

65. TsIAM 50.5.11976.

66. TsIAM 92.6.746.

67. TsIAM 142.4.81.

68. I was unable to thoroughly examine the records of the Moscow Commercial Court, which handled commercial bankruptcies, due to difficulties of access. The surviving documents represent no more than 10 percent of the original amount, after the intentional destruction of records in the 1930s, and those documents that remain seem to be in poor condition and are very grudgingly issued to researchers. Most of the bankruptcy cases discussed in this chapter were handled by criminal courts and therefore involved some allegations of fraud.

69. TsIAM 50.5.12850.

70. M. F. Vladimirskii-Budanov, *Obzor istorii russkogo prava*, 2nd ed. (St. Petersburg and Kiev, 1888), 538–539; Ya. Barshev, *Osnovaniia ugolovnogo sudoproizvodstva* (St. Petersburg, 1841), 165–166.

71. TsIAM 16.30.259 *(Delo ob osvobozhdenii dolzhnikov)* (1826).

72. TsIAM 142.1.862.

73. TsIAM 16.30.410 *(Delo o perestroike doma otdannogo Mosk. Gor. Obshchestvom pod pomeshchenie dlia vremennoi tiur'my neispravnykh dolzhnikov)* (1865–1866).

74. TsIAM 50.4.8960.

75. TsIAM 142.2.4.

76. Most merchants appear to have never surrendered their account books (if any) to creditors and thus were liable for criminal prosecution; whether one was initiated depended on the creditors' disposition and the court's attitude in each particular case.

77. TsIAM 50.5.12850.

78. TsIAM 142.3.264.

79. V. K. Rakhilin, *"Pervye rossiiskie gosudarstvennye lotereii"* (*Numizmaticheskii almanakh*, no. 2, 29–31; no. 3, 25–27; no. 4, 38–42, 1998), http://www.bonistikaweb. ru / NUMALMAN / rahilinlot.htm; Rakhilin, "V. K. Rakhilin *"Lotereia: chto eto?"* (*Numizmaticheskii almanakh*, no. 1, 25–29, 1998), http://www.bonistikaweb.ru / NUMALMAN/Rahilin.htm; Gettun, *"Zapiski,"* 67; P. I. Melnikov-Pecherskii, *"Babushkiny rosskazni,"* in *PSS*, vol. 1 (St. Petersburg, 1909), 201; N. S. Leskov, *"Zakhudalyi rod,"* in *PSS*, vol. 17 (St. Petersburg, 1903), 110.

80. TsIAM 16.4.2607.

81. Ibid.

82. Rakhilin, *"Pervye rossiiskie gosudarstvennye lotereii."*

83. This happened to Countess Zinaida Graziani in 1851. See TsIAM 16.17.95 (Graziani). Graziani also petitioned the tsar, who deferred to Count Zakrevskii's opinion (which was negative).

84. In post-Revolutionary France, a negotiated settlement known as "concordat" was more common than actual bankruptcy liquidation. Vause, "In the Red," 189.

4. Fraud, Property, and Respectability

1. Muldrew, *The Economy of Obligation*, esp. 95–118, 148; see also Randall McGowen, "Review: Credit and Culture in Early Modern England," *The Journal of British Studies*, 41 (2002): 120–131, esp. 128; Margaret Hunt, *The Middling Sort: Commerce, Gender, and the Family in England, 1680–1780* (Berkeley: University of California Press, 1996), 22–44. None of this literature addresses the issue of deception as an aspect of trust and risk, i.e., why deception was possible and how, why, and by whom was it carried out. See also Geoffrey Hosking, *Trust: A History* (Oxford: Oxford University Press, 2014).

2. William Reddy, *The Invisible Code: Honor and Sentiment in Postrevolutionary France, 1814–1848* (Berkeley: University of California Press, 1997), esp. 19, 115–122. See also Ann Goldberg, *Honor, Politics and the Law in Imperial Germany, 1871–1914* (Cambridge: Cambridge University Press, 2010); Robert Nye, *Masculinity and Male Codes of Honor in Modern France* (Berkeley: University of California Press, 1993); Edward Berenson, *The Trial of Madame Caillaux* (Berkeley: University of California Press, 1992); Bertram Wyatt-Brown, *Southern Honor: Ethics and Behavior in the Old South* (New York: Oxford University Press, 1982). See also Smail, "Credit, Risk, and Honor."

3. Reddy, *The Invisible Code*, 7

4. Sperber, *Property and Civil Society*, 109.

5. Nikolai Gogol, *Dead Souls*, tr. by Richard Pevear and Larissa Volokhonsky (Vintage, 1997).

6. *Sobranie pravil sokhrannoi i ssudnoi kazny pri Moskovskom i S. Peterburgskom Imperatorskikh Vospitatel'nykh domakh* (St. Petersburg, 1847).

7. Ostrovsky, *PSS*, vol. 3, 168.

8. Ibid., 237.

9. Ibid., vol. 2, 534.

10. Gettun, *"Zapiski,"* 46.

11. TsIAM 50.4.3167.

12. TsIAM 81.16.1998.

13. TsIAM 81.18.1259.

14. TsIAM 50.4.8264.

15. TsIAM 50.4.7229.

16. TsIAM 81.21.302.

17. TsIAM 50.4.5294(a).

18. Mann, *The Republic of Debtors;* Finn, *The Character of Credit;* Cohen, "The History of Imprisonment for Debt."

19. Finn, *The Character of Credit,* 152–196.

20. W. Bagehot, "Lombard Street," in *Collected Works,* ed. by N. St. John-Stevas, vol. 9 (1978), 191, quoted in P. J. Cain and A. G. Hopkins, "Gentlemanly Capitalism and British Expansion Overseas. The Old Colonial System, 1688–1850," *The Economic History Review* 39 (1986): 501–525. Conversely, a study of private credit in eighteenth-century Paris questioned the presumed dichotomy between informal and allegedly nonproductive pre-industrial credit and its capitalist and impersonal form, arguing that the former was efficient and rational, given the existing political and institutional framework. Philip T. Hoffman, Gilles Postel-Vinay, and Jean-Laurent Rosenthal, "Information and Economic History: How the Credit Market in Old Regime Paris Forces Us to Rethink the Transition to Capitalism," *The American Historical Review* 104 (1999): 69–94.

21. Zakharov, *Zapadnoievropeiskie kuptsy,* 206.

22. Steven Shapin, *A Social History of Truth: Civility and Science in Seventeenth-Century England* (Chicago: University of Chicago Press, 1995).

23. Quoted in Kupriianov, *Kul'tura,* 95–96; Bugrov, *Ocherki,* 198. For depictions of Russian merchants as untrustworthy and suspicious of the outside world, see Rieber, *Merchants and Entrepreneurs;* and Owen, *Capitalism and Politics.*

24. Nikiforov, *Vospominaniia iz vremen imperatora Nikolaia I* (Moscow, 1903), 52.

25. Ostrovsky, *PSS,* vol. 3.

26. Melnikov, *Nizhegorodskaia yarmarka,* 27, 266.

27. Ostrovsky, *PSS,* vol. 3, 241.

28. Makarov, *Izvlecheniia i vyderzhki,* 21, 25, 28–29.

29. For a similar point in the German context, see Richard J. Evans, *Tales from the German Underworld: Crime and Punishment in the Nineteenth Century* (New Haven: Yale University Press), 160.

30. S.Ya. Shtraikh, *Roman Medoks: Pokhozhdeniia russkogo avantiurista XIX veka* (Moscow, 2000); K. Medoks, *"Proiskhozhdenie russkikh dvorian Medoksov,"* *RA* 61 (1886): 262–265; R. M. Medoks, *"Moe predpriiatie sostavit' kavkazsko-gorskoe opolchenie v 1812 godu,"* *RS* 26 (1879): 709–713; K. P. Medoks, *"R. M. Medoks,"* *RS* 29 (1880): 221–222; E. A. Stogov, *"Roman Medoks,"* *RS* 28 (1880): 791–793; A. Zisserman, *"Samozvanets Medoks,"* *RS* 35 (1882): 620–624.

31. Nikolai Nadezhdin, *Son'ka zolotaia ruchka—koroleva vorov* (Rostov-na-Donu, 2012).

32. GARF 109.89.219, l. 49 ob.

33. For corpulence being a sign of prosperity, see Evans, *Tales*, 161.

34. Woodruff Smith, *Consumption and the Making of Respectability, 1600–1800* (Routledge, 2012); David Sunderland, *Social Capital, Trust and the Industrial Revolution 1780–1880.* (London: Routledge, 2007).

35. Gettun, *"Zapiski,"* 293.

36. Ogarkov, *Demidovy*, 76–79.

37. Hugh Hudson, *The Rise of the Demidov Family and the Russian Iron Industry in the Eighteenth Century* (Oriental Research Partners, 1986).

38. GARF 109.24.200, ch. 1.

39. N.N.Z., *Klub chervonnykh valetov;* V. M. Kostin, ed., *Vsevolod Alekseevich Dolgorukov: sbornik materialov* (Tomsk, 2013); M. O. Mel'tsin, *"Avtor odnogo iz pervykh putevoditelei po Novgorodu,"* *Novgorodika-2006*, ed. by S. A. Kovarskaia et al. (Novgorod, 2007), 257–264; Antonov, "Swindlers and Forgers of Moscow" (article in progress).

40. S. V. Shumikhin, ed., *Sud'ba avantiurista: Zapiski korneta Savina* (Novosibirsk, 2012).

41. GARF 109.89.219.

42. Ibid., l. 100.

43. N. A. Varentsov, *Slyshannoe. Vidennoe. Peredumannoe. Perezhitoe* (Moscow, 1999). Although Varentsov was writing about the second half of the century, I believe that his observations also apply to the period 1850–1870; see also N. I. Sveshnikov, *Vospominaniia propashchego cheloveka* (Moscow, 1996) and, for British examples, John Locker, "'Quiet Thieves, Quiet Punishment': Private Responses to the "Respectable" Offender, c. 1850–1930," *Crime, Histoire & Societes* 9 (2005): 9–31.

44. N.N.Z., *Klub chervonnykh valetov.*

45. Antonova, *An Ordinary Marriage.*

46. GARF 109.89.219.

47. On connections between swindlers and nineteenth-century political radicalism and secret police surveillance, see Evans, *Tales.*

48. GARF, 109.89.693/3, l. 26; 109.89.693/2, l. 75.

49. TsIAM 50.4.7742 (1861–1864); 7744 (1863–1864); and 7745 (1864–1865). The other three volumes of this case were denied by the archive.

50. TsIAM 81.18.1322.

51. TsIAM 16.23.208; 16.23.209.

52. TsIAM 50.4.8981.

53. TsIAM 50.4.765.

54. TsIAM 142.1.104.

55. TsIAM 142.2.154. In 1890 Saltykov was elected to the Board of Moscow Bar Association, the self-regulating body of Moscow's legal profession.

56. Evans, *Tales*, 151–153, 157–158. For the Russian case, this is documented in Evgenii Akeliev's excellent study of the infamous gangster Ivan Kain from the 1740s. Yevgeny Akeliev, *Povsednevnaia zhizn' vorovskogo mira Moskvy vo vremena Van'ki Kaina* (Moscow, 2012).

57. GARF 109.89.219, l. 83.

58. TsIAM 50.4.4416; 81.16.579; 50.4.4899.
59. This would not legally count as a confession because it was not made at a government office after the beginning of an official investigation.
60. Veselkin was sentenced to six years of hard labor in Siberia in 1854, and his brother was to be conscripted to the army. I was unable to determine what ultimately happened to Lefort.
61. Sandra Dahlke, "Old Russia in the Dock: The Trial against Mother Superior Mitrofaniia before the Moscow District Court (1874)," *Cahiers du Monde Russe* 53/1 (2012): 95–120. Dahlke argues that the post-reform legal establishment intended to make an example out of Mitrofaniia and to embarrass her patrons at the imperial court.
62. TsIAM 50.4.8208.
63. TsIAM 50.4.8968.
64. TsIAM 50.4.1983; 50.4.3389.
65. Robb, *White-Collar Crime.*

5. Kinship and Family

1. Hunt, *The Middling.*
2. For Germany, see Sperber, *Property and Civil Society,* 21.
3. John LeDonne, "Ruling Families"; Farrow, *Between Clan and Crown.*
4. Margot Finn, "Women, Consumption and Coverture in England, c. 1760–1860," *Historical Journal* 39 (1996): 703–722; Judith Spicksley, "Usury Legislation, Cash, and Credit: The Development of the Female Investor in the Late Tudor and Stuart Periods," *Economic History Review* 61 (2008): 277–301.
5. Marrese, *A Woman's Kingdom,* p. 237. Lee Farrow agrees with Marrese that "women in Imperial Russia enjoyed greater property rights than their Western counterparts." *Between Clan and Crown,* 120.
6. Galina Ulianova, *Female Entrepreneurs in Nineteenth-Century Russia* (London: Routledge, 2009).
7. Dolgorukov, *Povest',* vol. 1, 110–111.
8. Bolotov, *Zhizn' i prikliucheniia,* vol. 2, 104.
9. Finn, *The Character of Credit.*
10. TsIAM 50.4.8960.
11. Blagovo, *Rasskazy,* 179.
12. TsIAM 81.18.1259, l. 19.
13. Farrow, *Between Clan and Crown.*
14. Makarov, "Nastoichivost' i bor'ba s trudnostiami," in *Moi semidesiatiletnie vospominaniia* (St. Petersburg, 1881), 37–38.
15. Yu.N. Karpinskaia, "Iz semeinoi zhizni," *Istoricheskii vestnik* 70 (1897): 853–870.
16. TsIAM 92.10.611; 50.5.12279; 92.9.947.
17. PSZ 24:18001 (1797), 665.
18. TsIAM 142.4.1417.
19. TsIAM 92.6.746.
20. TsIAM 81.16.2079.

21. TsIAM 16.23.1107.

22. TsIAM 142.1.862.

23. TsIAM 50.4.4333.

24. TsIAM 50.4.8430. Kochnaia's name was also spelled in the case file as Khichnaia or Kichina.

25. TsIAM 50.5.12850.

26. TsIAM 81.17.2333.

27. TsIAM 50.14.1597 (urban mortgages, 1855); 50.14.1629 (rural mortgages, 1862).

28. TsIAM 92.9.947; 50.5.12279.

29. TsIAM 50.5.12292; 50.5.12294.

30. TsIAM 92.9.806

31. TsIAM 81.18.1277.

32. N. A. Reshetov, "*Dela davno minuvshikh dnei,*" *RA* 7 (1885): 428–441.

33. TsIAM 50.5.11976.

34. TsIAM 142.4.81.

35. TsIAM 50.4.8960.

36. TsIAM 142.4.1446 (Dzhakson) (1872).

37. TsIAM 91.2.704.

38. SZ 2/1:2438–2462 (1857), esp. 2449, 2450, 2455; SZ 10/2:3263 (n. 2). On the origins of Russian equity courts, see G. Barats, *Ocherk proiskhozhdeniia i postepennogo zatem uprazdneniia v Rossii sovestnykh sudov i suda po sovesti* (St. Petersburg, 1893) and N. N. Yefremova, "*Izmeneniia v sudebnoi sisteme Rossii vo vtoroi polovine XVIII v.,*" in *Istoriko-iuridicheskie issledovaniia: Rossiia i Angliia* (Moscow, 1990). For England, see J. H. Baker, *An Introduction to English Legal History* (London: Butterworths, 1990), 112–134.

39. TsIAM 91.2.322.

40. GARF 109.93.538. For Fedor Golitsyn, see Anna Nikitina, "*Rod Golit-synykh. Tverskie korni*" (*Tverlife,* July 12, 2015), http://www.tverlife.ru/news/69239.html.

41. N.N.Z., *Klub chervonnykh valetov,* 56–69.

42. TsIAM 16.21.425.

43. PSZ 5:2952 (1715); 13:10111 (1753).

44. Marrese, *A Woman's Kingdom,* 66–68; Pobedonostsev, *Kurs,* vol. 2, 130-135.

45. Marrese, *A Woman's Kingdom,* 68–69.

46. Ibid., 81–84; PSZ 16:11764 (1763), 166; 20:15022 (1780), 946; 26:20021 (1801), 795; 28:21926 (1805), 1259; 30:23685 (1809), 995; 40:20472 (1825).

47. Marrese, *A Woman's Kingdom,* 63–64, 130; PSZ 11:8300 (1740), 314; 26:19692 (1800), 452. See also PSZ 24:18001 (1797), 624. The decree of 1809 (PSZ 30:23685) applied to a merchant family and held that it was illegal for a wife to mortgage her property to the husband, despite the 1797 decree.

48. PSZ II, 21:20138 (1846), 622; see also Pobedonostsev, *Kurs,* vol. 2, 133.

49. SZ 11:1936 (1857) *(Ustav Torgovyi).*

50. TsIAM 92.6.741/1.

51. TsIAM 16.4.2522.

52. TsIAM 78.3.44 (Prokhorov) (1859).

53. TsIAM 81.21.302.
54. TsIAM 16, op. 23, d. 463 (Monakhov) (1857); see also TsIAM 50.4.4897 (Monakhov) (1857–1862).
55. TsIAM 142.4.81.
56. TsIAM 50.5.11967.
57. Karpinskaia, *"Iz semeinoi zhizni,"* 867.
58. TsIAM 91.2.704.
59. TsIAM 16.4.2522.
60. TsIAM 92.6.1082.
61. TsIAM 50.1.12053.
62. TsIAM 16.5.241.
63. TsIAM 50.4.8960.
64. TsIAM 92.6.741 / 1, l. 145–145 ob.
65. TsIAM 81.21.302.
66. Finn, "Women, Consumption and Coverture."
67. TsIAM 50.8.595.
68. D. I. Meier, *Russkoe grazhdanskoe pravo* (Moscow, 2003), 734 (originally published in 1858–1859); Pobedonostsev, *Kurs,* vol. 2, 124–127.
69. See Armand Pommier, *Madame la comtesse Dora d'Istria* (Brussels, 1863); Bartolomeo Cecchetti, *Bibliografia della Principessa Elena Ghika, Dora D'Istria,* 6th ed. (Florence, 1873); Dora d'Istria, "Italy" in *Woman Question in Europe,* ed. by Thomas Stanton (New York, 1884), 327.
70. TsIAM 81.18.1326.
71. TsIAM 81.18.1290, l. 26 ob.-27.
72. Ibid.
73. TsIAM 81.18.725.
74. TsIAM 81.18.1307, l. 2 ob.-3.
75. Ibid.
76. GARF 109.89.195.
77. TsIAM 81.16.675.
78. GARF 109.92.66.
79. GARF 109.87.489.
80. D. I. Nikiforov, *Moskva,* 50–52.

6. Debtors and Bureaucrats

1. Alexander Gerschenkron, *Economic Backwardness in Historical Perspective* (Cambridge: Belknap Press, 1962); Peter Gatrell, *The Tsarist Economy, 1850–1917* (London: Badsford, 1986). Critical accounts include Gregory, *Before Command;* Kahan, *Russian Economic History: The Nineteenth Century* (Chicago: University of Chicago Press, 1989); Rieber, *Merchants and Entrepreneurs;* Owen, *Capitalism and Politics;* see also Olga Crisp and Linda Edmondson, eds., *Civil Rights in Imperial Russia* (Oxford: Oxford University Press, 1989); Ronald Grigor Suny, "Rehabilitating Tsarism: The Imperial Russian State and its Historians. A Review Article," *Comparative Studies in Society and History* 31 (1989): 168-179.

2. Marc Raeff, *The Well-Ordered Police State: Social and Institutional Change through Law in the Germanies and Russia, 1600–1800* (New Haven: Yale University Press, 1983); Martin, *Enlightened Metropolis* (showing that the imperial social project persisted into the 1850s).

3. Wortman, *Scenarios of Power: Myth and Ceremony in Russian Monarchy,* 2 vols. (Princeton: Princeton University Press, 1995 and 2000); A. V. Remnev, *Samoderzhavnoe pravitel'stvo: Komitet ministrov v sisteme vysshego upravleniia Rossiiskoi imperii, vtoraia polovina XIX—nachalo XX veka* (Moscow, 2010).

4. Raeff, *Michael Speransky;* Wortman, *The Development;* W. Bruce Lincoln, *In the Vanguard of Reform: Russia's Enlightened Bureaucrats, 1825–1861* (DeKalb: Northern Illinois University Press, 1982); P. A. Zaionchkovskii, *Pravitel'stvennyi apparat samoderzhavnoi Rossii v XIX v.* (Moscow, 1978); Pintner, *Russian Officialdom.*

5. Schattenberg, *Die korrupte Provinz?,* 19, 243; Robbins, *Tsar's Viceroys;* Evtuhov, *Portrait;* LeDonne, *Absolutism;* David Ransel, *The Politics of Catherinian Russia: The Panin Party* (New Haven: Yale University Press, 1975); Smith, *For the Common Good;* Kupriianov, *Kul'tura;* Kamenskii, *Povsednevnost'.*

6. Hudson, "Modernization Through Resistance: War, Mir, Tsar, and Law in the World of the Pre-reform Russian Peasantry," *The Donald W. Treadgold Papers in Russian, East European and Central Asian Studies* 40 (2004).

7. See, e.g., Balzer, *Russia's Missing Middle Class.*

8. LeDonne, *Absolutism,* 121–157.

9. N. M. Kolmakov, "*Staryi sud,*" *RS* 11 (1886): 511–544; Robert J. Abbott, "Police Reform in the Russian Province of Iaroslavl, 1856–1876," *Slavic Review* 32 (1973): 292–302; Martin, *Enlightened Metropolis.*

10. SZ 10/2:84 (1857).

11. Ostrovsky, "*Beshenye den'gi,*" *PSS,* vol. 3, 246.

12. Nekrasov, "*Bez vesti propavshii piita,*" *PSS,* vol. 7, 42–69, esp. 64–68; see also "*Rostovshchik,*" ibid., 128.

13. Mann, *Republic of Debtors,* 20–29; W. J. Jones, *The Foundations of English Bankruptcy: Statutes and Commissions in the Early Modern Period* (Philadelphia: The American Philosophical Society, 1979), 15; in England by the eighteenth century, a debtor's "keeping house" was construed as "an intention to defraud his creditors." Blackstone, *Commentaries,* 385.

14. This provision was already found in the Law Code of 1649. See PSZ 1:112 (ch. 10, art. 264, 265, 271); PSZ 18:13212 (1768), 783. For military personnel, either one-half or one-third of the wages were subtracted. PSZ 15:10789 (1758), 124. In the nineteenth century, the amount varied from one-fourth to two-fifths, depending on the official's salary, with some categories exempted, thereby making them collection-proof. SZ 10/2:2230, 2231 (1857)

15. TsIAM 81.18.1259.

16. Wortman, *The Development,* 249, 255–257.

17. Hunt, *The Middling Sort,* 198, 203.

18. Nikiforov, *Moskva . . . Aleksandra II,* 130.

19. GARF 109.22.108.

20. Novitskaia, *Pravovoie*, 432.
21. On privacy in Victorian Britain, see David Vincent, *"I Hope I Don't Intrude": Privacy and Its Dilemmas in Nineteenth-Century Britain* (Oxford: Oxford University Press, 2015). For connections between privacy and taxation in imperial Russia, see Kotsonis, *States of Obligation*, esp. 92–95.
22. TsIAM 16.23.208; 16.23.209.
23. The procuracy oversaw the legality of other officials' actions. While rarely directly confrontational with the city government and the police, procuracy officials appear to have provided some minimum protections to imprisoned and arrested individuals.
24. TsIAM 81.16.1985.
25. TsIAM 81.16.1704.
26. "Enlightened" bureaucrats did not think much of the merchant judges sitting on Moscow courts. See M. A. Dmitriev, *Glavy iz vospominanii moiei zhizni* (Moscow, 1998), 306. Some of those merchants, according to Dmitriev, at least had "natural" intelligence and were willing to learn the legal procedure.
27. PSZ 20:14392 (1775).
28. PSZ.II 12/1:10303 (1837), 361.
29. Voropanov, *Regional'nyi factor*, 251–252; Viktoriia Yefimova, *"Pochemu general-gubernatory 1–i treti XIX v. utverzhdali prigovory po ugolovnym prestupleniiam,"* *Cahiers du monde russe* 53 (2012), 65–93.
30. SZ 2/1:2405 (1857).
31. I. V. Selivanov, *"Zapiski dvorianina-pomeshchika,"* *RS* 28 (1880): 289–316.
32. Selivanov, *"Zapiski,"* 728; A. A. Polovstov, *Russkii biograficheskii slovar'*, vol. 10 (Moscow, 1896–1918), 195–198 (includes references to memoirs about Count Zakrevskii); *Entsiklopedichskii slovar' Brokgauza i Efrona* (Moscow, 1890–1907); V. S. Aksakova, *Dnevnik, 1854–55* (Moscow, 2004).
33. N. V. Davydov, *Iz proshlogo* (Moscow, 1913), 7.
34. Selivanov, *"Zapiski,"* 725–726.
35. B. N. Chicherin, *Russkoe obshchestvo 40—50–kh godov XIX v. Chast' II. Vospominaniia B. N. Chicherina (Moskva sorokovykh godov)* (Moscow, 1991), 69.
36. Nikiforov, *Moskva . . . Aleksandra II*, 50–54.
37. Selivanov, *"Zapiski,"* 726–728, 731.
38. N. A. Reshetov, *"Dela davno minuvshikh dnei,"* *RA* 58 (1885): 539–547.
39. "Eliminating bribery was the last thing on his mind." Chicherin, *Vospominaniia*, 61.
40. TsIAM 50.4.4758. Serfs could purchase property with their landlord's permission, and after 1848 they could even do so in their own name, which in this case was somehow inconvenient.
41. Another example of Count Zakrevskii respecting property rights is the case of Countess Zinaida Graziani, who was heavily indebted and petitioned the governor to allow her to stage a lottery for her property and use the proceeds to satisfy her creditors. In denying Graziani's request, the count listed several reasons, including the fact that she had failed to obtain the creditors' permission. TsIAM 16.17.95.

42. Selivanov, *"Zapiski,"* 739.

43. TsIAM 16.23.208; 16.23.209.

44. Ibid.

45. TsIAM 50.3.8323.

46. TsIAM 81.18.1259.

47. The records of the Moscow governor general are poorly preserved due to Soviet-era archival policies.

48. TsIAM 16.23.1107.

49. GARF 109.89.693/1, l. 6–7. In the end, Rakhmanov did not pay even the reduced amount and was still sued in court.

50. GARF 109.89.369.

51. TsIAM 50.4.1983; 50.4.3389.

52. TsIAM 16.3.1254.

53. TsIAM 50.4.3167.

54. GARF 109.93.538.

55. GARF 109.89.195.

56. See also Madeleine Zelin, Jonathan Ocko, and Robert Gardelia, eds., *Contract and Property in Early Modern China* (Stanford: Stanford University Press, 2004), showing that the Chinese state in the late imperial period supported and enforced property rights.

57. Stephen Lovell, Alena Ledeneva, and Andrei Rogachevskii, eds., *Bribery and Blat in Russia: Negotiating Reciprocity from the Middle Ages to the 1990s* (New York: St. Martin's Press, 2001).

58. TsIAM 16.23.208; 16.23.209.

59. TsIAM 92.6.677.

60. TsIAM 50.4.8272.

61. Wortman, *The Development*, 191; Kolmakov, *"Staryi sud,"* 523.

62. Gettun, *"Zapiski,"* 279–280.

63. F.Ya. Luchinskii, *"Provintsialnye nravy za posledniie polveka,"* RS 91 (1897): 646–647, 655–656.

64. P. N. Kostyliov, *"Zapiski,"* RA 129 (1909): 123–168.

65. I. P. Bocharov, *"V pravitel'stvuiushchem Senate. 1840–1852 gg.,"* RS 44 (1884): 145–170.

66. Selivanov, *"Zapiski,"* 730.

67. Kolmakov, *"Staryi sud,"* 523.

68. TsIAM 50.4.1983; 50.4.3389.

69. TsIAM 50.4.4732.

70. TsIAM 81.16.1400.

71. Ibid.

72. Muldrew, "Credit and the Courts: Debt Litigation in a Seventeenth-Century Urban Community," *The Economic History Review* 46 (1993): 23–38.

73. Robert Mnookin and Lewis Kornhauser, "Bargaining in the Shadow of the Law: The Case of Divorce," *The Yale Law Journal* 88 (1979): 950–997.

74. Herbert Jacob, "The Elusive Shadow of the Law," *Law & Society Review* 26 (1992): 565–590.

75. On settlements, see SZ 10/2:1131–1137 (1857); on arbitration, see SZ 10/2:1138–1215; on pre-reform ad hoc arbitration commissions, see PSZ.II 2:1206 (1827), 573; for post-reform commissions, see PSZ.II 51/1:55466 (1876).

76. For an account of late imperial Chinese law as a small and relatively cheap system designed to resolve disputes that could not be settled through other means, see Melissa Macauley, *Social Power and Legal Culture: Litigation Masters in Late Imperial China* (Stanford: Stanford University Press, 1998).

77. Miliukov, *Dobroie,* 104.

78. Makarov, *Izvlecheniia,* 18.

79. TsIAM 50.4.8859.

80. TsIAM 50.4.8836.

81. On settling criminal cases, see SZ 15/1:169 and 171 (1857).

82. TsIAM 16.23.1107.

83. TsIAM 50.5.12292; 50.5.12294.

84. Blagovo, *Rasskazy babushki,* 29. On judicial mercy, see Nancy Kollmann, "The Quality of Mercy in Early Modern Legal Practice," *Kritika* 7 (2006): 5–22; Jane Burbank, "Mercy, Punishment, and Law: The Qualities of Justice at Township Courts," *Kritika* 7 (2006): 23–60.

85. Gettun, *"Zapiski,"* 295.

86. Ibid., 53, 66.

87. TsIAM 142.4.64.

88. TsIAM 81.18.1259.

89. TsIAM 81.16.1171.

90. TsIAM 78.4.275.

91. TsIAM 50.4.5022.

92. TsIAM 81.18.1322.

93. TsIAM 50.3.8323. It is unclear how the case ended, except that by July of that same year, Briukhatov was dead.

94. TsIAM 81.16.1998.

95. TsIAM 81.18.1277.

96. Ibid., l. 162.

97. S. V. Volkov, *Generalitet Rossiiskoi imperii,* vol. 1 (Moscow, 2009), 212.

98. TsIAM 81.18.1277, l. 112.

7. In the Pit with Debtors

1. Mikhail Gernet's study of the tsarist prison system did not discuss imprisonment for debt because it centered on imprisonment for political crimes. See *Istoriia tsarskoi tiur'my,* 5 vols., 3rd ed. (Moscow 1960–1963). For an overview of legislation, see V. V. Zakharov, *"Sposoby prinuditel'nogo ispolneniia v russkom prave XI—nachala XX veka: preemstvennost' i innovatsiia,"* (*Uchenye zapiski: elektronnyi nauchnyi zhurnal Kurskogo gosudarstvennogo universiteta,* no. 2 (2007)), http://scientific-notes.ru.

2. Vladimir Giliarovsky, *Moskva i moskvichi* (Moscow, 1926). It appears that he visited the Pit in the late 1880s before it was demolished, although much of his sketch is an urban tale.

3. Mann, *The Republic of Debtors;* Finn, *The Character of Credit;* Jay Cohen, "The History of Imprisonment for Debt."

4. For the Law Code of 1649, see PSZ 1:112 (ch. 10, art. 262, 263, 269).

5. Hellie, *Slavery in Russia,* 41–44.

6. PSZ 4:1805 (1700); 5:3140 (1718); 6:3717 (1718); 6:3959 (1722); D. I. Pikhno, "*Istoricheskii ocherk mer grazhdanskikh vzyskanii po russkomu pravu,*" *Kievskie Universitetskie Izvestiia* 8–10 (1874).

7. Zakharov, *Zapadnoevropeiskie,* 209.

8. PSZ 9:7013 (1736); Novitskaia, *Pravovoie,* 381.

9. TsIAM 16.1.598.

10. Ibid., l. 67.

11. PSZ.II 9:7443.

12. TsIAM 68.1.80.

13. TsIAM 16.1.715.

14. Luchinskii, "*Provintsial'nye nravy,*" 641.

15. SZ 10/2:326–414 (1857); A. Grinevich, "*O lichnom zaderzhanii v grazhdanskom protsesse,*" *Zhurnal grazhdanskogo i ugolovnogo prava* 1 (1873): 55–102. See also SZ 10/2:71, 1005–1034, 2217–2282 (1857).

16. SZ 10/2:2224 (1857).

17. PSZ.II 3:2440 (1828). Creditors were free to increase that amount but apparently never did so in practice; see also SZ 10/2:57–74 (1857).

18. Finn, *The Character of Credit.* On the Russian perception of French practices, see GARF 123.1.89. See also PSZ.II 15:13406 (1840).

19. GARF 123.1.62, l. 7.

20. TsIAM 78.3.44.

21. GARF 123.1.62, l. 34 ff.

22. TsIAM 142.4.64.

23. TsIAM 50.5.12754.

24. GARF 109.89.369.

25. TsIAM 142.5.1307.

26. TsIAM 16.23.1107.

27. TsIAM 16.44.6.

28. TsIAM 16.20.55.

29. Ibid.

30. GARF 123.1.89.

31. TsIAM 16.3.2521.

32. TsIAM 105.4.997.

33. TsIAM 50.4.8044; see also 16.30.410, l. 9–9 ob.

34. TsIAM 16.44.6.

35. GARF 123.1.62, l. 10.

36. On January 1, 1850, the Pit housed only 6 debtors, whereas during the year the overall number was 322. GARF 123.2.155.

37. GARF 123.2.155, ll. 85–86; 123.2.155, l. 9 ob.

38. GARF 123.2.302, l. 3.

39. GARF 123.1.322, l. 34.

40. GARF 123.1.446.

41. PSZ.II 54:59374 (1879); see also GARF 123.1.670.

42. Finn, *Character of Credit*, 109–196. Although debt imprisonment in the United States was officially abolished in the 1830s and 1840s, individuals can still be imprisoned for debt in a variety of situations. For recent media coverage, see, e.g., Jessica Silver-Greenberg, "Welcome to Debtors' Prison, 2011 Edition," *The Wall Street Journal* (March 16, 2011).

43. TsIAM 16.1.715.

44. Gernet, *Istoriia tsarskoi tiur'my*, vol. 2, 31.

45. SZ 14:96, app., par. 232 (1857) *(Ustav o soderzhashchikhsia pod strazhei)*.

46. P. V. Sytin, *Iz istorii moskovskikh ulits* (Moscow, 1958), 159.

47. TsIAM 68.1.547 *(o perevode vremennoi tiur'my)* (1803); by 1808 the prison had already been organized to house debtors.

48. TsIAM 16.3.2521.

49. TsIAM 16.44.6, l. 32–32 ob.

50. TsIAM 16.30.410, l. 26–29.

51. GARF 123.1.59, l. 210–211.

52. TsIAM 16.44.6.

53. GARF 123.1.89, l. 77.

54. *Entsiklopedicheskii slovar' Brokgauza i Efrona*, vol. 9 (St. Petersburg, 1893), 9 (showing 1856 as the founding date); R. S. Popov, ed., *Putevoditel' po Peterburgu* (St. Petersburg, 1886), 288; A. V. Kobak and V. V. Antonov, *"Uprazdnennaia tserkov' blag. vel. kn. Aleksandra Nevskogo pri dolgovoi tiur'me"* (Istoriko-kulturnyi internet-portal *"Entsiklopediia Sankt-Peterburga"*), http://www.encspb.ru.

55. *"Titovskii proezd,"* http: // www.yourmoscow.ru/city/street/titovskiy_proezd.

56. TsIAM 16.3.2521.

57. Ostrovsky, *PSS*, vol. 3, 243.

58. TsIAM 16.30.390, ll. 6–9 ob.

59. GARF 123.1.62, l. 17.

60. TsIAM 16.30.410.

61. TsIAM 16.30.390, ll. 10–24, art. 9.

62. TsIAM 50.4.8044.

63. TsIAM 16.30.259. Left out of these figures is one atypically large debt of 30,000 rubles.

64. See Finn, *The Character of Credit*. I did, however, see one (possibly sexualized) reference to the "family" *(semeistvo)* or "commune" *(obshchina)* of debtors by one prisoner who was confronting a moneylender and berating him for "making that family increase." See TsIAM 50.4.8044.

65. TsIAM 16.30.390.

66. For a detailed 1848 list of the Pit's staff and its salaries, see TsIAM 16.14.7. Staff turnover was much higher than at the Butyrskaia prison. The Petersburg rules are found in TsIAM 16.30.390, l. 10–24.

67. TsIAM 16.23.2078.
68. On the culture of food in the nineteenth century, see Smith, *Recipes for Russia: Food and Nationhood under the Tsars* (DeKalb: Northern Illinois University Press, 2011) and Bokova, *Povsednevnaia zhizn;* for prison conditions in England, see Finn, *The Character of Credit* and Philip Woodfine, "Debtors, Prisons, and Petitions in Eighteenth-Century England," *Eighteenth-Century Life* 30 (2006): 1–31.
69. For detailed instructions and rules in effect in 1865, see TsIAM 50.4.8044.
70. GARF 123.2.208, l. 51–54, 97.
71. TsIAM 16.14.7.
72. GARF 123.1.89.
73. GARF 123.1.322, l. 41 ob.
74. TsIAM 16.44.6, l. 29–30 ob.
75. TsIAM 16.23.2078.
76. TsIAM 1581.1.6.
77. TsIAM 50.2.4605.
78. TsIAM 50.4.8044.
79. Ibid.
80. TsIAM 142.2.232.
81. For the Butikov case, see TsIAM 16.23.208; 16.23.209.
82. On charity in imperial Russia more generally, see Galina Ulianova, *Blagotvoritel'nost' v Rossiiskoi Imperii. XIX-nachalo XX veka* (Moscow, 2005); Adele Lindenmeyr, *Poverty is not a Vice: Charity, Society, and the State in Imperial Russia* (Princeton: Princeton University Press, 1996).
83. Martin, *Enlightened Metropolis,* 269.
84. Riazanovskii, *Nicholas I and Official Nationality in Russia, 1825–1855* (Berkeley: University of California Press, 1967); A. L. Zorin, *Kormia Dvukhglavogo Orla . . . Literatura i gosudarstvennaia ideologia v Rossii v poslednei treti xviii—pervoi treti xix veka* (Moscow, 2001); Wortman, *"Ofitsialnaia narodnost' i natsional'nyi mif rossiiskoi monarkhii xix veka," Rossia/Russia* 3 (Moscow, 1999): 233–244.
85. Randolph, *The House in the Garden;* Antonova, *An Ordinary Marriage;* Martin, *Enlightened Metropolis,* 263–269.
86. Barry Hollingsworth, "John Venning and Prison Reform in Russia, 1819–1830," *The Slavonic and East European Review* 48 (1970): 537–556.
87. On Maria Fedorovna and her connection with Nicholas I's "family scenario," see Wortman, *Scenarios of Power,* vol. 1, 247–295. On the commemoration of Maria Fedorovna, see GARF 123.1.446, l. 65–66 ob.
88. Ironically, after the reforms of the 1860s greatly improved prison conditions, the Society wanted to become a completely private charitable institution. GARF 123.1.446.
89. Gernet, *Istoriia,* vol. 2, 139–145.
90. TsIAM 16.30.390; 1581.1.6.
91. Novitskaia, *Pravovoie,* 382; Bolotov, *Pamiatnik,* 93.
92. TsIAM 16.1.715.
93. *Moskovskie Vedomosti,* no. 76 (Sept. 23, 1797).
94. TsIAM 16.30.259. On Nicholas I's donations, see TsIAM 16.16.1368.

95. GARF 123.1.322, l. 54 ob; 123.1.446, l. 68; Other popular occasions in the 1860s were deaths of significant donors and commemoration days for Maria Fedorovna, Catherine II's death, and Alexander I's coronation. GARF 123.1.446, l. 65–66 ob.

96. TsIAM 16.20.55.

97. TsIAM 1581.1.6.

98. TsIAM 16.16.1368.

99. GARF 123.2.302, l. 17 ff.

100. GARF 123.1.446, l. 65–66 ob.

101. Bolotov, *Pamiatnik*, 93.

102. TsIAM 16.3.2431.

103. TsIAM 105.4.997.

104. TsIAM 1581.1.6.

105. GARF 123.2.302.

106. GARF 123.1. 322, l. 72.

107. TsIAM 68.1.799. For the 1860s, see GARF 123.1.353.

108. E. S. Shumigorskii, *"Grafinia A. V. Branitskaia," Istoricheskii Vestnik*, 79 (1900): 183–202; Blagovo, *Rasskazy babushki*, 412, n. 94.

109. TsIAM 54.12.222.

110. TsIAM 16.30.259.

111. GARF 109.89.369

112. TsIAM 16.30.259.

113. Ibid.

114. TsIAM 16.20.55.

115. Novitskaia, *Pravovoie*, 382; Bolotov, *Pamiatnik*, 93.

116. Pierre Bourdieu, *Outline of a Theory of Practice*, trans. by Richard Nice (Cambridge: Cambridge University Press, 1977), 193.

8. Intermediaries, Lawyers, and Scriveners

1. Macauley, *Social Power and Legal Culture*.

2. E. V. Vas'kovskii, *Organizatsiia advokatury* (St. Petersburg, 1893), 319–320.

3. Kolmakov, *"Staryi sud,"* 536.

4. Wortman, *The Development*. On the French lawyers' political role in the eighteenth century, see David Bell, *Lawyers and Citizens: The Making of a Political Elite in Old Regime France* (New York: Oxford University Press, 1994).

5. Vas'kovskii, *Organizatsiia*, 317–319.

6. William Pomeranz, "Justice from Underground: The History of the Underground *Advokatura*," *Russian Review* 52 (1993): 321–340.

7. A. N. Markov, *Pravila advokatskoi professii v Rossii* (Moscow, 2003) (originally published in 1913); Jane Burbank, "Discipline and Punish in the Moscow Bar Association," *Russian Review* 54 (1995): 44–64.

8. SZ 10/2:195 (1857) (art. 2214 in the 1842 edition).

9. PSZ.II, 6:4640 (1831), 462; PSZ.II, 8:6390 (1833), 469; PSZ.II, 9:7000 (1834), 299.

10. PSZ 10:8170 (1835), 644.

11. See, e.g., Vas'kovskii, *Organizatsiia*, 306–321.

12. Brian Levin-Stankevich, "The Transfer of Legal Technology and Culture: Law Professionals in Tsarist Russia," in Balzer, ed., *Russia's Missing Middle Class*, 223–249, esp. 224–230; A. D. Popova, *"Pravda i milost' da tsarstvuiut v sudakh" (iz istorii realizatsii sudebnoi reformy 1864 g.)* (Riazan', 2005).

13. Levin-Stankevich, "The Transfer," 225, 230.

14. I. V. Gessen, *Istoriia russkoi advokatury*, vol. 1 (Moscow, 1914).

15. Levin-Stankevich, "The Transfer," 226.

16. Mnookin and Kornhauser, "Bargaining in the Shadow of the Law," 986.

17. Lynn M. LoPucki and Walter O. Weyrauch, "A Theory of Legal Strategy," *Duke Law Journal* 49 (2000): 1405–1486.

18. Mnookin and Kornhauser, "Bargaining in the Shadow of the Law," 986.

19. Gessen, *Istoriia*, 1–25.

20. M. A. Dmitriev, *Glavy iz vospominanii o moei zhizni* (Moscow, 1998); Vodovozova, *Na zare zhizni;* Dolgorukov, *Povest.*

21. Pomeranz, "The Practice of Law and the Promise of Rule of Law: The *Advokatura* and the Civil Process in Tsarist Russia," *Kritika* 16 (2015): 235–262, esp. 244–245.

22. GARF 109.3.115.

23. For England, see J. M. Beattie, "Scales of Justice: Defense Counsel and the English Criminal Trial in the Eighteenth and Nineteenth Centuries," *Law and History Review* 9 (1991): 221–268; John Langbein, "The Criminal Trial before the Lawyers," *University of Chicago Law Review* 45 (1978): 263–72.

24. SZ, 15/2:145, 149, 164 (1857).

25. Vas'kovskii, *Organizatsiia*, 310.

26. SZ, 15/2:384, 445 (1857); PSZ.II, 25:24274 (1850), 570. Kolmakov also thought that private defenders were not allowed in criminal cases and that even in civil cases their role was limited. *"Staryi sud,"* 536.

27. Antonova, *An Ordinary Marriage*, 42–43.

28. GARF 109.89.369, l. 14–15.

29. Markov, *Pravila.*

30. TsIAM 142.2.154.

31. Lawrence Friedman, *A History of American Law*, 3rd ed. (New York: Touchstone, 2005); Mann, *The Republic of Debtors.*

32. TsIAM 92.6.677.

33. TsIAM 16.4.2522.

34. TsIAM 50.4.8434.

35. TsIAM 50.5.12287.

36. TsIAM 16.23.208; 16.23.209.

37. TsIAM 50.4.8960; 81.19.196.

38. N. A. Troitskii, *Advokatura v Rossii na politicheskikh protsessakh 1866–1904 gg.* (Tula, 2000).

39. TsIAM 81.18.1259.

40. TsIAM 50.5.12153.

41. GARF 109.92.66; 109.96.54; N.N.Z., *Klub chervonnykh valetov*, 444; Kolmakov, *"Staryi sud,"* 536.

42. GARF 109.94.503.

43. Ibid.

44. GARF 109.93.538.

45. N. I. Sveshnikov, *Vospominaniia propashchego cheloveka* (Moscow, 1996). For England, see C. W. Brooks, *Pettifoggers and Vipers of the Commonwealth: The "Lower Branch" of the Legal Profession in Early Modern England* (Cambridge: Cambridge University Press, 1986).

46. Aleksandrov, ed., *Moskovskaia starina*, 212.

47. Ostrovskii, *"Ne bylo ni grosha, da vdrug altyn,"* PSS, vol. 3, 407, 432.

48. Pomeranz, "Justice from Underground."

49. TsIAM 92.9.803.

50. TsIAM 50.4.8945.

51. Ibid.

52. TsIAM 50.5.12279.

53. TsIAM 92.6.1082.

54. TsIAM 91.2.338.

55. George L. Priest and Benjamin Klein, "The Selection of Disputes for Litigation," *The Journal of Legal Studies* 13 (1984): 1–55.

56. Marrese, *A Woman's Kingdom.*

57. TsIAM 81.18.1290.

58. TsIAM 81.16.1400.

59. TsIAM 50.4.4758.

60. TsIAM 50.4.6259.

61. TsIAM 50.4.1983; 50.4.3389.

62. TsIAM 50.4.8945.

63. TsIAM 50.4.4441.

64. TsIAM 50.4.8208.

65. TsIAM 50.4.7229

66. For the data on powers of attorney, see Table 8.1 and Appendixes D.1 and D.2

67. TsIAM 50.4.6259.

68. TsIAM 50.4.3167.

69. TsIAM 50.4.1983.

70. TsIAM 50. 4.4416; 81.16.579; 50.4.4899.

71. TsIAM 50.4.4758.

72. TsIAM 50.4.6164.

73. TsIAM 50.4.4727.

74. Locker, "'Quiet Thieves, Quiet Punishment.'

75. Troitskii, *Advokatura*, 183–184, 186; Gessen, *Istoriia.*

9. Creditors and Debtors in Pre-Reform Courts

1. See Table 0.2.

2. I. V. Gessen and A. I. Kaminka, eds., *Velikie reformy shestidesiatykh godov v ikh proshlom i nastoiashchem* (St. Petersburg, 1905); I. V. Gessen, *Istoriia;* I. A. Blinov, *"Sudebnyi stroi i sudebnye poriadki pered reformoi 1864 goda,"* in *Sudebnye ustavy*

20 noiabria 1864 g. za piat'desiat let, vol. 1 (Petrograd, 1914), 3–101; G. A. Dzhan-shiev, *Epokha velikikh reform,* 2 vols. (St. Petersburg, 1905).

3. Gessen, *Velikie reformy,* 10.

4. Ibid., 14–15.

5. Ibid., 17.

6. Ibid., 133.

7. Blinov, *"Sudebnyi stroi,"* 34–35.

8. Dmitriev, *Glavy;* Kolmakov, *"Staryi sud";* B. Bochkarev, *"Doreformennyi sud,"* in *Sudebnaia reforma,* ed. by N. V. Davydov and N. N. Polianskii, vol. 1 (Moscow, 1915), 205–241. D. N. Bantysh-Kamenskii, *"Shemiakin sud v XIX stoletii,"* *RS* 7 (1873): 735–784; I. N. Zakharin, *"Rasskazy iz prezhnei sudebnoi praktiki,"* *RS* 4 (1874): 777–780; Anonymous (I. S. Aksakov), *Prisutstvennyi den' ugolovnoi palaty. Sudebnye stseny iz zapisok chinovnika ochevidtsa* (Leipzig, 1874).

9. Kolmakov, *"Staryi sud,"* 513.

10. Bocharov, *"V pravitel'stvuiushchem";* P. N. Kostyliov, *"Zapiski,"* *RA* 129 (1909): 123–168.

11. Quoted in Gessen, *Velikie reformy,* 29–30; SZ 15/2:377 (1857).

12. Gettun, *"Zapiski,"* esp. 485.

13. Kolmakov, *"Staryi sud,"* 522.

14. Selivanov, *"Zapiski dvorianina-pomeshchika,"* *RS* 33 (1882): 625–636.

15. Gessen, *Istoriia,* 25.

16. Blinov, *"Sudebnyi stroi,"* 29–30.

17. Ye.I. Kozlinina, *Za polveka, 1862–1912* (Moscow, 1913), 1–16.

18. Samuel Kucherov, *Courts, Lawyers, and Trials under the Last Three Tsars* (New York, 1953).

19. LeDonne, *Absolutism,* 197–200.

20. For a detailed bibliography, see Wirtschafter, "Legal Identity."

21. Mironov, *A Social History;* Marrese, *A Woman's Kingdom;* Kollmann, *By Honor Bound;* Weickhardt, "The Pre-Petrine Law of Property" and "Due Process."

22. In part my approach is inspired by Paul Kahn, *The Cultural Study of Law.*

23. On the estate system, see Smith, *For the Common Good;* Confino, "The *Soslovie* (Estate) Paradigm"; Freeze, "The *Soslovie* (Estate) Paradigm"; Wirtschafter, *Structures of Society.*

24. Levin-Stankevich, "The Transfer," 228, 224.

25. SZ 2/1:2383 (1857).

26. Ye.A. Nefediev, *Souchastiie v grazhdanskom protsesse* (Kazan', 1891).

27. PSZ 20:14392, 340 (1775).

28. PSZ 22:16077 (1784–1788).

29. N. P. Eroshkin, *Istoriia gosudarstvenykh uchrezhdenii,* 141–142; M. F. Vladimirskii-Budanov, *Obzor istorii russkogo prava* (Kiev, 1908).

30. PSZ 26:20004 (1801).

31. PSZ 27:20284 (1802); PSZ.II, 2:862 (1827); PSZ.II, 27:26597 (1852); Voropanov, *"Izmeneniia v soslovnoi kompetentsii sudei na Urale i v Zapadnoi Sibiri v 1780–1866 godakh,"* *Izvestiia Cheliabinskogo nauchnogo tsentra* 3 (2003): 96–101.

32. N. Gartung, *Istoriia ugolovnogo sudoproizvodstva i sudoustroistva Frantsii, Anglii, Germanii i Rossii* (St. Petersburg, 1868), 192, 201.

33. PSZ.II, 23:22274 (1848).

34. TsIAM 92.9.1092.

35. Magistrate records were damaged particularly severely during the Soviet period.

36. I. A. Blinov, *"Sudebnyi stroi."*

37. TsIAM 92.9.806.

38. Selivanov, 725–752.

39. Provincial Chambers strictly required that every legal question first be examined by a lower court. See, for example, TsIAM 50.5.12153.

40. A civil case could be appealed to the Senate if the dispute involved more than 600 rubles.

41. TsIAM 92.6.679.

42. Gettun, *"Zapiski,"* 489.

43. SZ 10/2:78 (1857). Major permissible objections were (1) the debtor denied his or her signature on the debt document; (2) the debtor presented evidence of payment; and (3) debt was invalid because debtor was incompetent (for example, a minor).

44. SZ 10/2:202 and 14 (1857). If there were several defendants in a civil case who lived in different provinces or districts of the same province, the case was to be filed directly in the Civil Chamber of the guberniia "where the actions from which those suits arose, were effected *[sovershilis']*."

45. SZ 10/2:78, n. 2, 79 (1857).

46. For the rules of securing a lawsuit, see SZ 10/2:57–74 (1857).

47. SZ 10/2:297, n. (1857).

48. SZ 10/2:296, 289 (1857).

49. SZ 10/2:14, app, n. 2:57, 59; appropriate reasons for an interlocutory appeal included the rejection of a complaint, a ruling on jurisdiction, refusal to accept evidence, ruling on securing the suit or management of disputed property, removal of a judge, and delay.

50. SZ 10/2:1131–1137 (1857).

51. TsIAM 92.9.806. On Nicholaevan army, see Wirtschafter, *From Serf to Russian Soldier* (Princeton: Princeton University Press, 1990). Blaginin's service list suggests that his successful career was due to his skill at drill (six "gratitudes" from the tsar) as well as to his involvement in the administration of the infamous "military settlements" in South Russia.

52. TsIAM 92.6.677.

53. TsIAM 16.5.64.

54. SZ 10:1333, 648, 1324 (1842)

55. SZ 10 / 2:297, 447, 465 (1857).

56. See, e.g., LeDonne, *Absolutism;* Levin-Stankevich, "The Transfer."

57. Gettun, *"Zapiski,"* 259–260; see the same claim in Bocharov, *"V pravitel'stvui-ushchem Senate,"* 158.

58. TsIAM 50.5.12287.

59. TsIAM 50.4.3161.

60. Legally speaking, there were two types of denunciation—*izvet* ("notification") and *donos* (denunciation proper). SZ 15:914, 916, 934 (1842). An *izvet* did not have to be proven on pain of criminal penalty because, under Article 914, everyone was required to report crime.

61. TsIAM 50.4.8434.

62. TsIAM 50.4.1983.

63. For "sud po forme", see V. V. Zakharov, *"Sud po forme' kak osobyi poriadok rossiiskogo grazhdanskogo sudoproizvodstva v pervoi polovine XIX stoletiia"* (*Uchenye zapiski. Elektronnyi zhurnal Kurskogo gosudarstvennogo universiteta*, no. 2, 2008). http://scientific-notes.ru. For Savinov's case, see TsIAM 91.2.704.

64. LeDonne, *Absolutism*, 195.

65. Merryman, *The Civil Law Tradition: An Introduction to the Legal Systems of Europe and Latin America*, 3rd ed. (Stanford: Stanford University Press, 2007); Mirijan Damaska, "Presentation of Evidence and Factfinding Precision," *University of Pennsylvania Law Review* 123 (1975): 1083–1105.

66. Merryman, *The Civil Law*, 115.

67. LeDonne, *Absolutism*, 193. Levin-Stankevich ("The Transfer," p. 225) claimed that "the dominance of public law concepts since the Muscovite period left Russia with little in the way of a native private law tradition."

68. Merryman, *The Civil Law*, 126.

69. Cyril Glasser, "Civil Procedure and the Lawyers—The Adversary System and the Decline of the Orality Principle," *The Modern Law Review* 56 (1993): 307–324.

70. Ibid., 311.

71. Judith Resnik, "Managerial Judges," *Harvard Law Review* 96 (1982): 374–448.

72. Damaska, *The Faces of Justice and State Authority* (New Haven, 1986), 104–140. (A more active role for the court is desirable in matters of public interest or affecting the "integrity of the system").

73. J. A. Jolowicz, "Adversarial and Inquisitorial Models of Civil Procedure," *The International and Comparative Law Quarterly* 52 (2003): 281–295.

74. While "formal proofs" were abandoned, the desire to improve the law's predictability by reducing judges' discretion still exists today in many legal systems. Merryman, *The Civil Law*; Becker, *Medicine*; John Langbein, *Prosecuting Crime in the Renaissance: England, Germany, France* (Cambridge: Harvard University Press, 1974); Arthur Engelmann, *A History of Continental Civil Procedure* (Boston: Little, Brown, 1927); For the development of prosecution on the basis of circumstantial evidence, see Alexander Welsh, *Strong Representations: Narrative and Circumstantial Evidence in England* (Baltimore: Johns Hopkins University Press, 1992); Barbara Shapiro, *"Beyond Reasonable Doubt" and "Probable Cause": Historical Perspectives on the Anglo-American Law of Evidence* (Berkeley: University of California Press, 1991).

75. Merriman, *The Civil Law*, 126. Under Russian law, several imperfect proofs could add up to a perfect proof when there was no possibility "to wonder *[nedoumevat']*" about the defendant's guilt. SZ 15/2:1173, 1169 (1842). In Anglo-American law, there was an understanding that written proof was superior to oral testimony. Stephan Landsman, "From Gilbert to Bentham: The

Reconceptualization of Evidence Theory," *The Wayne Law Review* 36 (1990): 1149–1153; John Langbein, "Historical Foundations of the Law of Evidence: A View from the Ryder Sources," *Columbia Law Review* 96 (1996): 1168–1202.

76. See, e.g., Blinov, *"Sudebnyi stroi"*; Kozlinina, *Za polveka;* LeDonne, *Absolutism.*

77. Becker, *Medicine,* 35–38.

78. Becker noted that medical testimony was rarely challenged in pre-reform courts but would be discarded altogether if it did not fit the "other circumstances" of the case. Ibid., 34.

79. Ibid., 31.

80. Jennifer L. Mnookin, "Scripting Expertise: The History of Handwriting Identification Evidence and the Judicial Construction of Reliability," *Virginia Law Review* 87 (2001): 1723–1845.

81. Mnookin, "Scripting Expertise"; Randall McGowen, "From Pillory to Gallows: The Punishment of Forgery in the Age of the Financial Revolution," *Past and Present* 165 (1999): 107–140; "The Bank of England and the Policing of Forgery, 1797–1821," *Past and Present,* 186 (2005): 81–116.

82. Mnookin, "Scripting Expertise," 1764–74.

83. D. Michael Risinger, Mark Denbeaux, and Michael Saks, "Exorcism of Ignorance as a Proxy for Rational Knowledge: The Lessons of Handwriting Identification 'Expertise,'" *University of Pennsylvania Law Review* 137 (1989): 731–792; Michael J. Saks, "Merlin and Solomon: Lessons from the Law's Formative Encounters with Forensic Identification Science," *Hastings Law Journal* 49 (1998): 1069–1081.

84. A. V. Dulov and I. F. Krylov, *Iz istorii kriminalisticheskoi ekspertizy v Rossii: ekspertiza dokumentov* (Moscow, 1960).

85. I. F. Krylov. *Sudebnaia ekspertiza v ugolovnom protsesse* (Leningrad, 1963); Dulov, *Iz istorii.*

86. Dulov, *Iz istorii.* Also E. F. Burinskii, *Sudebnaia ekspertiza dokumentov: proizvodstvo i pol'zovanie eiu* (St. Petersburg, 1903).

87. SZ 10/2:348–354 (1857).

88. SZ, 10/2:350 (1857).

89. TsIAM 92.9.806.

90. TsIAM 16.21.425.

91. TsIAM 50.5.12292.

92. TsIAM 50.4.7368.

93. Another example of a small panel of seven secretaries is the forgery investigation of a prominent Petersburg lawyer, Bilbasov, in 1865. GARF 109.96.54, l. 35.

94. Mnookin, "Scripting Expertise," 1785.

95. TsIAM 371.2.214.

96. TsIAM 50.4.7731.

97. TsIAM 50.4.6191.

98. TsIAM 50.4.8434.

99. On connections between discipline and the law in Russia, see Engelstein, *The Keys to Happiness;* Burbank, "Discipline and Punish"; and Schrader, *Languages of the Lash.*

Acknowledgments

This project incurred a hefty debt burden to a number of organizations and to numerous friends and colleagues. The following represents an attempt at an accurate inventory, without, however, claiming anything like a complete discharge of all of my obligations.

Most importantly, I thank my mentor, Richard Wortman, for generously sharing his wealth of knowledge about imperial Russia and for his unceasing support of my intellectual efforts ever since I stepped into my first Russian Studies *kruzhok* meeting at Columbia back in 2002. I owe a huge debt of gratitude to Sam Moyn for his generous, cheerful, and truly enlightened spirit. I am equally in debt to Alex Martin for being a model colleague and mentor. Many friends, colleagues, and teachers have made this project possible in more ways that I can describe: through clever conversation and astute commentary, through comradeship, and by giving me many opportunities to present my research and develop my arguments in a variety of settings. I especially want to mention Susan Smith-Peter, Mikhail Dolbilov, Jane Burbank, Yanni Kotsonis, Anne Lounsbery, Will Pomeranz, Tarik Amar, Susan Heuman, Kim Lane Scheppele, Kathy Hendley, Tim Frye, Cathy Nepomnyashchy, Alison Smith, John Randolph, Bruce Mann, Erika Vause, Tom Luckett, Anatoly Pinsky, Anna Fishzon, Brigid O'Keeffe, Elissa Bemporad, Satadru Sen, and Bob Wintermute.

During the earlier stages of this project, I hugely benefited from the encouragement and support of Mark von Hagen, Madeleine Zelin, Irina Reyfman, Katharina Pistor, Isser Woloch, Susan Pedersen, Victoria de Grazia, Bradley Abrams, and Michael Stanislawski. Back in the early 2000s, Professor Benedict Kingsbury at the NYU School of Law encouraged and developed my growing interest in graduate work in legal history.

Several colleagues and friends in Russia have greatly facilitated my research and helped to place it in perspective, including Larissa Zakharova, Yurii Petrov, Boris Anan'ich, Leonid Borodkin, Maksim Shevchenko, Fedor Gaida, and Sofia Solomatina. These historians took their time to discuss my work and give useful advice and encouragement, and they generously invited me to attend some of their workshops, seminars, and—yes—parties. I am particularly grateful to Galina Ulianova and Natalia Datieva, fellow researchers at TsIAM, who in effect took *shefstvo* over me for the first research year in Moscow and afterward.

Research for this book was supported in part by a fellowship from the International Research and Exchanges Board, with funds provided by the U.S. Department of State through the Title VIII Program and the IREX Scholar Support Fund. My research was also supported by a fellowship from the Title VIII Program for Research and Training on Eastern Europe and Eurasia (Independent States of the Former Soviet Union), which is funded by the U.S. Department of State and administered by the American Councils for International Education (ACTR / ACCELS). None of these organizations are responsible for the views expressed herein. I am also grateful to the Harriman Institute at Columbia for its generous financial and institutional support of my research and writing over the years. Alla Rachkov and everyone else at the institute have been incredibly helpful and supportive. The History Department at Queens College, City University of New York, provided me with much-needed institutional affiliation and financial support.

This research could not have been carried out without the permission and good will of the archivists of TsIAM and, in particular, of its director, Ye.G. Boldina. I am extremely grateful to the warmhearted and cheerful reading room archivists at TsIAM for making my work there comfortable and almost home-like, as well as to TsIAM's document preservation staff, whose hard work with documents that had never before been requested by researchers was less public but just as strongly appreciated. I am also grateful to N. I. Abdulaeva and all the other archivists at GARF for providing a comfortable and efficient work environment, and especially to S. V. Mironenko, for his encouragement and support.

I am also deeply indebted to Andrew Kinney and Kathleen McDermott at Harvard University Press. Andrew's extremely helpful comments and suggestions during the final stage of preparing this manuscript are particularly appreciated.

I also wish to thank my colleagues and friends, whose encouragement and support have formed a brilliant network of personal credit, especially Alexey Akopyan, Vladimir Kobzar, Aline Voldoire, Leah Kaplan, and Owen Fletcher and his amazing family, and, more recently, Jennifer and Joe Mercurio.

Throughout this project, I have been ever conscious of my enormous debt to my teacher of Russian literature, Olga Stukalova, who always encouraged me to think rigorously and creatively. It was particularly satisfying to be able to thank Olga Vadimovna after so many years and to continue benefiting from her intellect and from her highest level of literacy and *kulturnost'*. My family in Moscow and in Augusta, including Galina, Sasha, Sergei Nikolaevich, Anna Fedorovna, Ninel' Timofeevich, Tatiana Nikiforovna, and Nadia, have been of incredible help all of my life, but in particular during my archival research trips, keeping me alive with their good humor, their wisdom, and their food. They made this book possible, but unfortunately not all of them will see the arrival of the final product. My in-laws, Dan, Chris, and Sandra Pickering, and the innumerable other Pickerings and Smits, have always treated me like their own son and helped me to survive the rigors of academic life.

Not simply this book as a discrete project, but all of my recent academic life would likely have remained a "what-if" alternative were it not for the intellect, character, and warmth of Katherine Pickering Antonova, who encouraged me to choose a life that I was truly created for and then ensured that the project was carried all the way through—by comforting my fears, by serving as an incredible editor and critic, and by sacrificing much of her own work time to allow me to research and to write, both in Moscow and in New York. Finally, the process has not always been facilitated, but definitely put into perspective, by the consecutive arrival of two extremely hilarious and rambunctious little fairies, who have more or less cheerfully limited their toy-banging agenda to allow me to write.

Index